Women's Education in Developing Countries

A World Bank Book

Women's Education in Developing Countries

Barriers, Benefits, and Policies

Edited by
Elizabeth M. King
M. Anne Hill

Published for the World Bank
The Johns Hopkins University Press
Baltimore and London

The photograph on the cover, by Antonia Macedo, shows girls in a classroom in Jamaica. The cover design is by George Parakamannil.

Library of Congress Cataloging-in-Publication Data

Women's education in developing countries ; barriers, benefits, and
   policies / edited by Elizabeth M. King, M. Anne Hill.
      p.   cm.
   Includes bibliographical references (p.).
   ISBN 0-8018-4534-3   ISBN 0-8018-5828-3 (paperback)
   1. Women—Education—Developing countries. 2. Women—Education—
Economic aspects—Developing countries. 3. Educational
equalization—Developing countries. I. King, Elizabeth M.
II. Hill, M. Anne.
   LC2572.W67   1993
   376.9'09172'4—dc20   93-9650
                                           CIP

Foreword

Education of girls may seem an odd topic for an economist to address. But enhancing women's contribution to development is as much an economic as a social issue. Economics, with its emphasis on incentives, provides a useful way to understand why so many girls are deprived of education and employment opportunities. And recent research and concrete calculations show that educating females yields far-reaching benefits for girls and women themselves, their families, and the societies in which they live. Indeed, during my tenure as chief economist of the World Bank, I have become convinced that once all the benefits are recognized, investment in the education of girls may well be the highest-return investment available in the developing world.

What is perhaps the most dramatic indicator of the special problems women face is found in the most basic of all national statistics—the demographic composition of the population. One might expect that the proportion of females in a population would be a biologically determined constant. Yet a survey of worldwide statistics reveals large differences in this proportion. Whereas women comprise 52.5 percent of the population in the industrial world, they account for only 51 percent of the population in Sub-Saharan Africa, less than 48 percent in East Asia, and less than 47 percent in South Asia.

Amartya Sen, who has calculated from numbers of this type that more than 100 million women are "missing" worldwide, describes the fate of these women as "one of the more momentous problems facing the contemporary world." Although some of the differential in the female composition of the population may be caused by census biases and the effects of migration, the overwhelming reason why 100 million women are missing is excess female mortality. In industrial countries, where basic necessities are available to all, women outlive men by an average of six years. But in many developing countries the spread is lower, and in large parts of South Asia a baby boy can actually expect to live longer than a baby girl.

Differential mortality of women and girls is only the most dramatic manifestation of systematic discrimination against them. Women and girls are more likely to be impoverished than men and boys. Studies have found evidence that girls are fed less than their brothers and that their illnesses are less likely to be treated. And it can come as no surprise that female literacy falls far short of male literacy.

There is no simple explanation for the extent of female deprivation or for its variation across time and space. Poverty does bear down especially hard on women, but it is striking that despite the very high poverty rates in Africa, the problem of excess female mortality is much less severe there than in South Asia. Although cultural factors must surely influence the extent of female deprivation, they do not explain why the female fraction of the population has changed substantially in some countries but not in others.

It is more accurate—and more fruitful as a guide to policy—to look at female deprivation as both a consequence and a cause in a vicious cycle. Parents fail to invest in their daughters because they do not expect them to be able to make an economic contribution to the family, a prophecy that becomes self-fulfilling. Two stories illustrate how the cycle works and how it can be broken.

- A poor family has six children. The mother never attended school, was married at age 15, and remains illiterate. Her husband earns most of the family's meager income and decides how it is spent. Since his own economic security depends on his sons' ability to support him in his old age, he insists that the boys go to school, while the girls remain at home to do chores. When his daughter becomes ill, he feels that he cannot afford to make the two-day trip with her to the medical clinic in the city. The daughter dies.
- A poor family has three children. The mother went to school for five years and is able to read and do arithmetic well enough to teach school in the village. As her last birth was extremely difficult, she and her husband adopted family planning. She now has more time and resources to spend on her family. Hoping for a better future for her children, she insists that they all go to school and practice their reading each night. When one of her daughters gets sick and does not seem to be getting better, she takes her to the medical clinic. The doctor gives the mother some ampicillin tablets and instructs her to give them to any of the children who fall ill. The daughter's strep infection is cured, as is the infection of the son, who is running a high fever by the time the mother returns home.

Some of the differences between these two situations are obvious enough. An uneducated mother without skills that are valued outside the home has less ability to influence choices within the family. Her daughters are uneducated as well, and a vicious cycle is perpetuated— girls grow up only to marry into somebody else's family and bear children. Girls are thus less valuable than boys and are kept at home to do chores while their brothers are sent to school. They remain un- educated and unskilled, and the conditions necessary for them to contribute to the economy are not created. The economy suffers, and young girls die of neglect.

By contrast, an educated mother faces a higher opportunity cost of time spent caring for the children. She has greater value outside the home and thus has an entirely different set of choices than she would without education. She is married at a later age and is better able to influence family decisions. She has fewer, healthier children and can insist on the development of all of them, ensuring that her daughters are given a fair chance. And the education of her daughters makes it much more likely that the next generation of girls, as well as of boys, will be educated and healthy as well. The vicious cycle is thus trans- formed into a virtuous circle.

Educating girls offers the best hope of breaking the cycle of female deprivation. Increased schooling has similar effects on the incomes of males and females, but educating girls generates much larger social benefits. Because of what women do with the extra income they earn, because of the extra leverage it affords them within the family, and because of the direct effects of greater knowledge and awareness, fe- male education has an enormous social impact.

There are those who say that encouraging girls to go to school, learn to read, and experience more of the world beyond their homes is a strategy that pays off only in the long run. I am reminded of a story that U.S. President John F. Kennedy used to tell, about a man who asked his gardener how long it would take for a certain seed to grow into a tree. The gardener said it would take a hundred years. The man replied, "Then plant the seed this morning. There is no time to lose."

Lawrence H. Summers
Vice President, Development Economics, and Chief Economist
The World Bank
January 1993

Contents

Preface

As we worked on this volume, we received numerous requests for copies of the preliminary draft. These requests came from staff members of international agencies and nongovernmental organizations who were designing or implementing projects promoting girls' education, from students who were writing their theses on economic development, and from researchers who were reviewing the literature on women's education. These requests, combined with the growing recognition of the critical importance of investment in education to economic development and social well-being, reinforced our belief in the value of this work.

The volume organizes recent data on the status of women's education in the developing world and links this information to indicators of development such as income per capita, mortality rates, and fertility levels. In an effort to identify effective policies, it also considers the factors that have slowed educational progress for women. The review suggests that future research on women's education will have to address methodological issues more seriously. Because of weaknesses in the analytical approaches used, many past studies cannot guide practitioners in the field as they design specific policies or interventions to improve female participation and performance in school.

This volume began as a collection of reviews of the literature commissioned by the Education and Employment Division and the Women in Development Division of the World Bank's Population and Human Resources Department in preparation for an interagency conference on this topic at the World Bank in June 1989. Each review focused on the literature pertaining to one developing region. The organizers chose authors either from or familiar with the region so that each review could cover literature sources (such as those in local languages) not available internationally.

After the conference, the editors substantially revised the regional papers for this compilation. Chapter 1 was added to provide a global view of the status of women's education and to present an analytical framework with which to assess the findings of the regional papers. We constructed cross-country, time-series data to examine the impact of women's education on child and maternal health, fertility, and economic growth. The estimates reveal that the amount of education women receive is a significant factor determining economic growth and the quality of life of their families. When we conducted this analysis, we knew of no other study that examined this broad set of relationships. Since then, we have been gratified to see similar efforts by other economists. Chapter 8 was added to review specific projects and program experiences in promoting women's education in various countries. It has received a lot of prepublication attention because few projects leave behind documentary evidence of lessons learned. Unpublished project documents made available to our study by the United Nations Educational, Scientific, and Cultural Organization, the U.S. Agency for International Development, and other funding agencies were critical in assembling the evidence presented in the chapter.

The book benefited from the ideas and advice of many friends and colleagues. We thank Ann O. Hamilton, who, as director of the Population and Human Resources Department, gave us her warm encouragement and support to press ahead with this compilation. Ann Duncan and Barbara Herz helped in conceiving the volume. Helen Abadzi, Ila Patel, and Maigenet Shifferraw wrote background papers on women's nonformal education; initial plans to include their papers in this volume were abandoned because much of the literature they surveyed offers little firm quantitative evidence. Jere Behrman, Rosemary Bellew, Birger Fredriksen, Deborah DeGraff, Lynel Long, and Adriaan Verspoor gave us many helpful comments along with their moral support at various stages of the study. Four anonymous referees for the World Bank's Editorial Committee provided useful suggestions for revisions.

We are also grateful to Charlene Semer, Helen Whitney Watriss, and Marianna Ohe, who painstakingly edited early drafts of the chapters. Jeanne Rosen, Nancy Levine, and finally Kenneth Hale took over from them and guided this volume to its completion. Jeanne Rosen worked tirelessly on each chapter, checked each table and figure, and made numerous editorial suggestions. Althea Skeete-Comedy provided superb secretarial support and excellent administrative assistance through much of the preparation of the volume, and we are heavily in her debt. Cynthia Cristobal patiently typed the final revisions. Finally, others who contributed to individual chapters are acknowledged separately by chapter authors.

1

Women's Education in Developing Countries: An Overview

M. Anne Hill and Elizabeth M. King

Widening access to education has been a major policy goal in most developing countries for the past three decades. This reflects a broad recognition that education is essential to economic and social development. The evidence is overwhelming that education improves health and productivity and that the poorest people gain the most. When schools open their doors wider to girls and women, as well as to boys and men, the benefits multiply. Indeed, failing to invest adequately in educating women can reduce the potential benefits of educating men. This failure exacts a high cost—in lost opportunities to raise productivity, to increase income, and to improve the quality of life. Yet women's education still lags far behind men's in most developing countries, with far-reaching adverse consequences for both individual and national well-being.

In this chapter we first review the state of women's education and the extent of the gender gap in education, using extensive data for 152 developing countries covering the period 1960 through 1985. Evidence from many countries (presented in detail in chapter 2) points to strong links between the education of women and national development. Most analysis of these links has focused on the *level* of women's education; the implications of the *gender gap* in education have yet to be fully explored. Our empirical research begins by assessing the considerable negative effects of gender disparities in schooling on economic and social development. We then seek to understand why these disparities nevertheless persist by considering the environment within which educational decisions are made. For a family, the costs and benefits of educating daughters may be quite different from those associated with educating sons. Specifically, many of the benefits of educating women in developing countries are public, whereas many of the costs are private. This leads to underinvestment in women's schooling and thus to the persistent gender gap.

State of Women's Education

Several indicators—including measures of literacy, enrollment, and years in school—reveal important patterns and trends in women's education in developing countries. Each of these indicators leads to the same conclusions: the level of female education is low in the poorest countries, with just a handful of exceptions, and by any measure, the gender gap is largest in these countries.

Literacy Rates

Literacy is one of the principal goals of education around the world. The ability to read and write is considered almost a basic human right. Yet low literacy rates prevail among women in many countries (figure 1-1).[1] In fourteen of the fifty-one developing countries for which school data or estimates are available for the 1980s, female adult literacy is less than 20 percent; in none is the male literacy rate as low. In Afghanistan, Burkina Faso, Nepal, Somalia, and Sudan, where fewer than 10 percent of adult women are literate, the percentage of men who are literate is three to four times larger. Among those countries with male literacy rates greater than 70 percent, the gender gap is notably large in Libya (30 percentage points), China (28), Zaire (26), Turkey (23), and Botswana (21). In contrast, the literacy rates for men and women are about equal in Colombia, the Dominican Republic, and the Philippines.

Primary School Enrollment

Low adult literacy rates are a result of past underinvestment in the education of women and thus do not necessarily reflect recent progress. We look next, therefore, at how the differences between primary school enrollment rates for boys and girls have changed over time.[2] Figure 1-2 illustrates the trend since 1960 for countries grouped by gross national product (GNP) per capita; figure 1-3 shows the trend by geographic region.

Without question, enrollment rates at all school levels have been rising in the developing world for both sexes. But this expansion has not substantially diminished gender disparities. The enrollment rates of girls remain much lower than those of boys, with the widest gap in the poorest countries. For the group of forty low-income countries, defined as those with a GNP per capita below $500 in 1988, the gap in

Figure 1-1. *Women's and Men's Literacy Rates in Developing Countries*

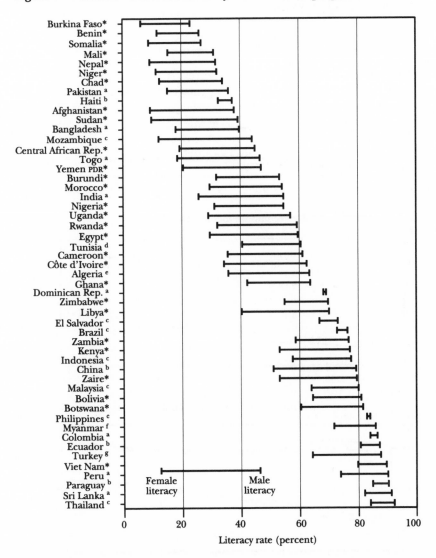

Note: The criteria for determining whether a person is literate can differ among countries; the definition used here is whether a person can with understanding both read and write a short, simple statement on his everyday life. Countries marked by an asterisk (*) do not have census-based literacy data after 1980. Most have data going back to the 1960s. For those countries the data reported are UNESCO estimates for 1985; for all other countries the latest survey-based data are used.

a. 1981. b. 1982. c. 1983. d. 1984. e. 1987. f. 1983. g. 1985.

Source: UNESCO data.

Figure 1-2. *Gross Enrollment in Primary and Secondary Schools by Income Group, 1960 - 88*

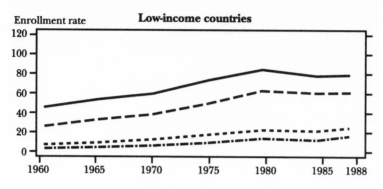

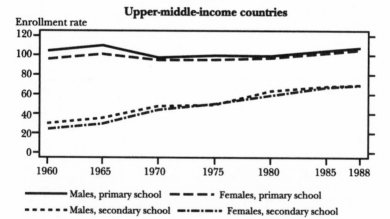

————— Males, primary school   — — — • Females, primary school

■ ■ ■ ■ ■ ■ Males, secondary school   ■—•—•—•• Females, secondary school

Note: The latest year for which data are available after 1985 is shown as 1988; for some countries, however, this date may be any year between 1985 and 1989.

Source: For gross enrollment rates, UNESCO data; for income groups (based on 1988 GNP per capita), World Bank data.

Figure 1-3. *Gross Enrollment Rates in Primary and Secondary Schools by Region, 1960 - 88*

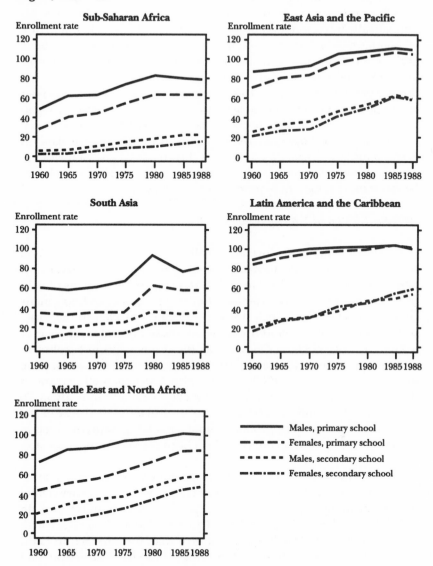

Note: The latest year for which data are available after 1985 is shown as 1988; for some countries, however, this date may be any year between 1985 and 1989.
Source: UNESCO data base.

primary school enrollment between boys and girls averages 20 percentage points. This gap has persisted in large part since 1960.

Both enrollment rates and gender disparities in enrollment differ dramatically by region. Except for South Asia and Sub-Saharan Africa, all regions have achieved nearly universal primary education for boys. Only in East Asia and in Latin America and the Caribbean, however, have enrollment rates for girls approached similar levels; in the other three regions they continue to lag behind. In South Asia the gender gap in primary enrollment has actually widened over the twenty-eight-year period because policies to expand the education system improved access for boys more than for girls. (Country-specific data for each region are discussed in chapters 3 through 7.) As countries approach universal primary education, the gender gap in enrollment becomes more apparent beyond the primary level.

Dropout Rates and Years of Schooling

Gross enrollment rates, which are usually reported for all primary and secondary classes, tend to mask some other important measures of educational progress. These include how many of the students remain in school, how many are promoted to the next grade, and how many complete each cycle. If high dropout rates prevail even in the lower primary grades, it is doubtful whether all those who enter school ever achieve functional literacy. As a result, the recent gains in enrollment in developing countries may overstate the progress in education since the 1960s. Data for the 1980s indicate that fewer than 60 percent of those who enter school in low-income countries, and only about 70 percent in lower-middle-income countries, reach the final year of the primary cycle. Moreover, primary school completion rates declined in the 1980s in the poorest countries (Lockheed, Verspoor, and associates 1991).

Dropout rates vary considerably from country to country. On average, 9.6 percent of girls in low-income countries leave primary school before finishing, compared with 8.2 percent of boys (table 1-1). In Sub-Saharan Africa as a whole and in the Middle East and North Africa, the dropout rate is higher for girls than for boys. But in Latin America and the Caribbean and in Congo, Lesotho, Madagascar, and the Philippines, girls are less likely than boys to drop out of primary school (Bellew and King 1991).

To illustrate the adverse effect of dropouts on the average level of education attained, consider the expected years of schooling implied by age-specific enrollment rates in selected countries (table 1-2). These are estimated by using a "synthetic cohort" approach—that is, by summing up the age-specific enrollment rates for boys and girls in

Table 1-1. *Primary School Dropout Rates, by Country Group and Region, 1988*
(percent)

Country group or region	Girls	Boys
Low-income countries	9.6	8.2
Lower-middle-income countries	6.1	5.9
Upper-middle-income countries[a]	6.2	6.3
Sub-Saharan Africa	8.6	7.3
South Asia (Sri Lanka only)	1.5	1.5
East Asia (Philippines only)	6.6	6.7
Latin America and the Caribbean	7.8	8.8
Middle East and North Africa	6.0	4.3

a. Data are available for only five countries in this group: Algeria, Gabon, Iran, Iraq, and Uruguay.

Source: UNESCO data.

a given calendar year to predict the likely educational attainment of those entering primary school in that year. One obvious shortcoming of this approach is its assumption that the enrollment rates of, say, today's seven-year-olds will be the same when they reach fifteen as those of today's fifteen-year-olds. This ignores improvements (or deterioration) over time in age-specific enrollment rates.

Table 1-2 shows that, despite the large increases in enrollment rates in most countries, expected attainment levels in the poorest countries remain low, especially for females. For example, a six-year-old girl entering school in Nepal in 1985 is expected to complete only 3.1 years of schooling by the time she reaches eighteen. For a girl in Burkina Faso, the figure is lower still, 1.5 years. Since 1965 the primary school enrollment rate for girls has increased fivefold in Nepal and almost threefold in Burkina Faso. But of all the girls enrolled in primary school in Nepal in 1985, almost 45 percent were in grade one and only about 10 percent were in grade five (the final year of the primary cycle). In Burkina Faso 26 percent were in grade one and 13 percent in grade five. In both countries the rate at which boys stayed in school, called the retention rate, was higher.

The gender gap in educational attainment, measured by years of schooling, tends to fall as one moves from low-income to middle-income countries. The expected years of schooling in 1985 ranged from averages of 2.7 and 4.8 years for females and males, respectively, in eight low-income countries to averages of 10.2 and 10.5 years, respectively, in eleven upper-middle-income countries. In the low-income group the expected length of schooling for males exceeds that for females. For example, in Nepal and Benin girls average 4.4 and 3.5 fewer years of schooling than boys, respectively. In the middle-income

Table 1-2. *Average Expected Years of Schooling by Age Eighteen in Selected Countries, 1985*

Economy	Females	Males	Difference males − females
Low-income			
Burkina Faso	1.5	2.6	1.1
Nepal	3.1	7.5	4.4
Bangladesh	3.3	5.6	2.3
Burundi	2.8	4.1	1.3
Benin	3.5	7.0	3.5
Somalia	1.2	2.3	1.2
Rwanda	5.0	5.4	0.4
Guinea	1.5	3.5	2.0
Lower-middle-income			
Lesotho	10.3	7.9	−2.4
Philippines	9.0	8.8	−0.2
Morocco	5.0	7.7	2.7
Bolivia	8.0	9.1	1.1
Honduras	8.6	8.1	−0.6
Nicaragua	9.4	7.7	−1.7
El Salvador	7.3	7.0	−0.3
Botswana	9.3	8.5	−0.8
Paraguay	7.8	8.2	0.3
Tunisia	8.5	10.7	2.2
Costa Rica	8.0	8.0	−0.1
Syrian Arab Republic	8.9	11.2	2.3
Upper-middle-income			
Hungary	10.7	10.6	−0.1
Poland	11.2	11.2	−0.1
Portugal	10.5	10.2	−0.2
Panama	10.0	9.9	−0.1
Algeria	8.0	10.3	2.3
Venezuela	9.5	9.0	−0.5
Greece	11.7	11.8	0.1
Ireland	11.2	10.7	−0.6
Trinidad and Tobago	10.6	10.2	−0.4
Hong Kong	11.4	11.0	−0.3
Iraq	8.1	10.7	2.6

Note: Economies were selected on the basis of availability of data on age-specific enrollment in 1985 in the UNESCO data base. They are listed by ascending order of GNP per capita in 1985.

Source: Computed from UNESCO data.

group, besides Bolivia, only countries in the Middle East and North Africa show a significant gender gap: girls can expect to be in school two or three years less than boys.

Although repeating grades can also have adverse consequences for completed schooling, we do not find significant gender differences in grade repetition rates at the primary level in cross-country data. It is easy to misinterpret this as proof that girls perform at least as well as boys under prevailing school conditions. But repetition rates can be estimated only for those girls who enter and remain in school. It is entirely possible that only a small, select group of girls (perhaps the best-off or the ablest) enter school at all and that this explains why they perform better on average than boys. Because repetition rates are conditional on access to school, they must be used with care in characterizing the state of female education.

Secondary School Enrollment

Progress at the secondary level since 1960 has been dramatic in parts of the developing world, as figures 1-2 and 1-3 indicate. Gross enrollment rates for females have increased from an average of 12 percent in 1960 to 44 percent in 1988 in lower-middle-income countries, and from 25 percent to 70 percent in upper-middle-income countries. Enrollment of females over this period rose faster than did that of males. A few low-income countries experienced major setbacks in enrollment in the early 1980s; China, for example, shows a decline of 5 percentage points for females and 8 percentage points for males.[3] On the whole, however, the average female enrollment rate for this group of countries has quadrupled since 1960.

Average secondary school enrollment rates for all five regions did not exceed 25 percent in 1960, with Sub-Saharan Africa's rate the lowest, at 3 percent. After twenty-five years of expansion, the regional pattern in enrollment rates had grown more diverse, especially for females. Africa's and South Asia's average enrollment rates in 1988 lagged behind East Asia's by about 40 percentage points. Indeed, the averages for Sub-Saharan Africa were still below the rates that East Asia had achieved twenty-five years earlier. Although the gender difference in secondary enrollment has narrowed in East Asia, it has widened in Sub-Saharan Africa and in the Middle East and North Africa, as well as in South Asia after 1965.

Most secondary school students can choose to follow either a general academic track or a vocational stream, which includes teacher training programs. A large majority of girls in secondary school are enrolled in general education programs (table 1-3). Of those students in vocational and technical education, women have generally been

Table 1-3. *Distribution of Female Enrollment at the Secondary Level,*
by Type of Education, 1970 and Most Recent Year
(percent)

	1970			Most recent year[a]		
Region	*General*	*Teacher training*	*Vocational and technical*	*General*	*Teacher training*	*Vocational and technical*
Sub-Saharan Africa	85.2	6.4	8.4	83.1	6.1	10.8
Asia	85.7	7.4	6.9	92.1	0.8	6.9
Latin America and the Caribbean	79.7	4.7	15.9	78.0	1.3	20.7
Middle East and North Africa	86.6	8.7	4.7	91.1	2.7	6.2

Note: Rows may not add to 100 percent because of rounding.
a. The most recent year for which data are available is usually early to mid-1980s.
Source: UNESCO data.

very much in the minority except in Latin America, where they make up half or more of the total enrollment in this stream (UNESCO 1983).

Women Teachers

The share of girls at the secondary level in teacher training has declined greatly in Asia and in the Middle East and North Africa since 1970 (see table 1-3). This decline accounts in part for the shortage of female teachers in low-income countries. Much importance is accorded to this shortage in discussions about improving the education of girls and women. Although the impact of female teachers on girls' school enrollment and performance has not been adequately examined, reported anecdotal evidence appears to confirm their positive role. Yet the percentage of women teachers at all levels of education in low-income countries is only about half that in middle-income countries. In low-income countries in 1985, women accounted for about a third of the primary teachers, fewer than a fourth of the secondary teachers, and roughly a tenth of college and university teachers (table 1-4).

In lower-middle-income countries, the percentage of primary and secondary teachers who are women has changed little in the past several decades. Women continue to constitute about half the teaching force at the primary level and a third at the secondary level. At the postsecondary level, however, women have made gains, going from 17 percent of all teachers in 1965 to 24 percent in 1985. In upper-middle-income countries, two-thirds of the primary school teachers are women. But the largest increase in female teachers in these countries has occurred at higher levels: by 1985 almost half the teachers at the secondary level and more than a fourth at the tertiary level were women.

Table 1-4. *Proportion of Females in the Teaching Force, by Income Group,
Selected Years, 1965–85*
(percent)

Country income group	1965	1970	1975	1980	1985
Primary level					
Low-income	0.20	0.24	0.31	0.30	0.32
Lower-middle-income	0.47	0.50	0.38[a]	0.51	0.49
Upper-middle-income	0.63	0.58	0.62	0.61	0.65
Secondary level					
Low-income	0.24	0.23	0.28	0.21	0.23
Lower-middle-income	0.34	0.32	0.34	0.36	0.34
Upper-middle-income	0.37	0.41	0.42	0.46	0.47
Higher level					
Low-income	0.12	0.11	0.15	0.15	0.14
Lower-middle-income	0.17	0.18	0.21	0.19	0.24
Upper-middle-income	0.18	0.19	0.23	0.26	0.28

a. The sharp drop for this year is due to missing data for one country, China, which
had a much higher female share in other years than the other countries in the group.
  Source: Computed from UNESCO data.

Enrollment in Higher Education

The broad trends and patterns in enrollment at the tertiary level are
similar to those at the secondary level. Enrollment rates in Sub-Saharan
Africa and South Asia are far below those in the other regions (table
1-5). In 1988 East Asia had the highest male enrollment rate of any region, but Latin America and the Caribbean led in female enrollment.
Averages in the Middle East and North Africa were close to those in
Latin America for males but were 4.4 percentage points lower for
females.

As chapters 3 through 7 make clear, throughout the developing
world women in institutions of higher education tend to be concentrated in certain fields of study. It is not surprising that female enrollment is heavily skewed toward the humanities, home economics, and
the arts. But women have gained ground in business and public administration programs and are expanding their numbers in medicine
and other science-related fields. With increased economic growth and
a labor market more open to them, women can be expected to continue their progress in higher education.

The Gender Gap in Education: A Brake on Development

The measures of educational attainment discussed above each reveal
clear gender disparities, which are costly to development. Develop-

Table 1-5. *Enrollment Rates at the Tertiary Level, 1965 and 1988*
(percent)

Country group or region	Females		Males	
	1965	1988	1965	1988
Low-income	0.2	1.1	0.7	2.8
Lower-middle-income	2.1	10.3	3.6	14.1
Upper-middle-income	3.1	15.6	5.9	18.3
Sub-Saharan Africa	0.1	1.1	0.6	3.3
South Asia	0.6	2.0	2.0	5.2
East Asia	4.1	14.6	6.7	18.9
Latin America and the Caribbean	3.1	16.2	5.7	16.4
Middle East and North Africa	2.1	11.8	5.6	16.2

Note: Although the latest year for which data are available is noted as 1988, the most recent year for some countries is any year from 1985 through 1989.

Source: UNESCO data.

ment, broadly defined, encompasses economic progress and improvements in the overall quality of life. What does female education contribute to these goals? This section assesses the effects of gender disparities on a country's economic and social well-being, as measured by GNP per capita, as well as by several social indicators of family welfare in the aggregate, including life expectancy (at birth), infant and maternal mortality rates, and total fertility rates.

A growing body of literature examines the benefits of educating women. Much of this work is described by T. Paul Schultz in chapter 2 of this book. A better-educated mother has fewer and better-educated children. She is more productive at home and in the workplace. And she raises a healthier family, since she can better apply improved hygiene and nutritional practices. Education can even substitute for community health programs by informing women about health care and personal hygiene, and it can complement such programs by raising income and promoting greater recognition of the value of these services. For example, in the Philippines an investigation of the determinants of chronic malnutrition among children found that mothers' schooling and the availability of safe drinking water explained health differences among children, whereas household income did not (Barrera 1990). See also Caldwell (1979) on Nigeria, Behrman and Deolalikar (1988) on Indonesia, and Behrman and Wolfe (1984) on Nicaragua.

So important is the influence of mothers' education on children's health and nutritional status that it reduces mortality rates. A study on India demonstrates that higher female education and wider availability and use of medical services are two crucial factors associated with the lower infant mortality in the state of Kerala (Jain 1985). And in Malaysia mothers' education was found to have a marked effect on infant mortality rates, especially in the second six months of life (Butz, Habicht, and DaVanzo 1984). In contrast, family income, although generally associated with infant mortality in cross-country analyses, proved to be altogether unimportant after taking into account mothers' education.

These benefits are also clearly evident from aggregate data. Figure 1-4 plots GNP per capita and three social indicators in 1985 against female enrollment rates in primary education in 1975. The results illustrate the expected negative correlation of education with fertility and infant mortality, and its positive correlation with income and life expectancy. These findings argue for increasing female enrollment rates at the primary level as part of any development strategy.

Extent of the Gender Gap

The benefits to economic growth and family welfare that come from educating women are undeniable. The evidence makes it clear that raising the level of women's education contributes in important ways to development. As we shall see, so too does closing the gender gap in education. Before turning to the effects of the gender gap, we look at the size of the gap in developing countries and at how it has changed.

Between 1965 and 1985 considerable progress was made in reducing the gender disparity in primary school enrollments (table 1-6). In 1965 nineteen countries had female enrollment rates that were less than 42 percent of male rates; only Chad and Yemen remained in that category in 1985. Similarly, the number of countries in which the ratio of female to male enrollment rates was between 42 and 75 percent fell from thirty-seven in 1965 to only seventeen in 1985.[4] The majority of these are low-income countries.

The gender gap in secondary school enrollments is more pervasive (table 1-7). In 1965 there were forty-five countries in which female enrollment rates were less than 42 percent of male rates; in another twenty-seven countries, the ratio was between 42 and 75 percent. By 1985 the number of countries with the widest gender disparities in secondary enrollment had fallen to sixteen, but twenty-seven countries still had a female to male enrollment ratio between 42 and 75 percent.

Figure 1-4. *Female Primary Schooling, Economic Productivity, and Social Well-Being*

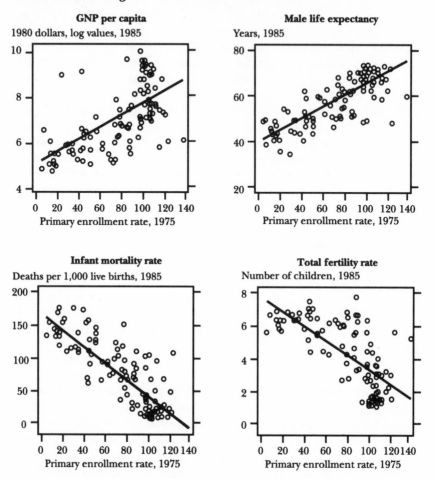

Note: The regression line in each graph is estimated from the scatter plots.
Source: Based on UNESCO and World Bank data.

Effects of the Gender Gap

For the analysis in the rest of this chapter, we combine information on gender disparities in primary and secondary enrollments to yield one measure of the gender disparity in education for a given country at a given time. What we henceforth refer to as the gender gap is the ratio of female to male enrollment at the primary or secondary level, whichever is smaller (that is, where the gap is larger).

Table 1-6. *Countries with Large Gender Differences in Primary School Enrollment Rates, by Level of Female-to-Male Ratio of Enrollment Rates, 1965 and 1985*

1965			1985	
< 0.42	0.42–0.75		< 0.42	0.42–0.75
Afghanistan	Algeria	Lao PDR	Chad	Afghanistan
Bhutan	Angola	Malawi	Yemen, Arab	Benin
Burundi	Bangladesh	Mali	Rep.	Bhutan
Central African	Benin	Morocco		Burkina
Rep.	Bolivia	Mozambique		Faso
Chad	Burkina	Niger		Central African
Comoros	Faso	Nigeria		Rep.
Ethiopia	Cambodia	Papua New		Ethiopia
Gambia, The	Cameroon	Guinea		Gambia, The
Guinea-Bissau	Congo	Rwanda		Guinea
Liberia	Côte d'Ivoire	Senegal		Guinea-Bissau
Libya	Egypt, Arab.	Sierra Leone		Mali
Mauritania	Rep.	Sudan		Mauritania
Nepal	Equatorial	Syrian Arab		Morocco
Pakistan	Guinea	Rep.		Niger
Saudi Arabia	Ghana	Tanzania		Pakistan
Somalia	Guinea	Tunisia		Senegal
Togo	India	Turkey		Somalia
Yemen, Arab	Iraq	Uganda		Togo
Rep.	Kenya	Zaire		
Yemen, PDR		Zimbabwe		

As a first look at the potential effects of this gender gap, consider a second set of scatter plots of female primary school enrollment rates against four development indicators. In figure 1-5 countries are divided into two groups according to the size of the education gender gap. The first subset consists of countries with a wide gender gap; that is, the ratio of female to male enrollment rates in primary education (F/M) is less than or equal to 0.75. The second subset consists of countries in which the female and male enrollment rates approach parity; that is, the ratio F/M exceeds 0.75. To emphasize the relationship observed, regression lines have been drawn for the two subsets of plotted points.

In each graph, the levels of fertility and infant mortality associated with a specific level of female education are much lower, and GNP per capita and life expectancy are much higher, in countries with greater equity between the sexes. Since these observations hold even for countries that have achieved gross female primary enrollment rates of 100 percent, the gender gap at the secondary level is apparently quite important too. Note also that in the graph for total fertility the slope for countries with a large gender gap is significantly flatter than the slope for countries with greater gender equity. This indicates that the widely known negative effect of education on fertility is weaker when

Table 1-7. *Countries with Large Gender Differences in Secondary School Enrollment Rates, by Level of Female-to-Male Ratio of Enrollment Rates, 1965 and 1985*

	1965		1985	
	<0.42	*0.42–0.75*	*<0.42*	*0.42–0.75*
Afghanistan	Mauritania	Albania	Bangladesh	Afghanistan
Bangladesh	Morocco	Algeria	Benin	Burkina Faso
Benin	Nepal	Angola	Bhutan	Burundi
Cambodia	Niger	Botswana	Central African	Cameroon
Cameroon	Pakistan	Burkino Faso	Rep.	Comoros
Central African Rep.	Papua New	Burundi	Chad	Egypt, Arab Rep.
Chad	Guinea	Denmark	Côte d'Ivoire	Ethiopia
Comoros	Rwanda	Fiji	Gambia, The	Ghana
Congo	Saudi Arabia	Gambia, The	Guinea	India
Côte d'Ivoire	Senegal	Guatemala	Guinea-Bissau	Iran
Egypt, Arab Rep.	Sierra Leone	Haiti	Malawi	Iraq
Equatorial Guinea	Somalia	Iran	Mauritania	Lao PDR
Ethiopia	Sudan	Jordan	Mozambique	Mali
Gabon	Syrian Arab Rep.	Korea, Rep. of	Niger	Mauritania
Ghana	Tanzania	Lao PDR	Pakistan	Oman
Guinea	Togo	Lebanon	Togo	Saudi Arabia
Indonesia	Tunisia	Malaysia	Yemen, PDR	Senegal
Iraq	Turkey	Mauritius		Somalia
Kenya	Uganda	Mexico		Syrian Arab Rep.
Liberia	Yemen, PDR	Mozambique		Tanzania
Libya	Zaire	Myanmar		Tunisia
Malawi	Zambia	Nigeria		Turkey
Mali		Portugal		Uganda
		Spain		Zaire
		Thailand		Zambia
		Zimbabwe		Zimbabwe

the education gender gap is larger. Therefore, to reduce total fertility rates in the future, female education levels must be raised until they are more nearly equivalent to the levels achieved by men—that is, until the gender gap is closed.

Figures 1-4 and 1-5 strongly suggest that important benefits for development goals accrue from improving women's education. Simple correlations can be misleading, however, because the level of female education is itself related to other factors such as national income, which in turn influences social welfare. To estimate correctly the magnitude of the education effect, the influence of all variables that determine income and social indicators must be considered concurrently.[5] In the following section the contributions of female education are explored using multivariate analyses for more than 100 developing countries (see appendix 1-1 for details). Moreover, to establish causality rather than simple correlation, measures of past investments in female education are used.[6]

Women's Education and Development: An Intercountry Analysis

The full impact of female education on development indicators can be
broken down into direct and indirect effects. Education bears a direct

Figure 1-5. *Gender Gap in Primary Enrollment, Economic Growth,
and Social Well-Being*

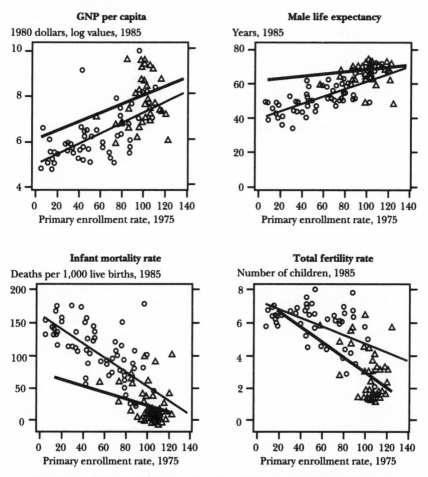

o Female enrollment rate less than or equal to 75 percent of male enrollment rate.
△ Female enrollment rate greater than 75 percent of male enrollment rate.

Note: The regression lines in each graph are estimated from the scatter plots of the
two groups of countries - those in which female enrollment rates are less than or
greater than 75 percent of male enrollment. The bold line is for countries with a
smaller gender gap.

Source: Based on UNESCO and World Bank data.

relationship to social well-being. (Chapter 2 describes these effects in detail.) As noted earlier, women's education influences infant mortality, perhaps because educated mothers are more likely to appreciate the importance of prenatal and neonatal care and so are more likely to use such health care services. But women's education also indirectly improves infant survival rates by leading to higher market productivity and income for women, and thus to better living standards for the family.[7]

We estimate an empirical model that examines both the direct and the indirect effects of female education. The model includes two recursive equations for each social indicator considered.[8] The first equation estimates a country's GNP, the determinants of which are modeled within a production function framework. The second equation specifies the factors that determine the level of each social indicator.[9] Both equations include female education as an explanatory variable. The level of female education is measured by gross enrollment rates for primary and secondary education. Although there are shortcomings to this methodology, enrollment rates are commonly used and widely available. An ideal measure would be one that reflects the actual stock of knowledge and skill in the female population; unfortunately, such a measure is not available for the countries considered.[10] In an attempt to represent the educational attainment of the population at present rather than current investments in education, we use enrollment rates lagged by ten years for primary education and by five years for secondary education.[11]

Each equation also includes a measure of the gender gap in education as an explanatory variable. On the basis of the inferences which we may draw from figure 1-5, we hypothesize that at a given level of enrollment, the education gap between men and women has an independent effect on social indicators. Yet the mechanisms by which gender inequality in education affects development are not well understood. Sen (1984) illuminates the potential for conflict between men and women over how family resources are used. If husbands and wives negotiate the distribution of resources within the family, and if men have access to greater resources outside the family through better job opportunities, for example, the household distribution may favor men. The gender gap in education may well affect the relative earning potential of husband and wife and, thus, the division of labor between them. If a husband is better educated than his wife, he is likely to command a higher wage in the labor market. To benefit most from this situation, the husband and wife specialize with respect to their family responsibilities: the husband devotes more hours to work in the market at the expense of work at home, whereas the wife increases her activities at home at the expense of her work in the market (see, for example, King and Evenson 1983). The wife and the rest of the family can benefit from returns to the husband's education through income transfers from him, but they cannot benefit as easily from the non-monetary returns to his education, such as greater skills and technical knowledge.

In many Sub-Saharan African countries men and women maintain separate budgets. There are well-established conventions concerning which expenditures are to be met from each income. Although men are expected to support their wives, the support varies widely among demographic groups. This separation of budgets implies that women's expenditures—for their farms, their children, and themselves—may be severely limited by their own productivity and access to credit and technology, which in turn are influenced by their own education, not their husbands' education.

Another effect of the gender gap is that the wife's role in decision-making may be weaker than the husband's when the husband's education is much greater than the wife's. Little control by women over their reproductive lives and over the allocation of resources for children may mean larger families and less healthy children. Thus, a large gender gap in education can lead to significant welfare losses.

The empirical results from estimating our recursive models are described in detail in appendix 1-1; a brief overview is provided here. Our findings are consistent with those of others in that we estimate the level of education to have a strong positive effect on GNP (see especially Lau, Jamison, and Louat 1991). As for the gender disparities in education, our GNP equations indicate that for given levels of female education, the size of a country's labor force, and its capital stock, those countries in which the ratio of female to male enrollment rates is less than 0.75 can expect to have a GNP roughly 25 percent lower than countries that are similar except for having a smaller gender gap. In other words, large gender disparities in educational attainment appear to reduce GNP. (See table 1-13 in the appendix to this chapter.)

GNP is but one measure of a country's well-being.[12] We also consider the effects of women's education on life expectancy, infant and maternal mortality, and total fertility. Table 1-8 extracts these estimated effects from the complete set of empirical results. (See table 1-14 in the appendix to this chapter.)

These results indicate that both the level of female enrollment and the gender disparity in enrollments influence social well-being, even after accounting for intercountry differences in GNP. They confirm what was observed from the scatter plots: higher levels of primary and secondary school enrollments for women are associated with longer life expectancy (with comparable benefits experienced by both men and women), lower infant mortality, lower maternal mortality, and

Table 1-8. *Effects of Female Education and the Gender Gap in Education on Social Indicators*
(regression coefficients)

Education variable	Female life expectancy (years)	Male life expectancy (years)	Infant mortality (deaths per 1,000 births)	Maternal mortality (deaths per 100,000 births)	Total fertility (number of children)
Female primary enrollment	0.10	0.09	−0.41	−3.31	−0.01
Female secondary enrollment	0.12	0.11	−0.56	3.02[ns]	−0.03
Female/male enrollment ratio					
<0.42	−4.80	−3.85	21.16	99.82[ns]	0.72
0.42–0.75	−3.41	−2.75	11.37	111.84[ns]	0.73
0.75–0.95	−0.69[ns]	−0.52[ns]	1.88[ns]	82.56[ns]	0.26[ns]

ns Not statistically significant at a 90 percent or greater level.
Source: Table 1–14 in the appendix to this chapter.

lower total fertility rates. These coefficients represent the net effect of the education variables on the social indicators and can be interpreted as follows, using infant mortality as an example. The coefficient of −0.41 implies that after taking into account the effects of GNP and other factors likely to be associated with infant mortality, an increase in the female primary enrollment rate by 10 percentage points can be expected to reduce the infant mortality rate by 4.1 deaths per 1,000 live births. If female secondary enrollment rose by the same amount, there would be an additional reduction of 5.6 deaths per 1,000 live births.

The results demonstrate, moreover, that even after accounting for the effects of GNP per capita and the levels of female enrollment, a large gender disparity in educational attainment reduces social well-being. The life expectancy of males is a case in point. Men living in those countries in which the female to male enrollment ratio is less than 0.42 would experience reductions of nearly four years in their average life expectancy, in relation to men in countries that were comparable except for having a smaller gender gap in schooling. Similarly striking results hold for the other social indicators. As countries approach greater gender equality in enrollments, the detrimental effect of the differential diminishes, with a gender gap of between 0.75 and 0.96 imparting effects which, although still negative, are not statistically significant.

We illustrate the importance of these results by conducting a series of policy simulations. We assume that gender disparities in education are reduced by raising female enrollment and then consider how this increase will influence national income and social well-being. As noted earlier, our measure of the gender gap depends on whether the enrollment disparity is greater at the primary or the secondary level. If the female to male enrollment ratio is lower (that is, if the gender gap is larger) at the primary level, we increase female enrollment in increments of 10 percentage points. If the ratio is lower at the secondary level, we increase female enrollment in increments of only 5 percentage points, since closing the gender gap would be more costly. Once a country reaches parity in both primary and secondary schooling, female enrollments are raised no further. The results of the simulations are summarized in figure 1-6.[13]

Qualitatively, the simulation results are the same for all country income groups. The magnitude of the effects differs, however, with gains usually being larger in poorer countries. To illustrate this, consider the simulation results for infant mortality rates. In 1985 the average infant mortality rate in our sample of low-income countries was 126 deaths per 1,000 live births, which is nearly 60 percent greater than the rate in lower-middle-income countries and more than double the rate in high-income countries (mostly those belonging to the Organization for Economic Cooperation and Development, OECD). Had the female enrollment ratio in low-income countries been 10 percentage points higher at the primary level in 1975 (or 5 percentage points higher at the secondary level in 1980), the average infant mortality rate in those countries would have been 7 percent lower than its actual 1985 level. In comparison, if female enrollment ratios were that much higher in lower-middle-income and upper-middle-income countries, the average infant mortality rates would be 6 and 9 percent lower than their actual 1985 levels, respectively.

One important conclusion we draw from these analyses of country data is that both the level of female education and the gender gap in education are important determinants of (aggregate) family well-being and economic growth. The benefits of improving female education go beyond increasing individual productivity and income. When fertility decreases, population pressure eases; when a family's health improves, life expectancy increases and the quality of life rises, not only for the family, but also for the community. Our results demonstrate that a country's failure to raise the education of women to the same level as that of men imposes a substantial cost on its development efforts. Unless the gender gap in education is closed, desired improvements in social indicators can be achieved only at much higher levels of economic growth.

Costs, Benefits, and Gender Differentials

If women's education is so important, why do women remain undereducated compared with men? Why do gender differentials in educa-

Figure 1-6. *Effect on Social Indicators of Closing the Gender Gap in Education (Simulation Results)*

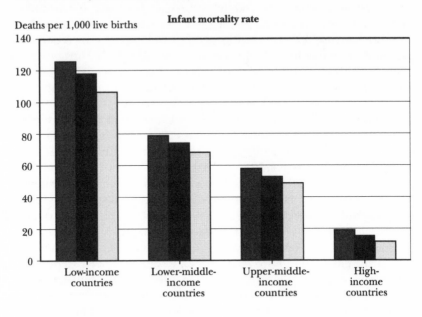

Deaths per 1,000 live births   **Infant mortality rate**

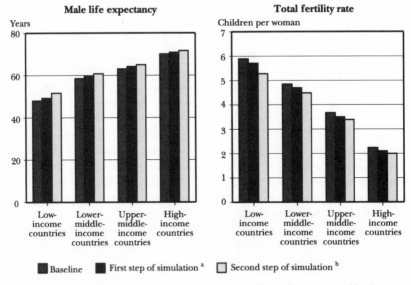

Male life expectancy   **Total fertility rate**

■ Baseline   ■ First step of simulation [a]   □ Second step of simulation [b]

Note: The education gap is "closed" in two steps, as explained in notes a and b. See text for a full explanation.
  a. Female enrollment in primary school increases 10 percent from the baseline; female enrollment in secondary school increases 5 percent from the baseline.
  b. Female enrollment in primary school increases 20 percent from the baseline; female enrollment in secondary school increases 10 percent from the baseline.
Source: Tables 1-12, 1-13, and 1-14.

tion persist? In this section we present a conceptual approach for organizing the factors that can explain the current state of women's education and for understanding the dynamics underlying educational outcomes. We propose, in short, that gender differentials in education endure because those persons who bear the private costs of investing in schooling for girls and women fail to receive the full benefits of their investment. This is especially true because much of the payoff in educating women is broadly social.[14]

The body of empirical work on the determinants of school enrollment in developing countries is expanding. The contribution of this literature is that it disentangles the many and complex influences on school enrollment. The studies are based, implicitly or explicitly, on a framework that treats education as a family or individual decision influenced by perceptions about current costs and future benefits. The decisionmaker weighs the benefits, net of costs, from spending family resources on education against the net benefits of keeping children out of school. The costs include those direct financial costs, indirect or opportunity costs, and nonpecuniary costs that are borne privately by the parents or the student. The benefits include returns both to the family (in higher earnings for the children, some share of which is returned to the parents) and to society (in improved quality of life, as evidenced in our earlier discussion).

Costs are often measured by the availability of, or distance to, school, for lack of better data on the costs that each parent or student faces.[15] A few studies have estimated the effect of the opportunity cost of schooling on enrollment or attainment in developing countries and have found a negative relationship (for example, Rosenzweig and Evenson 1977). Unlike costs, benefits do not usually find their way into empirical studies of school enrollment, primarily because of measurement difficulties (see chapter 2). Improved productivity in the workplace, as measured by expected earnings in the labor market corresponding to given levels of education, is easier to calculate than other returns to schooling, such as increased future productivity in unpaid labor, greater efficiency in taking care of one's children or one's health, or enhanced ability to deal with problems or "disequilibria" in one's daily life (Schultz 1975).

But how do these costs and benefits affect the schooling of men and women differently? Can they account for disparities in the amounts that parents are willing to invest in educating their daughters and their sons?

Although the returns to schooling go primarily to the student, the decision and the resources usually come from the parents, especially in the early school years. Thus the perception of parents may be the key factor. And parents may have different perceptions regarding their sons' and daughters' education.[16] In certain societies they tend to favor sons, not only in education but sometimes also in the allocation of food at mealtime or in the distribution of inheritance (Greenhalgh 1985, Rosenzweig and Schultz 1982). Such behavior on the part of parents may not be discriminatory in itself but may be a rational response to constraints imposed by poverty and to expected returns determined by labor market conditions and tradition. This does not make the consequences any less pernicious, however. When the expected returns to sending daughters to school do not exceed the costs of doing so, female education as an investment becomes unattractive to parents. Daughters will then be educated only to the extent that parents are willing to accept low economic returns. Appendix 1-2 presents a formal economic model that incorporates the effects of these factors.

Financial, Opportunity, and Psychic Costs

Even when education is public and tuition is free, school attendance still entails outlays from family resources. Miscellaneous school charges, learning materials, transportation, and boarding fees are some of the nontuition costs of sending children to school. Parental spending on education can be quite large. In Malawi, for example, a student at the secondary level paid K30 (Malawian kwacha) in tuition and K71 in boarding charges in 1982, or 38 percent of the total cost per student place (World Bank 1986). The families also incurred additional expenses for uniforms and transportation to school. In Korea in the mid-1960s about 70 percent of national educational expenses were paid for by parents and students. These contributions were used for the construction and operation of schools and for books, supplies, room and board, and transportation (McGinn and others 1980).

For a variety of reasons, some of these out-of-pocket expenses may be greater for girls than for boys. For example, parents' greater reluctance to send daughters to school without proper attire raises the cost of their attendance. And in some cultures, parents' concern for the physical and moral safety of their daughters makes them unwilling to let them travel long distances to school each day, necessitating costly boarding and lodging arrangements.

In addition, parents may not be able to afford the opportunity costs of educating their children. These costs vary by sex and from country to country. Although in some countries (for example, Botswana, Côte d'Ivoire, and some areas of the Philippines) boys perform a larger share of family labor, herding livestock or plowing the fields, in most places girls work more in the home and marketplace than boys. They cook, clean house, fetch water, and help their mothers care for younger children, especially those who are ill. In Nepal and Java, for example, most young girls spend at least one-third more hours per day working at home and in the market than boys of the same age; in some age groups this rises to as many as 85 percent more hours (table 1-9). In Malaysian households, girls between the ages of five and six who do home or market chores work as much as three-fourths more hours per week than boys of the same age. And in Chinese and Indian house-

Table 1-9. *Differences in Time Spent on Market and Household Activities by Girls Relative to Boys*

Author and location of study	Definition of work	Age group		
Cabañero (1978)		*6–8*	*9–11*	*12–14*
Philippines	Average annual hours in home			
	and market production	0.93	1.49	1.02
de Tray (1983)		*5–6*	*7–9*	*10–14*
Peninsular Malaysia	Annual participation rates in home and market production			
	Malays	1.82	1.17	1.10
	Chinese	2.50	1.78	1.31
	Indians	2.18	1.79	1.35
	Average hours per week if working			
	Malays	1.21	1.74	1.75
	Chinese	1.00	2.19	1.35
	Indians	1.76	2.49	1.80
King (1982)		*7–10*	*11–14*	
Philippines	Labor force participation rates			
	Youths in school	0.60	0.29	
	Youths out of school	—	0.37	
King and Bellew (1989)		*5–7*	*8–10*	*11–13*
Peru	Labor force participation rates			
	Youths in school	0.56	0.89	0.88
	Youths out of school	1.07	1.03	1.14
Mueller (1984)		*7–9*	*10–14*	
Rural Botswana	Proportion of total time in home and market production	0.93	0.92	
Nag and others (1980)		*6–8*	*9–11*	*12–14*
Indonesia	Hours per day in home and market production			
	Javanese village	0.97	1.74	1.85
	Nepalese village	1.32	1.29	1.36
Newman (1988)		*7–14*		
Côte d'Ivoire	Labor force participation rates	0.94		

holds in Malaysia, seven-to-nine-year-old girls work as many as 120–150 percent more hours than boys. Clearly, girls who work more than their brothers will be less likely to attend school or will be more overworked if they do (causing them to perform less well). These examples prove that gender inequality exists even at early ages.

Besides lost work, parents may feel that girls are forgoing important childcare, household, and craft training at home if they go to school. The relative importance of these training opportunities differs from country to country depending on the expected adult occupation. For example, if most women enter the informal labor market by continuing in a crafts tradition or in agriculture, relying on skills imparted by their mothers, then the cost of attending formal schooling must include not only the opportunity cost of current time but also the lost alternative training.[17]

Finally, in addition to the financial costs and the opportunity costs of schooling, educating girls may exact nonpecuniary or "psychic" costs as well. In certain settings, religion as well as sociocultural factors (such as norms delineating the societal, economic, and familial roles of women) strongly influence parents' choices by imposing a heavy cost on nonconformist behavior. These may bear significantly on schooling decisions. In countries in which females are usually secluded, for example, girls may attend only those schools that do not admit boys or employ male teachers. These concerns are usually stronger when girls reach puberty than earlier. Furthermore, parents may consider education itself a negative factor because of prevailing doubts about whether better-educated women make good wives. In many traditional societies, education beyond the acquisition of literacy is contrary to the social pressure for women to become wives and mothers and threatens their possibilities for marriage.

With economic development and expanding work opportunities for women, however, tension builds up between the family's adherence to traditional social norms and its desire to benefit from the changing conditions. The questions then become, when and to what extent will people respond to these shifts, and which families and individuals will respond? Economic theory does not deal formally with the impact of sociocultural forces on individual behavior, but it does predict behavioral adjustments to changes in incomes and prices that result from economic growth. For example, it predicts that a rise in women's wages, which in turn increases returns to their education, tends to increase parents' investment in their daughters' education. The magnitude and speed of their response depends on acquisition of new information and on the price and income elasticities of their demand for education. Clearly, parental preferences are both shaped by and shape the economic environment.

Benefits at Work and at Home

Even when the costs of educating girls and boys are identical, parents may still keep girls at home to work and send their sons to school. Although educating a girl benefits not only her parents but also the girl herself and her future family, as well as society at large, it may be parents' expectations of receiving greater returns from educating sons than from educating daughters that determine which of their children they will send to school.

Education enhances women's economic productivity in both the farm and the nonfarm sectors. In a study of the productivity of men and women farmers in Sub-Saharan Africa, the gain in productivity from education was found to be higher for women than for men. Studies on the determinants of wage earnings have found the marginal effect of education to be about as large for women as for men once labor force participation, work experience, and sector of employment have been taken into account. But discriminatory employment practices against women have limited their work opportunities and reduced the earnings they can expect to gain from education. Entry barriers against women, explicit or implicit, in certain occupations serve as deterrents to education; examples include restrictions on hiring married women in wage-paying jobs in the manufacturing or service sectors. Some of the barriers begin even at the primary school level, with teachers and textbooks projecting attitudes that discourage performance by girls, or promoting stereotypes of girls as less capable than boys of learning mathematics or technical subjects. Other barriers arise at the postprimary level with gender-specific admissions policies in certain areas of study.

Unless daughters transfer part of their future income to their parents, parents, who must bear some of the costs of their education, may not have sufficient incentives to do so.[18] For example, the earlier daughters marry and move in with their husbands' families, the less parents enjoy the benefits of their education. In Bangladesh 75 percent of women living in rural areas who have ever been married were married by the age of seventeen. In India 75 percent of this group were married by nineteen. Some evidence suggests that when girls do not marry so early but spend some time working in the labor force, parents are more willing to educate their daughters (see chapter 2 in this volume; Acharya and Bennett 1981). In Hong Kong, although custom dictates that sons take responsibility for their parents, girls who marry when they are older and help their parents in the interim appear to attain higher levels of schooling than others.

Although women with more education are generally better paid and more likely to find employment in the paid sector than those with less education, married women are more likely to withdraw from the labor market as their schooling increases from the primary to the secondary level. Pregnancy, childbirth, and childcare duties remove women from the paid work force for substantial periods or even permanently. Moreover, this pattern feeds back into employers' decisions about wages, causing them to place a lower value on female than on male workers. But the withdrawal from the labor force by married women is also due partly to the fact that education increases women's productivity in nonmarket activities too, and that unless better-paying jobs outside the home are available to those with secondary education, staying at home is often a superior option.

In the home the woman's education has a greater effect on family welfare than does the man's, as discussed earlier. Studies in demography, economics, medicine, and anthropology have found a strong link between a mother's schooling and a decrease in the incidence of mortality among her children—a link that appears to be strongest in low-income countries. These results show that an added year of education for a mother is associated with a reduction of between 5 and 10 percent in child mortality (see chapter 2).

We have also noted earlier that more schooling for the mother appears to lead to better hygiene, improved nutritional practices, and greater effectiveness in caring for her family's health. Does education encourage more use of health inputs and make possible more effective use of these inputs, or does education actually provide a mother with the capacity to cope with health risks and better manage her child's environment? Education enabled Nigerian mothers to exploit local public health services more effectively (Caldwell 1979). In the Philippines mothers' schooling was found to have a larger protective effect on child health in communities without piped water and water-sealed toilets and in communities that were farther from outpatient health care facilities than in areas that were better off (Barrera 1990). In general, schooling seems to equip mothers with the knowledge needed to be more effective in their roles at home.

A mother's schooling also improves her own health. One reason for this is that more schooling seems to accord her greater control over the frequency and spacing of childbearing and to influence her use of health services during pregnancy and birth. Frequent pregnancies take their toll on the mother, resulting in what is termed "maternal depletion syndrome," especially in poorer areas where the higher dietary requirements of pregnant or lactating women often remain unfulfilled. Among better-educated women in Latin America and Asia, through higher prevalence of contraception, fertility rates have declined and are approaching targeted levels (Cochrane and Sai 1991). It should be of interest to population planners to know that the wife's education has a stronger negative effect on fertility (by almost three times) than does the husband's education.

Similarly, a mother's schooling increases the educational attainment of her children, especially of her daughters. In many cases, it has been found to have a larger impact on children's schooling than the father's education (even though the father's education also implies an income effect). A study of female students enrolled in the public education system in Cairo found that differences in measures of their self-confidence were associated with their mothers' education. The more formal schooling a mother had, the more she gave praise and confidence to her daughters and the more her standards and expectations for her daughters differed from those of less-educated mothers.

Finally, education enhances women's ability to exercise their rights and responsibilities. The right to own land, for example, is diminished by not being able to read or understand contracts or to do simple arithmetic. The right to vote is meaningless unless women can inform themselves of the issues of the day. Violence against women in the home or on the streets has been associated not just with poverty but also with illiteracy, which prevents women from asserting their rights and protecting themselves through due process of law. These benefits are as important in the lives of women as the economic and welfare benefits we have discussed.

Table 1-10 summarizes the costs and benefits, both market and non-market, associated with women's education, as well as the agents who gain and those who pay. As this table emphasizes, educating women yields durable future benefits to individual women, to their families, and to society. The public benefits are large if often unmeasurable, but since the burden of costs is often borne by parents, the education that girls get is likely to be below the socially optimal level. It is hardly surprising, then, that in poorer countries women remain undereducated.

Determinants of the Gender Gap: A Summary of Regional Findings

In this chapter we have reported on our empirical research, which uses extensive data for 152 developing countries. This research indicates that the level of female education and the gender gap in education are both important determinants of aggregate family well-being and economic growth. To support the discussion in the chapters that follow, we have also presented a framework for analyzing how educational decisions are made within the family. This framework suggests that the degree to which many of the benefits of women's schooling are social, whereas many of the costs are private, accounts for the persistence of the gender gap in education.

Table 1-10. *Costs and Benefits Associated with Educating Girls*

Payer of costs or recipient of benefits	Market	Nonmarket
Current costs		
Private		
Parents	Uniforms, textbooks and supplies, examination fees	Opportunity cost of children's time in school
	Tuition, admission fees, tutorial fees	Psychic costs
	Travel	
	Board and lodging if living away from home	
Student	—[a]	Psychic costs
Social	Public expenditures for teachers' salaries, supplies, buildings	Forgone output of enrolled children[b]
Future benefits		
Private		
Parents	Higher family income	Improved social status for family
Student	Higher earnings	Higher life expectancy
	Greater occupational mobility	Greater fertility control
		Lower infant mortality
Social	Higher GNP; higher GNP per capita	Reduced population growth
	Increased labor productivity	Healthier population (lower infant mortality, longer life span)
	Faster GNP growth	
	Higher taxes on earnings	Better-functioning political processes

a. The assumption that the student does not bear any current "market" costs is realistic only at the primary or secondary level of education. Beyond the secondary level the student herself is likely to bear the costs of tuition and travel and to incur the opportunity cost of time spent in school.

b. This cost would have a larger market component for older than for younger girls.

Chapter 2 focuses on the multiple benefits that arise from increasing the education of women and on issues regarding the measurement of these benefits. It emphasizes the need to understand the sources of gender differentials in schooling and how these are affected by the structure of aggregate demand for labor, as well as by the costs of educating girls. The chapter also presents available microlevel evidence of the nonmarket benefits—evidence that helps flesh out the findings from the cross-country analysis in this chapter. The conclusion reached is that greater investments in the primary and secondary education of women are warranted on economic grounds.

Chapters 3 through 7 describe the regional settings within which schooling decisions are made, as well as the current status of women's education in each region. A brief summary of their findings and a note on methodology are given in this section. Finally, chapter 8 describes and analyzes various policy interventions intended to raise women's educational attainment and reviews specific examples of past and ongoing education programs to demonstrate what types of schemes have been effective.

The five regional chapters illustrate the vast differences in both the level of female education and the extent of the gender gap in the developing world. Furthermore, they depict the rich diversity of cultures, institutions, and economic conditions that result in distinct barriers to the education of women. Each chapter begins with a summary of the status of female education in the region and then surveys what the available literature—academic studies, government reports, project assessments, and the like—has to say about the factors that influence the schooling of girls and women. Interest in research on the education of women, and hence the amount of available data, vary widely by region. A strong and growing body of international research explores gender issues in education in South Asia, but only limited empirical research has been carried out for the Middle East and North Africa, even though female enrollment rates in this region lag behind male rates. And in Latin America, where primary school enrollment rates have generally been about the same for girls as for boys, most research on education does not focus on gender issues.

Despite clear regional differences in cultures and institutions, chapters 3 through 7 indicate striking commonalities in the factors that influence the educational attainment of women. Some of these factors are noted here, grouped not by the type of effect but by the context in which they operate—the family and home, the school, or the community. The regional chapters present a fuller discussion of these findings.

Family and Home

Parents' education has an important influence on gender differences in education. In Ghana female students in secondary schools are more likely than their male counterparts to come from families with more education. In Egypt, if income is held constant, parents' education has the most influence on the educational aspirations of children in both rural and urban areas. In some countries it is the father's education that appears to make a difference; in others, it is the mother's. A girl in Côte d'Ivoire with a university-educated father is thirty-five times more likely to enter an academic secondary school than the daughter of a man with no education. In Peru the father's education has twice as large an impact on the sons' schooling as the mother's education, whereas the effect of each parent's education on the daughters' schooling is equally strong and positive. In Thailand the father's, not the mother's, educational aspirations for daughters are important in determining their schooling, but this does not hold for sons. In Pakistan the large majority of illiterate women want only religious education for their daughters, but the bulk of those with some primary education want at least higher secondary education; in lower-income households, better-educated fathers tend to enroll their daughters in school more than do less-educated fathers.

In Sub-Saharan Africa the evidence is great that women bear a large part of the burden of educating their children, especially in areas where polygamous marriage is common or where male migration is widespread—that is, where women become de facto heads of households. And when women run the households, as in Botswana and Lesotho, girls are as likely as boys to go to school and to stay in school. Similarly, in Saudi Arabia, the higher the educational level of mothers, the greater their influence on their daughters' academic plans.

What does parents' education signify? The literature interprets the effect of this variable in different ways. First, it may be correlated with the value that parents attach to formal education. The expected direction of the relationship is that the more education parents have, the more they value formal education for their daughters as much as for their sons. Second, parents' education measures the degree to which parents are open to influences other than tradition. Even in a society that restricts the activities of girls and women, parents who are themselves educated are less likely to see formal education as a threat to their way of life. Third, parents' education serves as a limited measure of family income or wealth when more direct measures are not available. When estimates of family income are available, as in Malaysia, income has been found to have three times as great an influence on the probability that girls between the ages of twelve and eighteen will be enrolled in school as that boys of the same ages will be enrolled.

Another family factor that affects girls' education is the alternative demands made on their time. In countries such as Brazil, Chile, and Nicaragua, boys perform a larger share of family labor than girls, but in many other countries girls do more work in the home and marketplace than boys do (see table 1-9). In Ethiopia household duties are a primary reason for keeping boys out of school, whereas sending girls to school might be seen as a famine-fighting strategy because being literate allows girls to marry better or to find work. In Jordan and Nepal, however, girls drop out of school to help with domestic tasks, especially the care of siblings.

Schools and Teachers

The school environment exerts its own influence on female education. Compulsory education legislation, open admissions policies, and tuition-free education have not guaranteed equal access to education. For many other reasons, schools may be regarded as closed or inaccessible to girls and women. In Egypt, Morocco, and Tunisia parents are reluctant to send their daughters to distant schools because they fear exposing them to moral or physical peril. Even in the relatively more open societies of Malaysia and the Philippines, distance to school is a greater deterrent to girls' enrollment than to boys'. And school facilities themselves can be hostile to girls. In Bangladesh parents have withdrawn girls but not boys from schools without latrines. In Ghana and Kenya girls are overrepresented in secondary level institutions of low quality, usually implying their lack of access to science and math courses. Kuwait and Saudi Arabia (in contrast to Egypt and Morocco) illustrate how wealth has improved school facilities for girls, thereby mitigating the effects of cultural barriers.

A study on Brazil shows that teachers believe girls to be less capable than boys in mathematics; consequently, they fail to use teaching techniques that might improve girls' achievement in that subject. In Ghana and Kenya girls are channeled into domestic science, handicrafts, and biology and boys into chemistry, mathematics, and vocational subjects. Various studies have found that single-sex schools may be more effective than coeducational schools for girls' learning. In Thailand, such schools make a difference; even after controlling for such factors as socioeconomic background and school resources, girls achieve more in single-sex schools than in coeducational schools, whereas boys do better in the latter.

Employment and Marriage

Although we have focused in this chapter on the nonmarket benefits from educating girls, which are manifold, the regional reviews suggest that the returns to female education in the labor market are also important. In Nicaragua higher predicted earnings for the women in the household are significantly associated with greater educational attainment by the children. In Mexico visible returns to schooling, measured as the proportion of white-collar workers with high incomes, were more important for the decision to send girls to school than for the decision to send boys.

But even in East Asia and Latin America, where more women are entering the formal labor market, women are still concentrated in a few jobs—those that are generally characterized by low skills, low wages, and low mobility. In Malaysia boys expect higher salaries than girls do, and girls believe that the range of jobs open to them is restricted. These expectations, in turn, affect educational aspirations.

The sharp distinction between male and female socialization still persists in many countries. In Arab countries, such as Egypt and Morocco, the socialization of girls emphasizes the acceptance of the predominant sex roles, with marriage and family, not employment in the labor market, as the ultimate goals of women. In Ethiopia 20 percent of the primary school students surveyed in a study were already either promised, married, or divorced. Girls growing up under such conditions will be educated only if schooling is viewed as a positive factor in marriage. In Zaire a higher bride-price for better-educated girls induces some parents to send their daughters to school. But in northern Nigeria a social consensus seems to have emerged that education in Western schools is bad for girls and for society as a whole. This attitude is a barrier to female education even when the government or donor agencies finance the construction of schools, thus lowering private costs.

Limitations of Methodology

The study findings presented in the regional chapters and summarized here point to a host of factors that limit women's education, but they need to be interpreted with some circumspection. Past studies have examined the extent of the gender problem by comparing average schooling or achievement levels of both sexes, using either two-way tables or a dummy variable for sex in the case of multiple regression analysis. These comparisons, however, do not elucidate the more difficult question: what accounts for sex differences in education? To answer this, multiple regression models will need to examine whether family background, school-related variables, or individual characteristics besides sex have distinct effects on whether girls enroll in school, how long they stay in school, and how well they perform. This requires estimating separate regression parameters for girls and boys.

Conclusions regarding causality from aggregate two-way relationships can be misleading. For example, the marginal returns to education in terms of market wages have been found to be at least as high for women as for men (see chapter 2). That the average educational level is lower for women than for men does not necessarily mean that women's schooling does not respond to market incentives. Rather, the rate of return to female education may be higher simply because the average level of education is lower.

And even when the underlying research has been executed with great care, methodological and measurement problems persist.

Studies that attempt to quantify the strength of the different factors affecting, for example, the decision to continue in or drop out from a given level of schooling often fail to correct for the fact that the members of the sample studied (girls of a particular age group in school, in this instance) are not a random selection from the population at large (all girls in that age group). Certain family characteristics are highly associated with the probability that girls will ever enroll in school. To assess the relative strength of home, school, and other factors that affect continuation and attainment, it is necessary to control for the likelihood that girls already in school are a nonrandom sample from the relevant age cohort.[19]

The sampling problem is perhaps most obvious when dealing with female school populations that are a small percentage of the relevant age groups on a national or regional basis, but it also pertains when dealing with apparently high enrollment and continuance rates if there is a divergence in the types of school that males and females attend. For example, when both coeducational and single-sex institutions exist, it is very common for single-sex schools to be more selective, both academically and socially. A finding that girls in single-sex schools experience the highest achievement levels is of limited value unless statistical controls demonstrate that this effect remains after accounting for the backgrounds of those attending single-sex schools. Therefore, it is necessary first to correct for the types of girls who either attend school at all or attend a certain type or level of school before one can begin to make supported statements about those factors that can increase or decrease enrollment, retention, attainment, or scholastic performance.

The use of correlations, although illustrative and descriptive, does not provide adequate information on the net effect that a particular variable may have on the dependent variable. Often studies make no attempt to control for confounding factors when trying to identify those variables that influence women's education. For example, the attribution in Akande (1987) of differences in achievement and aspiration to urban or rural residence is problematic given that parental income, parental education, school quality, and labor market opportunities (to name only a few factors) are also highly correlated with living in urban or rural areas. Cooksey (1981) makes a similar point when he argues that comparisons of school populations in areas of high and of low enrollment are generally not valid because children in areas of low enrollment are usually chosen to be educated because of high ability, high socioeconomic status, or both.

Specifying incomplete models of educational choice, often as a result of measurement problems, also leads to biased estimates of the effects of various factors. Genetically determined ability affects learning and educational attainment, and thus income; but, because of the limited data on cognitive ability, the effect of this factor on education and income has been neglected in most studies of the determinants of schooling and its rate of return. Griliches and Mason (1972), in a study of the United States, estimated that failure to control for the effect of ability overstates the estimated rate of return to education by between 7 and 15 percent. Boissiere, Knight, and Sabot (1985), in a study of Kenya and Tanzania, found that controlling for ability lowered the estimated rate of return by about 60 percent.

Measurement problems regarding costs and benefits are pervasive, and without appropriate measures of these factors, our understanding of the sources of gender differentials in schooling is severely hampered. The gender difference in opportunity costs to the family, for example, has been measured by wages that boys and girls could command in the labor market. Yet many of the work activities that children engage in are outside the wage sector. Also, using time spent in alternative activities as a measure of the value of time is flawed since it is itself an outcome, determined by the value of time. The measurement of benefits as perceived by parents is even more elusive. Whereas the market and nonmarket benefits are plain to see in the aggregate, choosing appropriate measures that reflect individual or family differences in benefits presents problems. Is the wage that an individual receives in the labor market the correct measure of economic returns expected at the time schooling decisions were made? When explaining a student's likelihood to continue in school, whose wage is relevant?

Finally, sampling methods used in studies should be made explicit. Identifying the number and gender of pupils is not helpful even to the informed reader when the method of selecting the pupils or their background characteristics are not part of the report. Unfortunately, many studies do not describe their sampling methods adequately.

These estimation issues imply that readers of the literature should interpret findings with caution. It is reassuring, nevertheless, that the numerous studies reviewed in the following chapters demonstrate remarkable consistency across countries in the direction of the effects that perceived costs and benefits have on women's schooling. Such studies are useful for suggesting the broad directions policy should take to improve female education. Designing specific interventions, however, requires estimating more precise magnitudes of these effects, and this means paying greater attention to methodology.

Appendix 1-1. Description of the Data Sources

The data compiled for our analysis are derived primarily from United Nations statistical sources and World Bank documents.[20] The final analytical data base contains pooled time-series data covering 152 countries and quinquennial years during the period 1960–85.

Countries included in the data set span the entire globe, but we incorporate into our analysis only those reporting consistent data. Table 1-11 lists these countries by broad regional categories: Sub-Saharan Africa (42 countries), East Asia and the Pacific (7), South and Southeast Asia (17), Latin America and the Caribbean (31), the Middle East and North Africa (20, excluding Israel), and Other (34). Data for each of the variables were not always available in every year for every country. Details on the availability of data for each of the regressions are presented in table 1-12, which also displays variable definitions, sources, and means for each year. Tables 1-13 and 1-14 present regression results.

Appendix 1-2. An Economic Model of Gender Differences

To illustrate the potential mechanisms by which policy can affect gender differences in educational outcomes, one can specify a simple intergenerational model that depicts heuristically how parents in developing countries may choose to invest in their children's education. For simplicity, we assume that parental preferences embody no gender differences. Gender differences in education thus arise from social, economic, and cultural environments within which rewards and restrictions differ by sex.[21]

Suppose that parental preferences may be described by a simple two-period model, in which the first period represents the time during which children rely on their parents and the second period represents the time during which parents rely on their children:

$$(1) \qquad U = U(C_1, C_2)$$

where C_1 represents parents' consumption in the first period and C_2 represents parents' consumption in the second period.

We assume that during the first period parental income (V_1) is exogenous and that boys (m) and girls (f) may spend their childhood years in two activities, namely, investing in schooling (E_j) and working (L_j).

$$(2) \qquad T = E_j + L_j$$

where $j = f, m$. Child labor may be supplied to a well-developed market, or it may be employed in home production at wages (or shadow wages), w_m and w_f.

During the second period, we assume that parents rely solely on their children for economic support. Parents' income (and hence, their consumption) depends on both the income of their children (Y_j) and the rate at which the children may transfer income to parents (a_j).

Table 1-11. *Developing Economies (by Region) and Other Economies Included in the Analytical Data Base*

Sub-Saharan Africa

Angola	Côte d'Ivoire	Madagascar	Sierra Leone
Benin	Equatorial Guinea	Malawi	Somalia
Botswana	Ethiopia	Mali	South Africa
Burkina Faso	Gabon	Mauritania	Swaziland
Burundi	Gambia, The	Mauritius	Tanzania
Cameroon	Guinea	Mozambique	Togo
Cape Verde	Guinea-Bissau	Niger	Uganda
Central African Rep.	Kenya	Nigeria	Zaire
Chad	Lesotho	Rwanda	Zambia
Comoros	Liberia	Senegal	Zimbabwe
Congo			

East Asia and the Pacific

China	Korea, Rep.
Fiji	Mongolia
Hong Kong	Papua New Guinea
Korea, Dem. People's Rep.	

South and Southeast Asia

Afghanistan	Iran	Philippines
Bangladesh	Lao PDR	Singapore
Bhutan	Malaysia	Sri Lanka
Cambodia	Myanmar	Thailand
India	Nepal	Viet Nam
Indonesia	Pakistan	

Note: The data base contains quinquennial data beginning in 1960. For most countries it contains six data points.

$$(3) \qquad C_2 = C_2(a_m Y_m, a_f Y_f)$$

Each child's level of income, in turn, depends on his or her investment in education (E_j).[22]

$$(4) \qquad Y_j = y(E_j), j = f, m$$

where the function y, which can be interpreted generally as an earnings function, can differ for males and females (see empirical evidence for this in chapter 2).

Parents then face a clear tradeoff in choosing to educate their children. If children spend time in school, the parents' future income will rise, but only at the expense of current family consumption.

By substitution, we can simplify the problem to that of maximizing the objective function,

$$(1') \qquad U = U\{C_1; C_2 [a_m Y_m(E_m), a_f Y_f(E_f)]\}$$

Table 1-11 (continued)

Latin America and the Caribbean

Antigua and	Colombia	Guyana	Paraguay
Barbuda	Costa Rica	Haiti	Peru
Argentina	Cuba	Honduras	Puerto Rico
Bahamas	Dominica	Jamaica	Suriname
Barbados	Dominican Rep.	Martinique	Trinidad and
Belize	Ecuador	Mexico	Tobago
Bolivia	El Salvador	Nicaragua	Uruguay
Brazil	Guatemala	Panama	Venezuela
Chile			

Middle East and North Africa

Algeria	Jordan	Oman	Tunisia
Bahrain	Kuwait	Qatar	Turkey
Cyprus	Lebanon	Saudi Arabia	United Arab
Egypt, Arab Rep.	Libya	Sudan	Emirates
Iraq	Morocco	Syrian Arab Rep.	Yemen, Arab Rep.
			Yemen, PDR

Other

Albania	France	Israel	Portugal
Australia	Germany,	Italy	Romania
Austria	Democratic Rep.	Japan	Spain
Belgium	Germany, Federal	Luxembourg	Sweden
Bulgaria	Rep.	Malta	Switzerland
Canada	Greece	Netherlands	United Kingdom
Czechoslovakia	Hungary	New Zealand	United States
Denmark	Iceland	Norway	U.S.S.R.
Finland	Ireland	Poland	Yugoslavia

subject to

(5) $$p_1C_1 = V_1 + w_m(T - E_m) + w_f(T - E_f).$$

The first-order conditions imply that parents will choose the level of their sons' and daughters' education such that

$$\frac{\partial C_2/\partial(E_f)}{\partial C_2/\partial(E_m)} = \frac{w_f}{w_m}.$$

This equation implies that the benefits of educating sons relative to daughters (in terms of income transferred to the parents) must equal the relative opportunity cost of educating them (that is, income forgone while in school). Suppose then that the relative opportunity cost of educating daughters (w_f/w_m) rises. As long as there exist dimin-

Table 1-12. Definitions, Sources, and Mean Values for Variables Included in Intercountry Analysis

Variable	Definition	Mean value 1975	1980	1985
Ln GNP	1980 U.S. dollars	22.74 (126)	23.04 (125)	22.85 (124)
Female life expectancy	Expected years at birth	60.8 (148)	62.5 (147)	64.2 (147)
Male life expectancy	Expected years at birth	56.8 (148)	58.4 (147)	60.0 (144)
Infant mortality rate	Deaths per 1,000 live births	82.5 (138)	73.1 (138)	66.6 (144)
Maternal mortality rate	Deaths per 100,000 live births	382.0 (68)	269.9 (108)	—a
Total fertility rate	Children per woman	5.0 (126)	4.7 (125)	4.4 (125)
Ln capital stock (if reported)	Estimated by summing capital investments using quinquennial data; total depreciation over twenty years assumed	22.26 (104)	22.64 (109)	22.57 (114)
Ln labor force		15.39 (130)	15.53 (129)	15.65 (129)
Female primary enrollment	Gross enrollment ratio, lagged ten years	78.4 (126)	84.7 (125)	87.0 (116)
Female secondary enrollment	Gross enrollment ratio, lagged five years	35.4 (127)	43.5 (125)	48.4 (111)
Female/male enrollment ratio	Dummy variables based on primary or secondary ratio, whichever is smaller			
<0.42		0.30 (142)	0.20 (136)	0.15 (137)
0.42–0.75		0.23 (142)	0.25 (136)	0.24 (137)
0.75–0.95		0.24 (142)	0.28 (136)	0.30 (137)
Ln total population		15.49 (152)	15.61 (151)	15.71 (151)
Population (thousands) per physician (if reported)		12178.4 (58)	7764.8 (91)	7790.3 (108)
Percentage of population with safe water (if reported)		48.1 (92)	70.4 (21)	63.5 (104)

Note: Figures in parentheses are numbers of countries reporting data.

a. Only nine countries reported maternal mortality for 1985; we therefore excluded 1985 from our analysis of this variable.

Source: World Bank data base (includes data from IMF, UNESCO, and WHO).

Table 1-13. *Regression Results for GNP Models*

Independent variable	Coefficient	t-statistic
Intercept	2.52	3.66
Female/male enrollment ratio		
<0.42	−0.26	−1.74
0.42–0.75	−0.25	−1.95
0.75–0.95	0.02	0.21
Female secondary enrollment	0.03	2.46
Log capital stock	0.71	20.49
Capital × enrollment (× 100)	−0.20	−7.09
Log labor force	0.36	8.43
Labor force × enrollment (× 100)	0.12	1.46
Adjusted R^2	0.96	
F-statistic	239.37	
Sample size	289	

Note: The regression also includes dummy variables if missing capital stock measure, as well as dummy variable for year and for detailed regions.

Source: Authors' calculations.

ishing marginal returns to further education, the education of daughters would fall in relation to that of sons. Alternatively, if the relative returns to educating daughters

$$[\partial C_2/\partial(E_f)] \; / \; [\partial C_2/\partial(E_m)]$$

rise, relative parental investment in their daughters' schooling will also increase.

Without appealing to assumptions about tastes or preferences of parents, this model can explain why daughters might systematically attain less schooling than sons. As modeled, the parental return to education depends on both the manner in which education affects the child's income and the rate at which the child's income is transferred to the parents. Any factor that increases the return to educating sons more than the return to educating daughters will result in parents' providing relatively less education to their daughters. This may happen if the labor market rewards the education of males more than that of females. For example, parents may anticipate that the earnings prospects are poorer for their daughters than for their sons (that is, $\partial Y_m/\partial E_m > \partial Y_f/\partial E_f$). Or custom and social norms may dictate that sons, not daughters, take responsibility for their parents (that is, $a_m > a_f$). For example, a daughter may marry out of her own family into her husband's family, so that parents recoup little if any of the returns from their daughters' education.

Table 1-14. Effects of Female Education on Indicators of Social Well-Being

| | Life expectancy | | | | Mortality | | | | Total fertility | |
| | Female | | Male | | Infant | | Maternal | | | |
Independent variable	Beta	t	Beta	t	Beta	t	Beta	t	Beta	t
Intercept	40.2941	7.58	35.0791	7.10	186.4631	6.16	-996.6836	-1.42	6.5313	4.84
Female primary enrollment	0.0964	7.71	0.0915	7.87	-0.4130	-5.80	-3.3111	-1.98	-0.0064	-2.01
Female secondary enrollment	0.1224	5.52	0.1072	5.21	-0.5649	-4.48	3.0165	1.00	-0.0260	-4.62
Female/male enrollment ratio										
<0.42	-4.8044	-3.82	-3.8525	-3.30	21.1575	2.95	99.8237	0.65	0.7176	2.25
0.42-0.75	-3.4071	-3.20	-2.7511	-2.80	11.3668	1.89	111.8381	0.88	0.7300	2.72
0.75-0.95	-0.6856	-1.09	-0.5168	-0.88	1.8770	0.52	82.5575	0.98	0.2608	1.63
Ln GNP (predicted)	1.7773	4.01	1.7165	4.17	-10.7132	-4.24	-17.0170	-0.30	-0.2136	-1.90
Ln total population	-1.7254	-3.77	-1.6475	-3.88	11.7548	4.51	104.1428	1.68	0.2223	1.91
Population (thousands) per physician	-0.0279	-1.25	-0.0341	-1.65	0.2431	1.91	0.0105	3.72	-0.013	-2.30
Percentage of population with safe water	0.0136	1.11	0.0124	1.10	-0.0168	-0.24	-2.2997	-1.41	-0.0117	-0.38
Regions										
Eastern Africa	-2.2332	-0.96	-0.4342	-0.20	-25.2085	-1.90	180.9228	0.50	1.2033	2.03
Middle Africa	-6.3130	-2.58	-4.6285	-2.04	1.5855	0.11	347.0491	0.91	0.3535	0.57
Northern Africa	0.7706	0.34	3.5143	1.66	-4.6560	-0.36	280.5897	0.80	0.8885	1.54
Southern Africa	-9.3626	-3.54	-7.7855	-3.17	12.7618	0.85	358.8022	0.89	1.8227	2.71
Western Africa	-4.3821	-1.92	-2.7853	-1.31	6.2085	0.48	380.1984	1.05	1.0987	1.90

Caribbean	0.7682	0.32	2.5630	1.13	−16.6017	−1.20	271.6048	0.59	0.3122	0.51
Central America	0.9547	0.42	3.0891	1.47	−11.8763	−0.92	105.1453	0.29	1.2251	2.13
South America	−2.2592	−1.05	−1.0138	−0.51	5.7105	0.47	174.9261	0.51	0.7252	1.33
Eastern Asia	2.3547	1.11	3.3019	1.67	−21.4497	−1.77	−136.1847	−0.39	−0.6231	−1.15
Southeastern Asia	0.5069	0.22	2.5290	1.20	−24.9603	−1.93	8.8818	0.03	−0.3510	−0.61
Southern Asia	−0.5231	−0.22	4.8795	2.22	−20.8305	−1.55	44.5186	0.12	0.1105	0.18
Western Asia	0.9442	0.44	2.9308	1.45	−0.0608	−0.01	17.3155	0.05	1.7244	3.18
Northern Europe	−0.9263	−0.48	−0.1272	−0.07	−2.3011	−0.21	−85.8959	−0.26	0.2628	0.53
Southern Europe	1.7595	0.85	2.6271	1.37	−12.8484	−1.09	−55.9124	−0.14	−0.6410	−1.22
Western Europe	−1.0469	0.53	−1.0219	−0.55	0.1473	0.01	−1.1001	0.00	−0.1616	−0.32
Australia and New Zealand	−1.1982	−0.55	−0.5999	−0.30	0.3836	0.03	98.5990	0.27	0.2403	0.43
Melanesia	−1.8003	−0.64	2.2609	0.86	−27.2732	−1.69	733.8979	1.79	0.2571	0.36
Adjusted R^2	0.9378		0.9318		0.8948		0.5070		0.8463	
F-statistic	137.900		124.990		77.680		6.160		51.550	
Sample size	289		275		275		147		275	

Note: Regression also includes dummy variables for year and if missing data on population per physician or safe water measures. The equation for predicting GNP is displayed in table 1-13.

Source: Authors' calculations.

Notes

We are grateful to Joseph DeStefano for his excellent research assistance.

1. By definition, literacy rates indicate the proportion of the adult population that can read and write. These literacy data are obtained from censuses undertaken after 1980 and from estimates by the United Nations Educational, Scientific, and Cultural Organization (UNESCO) for 1985 for countries with no data for the 1980s; see note to figure 1-1. Concerning these estimates, UNESCO notes that the "methodology used is basically an extrapolation and an interpolation of the illiteracy rates observed in the past. They do not, for example, take into account the impact of literacy campaigns which are currently taking place . . . in several countries. The use of literacy rates to measure the population's educational level has been criticized for several reasons. The data are usually self-reported, and thus, less accurate; and literacy is sometimes defined only with respect to a selected major national language(s). Nonetheless, better indicators that reveal the results of a country's past school enrollment rates on education are very costly to collect for an entire population."

2. Gross enrollment rates are computed as the ratio (expressed as a percentage) of total enrollment in primary education to total population in the appropriate age group. Because of intake from younger or older age groups into the primary grades, or grade repetition, gross enrollment rates can exceed 100 percent. In spite of this shortcoming, gross enrollment rates are a favored measure of educational progress because they reflect the intake capacity of the system.

3. Since nearly all low-income countries saw an increase in enrollment rates between 1960 and the 1980s, those that experienced a decline deserve mention. Besides China, enrollment fell in Bangladesh (by 1 percentage point for males); Nepal (by 1 and 6 percentage points for females and males, respectively); Ghana (by 2 and 3 percentage points for females and males, respectively); Guinea (by 2 percentage points for both females and males); and Togo (by 6 and 18 percentage points for females and males, respectively).

4. The cutoff points of 0.42 and 0.75 indicate the twenty-fifth and fiftieth percentiles in the distribution of countries ranked from higher to lower levels of gender disparity.

5. Gujarati (1988, p. 188) provides one of the clearest explanations of the benefits of multivariate analysis by way of an agricultural example. Suppose that the simple correlation between crop yield and rainfall indicates that the two are not related. Both crop yield and rainfall are related, however, to a third variable, namely temperature. By holding constant the effect of temperature on crop yield as well as the effect of temperature on rainfall, a multivariate regression of crop yield on rainfall and temperature reveals the expected positive *net* effect of rainfall.

6. Past educational investments, even those undertaken ten years back, could nevertheless be correlated with current investments. These investments feed on themselves as a result of social and political pressure. The degree of simple correlation can be expected to be less, however, than for current investments.

7. Other indirect effects may work themselves out through variables other than income. Consider the effect of total fertility rates on infant mortality, for example, or of infant mortality rates on fertility. Research in this area (reviewed in King 1987) has argued that these two variables are interrelated and that the appropriate model for identifying their determinants would be one using simultaneous equations. As a result, the indirect effects of female education should also include its impact on fertility rates through its impact on infant mortality rates, and vice versa. We have simplified our empirical model, omitting the estimation of these other indirect effects, because of the lack of variables that satisfy the identification requirements of such a simultaneous equations model.

8. Except for a shift factor obtained using dummy variables for detailed regional groups (see table 1-14 in appendix 1-1), these estimates restrict the coefficients to be equal across all countries. Earlier empirical work allowed the education variables to vary by region; however, test statistics revealed that the regional slopes were not all significantly different in each equation.

9. In addition to the levels of primary and secondary education and measures of gender disparity in education, variables employed in the regression models include accumulated gross domestic investment used to measure the stock of physical capital (to predict GNP); the size of the labor force (to predict GNP); the ratio of population to physicians; and the percentage of population with access to safe drinking water. Each model does not, however, include all the variables. In addition, all the models contained control variables for year and detailed region. Tables 1-13 and 1-14 in appendix 1-1 display the estimation results for GNP and the social indicators, respectively.

10. Lau, Jamison, and Louat (1991) have recently estimated educational levels for the labor force in about sixty countries, using enrollment data. Their data were not publicly available when our analysis was being done. Their estimates are based on annual school enrollments for the primary and secondary levels, which are themselves backward trend extrapolations of actual enrollment data.

11. Sensitivity analysis supports this variable specification. The correlation between adult literacy rates, which is a stock measure, and primary enrollment rates improves significantly when lagged values of enrollment rates are used. The rank correlation coefficient between these stock and flow measures of education increases from 0.70 to 0.82 for a sample of thirty-five countries with 1980 data on both variables.

12. GNP may be measured only partially, since most accounting ignores the value of production at home or in the nonmonetized (informal) sector. According to a 1975 survey of the coverage of nonmonetary activities reported by Goldschmidt-Clermont (1987), countries differ widely with respect to what activities are included in the national accounts. Among seventy developing countries, all claimed to cover fully own-account (subsistence or noncash) agricultural production and rental incomes of owner-occupied dwellings. About two-thirds cover other own-account primary production, such as fishing, forestry, and house-building. About one-half cover own-account food processing and handicrafts. Only six countries include water collection; three include crop storage; and two include domestic activities.

13. Data for maternal mortality are available for only nine countries in 1985, hence this regression sample is smaller and the statistical results are weaker. These simulations focus on infant mortality, fertility, and male life expectancy. Results for maternal mortality and female life expectancy are comparable.

14. Although educating men involves substantial private costs and social benefits, men realize a higher proportion of the total benefits as labor market returns than women do.

15. The presence of primary and junior high schools in the community has been found to increase enrollment and years of completed schooling in Brazil (Birdsall 1985), Indonesia (Chernichovsky and Meesook 1985), and Nepal (Moock and Leslie 1986). Distance to a primary school was found to be negatively associated with enrollment and schooling attainment in Egypt (Cochrane, Mehra, and Osheba 1986), the Philippines (King and Lillard 1983), and Thailand (Cochrane and Jamison 1982). Similar effects have been found for secondary schools in Malaysia and the Philippines (King and Lillard 1987).

16. In an economic model, this can be shown by representing household utility as a function of two different commodities—the human capital stock of sons and that of daughters (Rosenzweig and Evenson 1977; Rosenzweig and Schultz 1982). Appendix 1-2 presents a model of demand for education that does not rely on this assumption but considers investments in education to be driven by market forces.

17. In some societies, still another opportunity cost of schooling is the earlier use that the family can make of the bride-price for daughters. Delaying marriage because of schooling postpones receiving the bride wealth and may even reduce its amount if greater value is placed on younger than on better-educated brides.

18. One attenuating factor may be that parents have preferences about the number of surviving grandchildren and that more highly educated daughters produce a greater number of surviving offspring than more highly educated sons. This could occur even in the absence of assortative mating (Becker 1973).

19. There is also the more general estimation problem related to analyzing schooling outcomes that are incomplete. When students are still enrolled in school, using educational levels attained so far as a measure of outcomes is essentially flawed. The final levels are, in reality, unobserved until schooling has stopped.

20. The Research Triangle Institute kindly provided information on seventeen variables from eighty countries. We expanded this initial data set with additional information taken from the United Nations' 1988 data base entitled Women's Indicators and Statistics (WISTAT) and from the World Bank data base containing UNESCO and WHO data. See also World Bank (1987, 1989, various years).

21. This model makes other simplifying assumptions, among them, (a) that the number of years attended by a student is a sufficient indicator of learning (this also disregards grade repetition) and (b) that the only costs to schooling are time costs—an assumption that is not appropriate when the family must

pay for learning materials and transportation and, as is often required in secondary schools, for tuition.

22. This model can be extended to allow for the effects of assortative mating. Education may enhance an individual's desirability as a marriage partner and therefore increase the child's future income by raising the expected income of the spouse.

References

Acharya, Meena, and Lynn Bennett. 1981. *The Rural Women of Nepal: An Aggregate Analysis and Summary of Eight Village Studies.* Tribhuvan University, Centre for Economic Development Administration, Katmandu.

Akande, B. E. 1987. "Rural-Urban Comparison of Female Educational Aspirations in Southwestern Nigeria." *Comparative Education* 23:75–83.

Barrera, Albino. 1990. "The Role of Maternal Schooling and Its Interaction with Public Health Programs in Child Health Production." *Journal of Development Economics* 32:69–91.

Becker, Gary S. 1973. "A Theory of Marriage: Part I." *Journal of Political Economy* 18(4):813–46.

Behrman, Jere R., and Anil B. Deolalikar. 1988. "Are There Differential Returns to Schooling by Gender?" Development Studies Project II Research Paper. Jakarta.

Behrman, Jere, and Barbara Wolfe. 1984. "The Socioeconomic Impact of Schooling in a Developing Country." *Review of Economics and Statistics* 66(2):296–303.

Bellew, Rosemary, and Elizabeth M. King. 1991. "Promoting Girls' and Women's Education: Lessons from the Past." Policy Research Working Paper 715. World Bank, Population and Human Resources Department, Education and Employment Division, Washington, D.C.

Birdsall, Nancy. 1985. "Public Inputs and Child Schooling in Brazil." *Journal of Development Economics* 18:67–86.

Boissiere, Maurice, John B. Knight, and Richard H. Sabot. 1985. "Earnings, Schooling, Ability, and Cognitive Skills." *American Economic Review* 75(5):1016–30.

Butz, William, Jean-Pierre Habicht, and Julie DaVanzo. 1984. "Environmental Factors in the Relationship Between Breastfeeding and Infant Mortality: The Role of Sanitation and Water in Malaysia." *American Journal of Epidemiology* 119(4):516–25.

Cabañero, T. A. 1978. "The Shadow Price of Children in Laguna Households." *Philippine Economic Journal* 17(1–2):62–87.

Caldwell, J. C. 1979. "Education as a Factor in Mortality Decline." *Population Studies* 33:395–413.

Chernichovsky, Dov, and Oey A. Meesook. 1985. *School Enrollments in Indonesia.* World Bank Staff Working Paper 746. Washington, D.C.

Cochrane, Susan H., and Dean Jamison. 1982. "Educational Attainment and Achievement in Rural Thailand." In Anita A. Summers, ed., *Productivity*

Assessment in Education. New Directions for Testing and Measurement 15. San Francisco, Calif.: Jossey-Bass.

Cochrane, Susan H., and F. T. Sai. 1991. "Excess Fertility." World Bank, Human Resources Department, Washington, D.C.

Cochrane, Susan H., Kalpana Mehra, and Ibrahim Taha Osheba. 1986. "The Educational Participation of Egyptian Children." EDT Discussion Paper 45. World Bank, Education and Training Department, Washington, D.C.

Cooksey, Brian. 1981. "Social Class and Academic Performance: A Cameroon Case Study." *Comparative Education Review* 25:402–17.

de Tray, Dennis. 1983. "Children's Economic Contributions in Peninsular Malaysia." Rand Note N-1839-AID. Rand Corporation, Santa Monica, Calif.

Goldschmidt-Clermont, Luisella. 1987. *Economic Evaluations of Unpaid Household Work: Africa, Asia, Latin American and Oceania.* Women, Work and Development Series 14. Geneva: International Labour Office.

Greenhalgh, Susan. 1985. "Sexual Stratification: The Other Side of 'Growth with Equity' in East Asia." *Population and Development Review* 2(2):265–314.

Griliches, Zvi, and William M. Mason. 1972. "Education, Income, and Ability." *Journal of Political Economy* 80(3), pt. 2:S74–S103.

Gujarati, Damodar. 1988. *Basic Econometrics.* 2d ed. New York: McGraw-Hill.

Haveman, Robert, and Barbara Wolfe. 1984. "Schooling and Economic Well-Being: The Role of Nonmarket Effects." *Journal of Human Resources* 19(3):377–406.

Heyneman, Stephen P., and William A. Loxley. 1983. "The Effect of Primary-School Quality on Academic Achievement across Twenty-nine High- and Low-Income Countries." *American Journal of Sociology* 88(6):1162–94.

Jain, Anrudh K. 1985. "Relative Roles of Female Education and Medical Services for Decreasing Infant Mortality in Rural India." In S. B. Halstead, J. A. Walsh, and K. S. Warren, eds., *Good Health at Low Cost.* New York: Rockefeller Foundation.

Kelly, Gail P., and Carolyn M. Elliott, eds. 1982. *Women's Education in the Third World: Comparative Perspectives.* Albany: State University of New York Press.

King, Elizabeth M. 1982. "Investments in Schooling: An Analysis of Demand in Low-Income Households." Ph.D. diss. Yale University, New Haven, Conn.

―――. 1987. "The Effect of Family Size on Family Welfare: What Do We Know?" In D. Gale Johnson and Ronald P. Lee, eds., *Population Growth and Economic Development: Issues and Evidence.* Madison: University of Wisconsin Press.

King, Elizabeth M., and Rosemary Bellew. 1989. "Gains in the Education of Peruvian Women, 1940 to 1980." Policy Research Working Paper 472. World Bank, Population and Human Resources Department, Education and Employment Division and Women in Development Division, Washington, D.C.

King, Elizabeth M., and R. E. Evenson. 1983. "Time Allocation and Home Production in Philippine Rural Households." In Mayra Buvinic, Margaret A. Lycette, and William P. McGreevey, eds., *Women and Poverty in the Third World.* Baltimore, Md.: Johns Hopkins University Press.

King, Elizabeth M., and Lee A. Lillard. 1983. "Determinants of Schooling Attainment and Enrollment Rates in the Philippines." Rand Note N-1962-AID. Rand Corporation, Santa Monica, Calif.

———. 1987. "Education Policy and Schooling Attainment in Malaysia and the Philippines." *Economics of Education Review* 6:167–81.

Lau, Lawrence J., Dean T. Jamison, and Frederic F. Louat. 1991. "Education and Productivity in Developing Countries: An Aggregate Production Function Approach." Policy Research Working Paper 612. World Bank, Office of Development Economics and Population and Human Resources Department, Washington, D.C.

Lockheed, Marlaine E., Adriaan M. Verspoor, and associates. 1991. *Improving Primary Education in Developing Countries* New York: Oxford University Press.

McGinn, Noel F., Donald R. Snodgrass, Yung Boo Kim, Shin Bok Kim, and Quee-Young Kim. 1980. *Education and Development in Korea.* East Asian Monographs. Cambridge, Mass.: Harvard University Press.

Moock, Peter R., and Joanne Leslie. 1986. "Childhood Malnutrition and Schooling in the Terai Region of Nepal." *Journal of Development Economics* 20:33–52.

Mueller, Eva. 1984. "The Value and Allocation of Time in Rural Botswana." *Journal of Development Economics* 15:329–60.

Nag, Moni, Benjamin N. F. White, and Robert C. Peet. 1980. "An Anthropological Approach to the Study of the Economic Value of Children in Java and Nepal." In Hans Binswanger, R. Evenson, C. Florencio, and B. White, eds., *Rural Household Studies in Asia.* Singapore University Press.

Newman, John L. 1988. *Labor Market Activity in Côte d'Ivoire and Peru.* Living Standards Measurement Study Working Paper 36. Washington, D.C.: World Bank.

Rosenzweig, Mark R., and Robert E. Evenson. 1977. "Fertility, Schooling, and the Economic Contribution of Children in Rural India: An Econometric Analysis." *Econometrica* 45:1065–79.

Rosenzweig, Mark R., and T. Paul Schultz. 1982. "Market Opportunities, Genetic Endowments, and the Intrafamily Distribution of Resources: Child Survival in Rural India." *American Economic Review* 72(4):803–15.

Schultz, Theodore W. 1975. "The Value of the Ability to Deal with Disequilibria." *Journal of Economic Literature* 13:872–76.

Sen, Amartya K. 1984. *Resources, Values and Development.* Cambridge, Mass.: Harvard University Press.

UNESCO (United Nations Educational, Scientific, and Cultural Organization). 1983. *Trends and Projections of Enrollment by Level of Education and by Age: 1960–2000 (as Assessed in 1982).* Paris.

———. 1986. "Education of Girls in Asia and the Pacific: Report of the Regional Review Meeting on the Situation of Education of Girls for Universalization of Primary Education." Regional Office for Education in Asia and the Pacific, Bangkok.

United Nations Statistical Office. 1988. *Women's Indicators and Statistics (WISTAT)—User's Guide.* New York.

World Bank. 1986. *Financing Education in Developing Countries: An Exploration of Policy Options*. Washington D.C.: World Bank.

————. 1987. *Financing Health Services in Developing Countries: An Agenda for Reform*. Washington, D.C.: World Bank.

————. 1989. *World Tables*. Washington, D.C.: World Bank.

————. Various years. *World Development Report*. New York: Oxford University Press.

2
Returns to Women's Education
T. Paul Schultz

The high returns to investing in the education of women are indisputable. Yet remarkably few detailed studies of these returns have sought to clarify public or private investment priorities. As a consequence, no explanation has been offered as to why the high returns to female education have not attracted more public and private investment, especially in those countries where women receive much less education than men do. Such an explanation must rest on an analysis of why returns to schooling differ by gender. The reasons for this may be related in part to the structure of aggregate demand for labor and in part to economic constraints such as income per capita and the costs of delivering school services (Schultz 1987). The differences in what a family is prepared to invest in a son's and a daughter's education may be perpetuated by regulations and incentives in public (and private) education systems. They may also reflect family decisionmaking and the preferences of parents who value greater productivity less highly in a daughter than in a son or who are unable to appreciate fully the enhanced nonmarket productivity of better-educated women. Understanding why this pattern of preferences occurs more in some settings than in others and which policy interventions can change family behavior poses a challenge for researchers and program designers alike.

Private and Social Rates of Return

As with other investments, so with education, the decision that a family—or a government—makes about how much to invest in this private and social good entails weighing the costs and benefits. Estimates of the rates of return to education are calculated in two forms. The *private return* is defined as the internal rate of return that equalizes the discounted present value of the private cost of attending school with the discounted present value of the private after-tax gains the individual recoups in subsequent productive activities. The *social return* includes, in addition to these private costs and benefits, the public cost of providing schooling and the gains in increased taxes that better-educated workers pay, as well as the broader social benefits—referred to as externalities—that education generates but that the individual does not capture.

The calculation of the private returns to education is rarely complete. In practice, few studies even deduct from labor earnings or wage rates what the more educated worker is likely to pay in increased taxes (both income and indirect), although doing so is not conceptually difficult. This deduction is irrelevant if the number of hours worked is independent of education and if taxes are proportional to wages—assumptions that may be plausible in analyzing the returns to male education. But the first assumption contradicts what is known about the behavior of working women.

The calculation of the social returns to education also tends to be flawed. In most empirical studies, the only distinction between private and social returns to schooling is that the latter adds public expenditures per student into the calculation of the internal social rate of return. Social returns to education are, therefore, predictably lower than private returns in proportion to the share of the total cost of schooling that the public sector absorbs. This gap between private and social returns to schooling is especially large for higher education in some of the poorer countries, where access to colleges and universities is rationed and the students who gain admission pay little or no tuition and may even receive cost-of-living stipends (Psacharopoulos and Woodhall 1985).

For primary and secondary education in tuition-free schools, the opportunity value of the time when students are removed from productive work in the family is the main private cost, augmented by any private outlays for books, school materials, uniforms, and transportation. Paying teachers is the main public cost in poorer countries, where teachers' salaries often absorb 80 to 95 percent of public spending on education (see UNESCO various years).

Investment Decisions

Private returns to schooling are the greatest incentive for individuals and families to invest in education. Decisions reflect the extent to which schooling is viewed as an economic investment in a person's future productivity. The consumption value of education (that is, the value put on learning for its own sake) provides another incentive.

This factor is not commonly observed, however, and therefore is not analyzed as a force affecting the level and mix of a society's educational investments. Families and individuals who have equal access to credit and face the same cost of capital would, if acting efficiently, invest in education as a form of human capital until the private returns to additional schooling declined to equal the private cost of capital. Applying efficiency criteria would predispose a family to invest differentially in the human capital of their children, depending on their perception of the ability and opportunities of each child, assuming ability and opportunity enhance the private returns to schooling (see, for example, Becker 1981).

Social returns to schooling offer one set of guidelines by which a society could efficiently allocate public resources and set priorities among alternative education programs that produce distinctive types of skills and workers. Individuals capture much of these social returns, however, so groups that derive high private returns from educating their children will be strong supporters of the status quo. In low-income countries, rent-seeking behavior in the middle and upper classes is commonly a potent political force that pushes the government to raise quality, maintain free access, and if necessary even ration entry into the better secondary and higher public institutions. High social returns signal the need to expand a specific segment of the school system. But if they are accompanied by high private returns, the public sector should consider using fees (and scholarships) to finance expansion or allowing private schools to satisfy the excess demand. If social returns are moderate primarily as the result of social externalities, and consequently private returns are on the low side, the public sector should expect to rely more on its own resources to finance school expansion.

An alternative criterion for allocating public resources to education could be to emphasize those activities for which the social externalities alone would justify public subsidies. Externalities from education are thought to be substantial at the primary level and to diminish at subsequent levels, since individuals capture more of the social benefits (minus taxes) from their continued education (Weisbrod 1964). Social externalities are well documented in studies of the effects of women's education, but they are rarely cited as a reason for expanding public education for women.

The research that is produced in conjunction with university education may itself generate external benefits that are an important source of economic growth. Most products of university research are freely available to firms and households, but, in part because of their limited accessibility, their productive value is difficult to assess. This potential externality of university training allied to research has not, to my knowledge, been quantitatively evaluated in many low-income countries. A possible exception is in the agricultural sciences, in which research and extension work are sometimes closely connected (Evenson 1988).

Overall Patterns in Private and Social Returns

Psacharopoulos (1973, 1985) has summarized several estimates of the rates of return to education by region and school level. Table 2-1, which is based on these estimates, implies several general patterns in these returns. The more developed the region, the lower the social return to education, both across regions and within regions over time. With notable exceptions, the higher the level of schooling in a region, the lower the returns. The social returns appear to be about twice as large in Africa and Latin America as they are in industrially advanced countries. Social returns in Asia fall between these extremes.

In many low-income countries, the private returns to higher education are twice the social returns because the public costs of education are a large share of total costs. The exception is Asia, where the social returns to secondary and higher education are not much lower than the private returns. In this region the public subsidies are only a moderate share of the total costs, whereas in Sub-Saharan Africa

Table 2-1. *Average Social and Private Rates of Return to Education, by School Level*

Region	Social			Private		
	Primary	*Secondary*	*Tertiary*	*Primary*	*Secondary*	*Tertiary*
Africa	27	19	14	45	28	33
	(12)	(12)	(12)	(9)	(9)	(9)
Asia	18	14	12	34	15	18
	(9)	(11)	(11)	(5)	(8)	(8)
Latin America	35	19	16	61	28	26
	(8)	(8)	(8)	(5)	(5)	(5)
High-income countries[a]	13[b]	10	8	19[b]	12	11
	(6)	(15)	(15)	(7)	(14)	(15)

Note: The number of countries in each group is reported in parentheses below the mean.

a. Europe, United States, New Zealand, and Israel.

b. Not calculable in the majority of high-income countries, where the comparison group without a primary education is small and highly unrepresentative at younger ages.

Source: Calculated by the author for most recent years when social returns were available at all levels or, for high-income countries, all but primary level. Original studies were summarized by Psacharopoulos 1973, table 14; 1985, table A-1.

and, to a lesser extent, in Latin America governments have provided large public subsidies for secondary and especially for higher education.

Many countries have only a single set of estimates available, and these come from the 1960s or early 1970s. With the slowing of economic growth in some countries in the late 1970s and 1980s, as in Argentina and Ghana, returns to education may have declined. The patterns shown in table 2-1 are therefore somewhat outdated. More recent studies tend to find lower returns to education in many parts of Sub-Saharan Africa and Latin America, and they document declining returns to primary schooling as the majority of new entrants to the labor force in these countries extend their schooling beyond the primary level.

The pattern of diminishing social returns to investments in human capital supports the view that public subsidies should focus on the expansion first of primary and then of secondary schooling. These not only offer the highest returns; they are also the most widely available and so are more likely to be equitably distributed among all economic classes. Private returns are high in Africa, where large educational investments began only recently, and in Latin America, where they may reflect the sluggish expansion of public secondary schools in recent decades. High-income countries, as well as parts of East and Southeast Asia, have already achieved substantial levels of human capital investment. In fact, some studies suggest that the social returns to schooling in these countries are roughly on a par with the private returns from physical capital after taxes. Thus in some regions, public investments in education could be increased efficiently and equitably, whereas in others with more rapid economic growth the case for public investment in school expansion depends in part on new evidence of social externalities (see, for example, Lucas 1985; Romer 1983).

Studies of the rates of return to schooling based on aggregate data are often replicated by estimating wage or earnings functions from survey data on individuals. In these logarithmic functions, the coefficient on years of schooling approximates the private internal rate of return to schooling (Mincer 1974; Rosen 1977). The estimated coefficient on years of schooling using this method tends to be slightly smaller than the estimated private return to schooling derived from tabulated data on earnings and education costs by age groups, as originally performed by Becker (1964). Wage function approximations of the private rate of return to education range from 13–25 percent in Latin America and Africa to 6–9 percent in high-income countries (see, for example, Psacharopoulos 1985, table 3).

This growing body of data and analysis leads to the conclusion that in most developing countries, the demand for better-educated labor appears to be increasing at least as rapidly as the supply of better-educated labor, although in some cases macroeconomic swings in economic growth cause temporarily high or low returns to schooling. Relatively little analysis has focused on how structural adjustment has affected private returns to education in the short run and in the long run. Moreover, all the calculations of returns to education neglect the consumption gains associated with schooling, as well as any externalities—that is, the "public good" attributes of education—because consensus is lacking on how to measure and value these benefits.

Problems in Estimating Returns to Schooling

Many difficulties arise in the empirical measurement of returns to schooling. The first class of problems involves the estimation bias introduced because the student's ability, the parents' background, and the school's quality are not adequately specified. Ideally, this bias could be corrected by careful specification and better data (Schultz 1988b). Most studies, however, must build on imperfect specifications and data. The direction of the bias that these problems may cause in estimating returns to education is unclear, as is their relative influence on the returns for women and for men.

A second class of problems has to do with the survey data on which estimates of wage functions depend. Only a portion of the population is asked to report the earnings and related productivity information. A bias is likely if selection into this sample is not independent of the relationship among schooling, wages, and productivity. The problem is likely to be even more serious if the criterion for including individuals in the sample is choice of occupation or migration; plausibly, both are linked to education. Such problems of sample selection involve explaining both the behavior of the labor market and the determinants of wages.

Other limitations in the use of intergroup comparisons for estimating returns to schooling are beyond the scope of this chapter; they are discussed elsewhere (see, for example, Griliches 1977; Schultz 1988b). One such limitation is the inadequacy of the statistical controls to account for individual ability or job characteristics—that is, the bias of omitted inputs or of selection by comparative advantage (Heckman and Sedlacek 1985; Willis and Rosen 1979). Another is the neglect of quality in the wage function; because the quality of schooling tends to be directly related to the quantity of schooling that individuals receive, the returns to additional years of schooling of a constant quality may be overestimated (Behrman and Birdsall 1983; Welch 1966).

No consensus exists on precisely which variables to include in the wage function or how to identify statistically those individuals who invest in schooling or who work for wages in the labor force. Different strategies for constructing the comparison groups may yield private rates of return to schooling that are sometimes substantially lower, and sometimes higher, than the simplest logarithmic wage function that includes years of schooling in linear or spline form and years of experience after finishing school in quadratic form (Mincer 1974). Fortunately, the controversies over the methods of estimating returns to schooling do not appear to be germane when comparing male and female education because most of these potential biases operate similarly for men and women, with the possible exception of the bias concerning labor supply. Nevertheless, assessing precisely the absolute level of returns to private and public resources invested in educating women remains an important, if subsidiary, objective.[1] The appendix to this chapter discusses these estimation problems more fully.

Market Returns to Education by Gender

Ten studies that report private rates of return to schooling separately for men and women are summarized in table 2-2. The studies are not

Table 2-2. *Returns to Education, by School Level and Gender, Various Economies*

Site and year	Estimation method	Primary Male	Primary Female	Secondary Male	Secondary Female	Tertiary Male	Tertiary Female
Bogotá, Colombia (1965)	II	18.2	nr	34.4	18.9	4.5	5.3
Kenya (circa 1960)	I	21.7	7.1	23.6	19.5	nr	nr
Malaysia (circa 1960)	—a	9.4	9.3	12.3	11.4	10.7	9.8
Brazil (1960)	—a	17.9	38.6	nr	nr	nr	nr
Korea, Rep. of (1971)	—a	nr	nr	13.7	16.9	15.7	22.9
Taiwan (China) (1982)	—a	8.4	16.0	nr	nr	nr	nr
Puerto Rico (1959)	—a	29.5	18.4	27.3	40.8	21.9	9.0
Andhra Pradesh, India (1977)	II	8.9	11.8	8.7	11.9	6.2	8.9
	I	7.2	0.3	6.8	2.41	5.5	5.5
Côte d'Ivoire (1985)	II	18.3	5.5	17.0	28.7	21.1	13.6

nr Not reported.

Note: I, includes participation rate in labor force to deflate returns, depressing female returns disproportionately. II, estimates wage rate relationship without labor force adjustment.

a. Estimation method not known.

Source: For Bogotá, Colombia, Schultz 1968, table 7, hourly wage; for Andhra Pradesh, India, Tilak 1987, table 6.8, average return for school level; for Côte d'Ivoire, van der Gaag and Vijverberg 1987, appendix 2; for other countries, Psacharopoulos 1973, table 4.5; 1985.

comparable, however, because they use different conceptual and empirical methods. Three aspects of the methodology need to be revised and standardized before such estimates can help determine investment priorities. First, how should the potential productivity gains attributable to schooling be adjusted when people work different amounts of time in the labor force? Second, how should the effect of education on nonmarket productivity be estimated and then combined with the effect on market productivity to yield average returns to schooling for the entire population? Third, how should these results be corrected for any bias that enters when direct observations on productivity are inevitably limited to a portion of the population—say, to those who report wages and hours worked?

The double entries in table 2-2 for Andhra Pradesh in India illustrate how sensitive the calculations of returns are to the treatment of the rate of women's participation in the labor force (Tilak 1989). Both the private and the social returns to schooling at virtually every school level are greater for women than for men when the returns are adjusted only for unemployment. When nonparticipation in the labor force is also factored into the calculation, as Becker (1981) has proposed, the private rate of return for women is less than it is for men. This same study also documents the lower public cost of female versus male education and the lower opportunity cost of time for female than for male students. The adjustment for nonparticipation of women apparently is not introduced to deflate the opportunity cost of female student time but only to deflate the stream of benefits from work in the labor force.

A study of Sri Lanka also confirms that the return to schooling, when not deflated by labor force participation rates, is greater for women than for men. The private rate of return to completing the general certificate exams at the end of secondary school is three times as high for women as for men in urban areas (36 compared with 13 percent) and twice as high in rural areas (14 compared with 7 percent). At the university level, however, the rates of return for men and women in Sri Lanka appear to converge (Sahn and Alderman 1988, table 17).

Table 2-3 summarizes the private rates of return to schooling for men and women in several Latin American countries. All the studies used a common conceptual and statistical methodology (Schultz 1980b). Although these estimates deal plausibly with the issue of labor supply by analyzing the hourly wage, which does not erroneously deflate the returns to educating women because they participate less in the labor force, they do not correct for the sample selection bias. Moreover, because the samples are small, some of the estimates are imprecise. Overall, however, these studies provide no clear evidence

Table 2-3. *Estimates of Private Returns to Education, Selected Labor Markets and Years*
(percent per year)

| | | Private rate of return | | | |
| | Year of | Ages 25–44 | | Ages 45–65 | |
Site	survey	Men	Women	Men	Women
Argentina, Buenos Aires					
(estimates similar in 1976)	1980[a]	9.3	6.6	10.0	11.0
Bolivia, La Paz					
(estimates similar in 1976)	1980	9.8	11.0	9.6	6.7
Brazil, São Paulo					
(estimates higher in 1980)	1971	5.4	6.3	6.0	6.1
Colombia					
(estimates lower in 1980)	1973	18.0	18.0	16.0	14.0
Paraguay, Asunción					
(estimates similar in 1977)	1979	11.0	8.0	10.0	11.0
Peru	1974	14.0	14.0	11.0	19.0

Note: Private returns refer to the estimated coefficient (times 100) on the variable years of completed education in a logarithmic hourly wage rate regression that also includes postschooling experience, experience squared, and some regional or migration origin variables. Samples vary in size from 21 to 3,478, but all estimates are statistically significantly different from zero at the 0.001 confidence level ($t > 2.83$). The selection only of workers in the labor force for whom wage rates could be calculated is not treated as a specific source of bias in these estimates.

a. The available age groups in Argentina are 25–49 and over 49.

Source: Schultz 1989.

that private returns to schooling differ systematically by gender. Returns do differ considerably across countries, however, presumably because of differences in macroeconomic conditions and in the level of past investments in schooling (Schultz 1988a).

Community and Household Fixed Effects

Fixed-effect estimation procedures provide another approach to eliminating the bias that may arise from certain types of unobserved or omitted variables.[2] A cross-section is drawn from a number of distinct localities in which the price and quality of market goods and public services may differ. If the local market variables of price and quality influence the productivity of schooling, then they should be controlled for in estimating the returns by varying only the years of schooling. In this case, introducing a fixed effect for every school district into the wage function removes any bias attributable to the omission of school quality, which might be correlated with the quantity of schooling received. The effect of other local market variables, such as size of schools, cannot be estimated, because they do not vary within the community. To the extent that the quality of local schools changes at different rates across regions and that individuals move from one region to another, attend more than one school, or work in a different region than the one where they attended school, the community fixed effect becomes a less adequate control for school quality.

Family background probably has its own impact on average ability, through genetic and environmental mechanisms that instill motivations and habits and also influence the quality of schooling that the children in a family receive. If these family characteristics affect productivity and are correlated with years of schooling, their omission from the wage function would in all likelihood bias upward the estimated rate of return to education. One strategy for dealing with these unobserved characteristics is to introduce fixed effects for each family. The estimates of returns to education are then based only on variations in productivity among workers in the same family. This procedure, however, may increase the relative importance of measurement errors by eliminating all variation among different families. Exaggerated measurement errors would bias to zero the fixed-effect estimates of schooling returns for a given family (Griliches 1977, 1979). Family or household fixed effects are, therefore, likely to represent a lower bound on the estimates of the effects of schooling on market productivity. Moreover, restricting the sample to those individuals residing in a family with at least one other wage earner may itself seriously distort the comparison group and so bias the return estimates in other directions.

Private rates of return to education have been estimated for men and women from a 1986 survey of Indonesia (Behrman and Deolalikar 1988). This study compares standard estimates of the wage function with those that include both community fixed effects (proxy for school quality and the like) and household fixed effects (proxy for family background correlates). Table 2-4 shows the rates of return for three types of schooling—primary, general senior high, and university.[3] In all cases the private rates of return to schooling for women exceed those for men. Furthermore, as expected, the estimates that include community and household fixed effects are between 9 and 24 percent smaller than those obtained from the standard regressions, which include intercommunity and interfamily variations. These estimates do not attempt to control for the potentially unrepresentative character of the sample of wage earners, nor are the two sets of estimates based on the same sample, because 16 percent of the wage earners included in the first set of estimates apparently did not reside in a household with another wage earner and are therefore excluded from the fixed-effect estimates (Behrman and Deolalikar 1988, table 3). Gender dif-

Table 2-4. *Implied Private Returns to an Additional Year of Schooling in Indonesia, by Gender*
(percent per year)

Gender and controls	Primary	Senior high	General university
Females			
Without fixed-effect controls	9.1	11.8	12.4
	(21.1)	(43.4)	(27.8)
With community and family fixed-effects	6.9	9.6	10.9
controls	(17.3)	(35.3)	(24.7)
Males			
Without fixed-effect controls	7.6	8.2	9.2
	(2.64)	(10.9)	(6.41)
With community and family fixed-effects	6.1	6.2	8.4
controls	(1.43)	(10.8)	(5.23)

Note: The absolute values of *t*-ratios are reported in parentheses beneath the coefficients for female returns; the values of *t*-ratios for the difference between the male and female regression coefficients are reported beneath the male returns. Thus, a significant *t*-ratio under a male return suggests that the rate of return to schooling for men and women differs by a statistically significant amount in this pooled earnings regression.

Source: Behrman and Deolalikar 1988, table 2.

ferences in the estimated private rates of return change moderately when fixed effects for the community and household are added: returns decrease at the primary level and increase at the university level.

Sample Selection

As already mentioned, many studies of the returns to education include only wage earners and thus exclude the self-employed and unpaid family workers for whom a wage is difficult to infer or measure precisely. This excluded group is a relatively small segment of the labor force in high-income countries, but it is a large segment in low-income countries, where nonmarket workers, the self-employed, and unpaid family workers together represent about half the adult male population and two-thirds of the adult female population (Schultz 1989). Thus, any bias from sample selection could be important in analyzing the educational returns for men, as well as for women, in low-income countries (Nakamura and Nakamura 1988).

Chiswick (1976) developed a technique for including self-employed workers in the estimation of an annual earnings function, thereby avoiding the bias from including only wage earners. She attributed a share of self-employed earnings to entrepreneurial capital or risk-taking. Her analysis of data on Bangkok from the 1971 Socioeconomic Survey of Thailand shows that male wage earners (not self-employed at all) received a 10.4 percent return on their years of schooling, whereas female wage earners received a 14.5 percent return. Including part-time and full-time self-employed persons increased the size of the sample by 39 percent for men and 53 percent for women; it reduced the returns to schooling only slightly, to 9.1 percent for men and 13.0 percent for women. In both cases the returns to schooling for women exceeded those for men, but those who were self-employed reported slightly lower returns than did wage earners. This is broadly consistent with the pattern that women with some education beyond primary school are more likely to work in wage jobs than women with only a primary school education. Whether underreporting of incomes by the self-employed distorts such estimated returns to schooling—and if so, by how much—is unclear.

A few studies of the links between wages and education have assessed how restricting the sample to wage earners biases findings (see, for example, Anderson 1982; Griffin 1987; King 1990; Mohan 1986; Schultz 1988b). These studies, however, often deal with either men or women alone and so do not help assess whether the bias due to sample selection systematically modifies comparisons of the estimated returns to education by gender, such as those reported in tables 2-4 (and later in table 2-5). This is an important issue for public policy but one that has received surprisingly little empirical study.

To appraise alternative methods of dealing with sample selection bias, Griffin (1987) analyzes the earnings of married women in the Philippines in 1980. He estimates a function for a nonmarket (reservation) wage and a function for market wage offers. The reservation wage function determines the shadow value of the nonmarket time of an individual and hence what wage would induce him or her to enter the labor market. Heckman (1979) also addresses the issue of sample selection. His selection-corrected model is identified within the context of the family or bargaining labor supply model. A standard log-linear specification of the earnings function is estimated with returns to education constant across schooling levels.[4] The selection-corrected maximum likelihood rate of return to education is 18 percent, compared with the estimate of 14 percent obtained without selection correction, by using only the one-third of the sample who earn wages. In this case correcting for sample selection increases the estimated returns to education for women. The selectivity term is statistically significant, implying that the sample of wage-earning women is not a random sample of the population with respect to their wage rates.

In another study King (1990) analyzes the earnings of women in the 1985–86 Peruvian Living Standard Survey. A probit equation for women in paid employment (that is, both wage earners and self-employed) is used to estimate an hourly earnings function in accordance with Heckman's (1979) two-stage procedure. This sample selection correction decreases the rate of return to women's education from 12.2 to 12.0 percent for primary school, from 8.0 to 7.8 percent for secondary school, and from 6.8 to −1.7 percent for the university (if a diploma is received after four years of study). As in Griffin's study, the family's assets and nonearned income and the husband's characteristics are included only in the paid-participation equation (along with the woman's marital status and a variety of more controversial identifying variables).

Khandker (1989) subsequently used the same Peruvian Living Standard Survey data to estimate the returns to schooling for both men and women. He restricts his analysis to wage earners, and he identifies the sample selection probit equation by the family's landholdings and nonearned income, as well as by the individual's marital status. The estimates appear to be relatively robust to variations in the list of identifying variables included only in the sample selection equation. For the country as a whole, the returns to women's education increase when controls are introduced for sample selection, and they become marginally larger than the returns for men at the secondary and higher levels. At the primary level in the metropolitan area of Lima, however, the returns are low for both sexes but lower for women than for men (2.0 percent compared with 2.5 percent). This pattern of low returns to primary schooling for women has been noted elsewhere in metropolitan Latin America (see Schultz 1968). Some researchers attribute it to the inclusion in the sample of female domestic servants, whom they then exclude when estimating wage functions because valuing the income they receive in kind, such as food, is difficult (Mohan 1986).

The 1976, 1981, and 1986 Socioeconomic Surveys of Thailand permit further evaluation of how sample selection can bias estimates of the private rates of return to education for both women and men. In this case the analysis incorporates two correction terms, representing the probability of being in the labor force and the probability of being a wage earner. The selection equations include family nonearned income, hectares of family land (irrigated or unirrigated), and the standard market wage rate determinants, including years of schooling completed at the primary, secondary, and higher levels. Land ownership and nonearned income raise the nonmarket reservation wage and thereby reduce the likelihood that a person will take a job or work at all in the market labor force.

Education does not exert a monotonic effect on the probability of a Thai woman's or man's working for a wage (Schultz 1989). A person with some primary schooling is less likely to be a landless wage laborer in this predominantly agricultural society than someone with no schooling. The more years of secondary schooling a person has, however, the greater the chance that she or he is working for a wage. And each year of university education strongly increases the likelihood of a person's working in a wage or salary job. This offers a clue why the sample selection bias can operate in different directions at different levels of schooling. Many landowners are also wage earners. But if they have enough land, they presumably withdraw from the wage market to cultivate their own land full-time. The critical question is whether land is exogenous (that is, not a consequence of labor supply choices) or merely a proxy for self-employment; in other words, is land a legitimate variable to use to identify the selection model?

Regional Labor Markets

An additional problem in specifying a wage function to estimate returns to education in low-income countries is how to model the regional segmentation of labor markets. Were there no interregional migration, wage functions could be estimated separately for each region; the wage differences linked to education would then be the appropriate parameter for determining priorities for private investment in schooling in that closed region. Interregional migration does occur, however, and the better-educated are more likely to migrate than others. Generally, they move from lower to higher wage markets and from rural to urban areas. In Colombia, for example, as much as half of the lifetime returns to education for rural children is associated with the increased likelihood that they will migrate to the urban labor market (Schultz 1988a). To analyze this situation would require knowing where people migrated from, the costs they incurred in moving, and where they went to school. An alternative is to hold constant statistically an individual's current regional labor market. This purges from the wage function an estimate of the return to schooling that arises from living in a higher-wage region, which is more frequent among the better educated (Schwartz 1976). Models with and without dummy variables for region provide a useful range of estimated returns to schooling. The greater the mobility, the stronger the case for treating the entire country as a single labor market when estimating returns to education.

Nominal wage differences among regional labor markets may reflect variations in the cost and quality of subsidized public services and therefore may not accurately measure real wage differences. High-wage urban regions typically have more and better schools; indeed, dummy variables for region in the wage function may also reflect regional differences in the quality of workers' schooling (Behrman and Birdsall 1983). Other prices, especially for housing, are also generally higher in high-wage urban regions. On balance, differences in nominal wages from region to region probably exceed differences in real wages if public services are a small part of a family's consumption. Estimating the participation and wage functions with and without regions as explanatory variables should at least help to assess the importance of migration when estimating returns to education. Unfortunately, the lack of information on migration in the Thailand survey data does not permit taking interregional migration into account in the analysis presented here.

Correcting for Sample Selection Bias: Returns to Education in Thailand

In table 2-5 private rates of return to schooling are estimated for Thailand, with and without selection corrections. The uncorrected figures are based on the ordinary least squares (OLS) estimates for wage earners, which ignore the potential bias arising from selecting only wage earners. For the corrected estimates, two selection probit equations predict the probability that the individual is in the labor force and is a wage earner (Catsiapis and Robinson 1982). Both the wage function and the two selection equations vary across regions in Thailand, which include the least-developed northeast region, the rural areas, the suburban sanitary districts, the urban municipal areas, and Bangkok. Because dummy variables for region are specified in the wage function, the private returns to education exclude the gains resulting from the migration of better-educated people to regions with higher wages.

For most of this century Thailand has invested heavily in primary education, which has been nearly universal for some time (see chapter 7). Still, it enrolls a smaller proportion of its population in secondary school than do many other countries at a similar stage of development, such as the Republic of Korea, Malaysia, the Philippines, Taiwan (China), and the two city states of Hong Kong and Singapore (Sussangkarn 1988). In contrast, the share of the Thai population enrolled in higher education is large for a country at its income level. The supply of workers by educational level would lead one to expect that the returns to education in Thailand are high at the secondary level and low at the university level compared with other countries at about the same stage of development.

Again in Thailand, the difference in enrollment rates by gender is small at the primary level. The difference is greater at the secondary level, although it is narrower in 1975–85 than in the preceding decade. And only about half as many women as men were enrolled in Thai institutions of higher education in the 1970s.

Table 2-5. *Estimates of Private Rates of Return to Education in Thailand, by Gender, with and without Statistical Correction for Sample Selection Bias*

Year and unit of earnings (sample of earners/ population)	Without correction[a]			With correction[b]		
	Primary	Secondary	Teritary	Primary	Secondary	Tertiary
I. 1986; monthly earnings						
Female	8.2	31.0	9.5	13.0	25.0	18.0
(2,709/8,606)	(4.75)	(18.7)	(4.31)	(7.00)	(9.84)	(5.45)
Male	14.0	18.0	12.0	17.0	6.8	7.8
(4,199/7,685)	(9.40)	(14.4)	(6.81)	(11.3)	(5.34)	(4.61)
II. 1981; monthly earnings						
Female	4.6	30.0	2.2	9.0	22.0	12.0
(2,419/8,816)	(2.41)	(19.7)	(.74)	(4.56)	(6.09)	(3.32)
Male	15.0	20.0	4.2	15.0	8.8	2.9
(4,525/7,986)	(10.2)	(17.4)	(1.72)	(9.22)	(6.24)	(1.22)
III. 1981; hourly earnings						
Female	5.2	34.0	1.6	10.0	25.0	11.0
(2,419/8,816)	(2.70)	(22.1)	(.55)	(5.00)	(6.77)	(3.04)
Male	16.0	24.0	5.4	14.0	13.0	4.1
(4,525/7,986)	(9.98)	(20.9)	(2.16)	(8.95)	(9.04)	(1.66)
IV. 1976; monthly earnings						
Female	11.0	17.0	7.8	11.0	31.0	17.0
(1,464/9,430)	(8.87)	(13.8)	(3.63)	(8.70)	(7.04)	(6.35)
Male	5.7	15.0	8.4	5.6	7.4	11.0
(3,783/8,836)	(6.37)	(16.5)	(5.50)	(5.33)	(7.65)	(6.85)

Note: Two correction terms for sample selection are included in the earnings functions to capture the probability of participation in the labor market and of selecting wage employment. (See text for identifying restrictions.) The estimation sample is restricted to wage and salary earners between the ages of twenty-five and fifty-four.

a. The absolute value of the *t*-ratio is reported in parentheses beneath the regression coefficient on years of education within each level of schooling.

b. The absolute value of the *t*-ratio is reported in parentheses, but it has not been adjusted for the selection correction procedure and is therefore potentially biased.

Source: Author's calculations following methodology outlined in text; for 1981 survey, Schultz 1989, tables 4, A-7, and A-8.

As table 2-5 shows, annual rates of return to schooling for Thai women, based on 1981 *hourly* earnings and with no correction for sample selection, are about 5 percent for primary education, 34 percent for secondary education, and 2 percent for university education. For men the comparable returns are 16, 24, and 5 percent, respectively. Applying a statistical correction for the two sample selection processes that might introduce a bias modifies the estimates markedly in four of the six cases. Three out of four selection terms are statistically highly significant (Schultz 1989). The return to primary education for women doubles to 10 percent, whereas the return to secondary school declines to 25 percent for women and to 13 percent for men. Private returns to higher education increase to 11 percent for women and decline to 4 percent for men.

The analysis is repeated with 1981 *monthly* earnings; this has the effect of including labor supply adjustments related to schooling as part of the private market returns. In four out of six comparisons, the corrected monthly returns are slightly lower than the corrected hourly returns. Those who are better educated work fewer hours a month or enjoy more leisure, responding to education as to a gain in wealth. Exceptions are women with a university education and men with only some primary schooling; these two groups increase their labor supply as their education increases. Overall, however, the data on hourly and monthly earnings yield similar results for the direction and the magnitude of the effect produced by correcting for sample selection. Unfortunately, only the monthly earnings functions can be estimated from the 1976 and 1986 Thai surveys because of a lack of data on how many hours the respondents worked during the previous month.

Between 1981 and 1986 returns to primary schooling increased for both women and men. Correcting for sample selection raises the 1986 returns for women still further. At the secondary level, women's high private returns to schooling are diminished somewhat by the correction procedure, but they are nevertheless more than three times as high as the returns for men. Finally, for higher education, private returns increase for both women and men; again, the correction has a greater effect for women, doubling their returns. Only at the primary school level are the returns greater to male than to female education. The pattern of returns to schooling in 1986 is roughly comparable to that for 1976. Higher education produced slightly higher returns for men in 1976 (11 percent) than in 1981 (3 percent) or in 1986 (8 percent). The rapid expansion of public "open" universities between 1976 and 1986 may have reduced the overall quality of a year of higher education.

Much more work is needed to assess alternative methods for coping with sample selection bias as it affects estimates of the returns to educating women compared with men. Nevertheless, these data from Thailand spanning eleven years suggest that estimates may be sensitive to this source of sampling bias. The overall tendency is for the sample selection correction to raise the returns to women's schooling and to lower those to men's schooling. With the exception of primary education after 1981, women's schooling appears to have a more favorable rate of return than does men's schooling in Thailand.

In estimating the market returns to education, an understanding of what determines how an individual allocates time is required to correct analyses that use data on wage earners to infer the effect of investments in education on the productivity of all people. The sample selection correction procedure used in the Thai example depends on what the family unit is that may pool resources and coordinate labor market behavior and on how these forms of family behavior are modeled. Two approaches are available. The bargaining model implies a few, possibly useful, differences between the empirical specification of the family Nash-bargained labor supply model and that implied by the unified family demand model.[5] On the whole, however, both models require similar variables for identification of the sample selection rule determining wage-earner status. Conclusions drawn from the analysis of market returns to education presented in this section are likely to be robust to changes in how the family decisionmaking process is eventually modeled.

Nonmarket Returns to Women's Education

The effects of schooling on market earnings are relatively well documented even if they are sometimes subject to uncertainty because of the problems of estimation discussed in the preceding section. Evidence about the effects of education on nonmarket production within the household is more fragmentary, however, and is inherently difficult to aggregate or summarize in a single measure such as the internal rate of return.

The more education a married woman has, the more likely she is to work in the labor market, given the husband's education and assets as a constant. This pattern has been observed frequently in low-income countries, especially in urban areas and in rural areas offering off-farm employment opportunities for educated women. Women who work in the labor market must either curtail their nonmarket production activities or find substitutes for their time in nonmarket production.

Women's education is also associated with quantifiable increases in home output—in the form of better health and nutrition, more attention given to each child, and so on—despite the fact that better-educated women are likely to spend less time in the home. This seeming paradox is only possible if the productivity of women at home increases as their education increases, indicating that nonmarket returns to schooling are positive.

Children's Health and Survival

Studies in demography, economics, anthropology, and sociology conclude that a strong inverse relationship exists between a mother's schooling and the incidence of mortality among her children. This is especially striking in low-income countries. The pattern has been widely replicated across comparative data bases, such as the World Fertility Surveys, and over time through repeated censuses. Many hypotheses have been advanced to explain this correlation (see, for example, Barrera 1988a; Farah and Preston 1982; Schultz 1984).

Data that are now widely collected from women in low-income countries on their age, children ever born, and children still living facilitate analyses of the determinants of child mortality. Additional information on the date of birth and the survival or date of death of each offspring improves the measurement of the mortality risk faced by each of a woman's children. These refinements are especially useful in comparing the child mortality experience of younger women. The link between more education and lower child mortality is not very sensitive to which method is used to compare with simple child survival (Preston and Trussell 1982). The statistical strength of this link and its replicability across surveys and societies is reminiscent of the "discovery" in the 1960s of the logarithmic wage function, which also depended centrally on education-based differences. One is a measure of the market rate of return to education, the other a form of nonmarket return.

An added year of maternal education tends to be associated with a fairly constant percentage decline in child mortality rates. Although mortality tends to be higher in rural than in urban areas in many low-income countries, the reduction in child mortality associated with an additional year of mother's schooling is about the same, between 5 and 10 percent. The effect of the father's education on reducing mortality is smaller, especially in rural populations (Mensch, Lentzner, and Preston 1986).

Studies in Latin America have noted that the differentials in child mortality associated with maternal education were narrower in Costa Rica and Cuba than in the rest of the region. One hypothesis is that strong public health programs in these two countries have improved access to health care, even among the least-educated mothers (Behm 1980). Other hypotheses for differences among countries in how strongly education affects child mortality are analyzed by Rosenzweig and Schultz (1982a; see also Schultz 1984; Thomas, Strauss, and Henriques 1987).

Is education simply correlated with the use of more health inputs, or does education improve a mother's ability to cope with health risks and manage her child's environment? An analysis of the 1973 census in Colombia indicated that controlling for household income, the husband's education, or the marital status of the mother did not eliminate or even greatly reduce the independent role of the mother's education as a partial explanation for her children's survival (Schultz

1980a). Studies elsewhere have shown that even after controlling for many lifetime events and for changes in socioeconomic status, the mother's education still has a substantial effect on child mortality rates (Farah and Preston 1982). In Brazil, for example, only a third of the effect of a mother's education on child mortality could be explained by family income variables (Thomas, Strauss, and Henriques 1987).

In addition to influencing child mortality, a mother's education undoubtedly influences many interrelated variables such as migration, labor market behavior, use of health care, and modern attitudes. Controlling statistically for such variables is therefore likely to result in an understatement of the net effect of schooling (Mensch, Lentzner, and Preston 1986).

The puzzle that remains is why a mother's education explains more of the variation in child mortality than do other variables such as access to health care, cost of health care, or even family income available for health care. Three competing hypotheses have been proposed: the better-educated mother uses a different mix of observable health inputs than does the less-educated mother; she uses these inputs more effectively; or her education is positively correlated with the use of many minor health inputs that are not observed and is credited with the effect of these inputs on child health (Schultz 1984).

The most important deliverer of health care to a child is the mother. How well she performs this task depends "on her schooling, which equips her with general and specific knowledge, and the means and confidence to seek new ideas" (Barrera 1988b). How does education influence the use of health inputs to reduce the probability of child mortality? The answer is sought by studying variations in such indicators of a child's health status as height and weight at birth. Physical (anthropometric) characteristics that can be measured at birth accurately predict lifetime health problems, mental and physical development, and age-specific mortality. Since the selection of some health inputs occurs in response to the mother's expectation of a good or poor birth outcome, the simple correlation between self-selected health care on the one hand and health outcomes on the other can be misleading. For example, early prenatal care is often sought if a pregnancy is difficult; so it is not surprising that early care is correlated with having a baby that is less healthy and weighs less at birth than the average. Yet early prenatal care is beneficial for the average woman or for a mother and unborn child whose initial health condition can be statistically held constant. In a United States study, the effect of the mother's education on birth weight is transmitted largely through the variation in four measured prenatal health inputs: age, parity (number of previous births), smoking, and timing of prenatal care (Rosenzweig and Schultz 1989). The effect of maternal education on child health is fully explained in this study by the effect of education on the use of observed health inputs.

The inputs that play an important role in producing good nutrition, good health, sound development, and survival in an older child are more difficult to measure. A statistical explanation must also be found for which mother uses each of these health inputs if their positive effect on child health is to be estimated without a self-selection bias.

Examining directly the impact on child health of the interactions between a mother's education and her constraints in caring for her children's health may be simpler than identifying the mechanisms or inputs through which they work, as in a production function. Estimates of the health consequences of these interactions document how maternal education exerts its elusive effect on child health. For example, Caldwell (1979) hypothesized that in West Africa a mother's education enabled her to exploit local public health care more effectively. He proposed that the interaction between a mother's education and the local public health infrastructure was complementary and positive: better-educated mothers gained most from local public health clinics. One can restate Caldwell's hypothesis to suggest that differentials in child health or mortality related to a mother's education should increase in communities served more intensively by a public health system. Rosenzweig and Schultz (1982a), however, found the opposite to be true in Colombia. There, differences in maternal education had a smaller impact on child mortality in urban populations that received more public and private hospital and clinic services per capita. Their findings can be viewed as consistent with the aggregate patterns reported in Latin America by Behm (1980) and Palloni (1981) and in Sri Lanka by Meegama (1981).

Other studies have examined the relationship between a mother's choice of health inputs and environmental constraints on child survival. Among households in Malaysia with poor water and sanitation facilities, breastfeeding was associated with reductions in child mortality (Butz, Habicht, and DaVanzo 1984). Estrey and Habicht (1987) found that safe water supplies reduced child mortality by a greater amount the more education mothers had, whereas access to toilets in the household reduced child mortality by a smaller amount the more education mothers had. Haines and Avery (1982) found that in Costa Rica an additional year of schooling for the mother reduced her children's mortality 6 to 7 percent when household sanitation, quality of the dwelling, child mortality rates in the community, and health care facilities were held constant. This study concluded that the gains in child health associated with a mother's education were smaller in urban than in rural areas, a result confirmed by Schultz (1980a) for Colombia and by Behm (1976) for several Latin America capital cities.

The studies on Malaysia and Costa Rica treated the household water and sanitation infrastructure, as well as the mother's breastfeeding, as exogenous, in other words, as not affected by maternal education or unobserved variables that might themselves have otherwise influenced child health outcomes. A study by Barrera (1988a) of household and community data from the Bicol province of the Philippines refined these earlier studies. He assumed that the water and sanitary facilities of households were endogenous choice variables that may be correlated with unexplained variations in child health. He first analyzed the relation between maternal education and child health, conditional on the community's average levels of water and sanitation but not on the household's actual variables, which are assumed to be spuriously correlated with the family's other choices. Barrera found that a mother's schooling had a larger protective effect on her children's health in unsanitary environments where signs of excreta were visible and in areas that were more distant (in time) from outpatient health care facilities. In a community where piped water was the predominant source of supply, the impact of a mother's education diminished; but in a community where water-sealed toilets were more prevalent, the impact of a mother's education increased. Because Barrera replaced measures of water and toilet facilities in the household with measures representing the availability of these facilities in the community, he obtained conclusions diametrically opposed to those of Estrey and Habicht (1987): the community water supply appeared to substitute for the mother's education, whereas modern toilets complemented it (Barrera 1988a, table 16). At the same time, Barrera showed that higher income and the mother's education increased the chances that a household had acquired piped water and water-sealed toilets.

The duration of breastfeeding, another important input to child health, is inversely related to mothers' education in many countries (see, for example, Blau 1984; Wolfe and Behrman 1982). Table 2-6 illustrates how in Africa, Latin America, and Asia, women with seven or more years of schooling tend to breastfeed their children seven or eight months less than do women with no schooling.

Breastfeeding is beneficial to child health primarily when it is supplemented by other foods before the end of the baby's first year. In Barrera's rural Philippine population, a mother's education shortened only the duration of unsupplemented breastfeeding (Barrera 1988a, table 23). Moreover, Barrera estimated that unsupplemented breastfeeding was beneficial only up to six months. The better-educated mother is more likely to replace her milk with sanitary substitutes. For the less-educated mother, Barrera hypothesized, supplementing breastfeeding before the baby was six months old was harmful. The optimal duration of breastfeeding and the optimal time to introduce

Table 2-6. *Women's Average Age at Marriage, Duration of Breastfeeding, and Use of Contraception, by Region and Education, World Fertility Survey Countries*

Region, number of countries, and years of school completed	Age at marriage (years)[a]	Duration of breastfeeding (months)[b]	Contraceptive usage (percent)[c]
Africa (8–12 countries)			
Years of school			
0	17.8	19.9	7
1–3	19.2	18.5	14
4–6	20.3	15.7	17
7 or more	23.0	13.4	27
Difference (7 or more − 0)	5.2	−6.9	20
Latin America and the Caribbean (13 countries)			
Years of school			
0	19.5	15.0	24
1–3	19.5	12.1	33
4–6	20.4	9.1	43
7 or more	22.6	5.4	53
Difference (7 or more − 0)	3.1	−8.7	29
Asia and Oceania (7–13 countries)			
Years of school			
0	20.2	20.1	16
1–3	19.5	18.4	26
4–6	20.6	16.0	28
7 or more	23.8	10.6	39
Difference (7 or more − 0)	3.6	−7.1	23

a. Singulate mean age at marriage in years.

b. Mean duration of breastfeeding in months using current status estimates based on surviving births only and using life table methods.

c. Percentage of currently married women age 15–49 currently using contraception, adjusted for age differences between education groups.

Source: United Nations 1987, tables 119, 121, and 122.

supplementary foods in the child's diet depended on the education of the mother, who had to provide sanitary substitutes for her own milk. In sum, maternal education and the duration of unsupplemented breastfeeding and education appear to be substitutes in their effect on child health. This finding may partially account for the fact that although mothers with more education breastfeed less, their children's health is better (Barrera 1988a, table 29).

Children's Schooling

Notwithstanding the material presented in the regional chapters of this volume, surprisingly few studies have systematically addressed the household determinants of school enrollment and attendance rates by gender in low-income countries. In most studies of the schooling of children in high-income countries, the mother's education has a larger effect than the father's, even though the father's education implies a larger effect on the family's income because he tends to receive a higher wage and to work more hours (King and others 1986; Leibowitz 1974). Evidence that the mother's schooling exerts a greater effect on the schooling of her daughters than of her sons is less well established (see, for example, de Tray 1988, table 5). This hypothesis requires further study.

Fertility

Better-educated women marry later, as shown in table 2-7 for the countries included in the World Fertility Surveys. In Africa women with seven or more years of schooling tend to marry five years later than women with no schooling; in Latin America and Asia the differential is about three years. This table examines how the median age when a women first gives birth varies by her education in eight African countries, with further disaggregation by age of the woman. The effect of her education on the age at which a woman begins bearing children is not uniform across Africa, but it is of growing importance in such countries as Kenya and Ghana, where overall fertility levels may soon begin to decline.

One of the important discoveries in research on nonmarket returns to women's education is the strong link between a mother's education and her fertility. Maternal education is associated with decreased breastfeeding, as already noted (see table 2-6). The best-educated mothers breastfeed seven to eight months less than mothers who have no schooling, with an accompanying drop in the interval between births of a month or so. But educated women are much more likely to practice contraception, which more than compensates in its impact on fertility for the shorter duration of breastfeeding. Total fertility rates are lower for women with seven or more years of schooling than for those with no schooling (table 2-8). The differences are larger in Latin America (3.6 fewer children) than in Africa (2.0 fewer children) or Asia (3.1 fewer children), but they are relatively uniform regardless of how fertility is measured. With marital status, or age at first marriage, held constant, differences in marital fertility by education are about a third less than differences in total fertility in Africa and Asia, but they are only one-fifth less in Latin America, where overall contraceptive prevalence is high but varies greatly by a woman's education. To compare children ever born, the figures are restricted to the group of women who have completed their childbearing (ages 40–49). These data do

Table 2-7. *Median Age of Women at Birth of First Child, by Age and Education, Selected Sub-Saharan African Countries, about 1980*

Country and years of school completed	Younger than 25 years	25–34	35 or older
Benin			
0	19.5	19.1	19.7
1–4	19.4	19.9	(19.8)
5–7	19.3	19.7	20.7
8 or more	20.2	21.2	21.0
Difference (8 or more − 0)	0.7	2.1	1.3
Cameroon			
0	18.2	19.3	20.6
1–4	18.4	18.8	19.7
5–7	19.0	19.0	19.1
8 or more	21.4	20.6	(24.3)
Difference (8 or more − 0)	3.2	1.3	3.7
Côte d'Ivoire			
0	18.3	18.7	19.3
1–4	17.6	19.2	20.2
5–7	18.2	18.7	19.9
8 or more	20.2	18.8	20.2
Difference (8 or more − 0)	1.9	0.1	0.9
Ghana			
0	18.9	19.3	20.0
1–4	18.6	19.7	20.3
5–7	18.8	20.2	19.3
8 or more	20.5	20.7	20.5
Difference (8 or more − 0)	1.6	1.4	0.5
Kenya			
0	18.2	18.4	19.4
1–4	18.6	18.2	19.3
5–7	19.1	19.3	19.2
8 or more	21.3	20.5	(21.5)
Difference (8 or more − 0)	3.1	2.1	2.1
Lesotho			
0	18.7	19.5	22.2
1–4	19.1	19.9	(19.8)
5–7	19.8	20.5	(21.1)
8 or more	20.8	22.9	22.8
Difference (8 or more − 0)	2.1	3.4	0.6
Senegal			
0	18.3	18.0	17.9
1–4	19.3	(18.6)	(19.6)
5–7	19.7	20.4	(21.0)
8 or more	22.4	(23.0)	(23.0)
Difference (8 or more − 0)	4.1	5.0	5.1

(Table continues on the following page.)

Table 2-7 *(continued)*

Country and years of school completed	Younger than 25 years	25–34	35 or older
Sudan			
0	18.0	18.5	20.0
1–4	17.6	18.6	20.1
5–7	19.1	(19.6)	(21.0)
8 or more	(20.3)	21.6	(23.6)
Difference (8 or more − 0)	2.3	3.1	3.6

Note: Means reported in parentheses are less reliable because they are based on fewer that fifty observations.

Source: World Fertility Surveys as tabulated by Eelens and Donne 1985, tables A.9–A.16.

not, therefore, provide information on reproductive patterns among younger women or on recent trends.

Another aspect of fertility measured by the World Fertility Surveys is women's desired family size. Desired fertility, like actual fertility, falls monotonically with a woman's education. Subtracting desired fertility from current total fertility suggests that the potential for increased contraception to reduce fertility toward desired levels is concentrated in Latin America among women with less than four years of schooling and in Asia among women with less than seven years of schooling. Among better-educated women in Latin America and Asia, total fertility rates are already approaching desired fertility levels (see table 2-8). This reflects the fact that women's education substitutes for family planning by helping women reach their desired reproductive goals (Schultz 1989).

Other studies confirm that the wife's education helps couples avoid exceeding their reproductive goals. This is partially achieved by delaying marriage (Cochrane 1979), but better-educated wives also have fewer unwanted conceptions and births in marriage (Rosenzweig and Schultz 1985, 1987). Although the husband's education may also enhance the effectiveness of contraception, the wife's education has at least as strong an effect on reproductive behavior, whether inferred from a respondent's own classification of conceptions as unplanned or derived from econometric analyses of the reproduction function and its residual (Rosenzweig and Schultz 1985, 1987, 1989).

Although fertility during a woman's lifetime appears to decrease as her education increases, in some cases the fertility of unschooled women is slightly lower than that of women with one to three years of schooling (see total fertility rates for Africa in table 2-8). This occasional reversal in the effect of women's schooling on fertility has been interpreted in two ways. Easterlin (1975) proposed a framework for describing the demographic transition that accommodates the ten-

Table 2-8. *Measures of Recent, Cumulative, and Desired Fertility: Averages for Women in World Fertility Survey Countries Reporting, by Region and Respondent's Education*

Region, number of countries, and years of school completed	Total fertility rate[a]	Marital fertility rate	Children ever born[b]	Desired family size[c]
Africa (8–10 countries)				
Years of school				
0	7.0	6.6	6.4	6.9
1–3	7.2	6.6	6.5	6.4
4–6	6.2	6.3	6.1	5.9
7 or more	5.0	5.4	4.8	5.0
Difference (7 or more −0)	−2.0	−1.2	−1.6	−1.9
Latin America (13 countries)				
Years of school				
0	6.8	6.8	7.1	4.8
1–3	6.2	6.2	6.8	4.7
4–6	4.8	5.2	6.0	4.2
7 or more	3.2	3.8	4.2	3.7
Difference (7 or more −0)	−3.6	−3.0	−2.9	−1.1
Asia and Oceania (9–13 countries)				
Years of school				
0	7.0	6.6	6.7	5.4
1–3	6.4	6.4	6.7	4.3
4–6	5.8	6.1	6.4	4.2
7 or more	3.9	4.7	4.9	4.0
Difference (7 or more −0)	−3.1	−1.9	−1.8	−1.4

a. Age standardized.
b. Age 40–49 years.
c. Age adjusted.
Source: United Nations 1987, tables 112, 115.

dency for birthrates to increase at the outset of modern economic growth before they then begin their secular decline. This early rise in fertility has been attributed to improved maternal health and decreased breastfeeding, both thought to increase reproductive potential before contraception was available and widely used. The rise in fertility among women with a few years of schooling could, therefore, be attributed to the enhanced reproductive potential of these women (Cochrane 1979, 1988).

A second explanation for the occasional rise in fertility associated with a few years of women's schooling has to do with family decision-making, as captured in the household economic model of fertility. This model focuses attention on the potentially different direction (positive or negative) of the effects of men's and women's schooling (or the value of their time) on their demands for children and hence on lifetime completed fertility (Schultz 1981). These differences in wage effects on fertility, by gender, follow from the customary tendency for women to devote more time to childcare than men do. The household economic model of fertility helps to account for the observed tendency in multivariate analyses for female education (or wages) to be inversely related to fertility but for male education (or wages), income from land or assets, and child wages to be directly related to fertility, at least in a traditional agrarian society (Schultz 1973). At a later stage in the development process, the effect of male education (or wages) on fertility may also be negative, in part because the parents invest more heavily in educating each child.

Thus, the frequently observed bivariate correlation between a woman's education and her fertility can be misleading. To estimate the *partial* effect of female education, one must hold constant the other main exogenous determinants of fertility. Failure to do so for men's education (or wages) undoubtedly reduces the estimated negative effect of women's early schooling on fertility. This is because the years of schooling of a husband and wife have a strong positive correlation in all societies, and men's education (or wages) is often positively related to fertility, at least at low levels of schooling.

Investing in the Next Generation

All these routes by which women's education may improve society— reduced child mortality, enhanced child health and nutrition, increased emphasis on schooling, and reduced fertility—involve benefits that are partly captured by a woman's own children. If parents are entirely altruistic toward their children or view their children's good as identical to their own, these nonmarket activities of women will be adequately encouraged within the family.

Yet this is often not the case. Parents may not view sons and daughters as equally important in the intergenerational family; or their perceptions of the payoff to education may be based only on its effect on wages in the labor force. Many societies have strengthened the rights of children and weakened the economic claims of parents—for example, through restrictions on the conditions of child labor, mandatory school attendance, and penalties for truancy. Also, many societies link improvements in women's education to increases in the level of investment in the human capital of children (Thomas 1989). A subsidy that favored women's schooling would help shift private household resources toward investments in the quality of the younger generation. Empirical studies have not yet widely appraised how responsive families would be to practical interventions that seek to educate women so that they, in turn, will increase their investment in the human capital of their own children, but some development projects are testing these linkages (Martin, Flanagan, and Klenicki 1986).

Social Returns to Education

The social costs of education are traditionally calculated by adding public spending on education to the private direct and opportunity costs of education. Hence, the social returns to education are lower than the private returns, often by 20 to 30 percent. If the public resources devoted to teaching women and men differ, the returns to educating women and men will differ. In many parts of the world higher education for women is focused on training for specific professions, such as teaching and nursing, which may be less costly to provide than other courses of study. Moreover, women in some countries receive much of their higher education in teacher training institutes (so-called normal schools) at a lower annual cost per student than if they attended regular academic institutions (see, for example, Birdsall and Fox 1985 for Brazil; Tilak 1987 for India). When the cost of educating men is higher, the social returns from their schooling should be commensurately lower. Much better data are needed on these differential costs, however, to be able to refine the differences in the social returns to men's and women's education.

If a government taxes labor earnings, it reduces the private returns to human capital and recovers some of its expenditures on education, health, and other public services. In most low-income countries, however, only wage and salary workers are effectively taxed, and no country has designed a tax on nonmarket production.[6] The tendency for more men than women to work for a wage and be taxed might appear to favor public investments in the schooling of males over that of females. This supposition depends, however, on how men and women respond to the market wage offered to them (after taxes). Most empirical studies of labor supply in both high-income and low-income countries indicate that women respond positively to an increase in their own market wages by working more but respond negatively to an increase in their husbands' market wages. Consequently, the taxable supply of female labor rises with an investment in women's capabilities and decreases with a comparable investment in men's capabilities. Moreover, estimates of male labor supply often reveal a tendency for men to reduce how much they work as their wages rise.[7] To the extent that governments recoup some of the public cost of investing in human capital by taxing wages, the social return from investing in women should be greater than that from investing in men.[8]

A more widely accepted rationale for public spending to educate both men and women is that an educated population enjoys a higher level of welfare. This gain is not entirely captured by the educated individuals or their families. That human capital may be a source of increasing returns—because of the effect of education on technological progress, for example—helps to explain the puzzle of modern economic growth (Kuznets 1966; T. W. Schultz 1988).

Supporters of public education may also argue that a better-educated society is more capable of managing a political system that protects individuals' rights and facilitates efficient and equitable growth. Although these claims may be difficult to substantiate statistically, some evidence indicates that a higher level of schooling for females is associated with these benefits (World Bank 1991).

Directions for Research and Policy

Investments that increase the primary and secondary schooling of women are economically warranted on several grounds, based on the currently available evidence from many countries. The direct and opportunity costs of women's schooling, both private and social, appear to be recovered fully by increases in market productivity or wage gains experienced by better-educated women during their adult years. When internal rates of return are calculated using the private costs of attending school and the potential wage gains, the returns tend to be at least as high for women as for men, varying from 30 percent in less-developed countries to 10 percent in more-developed countries (Psacharopoulos 1973, 1985).

Social rates of return, calculated to include public spending on education, are only slightly lower than private rates of return at the primary school level. In contrast, the social returns to higher education are in some instances markedly lower than private returns because of the relatively high cost of university training in low-income countries and the reluctance of governments to cover the cost by raising tuition. The public sector may even pay for the opportunity cost of students' time by providing scholarships and cost-of-living stipends regardless of financial need (World Bank 1986).

Although public expenditures for education are rarely disaggregated by sex, these costs are likely to be lower for women than for men, for reasons suggested in the preceding section. If this is so, the social returns to education are correspondingly higher for women than for men, at least at the university level, all else being equal.

Evidence is accumulating that schooling increases the nonmarket productivity of women. For example, a mother's education can improve her children's health, measured by their birth weight, nutritional status, and survival rate. Research surveyed earlier in this chapter and elsewhere in this volume describes how maternal education produces these child health benefits. The way in which maternal education interacts with program and policy interventions has also been investigated. In some circumstances public health and family planning services appear to substitute for maternal education (Schultz 1984). Nonmarket returns to maternal education are greatest when such programs are least developed. Differentials in child mortality by the mother's education are smallest in urban areas served by comparatively well-funded public health programs and largest in rural areas lying beyond the reach of hospitals and of public health and family planning clinics.

The education of a woman is also associated with her fertility, her regional and occupational mobility, and the educational achievement of her children. Although less widely studied than the link between maternal education and child health, these relationships also confirm the contribution of female education to nonmarket productivity. For the most part the woman and her family capture these benefits and so are compensated for at least some of the cost of her education. The nonmarket returns to women's education may also represent a broader social externality, however, and may therefore warrant a special public subsidy insofar as the society as a whole benefits from reduced fertility, diminished population growth, improved health and education for children, and increased population mobility.

Investments in female education encourage women to shift from home-based to market-based work. Market-based work is counted in conventional national income accounts—and hence adds to GNP—whereas home-based work is not. This in itself is no reason to encourage female education. But the shift in how women allocate their time may have other desirable consequences for the productive use of social resources. For example, because better-educated women are more likely than less-educated women to work for wages, they tend to pay more direct and indirect taxes; given the government's need for resources, this lowers the tax rates for others. Increases in men's education that contribute to raising their wages tend to reduce the number of hours their wives work in the market labor force, and frequently the men work fewer hours as well. So women's education, which returns more in taxes to support public services, including schooling, has a higher social rate of return than men's education.

Education, Fertility, and Child Mortality

Social scientists and statisticians studying how education is linked to fertility and to child mortality have used a wide variety of methods to estimate these relationships. Unless the common core of important exogenous economic variables is held constant, findings on the partial effects of women's education on fertility and child mortality will be unstable and potentially misleading. Any survey of the literature in these fields requires setting forth a clear research methodology.

Although couples universally prefer to reduce child mortality, they do not always wish to limit their fertility. The impact of a variable such as the wife's education on fertility includes both its effect on desired fertility (if birth control were without cost and perfectly reliable) and its effect on unwanted fertility (by reducing the cost of using birth control with greater effectiveness). Therefore, surveys of the relationship between female education and fertility that do not control for the economic resources available to a woman from her husband and from nonearned family income, and for the relative benefits and costs of children, do not always find this relationship to be a monotonic inverse one. Consistent use of the household economic model of fertility should make assessments of this important determinant of fertility more uniform across low-income countries.

Regional and Occupational Groups

Returns to education are sometimes calculated for specific subpopulations. If these subpopulations are defined by characteristics that are fixed for individuals, such as sex, race, or caste, the interpretation of the returns for each group is straightforward. But if the subpopulations are open rather than closed, as regional or occupational groups are, empirical estimates of the returns to education for each group are potentially misleading.

Better-educated men and women are more likely than those who are less educated to migrate from one region to another, assuming that migration leads to higher wages (Schwartz 1976). For example, estimates of the returns to schooling in a sector experiencing economic decline, with wages that are generally lower than elsewhere, are likely to introduce a downward bias into estimates of the returns to schooling. This is because part of the return to schooling in the declining sector involves migrating out of that sector. So, for example, estimates of educational returns for rural and urban subpopulations are potentially misleading unless the groups can be defined by place of birth or schooling. When men and women migrate from a sector at different rates, this bias may also distort the comparison of the estimated returns to schooling for each gender.

Similarly, assessing the returns to schooling among the self-employed is difficult. In rural areas the self-employed tend to be landholders or tenants, and in urban areas, small businessmen. The probability of being self-employed generally increases over a person's lifetime in low-income countries. Therefore, wage functions estimated across ages for the self-employed cannot be readily interpreted in the human capital life-cycle framework to determine returns to schooling (Mincer 1974). The assessment of market returns to schooling may be more accurate if the analysis is restricted to wage earners, whose wage rates approximate hourly productivity. Such an analysis must be corrected, however, for the systematic bias introduced because only wage earners compose the sample. This brings us again to the importance of correcting for the bias introduced by how the sample is selected. The absence of such a correction has emerged repeatedly in this chapter as a crucial limitation in existing research on returns to educating women.

Allocation of Time

To evaluate the intensity with which resources are used in the educational process, more detailed information is needed on how much time students and teachers devote to it. A student's resource input is the private opportunity cost of the time allocated to attending school and doing homework. A teacher's input is time, adjusted for the number of students taught in a class and for the amount of time needed to prepare. These resource inputs may differ for female and male students even though they are enrolled in the same level of a school system. More accurate measures of the private and social costs of a year of schooling for females and for males in specific branches of the education system might help explain subsequent differences in their adult productivity and might in turn modify estimates of the private and social returns to schooling for women and for men.

Increasing Female School Enrollment

The situation of women varies widely within and across countries. The challenge in every country is to give priority to those programs and policies that are most likely to raise female enrollment rates in the society. Because the direct and indirect effects of many of these interventions are uncertain given the great variety of circumstances, collecting baseline and longitudinal data on populations served by pilot programs and new policies is important. Such data would permit future evaluation of how programs and policies affect the educational attainment of women, the productivity and choices of both women and men, and the welfare of their families, communities, and countries.

Parents appear to be responding to the growing evidence in the developing world that educated sons and daughters get much better jobs. Generally, their offspring will eventually earn more than enough to justify the sacrifices made to send them through school. Micro-economists have amassed enough data supporting the link between more education and higher earnings to explain the growth in school enrollments in most low-income countries.

A quantitative assessment of how better-educated mothers produce healthier children who have a greater chance of surviving to adulthood is more difficult. And appraising the effect of maternal education on children's nutrition, cognitive development, and school achievement is more difficult still. The majority of parents may not yet fully appreciate these links, which are complex and may extend over a lifetime. Indeed, social scientists do not yet fully understand them. Even if the clues in the current literature are confirmed by new, more thorough analyses and surveys, parents will still need time to digest and act on this body of evidence.

How will this information, as it diffuses through society, affect behavior? Young men, encouraged by their parents, should be willing to "pay" more, modifying their traditional attitudes, to marry a better-educated woman, even when she is not expected to work in the labor force. As this increased demand for the nonmarket productivity of educated wives becomes obvious, parents may perceive the monetary and psychological benefits they will gain by investing more heavily in educating their daughters.

The historical record has not been adequately analyzed, but the gains in nonmarket productivity associated with women's education may be a relatively recent phenomenon in some parts of the world. In the past, when modern health inputs such as antibiotics, vaccines, and oral rehydration salts were not readily available to the poor, the ability of a mother, even if she was educated, to protect her child from health risks may have been much more limited. But now, modern inputs to home production activities may be especially useful to better-educated women, who can control their reproduction with greater ease and certainty than ever before because of the widening range of available birth control techniques. Nonetheless, until more women participate in the paid labor force, parents may persist in their belief that educating their daughters is less important than educating their sons.

Given the growing understanding of the negative consequences of the gender gap in education, the current allocation of resources in many countries is now viewed as uneconomic. Existing policy research, however, has not addressed the question of how governments might compensate for this traditional bias. What policies should be encouraged, given the accumulating evidence that the market returns to women's education are at least as high as those to men's education, and that nonmarket productive returns to women's education are associated with important social externalities—in fertility, nutrition, and children's health and schooling—that many societies want to subsidize? Better research in a wide variety of settings could bolster the case for policy interventions. Development agencies should launch pilot programs and experimental policy changes now to begin identifying promising, cost-effective options. Even before the pilot programs can be fully evaluated, however, governments can help initiate the research needed to document the local returns to women's education, both in market wage increases and in nonmarket productivity gains. Research and action must go hand in hand if the gender gap in education is to be closed in the next century.

Appendix. Issues in Estimating Returns to Education

In the early studies of the association between education and labor earnings, private rates of return were calculated with the assumption that better-educated people benefit from schooling only to the extent that they hold a job in the labor force (and report earnings). If a year of additional schooling raised the wage rates of men and women by x percent a year, and if both men and women worked full-time in the labor force, the lifetime internal rate of return to the opportunity cost of attending school for that year was x percent for men and women. But if women worked only half-time in the labor force after completing their schooling, whereas men worked full-time, the conclusion was that women earned only half the rate of return that men earned on their additional year of schooling.

Becker (1964), in his seminal contribution on this subject, observed that the lower returns to women's education attributable to their lower participation in the labor force were consistent with the fact that a smaller percentage of women than men attended college in the United States in the 1950s. Later empirical studies and surveys that specifically addressed gender differences in rates of return to education used Becker's methodology (Hines, Tweeten, and Redfern 1970; Psacharopoulos 1973; Thias and Carnoy 1969; Woodhall 1973). The implicit assumption underlying this research was that schooling had no effect on the productivity of people working outside the market labor force.

Many subsequent empirical studies have challenged this assumption. They indicate that education increases the productivity of time in nonmarket production, especially for women (Haveman and Wolfe 1984; Michael 1982). Moreover, the opportunity cost of the time spent by females in school was not symmetrically discounted; girls were implicitly assumed to be giving up a full-time job in the labor force to attend school, a pattern that might not have been so. These working assumptions exert a downward bias on the rates of return to groups, such as women, that participate in the labor force less than the average person does or that serve more often as unpaid family workers.

Becker (1964) and Mincer (1974) also analyzed the differences among individuals in annual earnings, combining the potential effect of schooling on the worker's hourly productivity with its potential effect on market labor supply and unemployment. The empirical consequence of this decision is not theoretically obvious, but any empirical tendency for unemployment rates to be lower and labor supply to be larger among the better educated would bias estimates of the rate of return to schooling upward when the dependent variable used is the logarithm of annual or monthly earnings rather than the (preferable) logarithm of the hourly wage rate.

The usual assumption in labor economics is that people enter the market labor force when the market wage they are offered (after taxes and fixed costs of entering the labor force) exceeds the reservation wage that is determined by their marginal productivity in nonmarket or home activities. When an individual shifts time from nonmarket to market work, national income may increase, but the broader welfare indicator of "full income" (Becker 1965), or the potential productivity of the human agent, remains unchanged. As people vary the hours they work in the market labor force, the observable market wage rate continues to approximate their nonmarket productivity. Only when they leave the labor force entirely can we infer that their nonmarket productivity exceeds their market wage offer. The problem is how to estimate the productivity of nonmarket time for nonparticipants in the labor force, by years of schooling, so as to incorporate this information into the calculation of the returns to education. Estimating the nonmarket productivity of nonparticipants requires that we specify the mathematical function for nonmarket productivity (for example, linear or nonlinear) and show how its parameters are identified. No consensus exists on how this should be done, and it is not attempted here.

The original methodology of Becker and Mincer for estimating the returns to schooling can be improved by assuming that education affects hourly labor productivity in market and nonmarket work by the same amount, or that it is neutral between these sectors. The coefficient on years of schooling in a logarithmic hourly wage function is then an estimate of the private rate of return to schooling. Research must now appraise the severity of the bias remaining in this revised simple estimation methodology because of the underestimation of the nonmarket productivity of those not participating in the labor force.

Fixing the effect of schooling on nonmarket productivity to zero appears, with hindsight, to have been unjustified and to have led to a large downward bias in the estimated rates of return to education for women. The bias in the estimated rates of return attributable to analyzing annual earnings, rather than the hourly wage rate, cannot be generally described since it depends on the joint determination of labor supply behavior and wage functions in a specific society. Similarly, research is only beginning to evaluate the bias on estimates of the returns to women's schooling that is attributable to how the sample of wage earners is selected. This bias could overstate or understate the true rate of return to education for the entire population (Heckman 1979, 1987).

Theoretically, the variable needed to identify the nonmarket productivity (or reservation wage) function is a household fixed productive factor that affects the individual's nonmarket productivity but does not alter his or her labor productivity to a firm in the market. In the short run, children have been viewed as such a variable in that they raise a woman's productivity only in the home (Gronau 1974). Over the life cycle, however, this variable is also both determined by and responsive to labor market wage rates, so it should be viewed as endogenous or as determined within the same framework (Schultz 1981). Landownership, family business assets, and the market productivity of a person's spouse may be more satisfactory measures of fixed household endowments that enhance the value of an individual's time in nonmarket activities. The choice of this identifying restriction determines how the estimates of the market wage function are interpreted and hence whether the implied rate of return to schooling is a satisfactory estimate for the entire population or only for the nonrandom sample of wage earners.

If more than one selection process is used to define the sample for estimation, and the selection processes have different determinants, multiple sample selection equations and corrections are used (see, for example, Catsiapis and Robinson 1982). Participation in the market labor force and acceptance of wage employment may be responses to different home and market constraints. If the marginal product of labor is measured with less error for wage and salary workers than for self-employed workers, this scheme of double sample selection may be an appropriate way to reduce measurement error, despite the loss in the final sample size.

Labor Supply and Unemployment

Individuals with different levels of education may choose to work different numbers of hours. The rates of return to education will vary depending on whether they are based on comparisons of hourly wage rates or annual earnings (Schultz 1968). Adjusting for how people allocate their time to market work in constructing the benefit stream from female education can be important in low-income countries.

According to Mincer's (1974) equilibrium investment framework, the present value of the *sum* of human and physical capital is not affected by investments in schooling. In this case, the total wealth effect of schooling should be unimportant (see Lindsay 1971).

The voluntary response in the labor supply to the increased wage rate offered to better-educated workers can be decomposed into an income effect and an income-compensated price (wage) effect. Mincer's framework implies that education is associated with a relatively small income effect. He assumes that all individuals can borrow at the same interest rate, but this assumption may not be tenable in countries without well-developed loan markets. Where liquidity constraints explain why low-income groups invest less in their children, those with more education should tend to work *fewer* hours because education will be associated with a wealth advantage and thus will be reflected in a demand for more leisure time. This tendency would lead to underestimating the private returns to schooling if the comparisons are framed in terms of monthly or annual earnings (see the analysis of Thailand accompanying table 2-5). The better educated would receive part of their returns to schooling in the form of increased nonmarket activities, including leisure (see, for example, Mohan 1986 for Colombia). Conversely, they might tend to work longer hours in societies where family wealth is more equally distributed and where student loans and fellowships help the poor invest in human capital. The income-compensated price (wage) effect associated with a worker's education would encourage the better educated to work longer hours, perhaps because of the debt they have assumed to get an education. If this were the only effect of education on labor supply, comparisons of annual earnings would overstate the private returns to schooling.

The partial association of education and hours of market work tends to be positive for youth and married women if other sources of income, such as family's or husband's, are held constant. When returns to schooling are based on variations in annual earnings, the private returns may be overstated because the offsetting loss of nonmarket production and leisure among the better educated is not deducted from the gains in market earnings. The change in wage rates (measured, for example, by annual earnings divided by hours) attributable to education is therefore a better approximation of the private welfare benefits from schooling than are changes in weekly, monthly, or annual earnings, especially for women. The preferred dependent variable in the earnings function used to estimate private returns to schooling is the logarithm of the *hourly wage rate*, deflated by local prices.[9]

Unemployment may be a productive period during which workers search for job opportunities that match their skills. If unemployment is greater among more highly educated youth during a relatively short period after they complete their schooling, the opportunity cost of their job search should be included along with the other costs of schooling that eventually will be recouped by enhanced earnings in employment (Berry 1975; Berry and Sabot 1984; Blaug 1976; Gregory 1980; Turnham and Jaeger 1971). Unemployment is generally lower among the more educated than among the less educated a decade after they enter the labor market. If this pattern does not reflect a current choice of the worker between nonmarket activities and market work, then unemployment may be called involuntary. One of the private gains from increased schooling is enhanced access to regular work opportunities in the market labor force and hence a lower incidence of involuntary unemployment. Typically, analysts only address patterns of unemployment by level of education among men; no studies were found on the differential effects of unemployment on returns to schooling for women (see Tilak 1987 for some evidence).

Occupational Choice

Returns to education are often calculated for subpopulations, such as occupational groups.[10] Possibly the most important occupational distinction is between those who earn a wage or salary and those who are self-employed. Most research on returns to schooling focuses on employees because their labor earnings can be observed more directly; self-employed respondents must be asked to deduct purchased and imputed values of inputs from gross income. Yet relatively few studies analyze how selection into the employee sample could bias the estimated returns to education (see, for example, Anderson 1982; Griffin 1987).

The probable covariance between an individual's choice of whether to be a wage earner or to be self-employed and that person's potential productivity can be ignored to simplify the problem. Separate estimations are then reported without correcting for sample selection in each wage function for the wage earners and the self-employed. The coefficients on a worker's years of schooling are then compared within the two subgroups. The proportionate upward shifts in wage rates or earnings associated with schooling tend to be of a similar magnitude in Colombia (Fields and Schultz 1982), Israel (Ben-Porath 1986), and Thailand (Chiswick 1979). The increase in transitory income variations in the earnings of the self-employed is often emphasized in the economics literature, but its relevance to the returns realized from education has not been explored.

These comparisons of wage earners and the self-employed have two weaknesses. First, they assume that the self-employed are willing and able to report their labor earnings net of the value of purchased and owned inputs, such as the rental value of owned land and business capital. In fact, in developed countries such as the United States, farmers and unincorporated entrepreneurs report incomes to surveys and tax authorities that are much lower than the incomes the national accounts impute to them. How this understatement of self-employed income would bias comparisons among groups with differing amounts of education is unclear. To reduce this potential source of reporting bias, Teilhet-Waldorf and Waldorf (1983) followed a small sample of self-employed people in the informal sector of Bangkok to derive their own estimates of the net hourly returns to the labor of the self-employed. The returns to schooling appeared to be no less for them than for wage earners, although obtaining more education predisposed men in the Bangkok sample to obtain wage employment.

The second weakness is that the fraction of the labor force that is self-employed often increases with age. The process of accumulating skills, experience, contacts, and physical capital appears to increase the likelihood that an individual will become self-employed (Ben-Porath 1986; Fields and Schultz 1982). Approaching retirement, a person may gain more flexible work opportunities from self-employment than from wage employment (Fuchs 1980). A secular tendency exists, however, for the share of self-employed workers in the labor force to decline with economic development (Kuznets 1966). Little empirical evidence is available to help disentangle the effects of life-cycle changes from those attributable to the secular changes accompanying development.

Nonmarket Returns to Education and Sample Selection Bias

Nonmarket returns to education cannot be valued in comparable monetary terms and readily aggregated. Therefore, evidence of the returns to women's schooling tends to rely on analyses of differences in productivity among wage earners who have different amounts of education. The central problem in constructing the statistical comparisons from which to estimate the returns to schooling for women is to correct for any potential bias that might be introduced into the analysis because women who work for wages may be more (or less) productive than the average person.

Statistical procedures designed for dealing with such a problem of sample selection bias have been developed in economics in the past decade or so (Heckman 1979, 1987). They require information on a variable for the entire population that is statistically correlated with the probability of being in the sample of wage earners, but the variable must not be related to variation in market productivity (wages) that is left unexplained after controlling for education, experience, and so on.

This sample selection methodology permits estimation of the effect of education on the average person's market productivity so that an unbiased estimate can be obtained of the private and social returns to schooling. If someone does not work in a wage job, it is because that individual can work in a more productive job at home or by being self-employed, or because the extra costs of finding and holding a wage job exceed the financial gain. To correct an analysis of wage functions for this potential sample selection bias requires a variable that influences a person's net nonmarket reservation wage but not her or his market wage offer. Such a variable, it was argued earlier, could be the family's nonearned income, land, or other assets that raise the persons's productivity in self-employment and also increase her or his demand for leisure, assuming leisure is a "normal" economic good.

Sample selection corrections should be performed routinely in the estimation of wage functions designed to estimate the average private returns to schooling for women and for men. Although this practice is spreading, the methodology generally has not been identified by a common set of economically justified variables. The correction procedure may be especially important for low-income countries, because they often have a higher share of family workers and self-employed workers, and for women, because the share who earn wages may be small.

Correcting for this sample selection bias by identifying satisfactory restrictions sometimes substantially changes the estimated private rates of return to schooling. We do not know why these differences occur in certain countries and not others, or why they vary by level of schooling. Improving the empirical research methods should raise our confidence in the basic facts and refine our forecasts of educational investment priorities, by school level and gender, over the course of economic development in a given country. These improved empirical estimates of the returns to schooling should also help explain long-run, simultaneous shifts in the aggregate supply of and demand for educated labor that occur in the course of modern economic growth.

Notes

1. For example, if more-able students select themselves into the better-educated comparison group, the returns to education could be overstated unless a selection-corrected measure of the private returns to schooling is computed (Willis and Rosen 1979). But this form of selection may not bias the comparison of the directly measured returns to the education of men relative

to women if ability has a similar influence on who goes to school among both boys and girls.

2. For a discussion of the fixed-effects model, see the seminal works of Maddala (1971) and Nerlove (1971).

3. A logarithmic monthly earnings function is estimated pooling men and women; this function includes dummy variables for nine levels of schooling and a quadratic in age. Parameters are estimated for the difference between male and female coefficients for all variables, including the intercept. The community and household fixed effects are believed to control for possible variation in school quality and for the effect of family background on earnings. Unfortunately, the ordinary regression estimates and those including the fixed effects are for different samples, raising the possibility that the differences reported in table 2-4 may be due to the different samples and not to the introduction of the fixed-effect controls.

4. The nonmarket (reservation) wage of the wife is affected by the family's landownership, ownership of a business, assets, and nonearned income, as well as her husband's education and experience. These variables are added to the wage-status probit equation. The Heckman (1979) two-stage estimate, which is less efficient, yields an estimate of private returns to schooling of 0.16 (Griffin 1987, table 3).

5. For a discussion of the Nash-bargained labor supply model see Manser and Brown (1980).

6. Taxes on personal income are a relatively small portion of government revenues in low-income countries. Latin America may be an exception if "social security" taxes are included (World Bank 1988, p. 84) According to Thailand's National Statistical Office, in Thailand in 1981 direct taxes on personal incomes amounted to less than 5 percent of household expenditures, and they were only 10 percent of expenditures for wage recipients in Bangkok. Most government revenue in low-income countries comes from trade and excise taxes on companies and commodities. Adjusting for taxes may be of secondary importance in these countries, but it could be quite important in industrially advanced countries and moderately important in Latin America.

7. The marginal tax revenue, dR, generated by the expansion of education for women, E_w, and men, E_m, can be expressed as:

$$dR \mid dE_w = tw_w\alpha_{1w}(\beta_{1w} + \beta_{2m})$$

$$dR \mid dE_m = tw_m\alpha_{1m}(\beta_{1m} + \beta_{2w})$$

where α_{1m} and α_{1w} are the private rates of return to schooling of men and women, which are assumed equal; $\beta_{1w} > 0$ is the wife's uncompensated own wage effect; $\beta_{2w} < 0$ is the wife's uncompensated husband's-wage effect; $\beta_{1m} \leq 0$ is the husband's uncompensated own-wage effect; and $\beta_{2m} \cong 0$ is the husband's uncompensated wife's-wage effect. The signs indicated here are those commonly obtained in static instrumented family labor supply models (Cogan 1980; Schultz 1981).

8. A parallel public finance argument can be made for imposing heavier taxes on inelastically supplied factors, if the goal is not to distort the optimal (that is, untaxed) allocation of factors. This tax criterion implies that, given

the labor supply parameters outlined in note 7, male labor outcomes should be taxed more heavily than female labor outcomes because male labor supply is inelastically supplied.

9. To introduce measures of labor supply among the explanatory variables in the wage function is clearly inappropriate unless they are treated as endogenous variables that could also respond to education. Another serious problem in estimating returns to schooling is to explain the variation in annual or monthly earnings by the variation in the number of hours or weeks that individuals work.

10. It is still tempting to decompose the effects of such exogenous traits as education, race, or gender on earnings and to appraise what portion of the effect occurs because of occupational sorting and what portion occurs within occupations (Polachek 1979). Because the stochastic processes determining occupation and earnings are undoubtedly affected jointly by unobserved factors, this form of decomposition of a simultaneous equation system is feasible only when identifying restrictions are known a priori; that is, a factor known to influence occupational choice or placement, but not earnings, can be used to explain occupational sorting but justifiably can be omitted from the structural wage equation. Studies nonetheless assume, without justification, that occupational choice and earnings are stochastically independent and can therefore be modeled as block-recursive.

References

Anderson, K. H. 1982. "The Sensitivity of Wage Elasticities to Selection Bias and the Assumption of Normality." *Journal of Human Resources* 17 (Fall):594–605.

Barrera, Albino. 1988a. "Maternal Schooling and Child Health." Ph.D. diss. Yale University, New Haven, Conn.

———. 1988b. "The Role of Maternal Schooling and Its Interaction with Public Health Programs in Child Health Production." Economic Growth Center Discussion Paper 551. Yale University (forthcoming in *Journal of Development Economics*).

Becker, Gary S. 1964. *Human Capital: A Theoretical and Empirical Analysis with Special Reference to Education.* New York: Columbia University Press.

———. 1965. "A Theory of the Allocation of Time." *Economic Journal* 74 (December):493–517.

———. 1981. *A Treatise on the Family.* Cambridge, Mass.: Harvard University Press.

Behm, H. 1976. *La Mortalidad en los Primeros Años de Vida en los Países de America Latina.* San José: Centro Latinoamericano de Demografía.

———. 1980. "Socioeconomic Determinants of Mortality in Latin America." In World Health Organization, *Socioeconomic Determinants and Consequences of Mortality.* Geneva.

Behrman, Jere R., and Nancy Birdsall. 1983. "The Quality of Schooling: Quantity Alone Is Misleading." *American Economic Review* 73 (December):928–46.

Behrman, Jere R., and Anil B. Deolalikar. 1988. "Are There Differential Returns to Schooling by Gender?" Development Studies Project II Research Paper. Jakarta.

Ben-Porath, Yoram. 1986. "Self Employment and Wage Earners in Israel." In U. O. Schmeiz, ed., *Studies in the Population of Israel* vol. 30. Jerusalem: Hebrew University, Magres Press.

Berry, Albert. 1975. "Open Unemployment as a Social Problem in Urban Colombia." *Economic Development and Cultural Change* 23:276–91.

Berry, Albert, and Richard H. Sabot. 1984. "Unemployment and Economic Development." *Economic Development and Cultural Change* 33:99–116.

Birdsall, Nancy, and M. L. Fox. 1985. "Why Males Earn More: Location and Training of Brazilian School Teachers." *Economic Development and Cultural Change* 33 (April):533–56.

Blau, David. 1984. "A Model of Child Nutrition, Fertility and Women's Time Allocation." In T. Paul Schultz and Kenneth I. Wolpin, eds., *Research in Population Economics,* vol. 5. Greenwich, Conn.: JAI Press.

Blaug, Mark. 1976. "The Empirical Status of Human Capital Theory: A Slightly Jaundiced Survey." *Journal of Economic Literature* 14 (September):827–55.

Butz, William, Jean-Pierre Habicht, and Julie DaVanzo. 1984. "Environmental Factors in the Relationship between Breastfeeding and Infant Mortality." *American Journal of Epidemiology* 119:516–25.

Caldwell, J. C. 1979. "Education as a Factor in Mortality Decline." *Population Studies* 33:395–413.

Catsiapis, George, and Chris Robinson. 1982. "Sample Solution Bias with Multiple Selection Rules: An Application to Student Aid Grants." *Journal of Econometrics* 18:351–68.

Chiswick, Carmel U. 1976. "On Estimating Earnings Functions for LDCs." *Journal of Development Economics* 4:67–78.

———. 1979. "The Determinants of Earnings in Thailand." Research Project 671-36. World Bank, Washington, D.C.

Cochrane, Susan H. 1979. *Fertility and Education: What Do We Really Know?* Baltimore, Md.: Johns Hopkins University Press.

———. 1988. "The Effects of Education, Health and Social Security on Fertility in Developing Countries." Policy Research Working Paper 93. World Bank, Population and Human Resources Department, Population, Health, and Nutrition Division, Washington, D.C.

Cogan, John F. 1980. "Married Women's Labor Supply: A Comparison of Alternative Estimates." In J. P. Smith, ed., *Female Labor Supply.* Princeton, N.J.: Princeton University Press.

de Tray, Dennis. 1988. "Government Policy, Household Behavior and the Distribution of Schooling: A Case Study of Malaysia." In T. Paul Schultz, ed., *Research in Population Economics: A Research Annual,* vol. 5. Greenwich, Conn.: JAI Press.

Easterlin, R. A. 1975. "An Economic Framework for Fertility Analysis." *Studies in Family Planning* 6 (March):54–63.

Eelens, Frank, and L. Donne. 1985. "The Proximate Determinants of Fertility in Sub-Saharan Africa." IPD Working Paper 1985-3. Vrije Universiteit, Brussels.

Estrey, S. A., and J. P. Habicht. 1987. "Maternal Literacy Modifies the Effect of Toilets and Piped Water on Infant Survival in Malaysia." Cornell University, Ithaca, N.Y.

Evenson, R. E. 1988. "Economic Issues in Agricultural Extension Policy." Yale University, Economic Growth Center, New Haven, Conn.

Farah, A. A., and S. H. Preston. 1982. "Child Mortality Differentials in Sudan." *Population and Development Review* 8 (June):365–83.

Fields, Gary, and T. Paul Schultz. 1982. "Income Generating Functions in a Low-Income Country: Colombia." *Review of Income and Wealth* 28:71–87.

Fuchs, V. R. 1980. "Self-Employment and Labor Force Participation of Older Males." NBER Working Paper 584. National Bureau of Economic Research, Cambridge, Mass.

Gregory Peter. 1980. "An Assessment of Changes in Employment Conditions in Less Developed Countries." *Economic Development and Cultural Change* 28 (4):673–700.

Griffin, C. G. 1987. "Methods for Estimating the Value of Time with an Application to the Philippines." University of Oregon at Eugene.

Griliches, Zvi. 1977. "Estimating the Returns to Schooling." *Econometrica* 45:13 (January):1–22.

———. 1979. "Sibling Models and Data in Economics." *Journal of Political Economy* 87 (October):S37–S64.

Gronau, Reuben. 1974. "The Effect of Children on the Housewife's Value of Time." In Theodore W. Schultz, ed., *Economics of the Family*. Chicago, Ill.: University of Chicago Press.

Haines, M. R., and R. C. Avery. 1982. "Differentials in Infant and Child Mortality in Costa Rica, 1968–73." *Population Studies* 36:31–44.

Haveman, Robert, and Barbara Wolfe. 1984. "Education and Economic Well-Being: The Role of Nonmarket Effects." *Journal of Human Resources* 19(3):377–407.

Heckman, J. J. 1979. "Sample Bias as a Specification Error." *Econometrica* 47 (January):153–62.

———. 1987. "Selection Bias and Self Selection." In *The New Palgrave: A Dictionary of Economics*. London: Macmillan.

Heckman, J. J., and G. Sedlacek. 1985. "Heterogeneity Aggregation and Market Wage Functions." *Journal of Political Economy* 93 (December):1077–125,

Hines, Fred, Luther Tweeten, and Martin Redfern. 1970. "Social and Private Rates of Return to Investment in Schooling, by Race-Sex Groups and Regions." *Journal of Human Resources* 5 (Summer):318–40.

Khandker, Shahidur R. 1989. "Labor Market Participation, Returns to Education, and Male-Female Wage Differences in Peru." Policy Research Working Paper 461. World Bank, Population and Human Resources Department, Women in Development Division, Washington, D.C.

King, Elizabeth M. 1990. *Does Education Pay in the Labor Market? The Labor Force Participation, Occupation, and Earnings of Peruvian Women.* Living Standards Measurement Study Working Paper 67. Washington, D.C.: World Bank.

King, Elizabeth M., Jane R. Peterson, Sri Moertiningsih Adioetomo, Lita J. Domingo, and Sabiha Hassan Syed. 1986. *Change in the Status of Women across Generations in Asia.* Santa Monica, Calif.: RAND.

Kuznets, Simon. 1966. *Modern Economic Growth: Rate Structure and Spread,* New Haven, Conn.: Yale University Press.

Leibowitz, Arleen 1974. "Home Investments in Children." In Theodore W. Schultz, ed., *Economics of the Family: Marriage, Children, and Human Capital.* Chicago, Ill.: University of Chicago Press.

Lindsay, C. M. 1971. "Measuring Human Capital Returns." *Journal of Political Economy* 79 (November–December):1195–215.

Lucas, R. E. 1985. *On the Mechanics of Economic Development.* Marshall Lecture, Cambridge University. London: Basil Blackwell.

Maddala, G. S. 1971. "The Use of Variance Components in Polling Cross Section and Time Series Data." *Econometrica* 39:341–58.

Manser, Marilyn, and Murray Brown. 1980. "Marriage and Household Decision-Making: A Bargaining Analysis." *International Economic Review* 21(1):31–44.

Martin, L. G., D. R. Flanagan, and A. R. Klenicki. 1986. "Evaluation of the Bangladesh Female Secondary Education Scholarship Program and Related Female Education and Employment Initiatives." 8563-032. U.S. Agency for International Development, Office of Population, Washington, D.C.

Meegama, S. A. 1981. "The Decline in Mortality in Sri Lanka in Historical Perspectives." In *Proceedings of the IUSSP Conference.* Manila.

Mensch, B., H. Lentzner, and S. Preston. 1986. *Socioeconomic Differentials in Child Mortality in Developing Countries.* New York: United Nations.

Michael, R. T. 1982. "Measuring Nonmonetary Benefits of Education." In W. W. McMahon and T. G. Geske, eds., *Financing Education.* Urbana: University of Illinois Press.

Mincer, Jacob. 1974. *Schooling, Experience, and Earnings.* New York: Columbia University Press.

Mincer, Jacob, and S. W. Polachek. 1974. "Family Investments in Human Capital: Earnings of Women." In Theodore W. Schultz, ed., *Economics of the Family: Marriage, Children, and Human Capital.* New York: Columbia University Press.

Mohan, Rakesh. 1986. *Work, Wages and Welfare in a Developing Metropolis: Consequences of Growth in Bogotá, Colombia.* New York: Oxford University Press.

Nakamura, Alice, and Masao Nakamura. 1988. "Selection Bias: More Than a Female Phenomenon." University of Alberta, Edmonton, Canada.

Nerlove, Marc. 1971. "Further Evidence on the Estimation of Dynamic Economic Relations from a Time Series of Cross Sections." *Econometrica* 39:359–82.

Palloni, Alberto. 1981. "Mortality in Latin America: Emerging Patterns." *Population and Development Review* 7:623–50.

Polachek, S. W. 1979. "Occupational Segregation among Women." In C. B. Lloyd, E. S. Andrews, and C. L. Gilroy, eds., *Women in the Labor Market*. New York: Columbia University Press.

Preston, Samuel, and James Trussell. 1982. "Estimating the Covariates of Childhood Mortality from Retrospective Reports of Mothers" [author's translation]. *Notas de Población* 10(29):71–118.

Psacharopoulos, George. 1973. *Returns to Education*. San Francisco, Calif.: Jossey-Bass.

————. 1985. "Returns to Education: A Further International Update and Implications." *Journal of Human Resources* 20 (Fall):583–604.

Psacharopoulos, George, and Maureen Woodhall. 1985. *Education for Development: An Analysis of Investment Choices*. New York: Oxford University Press.

Romer, Paul. 1983. "Dynamic Competitive Equilibria with Externalities, Increasing Returns and Unbounded Growth." Ph.D. diss. University of Chicago, Chicago, Ill.

Rosen, Sherwin. 1977. "Human Capital: A Survey of Empirical Research." In R. G. Ehrenberg, ed., *Research in Labor Economics,* vol. 1. Greenwich, Conn.: JAI Press.

Rosenzweig, M. R., and T. Paul Schultz. 1982a. "Child Mortality and Fertility in Colombia: Individual and Community Effects." *Health Policy and Education* 2:305–48.

————. 1982b. "Market Opportunities, Genetic Endowments and the Intrafamily Distribution of Resources." *American Economic Review* 72(4):803–15.

————. 1985. "The Demand and Supply of Births." *American Economic Review* 75 (December):992–1015.

————. 1987. "Fertility and Investment in Human Capital: Estimates of the Consequences of Imperfect Fertility Control in Malaysia." *Journal of Econometrics* 36:163–84.

————. 1989. "The Stability of Household Production Technology: A Replication." *Journal of Human Resources* 23(4) (Fall):535–49.

Sahn, D. E., and H. Alderman. 1988. "The Effect of Human Capital on Wages and the Determinants of Labor Supply in a Developing Country." *Journal of Development Economics* 29(2):157–84.

Schultz, T. Paul. 1968. *Returns to Education in Bogotá, Colombia*. Santa Monica, Calif.: Rand Corporation.

————. 1973. "A Preliminary Survey of Economic Analysis of Fertility." *American Economic Review* 63 (May):71–78.

————. 1980a. "Estimating Labor Supply Functions for Married Women." In J. P. Smith, ed., *Female Labor Supply*. Princeton, N.J.: Princeton University Press.

————. 1980b. "Interpretation of the Relations among Mortality, Economics of the Household, and the Health Environment." In World Health Organization, *Socioeconomic Determinants and Consequences of Mortality Differences*. Geneva.

————. 1981. *Economics of Population*. Reading, Mass.: Addison-Wesley.

————. 1984. "Studying the Impact of Household Economics and Community Variables on Child Mortality." In W. H. Mosley and L. C. Chen, eds., *Child Survival*. Supplement to *Population and Development Review*, vol. 10.

————. 1987. "School Expenditures and Enrollments, 1960–1980." In D. Gale Johnson and R. Lee, eds., *Population Growth and Economic Development*. Madison: University of Wisconsin Press.

————. 1988a. "Educational Investment and Returns." In Hollis Chenery and T. N. Srinivasan, eds., *Handbook of Development Economics*, vol. 1. Amsterdam: North-Holland.

————. 1988b. "An Individualistic Approach to Family Labor Supply and Fertility." Yale University, New Haven, Conn. (Revised April 1989.)

————. 1988c. "Women's Changing Participation in the Labor Force: A World Perspective." Paper presented at the Population Association of America meeting, New Orleans, April, 1988. Yale University, New Haven, Conn. (Revised June.)

————. 1989. "Women and Development: Objectives, Framework and Policy Intervention." Yale University, New Haven, Conn.

Schultz, T. W. 1988. "On Investing in Specialized Human Capital to Attain Increasing Returns." In G. Ranis and T. P. Schultz, eds., *The State of Development Economics*. London: Basil Blackwell.

Schwartz, Aba. 1976. "Migration, Age and Education." *Journal of Political Economy* pt. 1, 84 (August):701–19.

Sussangkarn, C. 1988. "Production Structures, Labour Markets and Human Capital Investments: Issues of Balance for Thailand." Bangkok, Thailand Development Research Institute.

Teilhet-Waldorf, Saral, and William H. Waldorf. 1983. "Earnings of Self-Employed in the Informal Sector: A Case Study of Bangkok." *Economic Development and Cultural Change* 31 (April):587–607.

Thias, Hans Heinrich, and Martin Carnoy. 1969. "Cost-Benefit Analysis in Education: A Case Study on Kenya." Report EC-173. World Bank, Economics Department, Washington, D.C.

Thomas, Duncan. 1989. "Intra Household Resource Allocation: An Informational Approach." Economic Growth Center Conference Paper. Yale University, New Haven, Conn.

Thomas, Duncan, J. Strauss, and M. H. Henriques. 1987. "Child Survival, Nutritional Status and Household Characteristics." Economic Growth Center Discussion Paper 542. Yale University, New Haven, Conn.

Tilak, Jandhyala B. G. 1987. *The Economics of Inequality in Education*. New Delhi: Sage Publications.

————. 1989. "Female Schooling in East Asia: A Review of Growth, Problems and Possible Determinants." PHREE/89/13. World Bank, Population and Human Resources Department, Washington, D.C.

Turnham, David, and Ingelies Jaeger. 1971. *The Employment Problem in Less Developed Countries: A Review of Evidence*. Paris: Organization for Economic Cooperation and Development, Development Centre.

United Nations, Department of International Economics and Social Affairs. 1987. "Fertility Behavior in the Context of Development." Population Studies 100. New York.

UNESCO (United Nations Educational, Scientific, and Cultural Organization). Various years. *Statistical Yearbook*. Paris.

van der Gaag, Jacques, and Wim Vijverberg. 1988. *Wage Determinants in Côte d'Ivoire*. Living Standards Measurement Study Working Paper 33. Washington, D.C.: World Bank.

Weisbrod, B. A. 1964. *External Benefits of Public Education*. Princeton, N.J.: Princeton University, Industrial Relations Section.

Welch, Finis. 1966. "Measurement of the Quality of Schooling." *American Economic Review* 56 (May):379–92.

Willis, Robert J., and Sherwin Rosen. 1979. "Education and Self-Selection." *Journal of Political Economy* pt. 2, 87 (October):S7–S36.

Wolfe, Barbara, and Jere R. Behrman. 1982. "Determinants of Child Mortality, Health and Nutrition in a Developing Country." *Journal of Development Economics* 11 (October):163–93.

Woodhall, Maureen. 1973. "Investment in Women: A Reappraisal of the Concept of Human Capital." *International Review of Education* (Spring):9–28.

World Bank. 1986. *Financing Education in Developing Countries: An Exploration of Options*. Washington, D.C.

———. 1988. *World Development Report 1988*. New York: Oxford University Press.

———. 1991. *World Development Report 1991*. New York: Oxford University Press.

3

Sub-Saharan Africa

Karin A. L. Hyde

Some of the world's poorest countries, with some of the world's highest illiteracy rates, lie in Sub-Saharan Africa. Education in this vast, diverse group of nations has been shaped by a mix of influences, among them indigenous cultures, Christianity, Islam, and a network of Western-type schools set up by missionaries and colonial governments. The region encompasses Nigeria, where school enrollment of girls in the Muslim north is lower than in the rest of the country, and Sudan, where school enrollment of girls in the Muslim north is higher than in the Christian and traditional south. And it includes Chad and the Central African Republic, where women make up less than 10 percent of the students in institutions of higher learning, as well as Lesotho, where women make up more than 60 percent of such students.

Amid the cultural and economic diversity, and despite the widespread poverty, Sub-Saharan Africa has made spectacular progress in expanding education since the countries achieved independence. Gross primary school enrollment was only 36 percent in 1960, half the rates of Asia and Latin America at the time. Between 1960 and 1983, striving to meet the needs of independence and economic growth, the region quintupled student enrollment in schools at all levels to 63 million, a higher growth rate than in any other developing region. But fast-growing populations and adverse economic conditions caused enrollments to stagnate and educational quality to decline in much of the region in the early 1980s. The challenge, given fiscal constraints and continuing population growth, is to diversify the means of financing education, to maximize the efficiency and quality of the existing system, and to expand the education infrastructure selectively. A central concern is narrowing the educational gap between men and women by removing the barriers to sending girls to school and keeping them there.

This chapter begins by examining several aspects of girls' and women's education in Sub-Saharan Africa, including enrollment, wastage (caused by dropout and grade repetition), and attainment. It then reviews what has been written about the factors that affect these aspects of education, assesses policies that have been implemented in various countries, and proposes a framework for further research, policy formulation, and action.

The Educational Setting

Most Sub-Saharan African countries can be characterized as low-income (table 3-1). The median GNP per capita for the region in 1987 was $300, ranging from a low of $130 in Ethiopia to a high of $2,700 in Gabon. Total fertility rates are high, with a median of 6.5 children in 1987 and a range from 2.1 in Mauritius to 8.0 in Rwanda. Despite this, the median annual rate of growth in the number of children of primary and secondary school age in the region as a whole increased only slightly, from 2.7 percent in 1960–70 to 2.8 percent in 1970–80. This growth rate actually declined in nearly half the countries.

Literacy rates have improved dramatically since 1960, rising from a mean of 9 percent in that year to 42 percent in the mid-1980s. But a great deal of variation across countries remains, as table 3-2 shows, and the differences between men and women persist. In Burkina Faso the most recent data indicate that fewer than 5 percent of women are literate, compared with 15 percent of men. In Swaziland literacy rates are much higher for both women and men, although women's literacy still lags by about 4 percentage points.

School Enrollments

One of the most enduring kinds of educational inequality is between males and females. Although many countries have made tremendous progress in widening the reach of education, in no country have males and females benefited equally. In the poorest countries, this inequality is reflected in lower enrollment rates, higher dropout and repetition rates, and lower levels of attainment for girls. Inequality is also apparent in the different curriculum choices offered to or made by men and women at the secondary and tertiary levels, most notably in the low enrollment figures for women in scientific and technical fields.

Africa may stand out because it is the poorest region and has the lowest levels of education, but it is also the region that has made the most progress in increasing schooling for girls and women in the past

Table 3-1. *GNP Per Capita and Growth of School-Age Population,*
Sub-Saharan Africa, 1960–80

Country	GNP per capita 1987 (dollars)	Growth rate of school-age population (percent)[a] 1960–70	1970–80
Low-income			
Angola	—	2.3	2.7
Ethiopia	130	2.8	2.9
Chad	150	2.3	1.9
Zaire	150	2.0	2.1
Malawi	160	2.8	2.9
Mozambique	170	2.5	4.6
Guinea-Bissau	170[b]	2.8	2.8
Tanzania	180	3.4	3.5
Burkina Faso	190	2.2	2.4
Madagascar	210	2.8	2.7
Mali	210	2.7	3.0
Gambia, The	230[b]	2.5	2.9
Burundi	250	1.7	2.5
Zambia	250	3.0	3.6
Niger	260	3.0	2.7
Uganda	260	4.3	3.5
Somalia	290	4.7	1.4
Togo	290	3.2	2.7
Rwanda	300	3.5	3.9
Sierra Leone	300	1.8	1.3
Benin	310	2.9	2.9
Central African Rep.	330	1.7	3.2
Kenya	330	4.1	3.8
Sudan	330	2.2	3.2
Lesotho	370	2.6	2.4
Nigeria	370	2.6	2.7
Ghana	390	2.6	2.5
Mauritania	440	2.7	2.2
Liberia	450	2.9	2.3
Guinea	—	1.4	1.7
Middle-income			
Senegal	520	2.6	2.5
Zimbabwe	580	4.0	3.8
Swaziland	600[b]	3.6	3.5
Côte d'Ivoire	740	3.3	5.6
Congo	870	2.6	4.0
Cameroon	970	2.5	3.0
Botswana	1,050	3.2	4.2
Mauritius	1,490	2.6	0.0

Table 3-1 *(continued)*

Country	GNP per capita 1987 (dollars)	Growth rate of school-age population (percent)[a]	
		1960–70	*1970–80*
Upper-middle-income			
Gabon	2,700	1.0	2.2

— Not available.

a. Average annual growth rate of population of children of primary and secondary school age.

b. 1986 data.

Source: World Bank 1988, 1989.

three decades (UNESCO 1983).[1] Table 3-3 gives primary, secondary, and tertiary school enrollment rates in Sub-Saharan Africa. Of the thirty-nine countries included, twelve apparently had universal primary school enrollment in the mid-1980s; gross enrollment rates were close to or more than 100 percent,[2] and girls accounted for at least 46 percent of enrollment.[3] Tanzania and Rwanda—countries with high but not universal primary school enrollment—appear to have been more successful than many other countries in extending educational access to girls.

Enrollments in secondary schools were far lower than in primary schools. Only in Congo and Mauritius did more than half the relevant age group attend secondary school in the mid-1980s. The rates in most countries were less than 20 percent, and Burundi, Malawi, and Tanzania are notable for having enrollments that have remained at less than 5 percent since 1960. The higher the school level, the lower the representation of girls.[4] Only in Botswana, Lesotho, Mauritius, and Swaziland were female enrollment rates roughly equivalent to or greater than male rates in secondary schools. At the tertiary level only Lesotho achieved parity between males and females; few other countries came even close.

The effects of South Africa on its neighbors, the so-called frontline states, are myriad, but two in particular affect school enrollment. First, the economy of South Africa generates a high demand for labor, which is met in part by migrants, usually young men from neighboring states. Second, the quality of education available to blacks in the frontline states is better than that available to most black South Africans, so a substantial share of South Africa's demand for black skilled workers is met by recruiting noncitizens. Consequently, all the neighboring states experience large flows of young men out of secondary and tertiary schools and into jobs in South Africa. In addition, the use of boys as herders outside settled areas in their own countries increases the drain of males out of the school system. This explains why a

Table 3-2. *Adult Illiteracy Rates by Gender, Selected Sub-Saharan African Countries, Various Years*

Country	Year	Female	Male
Low-income			
Benin	1979	90.5	74.8
Burkina Faso	1975	96.7	85.3
Chad	1963	99.4	87.9
Ethiopia	1970	99.8	91.7
Ghana	1970	81.6	56.9
Guinea	1965	96.0	86.0
Liberia	1974	89.0	71.0
Malawi	1966	87.7	66.3
Mali	1976	94.3	86.5
Mozambique	1980	87.8	56.0
Niger	1960	99.7	98.5
Rwanda	1978	73.4	49.2
Sierra Leone	1963	96.1	90.4
Somalia	1975	52.1	39.1
Sudan	1973	82.1	55.2
Tanzania	1978	68.6	37.8
Togo	1981	81.5	53.3
Zambia	1969	65.5	39.0
Middle-income			
Botswana	1971	56.0	63.1
Cameroon	1976	70.9	45.4
Senegal	1961	98.9	89.6
Swaziland	1976	46.5	42.7
Upper-middle-income			
Gabon	1960	95.2	77.8

Note: The countries omitted are those for which data are not available.
Source: UNESCO, *Statistical Yearbook,* 1990.

majority of primary and secondary school students in both Botswana and Lesotho are female.

Repetition, Dropout, and Attainment

Wastage is a term that includes both grade repeaters (that is, children who are held back for one or more years, frequently for poor performance on the end-of-year or promotion examination) and dropouts (that is, children who leave school before they have completed a cycle and who do not reenroll). The extent of these two problems in Sub-Saharan Africa is difficult to quantify because record-keeping at all levels of schooling is poor. It is clear from table 3-4, however, that repetition at the primary level can be a serious problem.

Table 3-3. *Gross Enrollment Rates in Primary, Secondary, and Tertiary Education, 1980s, and Annual Growth Rates since 1960, Sub-Saharan Africa*
(percent)

Country	Primary 1986	Primary Growth rate	Secondary 1985	Secondary Growth rate	Tertiary 1987	Tertiary Growth rate
Low-income						
Angola	134[a]	29.92	12[b]	22.73	0.4[c]	−1.43
Benin	65	5.77	17	30.00	2.4	135.29
Burkina Faso	29	8.55	5	16.00	0.7	19.05
Burundi	53	5.86	4	12.00	0.8	17.65
Central African Rep.	77	6.03	16	60.00	1.2	64.71
Chad	43	5.88	6	56.00	0.4	4.76
Ethiopia	34	14.84	13	48.00	0.9	20.59
Gambia, The	68	14.84	17	13.00	—	—
Ghana	72	2.17	39	4.21	1.4	22.22
Guinea	30	1.92	10	16.00	1.3[d]	7.29
Guinea-Bissau	56	5.13	7	5.33	—	—
Kenya	98	4.17	21	38.00	1.2[c]	20.00
Lesotho	113	0.88	19[b]	24.24	1.7[c]	30.00
Liberia	35	−0.11	21	38.00	2.4[d]	14.62
Madagascar	104	3.30	15	11.00	3.6[d]	65.38
Malawi	62	2.43	4	12.00	0.6	3.70
Mali	23	5.98	7	24.00	0.7	14.71
Mauritania	49	27.56	15	56.00	3.5	21.43
Mozambique	86	2.64	7	10.00	0.2	−1.96
Niger	28	14.10	6	76.00	0.6[d]	16.67
Nigeria	77	3.21	23	26.67	2.6[c]	48.00
Rwanda	63	1.10	6	8.00	0.4	5.88
Sierra Leone	54[a]	7.39	15	26.00	0.9[c]	14.00
Somalia	15	4.40	9	32.00	2.5[c]	35.00
Sudan	50	5.77	20	22.67	1.9[d]	14.42
Tanzania	72	7.69	3	2.00	0.2	0.00
Togo	95	4.46	21	38.00	2.5	23.53
Uganda	70	1.88	13	13.33	0.8[d]	11.54
Zaire	76	1.57	23	42.00	1.5[d]	53.85
Zambia	99	3.62	17	30.00	1.3[d]	14.06
Middle-income						
Botswana	108	6.80	30	116.00	2.6	19.48
Cameroon	108	3.44	24	44.00	2.6[d]	26.25
Congo	163[a]	4.40	87[b]	94.32	6.0[c]	58.33
Côte d'Ivoire	70	2.42	19	34.00	2.4[c]	92.00
Mauritius	105	0.45	51	5.27	1.4	48.15
Senegal	57	4.27	14	14.67	2.8	17.04

(Table continues on the following page.)

Table 3-3 *(continued)*

Country	Primary		Secondary		Tertiary	
	1986	Growth rate	1985	Growth rate	1987	Growth rate
Swaziland	107	3.37	43	30.40	3.5	28.43
Zimbabwe	135	3.17	41	23.33	3.7[d]	43.59
Upper-middle-income						
Gabon	118[a]	5.15	23[b]	30.30	3.3[c]	110.71

— Not available.
a. 1983.
b. 1982.
c. 1984.
d. 1986.
e. 1985.
Sources: World Bank 1988; UNESCO, *Statistical Yearbook,* 1989.

Repetition and dropout rates reflect ineffective teaching and a weak demand for education, but they are also accepted strategies within the education system for maintaining standards and for lowering the demand for school places at both the primary and secondary levels (see Bali and others 1984; Chishimba 1984). Expelling students for academic failure and for nonpayment of school fees is widely accepted as a legitimate policy. Such expulsions are not distinguished in the data from voluntary exits. In some countries where intense competition for secondary school places exists (as in Kenya and Nigeria), affirmative action takes the form of setting lower pass marks for pupils from less-advantaged areas. As a result large-scale, although largely undocumented, transfers into the last year of primary school have taken place in these disadvantaged regions (Nkinyangi 1980). Pupils have switched schools to raise their prospects for admission to a secondary school, and they have changed their names and resorted to other subterfuges to conceal their past school histories (Nkinyangi 1982). In Kenya, for example, dropout rates in primary schools in the least-developed areas were consistently negative in the period 1970–76 (Nkinyangi 1980).

The mean educational attainment of girls in Sub-Saharan Africa is low because enrollment is low and wastage is high. In most countries more girls than boys never enter school at all. Among those who do enroll, the retention rates are lower for girls than for boys, with a difference of almost 20 percentage points in Côte d'Ivoire and Malawi (table 3-5). The result, in these countries and many others in the region, is a large and persistent gender gap in educational attainment.

Table 3-4. *Grade Repetition at the Primary Level, Selected Sub-Saharan African Countries, Various Years*
(percent)

Country	Year	Total	Female
Low-income			
Benin	1985	27	28
Burkina Faso	1984	14	15
Burundi	1984	15	16
Central African Rep.	1982	35	37
Chad	1976	38	36
Ethiopia	1981	12	14
Gambia, The	1985	17	16
Ghana	1980	2	2
Guinea	1985	27	31
Guinea-Bissau	1984	50	50
Kenya	1981	13	13
Lesotho	1985	23	21
Liberia	1978	11	12
Malawi	1984	16	15
Mali	1983	30	30
Mauritania	1980	14	17
Mozambique	1985	24	24
Niger	1986	15	15
Rwanda	1985	12	12
Tanzania	1982	1	1
Togo	1984	37	38
Uganda	1982	10	11
Zaire	1983	19	19
Zambia	1981	1	1
Middle-income			
Botswana	1985	6	6
Cameroon	1984	29	28
Congo	1985	30	29
Côte d'Ivoire	1984	29	28
Senegal	1984	16	16
Swaziland	1984	13	11
Zimbabwe	1984	1	1
Upper-middle-income			
Gabon	1983	33	33

Note: The countries omitted are those for which data are not available.
Source: UNESCO, *Statistical Yearbook,* 1987.

Table 3-5. *Retention Rates at the Primary Level, Selected Sub-Saharan African Countries, 1980s*
(percent)

Country	Girls	Boys
Benin	53.3	57.0
Botswana	79.3	76.0
Burkina Faso	55.4	58.0
Burundi	12.8	13.0
Cameroon	46.5	52.0
Central African Rep.	28.6	44.9
Chad	22.2	36.9
Congo	57.3	61.8
Côte d'Ivoire	45.9	63.9
Gabon	33.9	42.4
Kenya	68.5	76.8
Lesotho	45.5	32.2
Madagascar	20.1	20.7
Malawi	26.9	45.9
Mali	42.7	48.8
Mauritania	52.5	53.6
Niger	49.7	55.3
Rwanda	33.0	37.1
Senegal	63.1	72.3
Swaziland	64.4	59.3
Tanzania	49.3	65.6
Togo	52.8	66.9
Zaire	28.1	42.4
Zambia	64.3	84.8

Note: The countries omitted are those for which data are not available.
Source: Robertson and Berger 1986, ch. 6.

Factors Influencing Women's Educational Status

The purpose of this review is to develop a basis for policy and intervention. The emphasis, therefore, is on those studies that have tried to identify the factors responsible for the largely second-class status of women within the educational systems of Sub-Saharan Africa. Many, if not most, of the issues touched on here are not unique to this region. Ultimately, the reasons why women are seldom as well educated as men lie outside the education system. Ideas about the appropriate roles for women in the labor market or in society, about the biological unsuitability of women for science, and about the gender-based division of work in the household and on the farm influence decisions about schooling, as do income, class, religion, and rural or urban residence.

Several limitations of this review need to be clarified. First, it focuses on formal educational systems derived from Western models, although informal education is an essential and expedient means of increasing female participation. Second, the studies compare men and women in the same environment when looking at measures of educational status. Using such comparisons to highlight specific levels of schooling, geographic areas, and socioeconomic groups in which females are at the greatest educational disadvantage is natural and appropriate. But when unusual circumstances prevail—as in southern Africa—such comparisons may yield misleading or inadequate results. In Lesotho more females than males are enrolled at every level of education and in every age group; the situation is similar, though not as extreme, in Swaziland and Botswana.

A third limitation is that, although these studies identify various factors that have affected women's education in Africa, data are missing for a large number of countries. Educational statistics from Africa are generally poor and often outdated. Seldom are they collected in a way that is useful for gender-specific analysis, with females treated separately. And finally, authors occasionally neglect to use satisfactory tests of statistical significance, an appropriate sampling methodology, or adequate controls, and these shortcomings may call the strength and robustness of particular effects into question.

The studies reviewed here were selected on the basis of three criteria: they are empirical, that is, they either use collected data or analyze other studies that collected data; they were published after 1979, because a number of extensive reviews undertaken about then covered earlier work; and they treat gender explicitly. All studies meeting these criteria that could be identified and obtained have been included.

The various aspects of educational participation—enrollment, attainment, wastage, and achievement—all reveal the lower educational status of women than men in Sub-Saharan Africa. Although these aspects are considered separately because they can be measured separately, they are linked statistically in at least two ways. First, the levels of attainment, wastage, and achievement are all conditional on the initial decision of whether or not to enroll. Second, because the factors that affect any one aspect of participation also affect the others, levels of attainment, wastage, and achievement are interdependent. For example, how a student performs can lead to a reevaluation of plans for continuing in school or dropping out, although the relationship is not a simple one (see Mann 1986 for the United States; Gambetta 1987 for Italy).

A Framework for Educational Decisionmaking

Decisions to continue in school or drop out are contingent first on the decision to enroll and then on a continuing reassessment of the student's school situation, aided by feedback on achievement. The recurring and sequential nature of decisions about schooling has theoretical and methodological implications. Actions that result in entering, continuing, or dropping out of school occur at several sequential points or decision nodes. At each point the decision for or against schooling may be influenced by characteristics of the individual, the home, the community, the school, and the school system.

With regard to whether a child enters school, the factors that influence the decision include competing activities, primarily to satisfy the household's demand for child labor; competing ideologies, in the form of community disagreement over the mores and values taught or perceived as being taught in school; and an estimate of the expected costs and benefits of attending school. The relevant decisionmakers may vary for each of these factors. The family, each parent, the community at large, and even the child will have opinions that carry differing weights. In addition, institutional factors, such as the supply of places, may impose constraints on school entry.

Once a child is in school, the characteristics of the school become more salient, influencing what parents or other adults decide about keeping the child in school. The child also becomes more involved in the decisionmaking process. The school may directly affect the outcome by resorting to suspension or expulsion. How important is each of these factors in keeping children in school? How do gender bias in the school, or teachers' expectations, influence these decisions? As a child progresses through school, the costs frequently increase and the balance of actual costs and perceived benefits changes. Is this an important factor in the early dropout of girls from school? Do the curriculum choices offered to girls differ from those offered to boys, and if so, what are the short-term and long-term consequences? The capacity of the school system is also critical. Virtually all school systems in Sub-Saharan Africa expect only a minority of students to proceed to the secondary level. Achievement is an important factor in determining who stays in school beyond the primary level, but it is not the only one.

As a girl approaches puberty, still other factors come to the fore. Social and cultural pressures surrounding engagement, marriage, and initiation rites may keep girls from remaining in school. Girls who become pregnant are usually asked to leave school and may experience difficulty reenrolling even in different institutions. Marriage often marks the end of schooling. Decisions about leaving school are also related to the labor market, which can exert both a push and a pull. If the eventual gains from staying in school exceed the immediate gains from leaving, a girl is likely to continue her education.

Besides these specific factors, which have an impact at different ages of the student and different levels of schooling, general societal factors can affect decisions about a child's school life. The country's level of economic development may be significant. Religion, language policy, rural or urban residence, the general availability of schools, and the economic opportunities open to females all play a role.

Figure 3-1 seeks to capture the underlying structure of the decision-making process that determines whether a girl enters school and, if she does, how long she continues. The diagram underscores the inter-connectedness of the outcomes of these decisions, as well as their cumulative nature. It emphasizes the option of exit not only at the points of entrance or transition but also at the end of every week, every term, and every year, as family and school continuously adjust to changing conditions. A further refinement would be to add branches at the points of transition to secondary or higher education to indicate options in the types of institutions girls enter.

Most studies on girls' school enrollment in Sub-Saharan Africa focus on the initial decision to enter primary school, but a few deal with factors that encourage the enrollment of girls and women in secondary or tertiary schools or that influence what types of secondary or higher institutions they enter (Eshiwani 1982; Weis 1981). The variables that appear to affect female participation have been grouped, for the purpose of discussion, into family factors, societal factors, and school factors.[5]

Family Influence

The socioeconomic background of parents, their attitudes about educating girls, and the mother's education contribute to shaping deci-

Figure 3-1. *Decision Structure of Educational Participation*

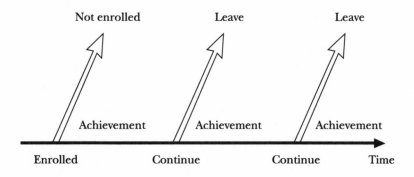

Source: Modified from Gambetta 1987.

sions about schooling for daughters. A family's need for child labor may add a high opportunity cost to any other reasons for not sending daughters to school.

Social Class. Girls who come from socioeconomically advantaged families are much more likely to enter and remain in secondary school than are girls from disadvantaged families. Assie (1983) has shown that in Côte d'Ivoire a girl with a university-educated father was more than thirty-five times as likely to enter an academic secondary school as was the daughter of a man with no education. For a son the comparable added likelihood was only a tenth as large. The great benefit experienced by girls from homes with high socioeconomic status is reflected, in Assie's sample, in their high representation in elite *lycées*, the academic secondary schools that prepare students to enter the university. Although only 25 percent of all students in the *lycées* were female, 41.7 percent of those in elite *lycées* were female.

Weis (1981) found that female students at the secondary level in Ghana were also disproportionately drawn from educated families compared with male secondary school students. The class advantage was even more striking when contrasted with historical patterns of male enrollment. Even when the Ghanaian educational system was much smaller, the sons of uneducated fathers were not unduly at a disadvantage. Despite their higher socioeconomic status, however, female students were more likely to attend inferior schools; that is, the growing numbers of female students were finding their way primarily into the newer and less-established secondary schools. This pattern differs, however, in Côte d'Ivoire, where the smaller size of the school system and the lower proportion of female students may explain why girls are as likely as boys to attend good schools. Another possible explanation is that the growing enrollments in Ghana were made possible mainly by providing new schools rather than by expanding existing ones. Thus, the opportunities for girls and other disadvantaged groups to gain entrance were greater in the new institutions.

The educational advantages conferred by high socioeconomic status are even more pronounced at the university level. Biraimah (1987) points out that women students at the tertiary level in Nigeria have been drawn disproportionately from more privileged families.

Parental Attitudes. The wish to protect daughters from undesirable influences appears strongest in areas that are still very traditional. This explains, for example, why northern Nigeria stands in sharp contrast to other parts of the country in the percentage of girls not enrolled in school. The reasons for the relative underdevelopment of education in Muslim northern Nigeria are often held to arise from the

British government's laissez-faire attitude toward the region and from the resistance of the emirs to the introduction of Christian missionaries and the spread of Western education (Denzer 1988; but see also Tibenderana 1988 for a contrasting view that the lack of schooling in the north was a result of British thrift rather than the emirs' resistance). According to Callaway (1984) the education of girls was hampered because northern Nigeria was the only area in Sub-Saharan Africa that observed *purdah,* and the only area in the world that observed it so strictly and extended it to both rural and urban women.[6] Western education was regarded as a threat to both Muslim and Hausa values, a threat seen as especially dangerous for women, whose duty it was to protect the traditions. Csapo (1981) reviewed a number of unpublished theses from Ahmadu Bello University in northern Nigeria, as well as editorials and articles from newspapers published in northern Nigeria, on the subject of female education. The consensus appeared to be that it was bad for society in general, and for girls in particular, to be educated in Western schools. Csapo's review does not, however, give any measure of the prevalence and strength of these views or of the extent to which girls and women themselves subscribed to them.

As Robertson (1986) points out, however, Islam should not be held responsible for the low enrollment of girls in Africa. Sudan stands as a counterexample: the Muslim north has significantly higher school enrollment rates than the Christian and traditional south. Robertson claims that, since independence, the predominantly Muslim countries in Africa have had the highest enrollment growth rates.

Mother's Education. Evidence from a number of countries indicates that African women bear a large part of the burden of educating their children (Robertson 1977 for Ghana; Tripp 1988 for Tanzania). A mother's ability to pay school fees and to provide encouragement to her children to continue attending school is an important factor in explaining enrollment and attendance. In areas where polygamous marriage is common, many women are the prime movers with respect to their children's education (Bledsoe 1988), and their own levels of education and command of resources are important factors in their ability to keep their children in school.

This is especially true where male migration is widespread and women become de facto heads of households (Kossoudji and Mueller 1983). Households headed by educated females are more likely to send girls as well as boys to school, and to keep them there longer, than households headed by uneducated females or by males (Chernichovsky 1985; Kossoudji and Mueller 1983; both for Botswana). These women's ability to support themselves and their children in part depends on their own schooling, since education is usually what allows women to find jobs in the formal sector, with its higher and more dependable income stream. Also, because work in the formal sector complicates childcare, women with such jobs are usually more willing to have the school help care for their children and more able to incur school expenses.

Child Labor. Mothers' time appears to be very constrained, especially in rural areas where households must commit many hours to such activities as collecting water or firewood (McSweeney and Freedman 1980). The high fertility rates in Sub-Saharan Africa may be an adaptive response to the time-consuming household and farm tasks that make women's time a scarce commodity. One of the advantages of polygamous marriage is the sharing of household tasks; perhaps as a consequence, women in polygamous marriages have fewer children than other women (Garenne and van de Walle 1988; Smith and Kunz 1976).[7] The majority of African women are not in polygamous marriages, however, and it is natural for them to turn to their children or other young relatives for additional help with time-intensive, low-skill jobs in the household and on the farm.

The extensive use of child labor has obvious implications for school enrollment. Using 1974 data from Botswana, Chernichovsky (1985) showed that the enrollment of children seemed to be influenced by the presence in the home of elderly people (who can be seen as substitutes for child labor) and by the household's possession of capital (for example, livestock) that may involve children in income-producing activities. Children were more likely to be enrolled in school if their grandparents lived in the household. They were less likely to remain in school if, at intermediate levels of family wealth, the household had more livestock.[8] But boys' schooling was more affected than girls' by the household's ownership of livestock because boys' herding activities were more likely to take them away from home and school. Similarly, in rural Ethiopia labor demands fall more heavily on boys than on girls. Results from interviewing a sample of 576 households indicate that household duties are the primary cause of school absenteeism among 57 percent of boys but only 32 percent of girls (Biazen and Junge 1988).

In other areas the demand for household labor falls more heavily on girls. Muslim women who live in seclusion in northern Nigeria depend on children to help with their market activities. Ironically, being in seclusion does not exempt these women from family obligations that require cash. Their husbands are unlikely to assume responsibility for the obligations that are involved in supporting the woman's position in her own lineage (Remy, as cited in Fapohunda 1978). Consequently, women in *purdah* engage in several kinds of production for the market, especially food preparation and handicrafts. Confined as they are to their households during daylight, they depend on daughters or young female relatives to sell their wares in the street or marketplace. They also rely on their children to collect raw materials and help with production and sales. Sending children to school may curtail the income-generating activities of these women.

Selective Education of Children. In large families not all the children may be needed to work at home or on the farm. Chernichovsky (1985) found that higher educational levels were associated with more school-age children in a family. An examination of the education within each family, however, showed a large inequality among children. Those who went to school attended for longer periods, but those not enrolled were more likely never to have been enrolled. This pattern suggests that parents select certain children for Western education. The reason Chernichovsky gives is the diminishing returns to labor in a household with a given amount of assets. Some children are reserved for productive activity in the household or farm, and others are allowed to study. In Botswana, Lesotho, and Swaziland this calculus appears to operate to the advantage of girls because they are chosen to fill their families' need to have educated children. In most other countries, however, boys are more likely to gain this educational advantage.

The selection of specific children for education need not be gender-biased. In the face of limited resources, the education of children can represent a strategy to disperse risk; formal education can reduce the likelihood that a particular child has to earn a living from agriculture and increases the possible sources of income for the intergenerational family. The structure of the formal labor market generally gives boys an advantage, however. Similarly, faced with high dropout rates, parents may decide to educate only those children who they expect will do well in school and will succeed in getting a remunerative job in the modern sector after finishing school.

Children may also be kept out of school because they need the time to learn traditional skills (Bowman and Anderson 1980; Robertson 1984). Even in an urban setting, the forgone learning can be so costly as to deter the enrollment of girls in school (Robertson 1984). Girls and women are overwhelmingly employed in the traditional or informal sectors, and school attendance means that they have less time to learn from their mothers or to apprentice with other older women.

Schooling also entails direct monetary costs—for fees, uniforms, books, and the like—which may be low relative to incomes in the modern sector but are high if a family's principal income-generating activities lie in the traditional sector. At the same time, the earnings from jobs in the modern sector are much lower for women than for men. Given the costs associated with schooling and the lower monetary return to girls' education than to boys', the choice of whom to enroll in school is often made in favor of boys. Studies of spending on girls and boys in Nigeria show that parents both expect to spend and actually do spend more to feed and educate their sons than their daughters (Orubuloye 1987).

Societal Influence

Work—for the family or in the labor market—often keeps older girls out of school.[9] Other activities as well, including marriage and childbearing, compete with school for older girls' time. A few studies have also looked at how place of residence, rural or urban, and government spending on education affect the schooling of girls in Sub-Saharan Africa.

Marriage and Childbearing. Although initiation rites at puberty are becoming more flexible, they can require extensive periods away from school, especially if parents wish a daughter to become engaged or to marry at this time. The young age at which females marry in much of the region (table 3-6) makes marriage an important reason why they do not enter secondary or higher institutions or, having entered, leave before completing the cycle. Although the enrollment of married students is not unheard of, pregnancy and childbirth usually end a school career. For older female students, therefore, the competing activity of family formation is an additional deterrent to schooling. Marriage can affect primary school children in societies where the schools have significant numbers of overage children or where betrothal takes place at a very young age. In Ethiopia, for example, 20 percent of the primary school students surveyed in a study reported by Biazen and Junge (1988) were either promised, married, or divorced. Both boys and girls were affected, but this was the most common reason given for the nonenrollment of girls. Yet Wrzesinska (1980) reports that in Zaire the higher bride-price paid for educated daughters was a reason that parents sent their daughters to secondary school.

Rural-Urban Differences. A number of studies (Akande 1987; Assie 1983; Bedri and Burchinal 1985; Chernichovsky 1985) have suggested that area of residence is predictive of enrollment and attainment at all levels of education. The mechanisms through which this factor operates are not always clear, however. The greater availability of schools in urban areas, the higher opportunity cost of a rural girl's time, the greater wealth of urban families, the more open attitudes among ur-

Table 3-6. *Median Age of Marriage for Ever-Married Women and Men, Selected Sub-Saharan African Countries, Various Years*

Country	Year	Women	Men
Angola	1970	18	23
Benin	1961	20[a]	24
Botswana	1971	24	30
Burkina Faso	1975	17	27
Burundi	1970–71	21	23
Cameroon	1976	18	26
Chad	1964	17[a]	22
Ghana	1971	19	—
Guinea	1954–55	20[a]	26
Kenya	1969	19	25
Lesotho	1966	19	25
Liberia	1974	18	26
Malawi	1977	17	22
Mali	1976	17	27
Mauritius	1972	22	27
Mozambique	1970	19	24
Rwanda	1970	20	22
Senegal	1972	18	28
Seychelles	1977	30	32
Sudan	1973	18	25
Tanzania	1967	17	23
Togo	1970	18	25
Uganda	1973	20	30
Zaire	1955–58	18	23
Zambia	1969	18	24

— Not available.

Note: The countries omitted are those for which data are not available.

a. Precise age cannot be determined; figure represents a maximum estimate.

Source: Newman 1984, table 6.2.

ban parents toward having girls attend Western schools, and the greater opportunities for girls in urban areas to obtain jobs in the modern sector may all be relevant. Evidence by which to judge the relative strength of various possible explanations, however, is largely lacking.

A recent study on Ethiopia (Abraha and others 1991) observes that urban girls enrolled in school are more likely than rural girls to persist, both in absolute terms and compared with boys (table 3-7). Female persistence, measured as the ratio of enrollment in grade four to enrollment in grade one for each school included, is higher in urban schools (0.61) than in rural schools (0.42). Moreover, enrollment equity, measured as the ratio of female to male enrollments in grades four through six, is significantly higher in urban schools (0.84) than in

Table 3-7. *Urban-Rural Difference in Girls' Enrollment and Performance, Ethiopia, 1986*

Measure	Urban	Rural	F-ratio
Grade 4 female	0.61	0.42	5.88[a]
persistence	(39)	(135)	
Grades 4–6 enrollment	0.84	0.49	31.29[b]
equity	(41)	(141)	
Percentage of girls passing	0.81	0.88	5.37[a]
national exam	(36)	(119)	
Pass-rate equity ratio	0.89	1.04	1.11
	(36)	(119)	

Note: Numbers in parentheses are sample sizes. Grade 4 female persistence is the ratio of grade 4 to grade 1 enrollment. Grades 4–6 enrollment equity is the ratio of female to male enrollments in grades 4–6. Pass ratio is the proportion of girls to boys passing the national exam.
a. $p < 0.5$.
b. $p < .001$.
Source: Abraha and others 1991.

rural schools (0.49). Surprisingly, the share of girls passing the national exam appears to be lower in urban areas, a result perhaps of the greater selectivity exercised in sending rural girls to school.

The impact of urban residence is misleading, however. Once both the school and the teacher are taken into account in a multivariate analysis, the force of the community variables weakens (Abraha and others 1991). Chernichovsky (1985) found that when the effects of family and other factors affecting schooling are carefully considered, the correlation between educational attainment and the size of the community vanishes. Residence in larger villages primarily affects enrollment probabilities; other factors explain the level of education attained.

National Patterns. Three other variables characterizing the society as a whole have been found to influence access to education for girls: overall levels of enrollment, percentage of the labor force engaged in agriculture, and percentage of GNP spent on education. These variables are indicators of the level of development of a country and of its education system.

Adams and Kruppenbad (1987) suggest in their comparison of four countries (Botswana, Liberia, Niger, and Somalia) that the overall level of enrollment is one of the factors that explains female access to primary school. Countries enroll boys first; girls gain access at a delayed rate. Another factor was the overall level of economic development, with richer countries having higher levels of female enrollment than poorer countries. With a larger sample of countries, however, Robertson (1986) found very little correlation between growth rates in girls' enrollment and either GNP or income per capita.

Analyzing data for all developing countries in Africa and Asia, Wood, Swan, and Wood (1986) reported that the percentage of the labor force engaged in agriculture was the economic factor that most strongly predicted a nation's school dropout rate. They hypothesized that the size of the agricultural labor force was a measure of the demand for child labor. Especially in areas still using traditional farming methods, the payoff to education was sufficiently low that parents did not feel the need to send their children to school, nor were opportunities for off-farm employment likely to be numerous. Although this argument is not specific to girls, it suggests that in areas where most of the farming is done by women, labor demands are greater on girls than on boys. The situation in Botswana, noted earlier, illustrates the effects when boys' labor is in greater demand than girls'.

Wood, Swan, and Wood (1986) also identify government spending on education as an important predictor of the national dropout rate. Committing a greater percentage of GNP to education is related to placing a high value on education. Expenditures on education are probably also related to the number of school places and hence to the likelihood that students will not be asked to leave school because of a shortage of places.

School Characteristics

Finally, school-related factors can be an important determinant of whether girls enter and remain in school. The quality of the schools, especially the courses offered, and the messages about sex roles conveyed by educational materials and by teachers influence how parents, as well as students themselves, make schooling decisions.

School Quality and Curriculum. Schools of poor quality inhibit the educational attainment of girls and affect the choices they make about what to study. In Kenya (Eshiwani 1982) and in Ghana (Weis 1981) girls were overrepresented in secondary schools of low quality, that is, in institutions that were less successful than others in preparing their students for the "O-level" and "A-level" examinations that are often prerequisites for continued study or employment in the formal sector. One of the greatest disadvantages experienced by girls was a lack of access to science and mathematics, fields often regarded as unfeminine.[10] The majority of girls in secondary school in Kenya were in harambee schools (schools created and maintained through community self-help); few of these schools offered any science courses, and those that did were without the infrastructure needed to teach them effectively. In Swaziland, as reported by Wheldon and Smith (1986), girls in single-sex schools were less likely to choose physical sciences than were girls in mixed schools, despite the fact that the single-sex schools in their sample admitted students selectively and were well equipped. The lack of access to science in secondary school usually proves decisive; the European type of education system still in use in African countries ensures that options not taken are usually options lost for good, since changing fields of study at a later time is rarely possible. In higher education, disparities in the fields of study chosen by men and women are glaring (table 3-8).

The poor quality of the institutions they attend and their constricted curriculum choices also put women at a disadvantage after leaving school because they are less likely to have acquired permanent functional literacy and the skills that employers value in educated workers. This disadvantage is distinct from any distaste or discrimination that may have existed among employers. Some evidence indicates, however, that those women who did manage to complete their education successfully may have suffered pronounced discrimination on the job. Female engineers, for example, were sometimes not allowed on construction sites or had great difficulty obtaining internships during their training (Adjebeng-Asem 1988 for Nigeria).

Several authors have attributed the reluctance to send girls to school in part to a society's response to a perceived lack of fit between the vocations for which schooling is supposed to prepare students and the vocations that are regarded as suitable for girls. Csapo (1981) suggests that in northern Nigeria the only approved role for women was that of wife and mother and that therefore school was deemed unnecessary. Wrzesinska (1980) reports that this role was the only one in which the subjects of her study, secondary school girls, appeared to take an interest.

These views are associated with two other issues: the availability of job opportunities for women in the modern sector and the segregation by gender into alternative courses of study, which often starts in the higher grades of elementary school and continues on to the secondary and tertiary levels. Girls are channeled into domestic science, handicrafts, and biology, whereas boys study chemistry and mathematics, or go directly into vocational subjects (Eshiwani 1982 for Kenya; Harding 1985).[11] One of the results of women's not being prepared to enter the labor market may have been the drop in female participation in the labor force in Sub-Saharan Africa from 45 percent in 1960 to 42 percent in 1981, despite a massive expansion in education in the same period (Kelly 1988). The evidence indicates that the causes for

Table 3-8. Female Enrollment in Higher Education, Overall and in Selected Fields of Study, Selected Sub-Saharan African Countries, Most Recent Year

(percentage of total enrollment)

Country	Total	Education and teacher training	Commerce and business administration	Home economics	Natural science	Medicine and Health-related sciences	Engineering
Benin	16.4	16.2	18.7	0.0	18.6	16.0	3.7
Botswana	40.1	47.6	43.3	0.0	26.1	0.0	0.0
Burkina Faso	22.2	0.0	50.0	0.0	16.9	19.7	0.0
Burundi	26.9	25.8	37.6	0.0	19.6	21.0	1.6
Cameroon	—	18.6	17.8	0.0	14.7	21.0	—
Central African Rep.	9.9	13.4	21.8	0.0	3.6	11.5	0.0
Chad	8.6	1.7	0.0	0.0	5.1	0.0	0.0
Congo	13.4	13.1	38.7	0.0	6.1	20.9	0.0
Côte d'Ivoire	—	—	46.0	0.0	10.6	32.3	3.6
Ethiopia	17.9	19.1	34.4	37.5	7.5	14.3	3.3
Gabon	27.0	14.8	48.7	0.0	15.9	42.1	4.8
Ghana	17.1	25.7	14.4	90.4	12.1	20.9	1.8
Guinea	14.4	11.7	31.0	0.0	16.2	14.6	3.8
Kenya	26.2	37.0	38.3	89.2	13.9	24.6	1.7

(Table continues on the following page.)

Table 3-8 (continued)

Country	Total	Education and teacher training	Commerce and business administration	Home economics	Natural science	Medicine and Health-related sciences	Engineering
Lesotho	63.2	72.1	52.0	0.0	29.8	69.2	0.0
Liberia	27.7	23.4	33.4	0.0	15.8	55.9	0.0
Madagascar	38.4	31.6	34.2	0.0	36.9	43.6	7.4
Malawi	27.5	33.6	13.6	0.0	12.3	71.1	0.0
Mali	11.3	43.5	17.4	0.0	0.0	12.8	2.1
Mauritius	27.2	33.3	22.1	0.0	0.0	25.0	4.0
Mozambique	23.0	33.0	0.0	0.0	30.4	50.6	7.8
Niger	18.4	20.5	0.0	0.0	24.7	18.4	0.0
Rwanda	13.4	20.5	—a	31.6	11.6	11.9	0.0
Senegal	20.8	11.0	—a	0.0	11.3	34.6	14.0
Sudan	30.5	33.2	27.0	0.0	38.0	32.0	7.4
Swaziland	38.2	49.1	40.6	100.0	26.6	0.0	0.0
Tanzania	13.6	20.0	20.8	0.0	22.4	11.9	3.9
Togo	15.0	22.0	—a	0.0	6.0	21.3	0.0
Uganda	21.9	24.2	24.7	0.0	13.7	21.2	3.4
Zambia	17.3	19.2	21.1	0.0	9.1	31.1	0.0

— Not available.

Note: The countries omitted are those for which data are not available.

a. Data included in another category.

Source: UNESCO, *Statistical Yearbook*, 1987.

this seeming anomaly may have arisen both from the curriculum choices women were given and from the quality of the schools they attended (Eshiwani 1982, Weis 1981).[12]

Consequently, neither the belief that women need only prepare to be housewives (refuted by the overwhelming evidence that most women engage in economically productive activities in the informal and traditional sectors)[13] nor the assumption that girls in secondary school are predominantly interested in becoming wives and mothers (since attitudes are shaped by the training girls are exposed to in school) is a useful generalization about the social or personal expectations of African girls. Yet this assumption, however unrealistic, affects the supply of places as well as the demand for schooling.

Lack of Role Models. Unfortunately, learning materials used in schools too often exaggerate and perpetuate the unrealistic idea that a woman's role is confined to that of wife and mother. Tembo (1984) surveyed a number of primary and lower secondary school textbooks from Zambia as part of a UNESCO project on gender stereotypes in textbooks. The methodology was simple: the number of occurrences of male and female characters were tallied and their activities and characteristics noted. The results were instructive. The books contained many more male than female characters, and those female characters who appeared did so primarily in domestic roles and were presented as passive, stupid, and ignorant. Men's activities were admired, women's ignored. No study that attempted to measure the impact of such stereotypes on girls in this region was found. One can conjecture, however, that the probable educational and occupational aspirations of girls will be those of wife and mother when those roles are portrayed as the only appropriate ones for women. The presence of female teachers in schools and classrooms is often held to be a strategy for countering these images.

Raising Female Achievement

Data on the educational achievement of girls usually comes from comparing test results, often on national examinations. Research on the relationship between gender and achievement yields mixed results. For example, Heyneman (1975) found that gender was the single most important variable in explaining differences in achievement (measured as performance on the Primary Leaving Examination) in Ugandan schools before 1975, with boys performing notably better than girls. Amuge (1987), using a national sample of secondary school leavers in Tanzania, found that boys outperformed girls in secondary school in almost every subject. Yet an intensive study of performance in primary schools in Mauritius found that girls outperformed boys in both urban and rural areas (Chinapah 1983). Another study found that girls in government and government-aided secondary schools in Nairobi performed as well as boys, but also that pupils in single-sex schools performed better than those in mixed schools (Boit 1986).

Unfortunately, none of the studies on Sub-Saharan African countries attempted to investigate directly the factors important for the achievement of girls. Several factors are probably relevant, including family influences and school characteristics. The findings related to family factors have already been discussed. Girls are more likely than boys to be burdened with household tasks, and these are more likely to take precedence over schoolwork for them than for their brothers (Fapohunda 1978; Wrzesinska 1980; see also Wheldon and Smith 1986). Less time for studying is likely to lower achievement.

Among school factors, the quality of schools is salient.[14] Eshiwani (1982) reports that in Kenya girls primarily entered harambee schools that had poorer equipment, less-qualified teachers, and more-limited curricula than did the government or government-aided schools that boys were more likely to attend. Weis (1981) indicates that 86 percent of secondary school girls in Ghana were enrolled in low-status schools, compared with 43 percent of secondary school boys. Akande (1987) found that female students in urban schools achieved more than those in rural schools, but he did not discuss the mechanisms of this advantage.

Given the financial constraints that most African governments face, extensively upgrading physical facilities, providing more textbooks, and increasing the number of qualified teachers may be difficult in the near future. Nevertheless, schools could make some changes that would improve school quality without necessarily incurring substantial new costs by addressing what Dreeben and Barr (1988) call technological choices in the classroom. For example, Lockheed and Komenan (1988) show that teaching practices rather than teacher quality were predictive of higher attainment in schools. Barr and Dreeben (1983) make a similar point in the context of the United States: the organization of classroom time and the use of classroom materials can raise achievement levels, independent of the ability of students. Eshiwani (1982), focusing outside the classroom, strongly urges organizational changes in the education system to remove or weaken the disadvantages for girls.

Increasing the number of female teachers is often recommended as a strategy for raising achievement as well as attainment among girls and women. Unless female (and male) teachers are trained to be sensitive to gender equity, however, increasing the number of female teachers may not have the desired result. A few studies have looked at the effect of teachers' attitudes on achievement, but they do not report the gender of the teachers. Nevertheless, the point has been made that a negative attitude toward the ability of girls, and even in some cases toward their right to an education, is surprisingly prevalent among teachers. From Ethiopia, Wondimagegnehu and Tiku (1988) report that eighteen of the thirty-one teachers interviewed felt that boys were better than girls in all academic subjects. Boit (1986) found that only 40 percent of the Nairobi teachers and heads of schools interviewed thought that girls would do as well as boys if given the same opportunities. Amara (1987) concluded from an informal survey that teachers in Sierra Leone had higher expectations for boys than for girls.

Evidence on the effectiveness of single-sex schools in raising girls' performance at the secondary level is mixed (table 3-9). In a sample of third-year students from Nairobi secondary schools, Boit (1986) found that girls in single-sex schools performed as well as boys in single-sex schools and significantly better than both boys and girls in coeducational schools when tested for achievement in mathematics. In Swaziland Wheldon and Smith (1986) found that the relative pass rate in science was the same for girls in both types of schools. Girls in single-sex schools were more likely to choose mathematics and agriculture than the physical sciences, however, a pattern that may have accounted for Lockheed and Komenan's (1988) finding of superior mathematics achievement by girls in single-sex schools in Nigeria and Swaziland. These authors found that in both countries girls in single-sex schools outperformed girls in other schools. Although the reasons for the better performance in girls' schools is not directly explored, the authors state: "The picture that emerges from this comparison between high, average and low performing schools/classes is one of substantial differences between students, teachers and teaching practices" (p. 25).

Table 3-9. *Studies of Effects of Single-Sex Secondary Schools on Girls'*
Achievement, Selected Sub-Saharan African Countries

Source	Country	Sample	Comment
Amuge (1987)	Tanzania	National, 4,181 Form IV students	No effect
Boit (1986)	Kenya	Nairobi government schools, third-year math class	Positive
Lockheed and Komenan (1988)	Nigeria Swaziland	Eighth grade, eight southern states Eighth grade, volunteer	} Positive
Wheldon and Smith (1986)	Swaziland	Cambridge Overseas School Certificate entrants (1985)	Positive

The implication is that all-female schools attract higher-quality students and teachers and that they provide more effective teaching than other schools. Although single-sex schools in Britain have less gender bias than do mixed schools, gender bias was greater in single-sex schools in Swaziland (Wheldon and Smith 1986). Swazi girls in mixed schools may be taking advantage of curriculum offerings intended for boys, or single-sex schools may not be able to hire female teachers to teach subjects such as physics and chemistry.

Amuge (1987) found that among a sample of fourth-year secondary school students in Tanzania, no significant difference was apparent between the performance of girls in single-sex and coeducational schools in a wide range of subjects (commerce, agriculture, English, verbal ability, home economics, mathematics, math aptitude, Swahili, and technical subjects). Boys outperformed girls in all subjects except commerce, however.

Summary and Conclusions

The factors that have affected girls' educational status in African countries include negative parental and community attitudes toward the Western education of girls; the opportunity cost of a girl's school time and, indirectly, of her mother's; general levels of wealth and economic development; disparities between urban and rural areas; unfavorable labor market opportunities; and low-quality schools with limited curriculum choices. Some of these factors are more amenable to intervention than others. Except for improving curriculum options, revising textbooks, and increasing the number of female teachers, all require strategies that reach beyond the school to the family and the community.

Conspicuous by its absence is any study that uses the shortage of places in primary school to explain the disparity between boys' and girls' enrollment rates. The tacit, and perhaps valid, assumption would be that even if enough places were available for all children of primary school age, girls would still be underrepresented in many countries, and school places would go unused (Bowman and Anderson 1980). The study that comes closest to linking supply factors to school enrollment found that, on average, primary school students lived closer to the school than did most of the people in the community (Biazen and Junge 1988 for rural Ethiopia). The conclusion is either that school enrollees are disproportionately drawn from families living close to the school or that those students who are enrolled in a school move closer to it.

One of the more fruitful approaches to increasing female schooling may be a strategy directed not at school-age girls themselves but at their mothers. Such a strategy would have at least two prongs: to reduce the mother's dependence on the labor of her children and to raise the educational levels of mothers themselves. The first prong involves introducing time-saving amenities such as a convenient water supply and fuel for the household. At least two projects have used such technological innovations to reduce the time constraints on women and to free them for education: a UNESCO project in Burkina Faso, which provided women with new home technology (McSweeney and Freedman 1980); and a soil and water project on agricultural innovation funded by the U.S. Agency for International Development (USAID) in Kenya (Knowles 1988).

The second prong involves literacy programs, which are an ongoing feature in many African countries, such as Tanzania, that have had success in educating females. These programs should be continued. Closer integration with existing formal education structures and with grass-roots organizations such as cooperatives could lower the cost of these programs and integrate them into the lives of newly literate women. Organizational needs, such as record-keeping, can spur demands for literacy and encourage its maintenance by providing opportunities for its use.

Increasing Access

Such factors as general levels of school enrollment, levels of economic development, and job opportunities for women are linked to long-term economic and planning initiatives. Evidence from other continents gives some cause for pessimism about the impact such changes would have on closing the gender gap in education. These changes may be necessary, but they are far from sufficient. Economic development may increase female enrollment, but its effect on other aspects of women's participation in education, and indirectly on their social and economic welfare, is dubious in the absence of committed efforts and specific policies directed toward women.

Only a few programs by government agencies have been directed specifically at increasing schooling for girls and women (Damiba 1982; de Souza 1982). Nongovernmental organizations and international donors have made some efforts to raise the level of female schooling, but the results appear to have been negligible, largely because these efforts have been small-scale and limited (Stromquist 1987). In addition, sponsorship by foreign organizations may reinforce traditional beliefs about protecting women from Western corruption, which in turn can pose obstacles to improving their schooling.

Expansion of education systems has led to increases in access for girls with historically low levels of school participation. It has been successful in increasing female enrollment and attainment but less successful in reducing or eliminating gender differentials. For example, providing 100 new primary schools in Kano state in Nigeria between 1976 and 1981 quadrupled girls' enrollment rate, but their relative share of school places only increased from 25 to 30 percent (Callaway 1984). Expansion is also a very expensive option. Extending schooling to those who do not now have access by expanding the system would entail administrative and financial costs that would strain most African education budgets.

Chamie (1983) has suggested the multiple use of teachers and buildings as a way of expanding school places without incurring large capital costs. Countries have tried this option with some success. Such a strategy may widen regional gaps, however, because those regions already well provided with schools would be able to generate the largest number of additional school places. Moreover, unless teachers are paid extra, they are likely to resist taking on an increased workload.

Countries with fiscal constraints and less-developed educational systems will find it impossible to provide additional years of public schooling to all children. Nigeria has used public expansion and Kenya has used private expansion to increase access to education, yet neither has achieved universal primary enrollment. Alternative educational services that can supplement public services need to be developed, but privatization is only part of the answer, and in some countries only a small part.

Stromquist (1987) recommends the use of women's organizations and other nongovernmental organizations to promote nonformal education systems that could supplement formal systems. She reports that the record of these organizations in working with international aid agencies has generally been positive. Nongovernmental organizations already have a framework in place and are oriented toward cost-effective, community-level work. Women's organizations, both traditional and international, already exist in African countries, and they serve women in various nonformal educational settings. Women can overcome the deficiencies of public and private formal educational systems by seeking training in such settings. The existence of nonformal alternatives also tends to relieve the pressures for reforming formal education systems. The danger, however, is that these organizations may be overburdened by such demands.

Religious education systems can also be developed. Morgan and Armer (1988), with reference to the education of boys in northern Nigeria, point to the vigor and growth of Koranic education alongside Western education. In parts of West Africa, such as Nigeria and Sierra Leone, Muslim organizations (including women's groups) have opened schools that presumably do not engender fears that formal education will lessen girls' commitment to Islam or encourage non-Muslim values.

Setting Policy

Policies promoted by international agencies have improved women's participation in education. The package of structural adjustment policies being advocated by the World Bank and the International Monetary Fund for many African countries could have some negative consequences for women's education, however. This applies to cutbacks in the public sector, which is a disproportionately large employer of women, including in education.[15] The cutbacks can be regarded as an attack on two fronts: school places could be imperiled, and employment opportunities for those who do attend school could be reduced—a situation that could further erode the already low labor market returns to education for women. In addition, the privatization of the public sector, including education, could widen the chasm between those girls who get an education and those who do not. As more of the cost of an education is shifted to the students' families, the strong consumption aspect of a Western education for girls at the secondary and tertiary levels will discourage many parents from keeping their daughters in school. And in those areas where primary school enrollment is universal or nearly so, privatization may introduce an economic consideration into a decision that had become automatic. Recommendations made in the World Bank's policy study on education in Sub-Saharan Africa (World Bank 1988) appear more sensitive to the problems women face as they try to enter and move through the education system. Reconciling these recommendations with World Bank fiscal policy will not be easy, however.

The African Development Bank's *Education Sector Policy Paper* (1986), points to access and equity, including gender equity, as the first of five main problem areas that will guide its funding policies. Support for projects that try to remedy inequalities and to ease enrollment in institutions in which women have been underrepresented will be a special priority (p. 15). Such an emphasis presumably will be affected by the willingness of member states to propose and support such projects. A brief review of the most recent development plans from African countries suggests that gender inequality does not appear to have received much attention at the national level; instead, general economic development and fiscal stability appear to be the prime concerns (Metra Consulting 1983).

Future policies and actions need to be firmly grounded in an accurate understanding of the barriers to women's education. Research needs to focus on specific contexts on a national or even regional basis. An important initial step would be to learn from research already completed, but not made generally available, by research institutes, university departments of education, teacher training institutions, and ministries of education within each country. Enough data are available on most countries to describe fully how gender inequality manifests itself in the education system. But more analysis is needed of the process—that is, of how females become disadvantaged—before effective remedial strategies can be designed. The analysis requires a multivariate approach, with appropriate controls for the socioeconomic status of the relevant household. Armed with the results of this research and analysis, policymakers will be better able to direct scarce resources to programs that will benefit girls and women the most.

Notes

I am grateful to Peter Kim and Gilbert Valverde for research assistance. Peter Kim and Frank Norfleet assembled some of the tables. Mette Shayne and the staff of the Melville J. Herskovits Library of African Studies at Northwestern University provided invaluable assistance. Discussions with Josephine Beoku-Betts and Nelly Stromquist were stimulating. Several useful suggestions came from John Craig, Gail Kelly, Robert Willis, Marie Thourson Jones, Michael Brien, and Elizabeth Hyde.

1. Obviously, floor effects are operating here, but this progress may nevertheless suggest the absence of intransigence in Africa toward the idea of equal education for women and men.

2. See chapter 1 for an explanation of how the calculation of gross school enrollment can lead to rates greater than 100 percent.

3. Regional variation exists within countries. In some districts of Kenya, for example, girls compose only a fourth of enrollments (Eshiwani 1982).

4. Although it can be argued that the enrollment figures at the higher levels of schooling reflect the histories of earlier cohorts, there is no evidence that these relative positions have been changing. High repetition and dropout rates among girls imply both that schools are ineffective in teaching or retaining girls and that girls are weakly motivated to attend school and learn. Parental attitudes (against exposing girls to "foreign" influences and expending resources on girls), levels of parental education, and the demand for child labor at home are some factors that may affect motivation.

5. Under family factors are grouped studies on social class (Assie 1983; Biraimah 1987; Weis 1981); parental attitudes toward sending girls to school (Csapo 1981); level of maternal education (Chernichovsky 1985; Kossoudji and Mueller 1983); demand for child labor (Biazen and Junge 1988; Chernichovsky 1985); and selective education of children (Chernichovsky 1985; Orubuloye 1987). Societal factors include studies on marriage and other competing activities (Amon-Nikoi 1978); urban residence (Akande 1987; Assie 1983; Bedri and Burchinal 1985; Robertson 1986); overall levels of enrollment

(Adams and Kruppenbad 1987); agricultural labor force (Wood, Swan, and Wood 1986); and government expenditures on education (Wood, Swan, and Wood 1986). School factors include school quality (Eshiwani 1982; Weis 1981); vocational training opportunities within schools (Csapo 1981; Eshiwani 1982; Robertson 1986); and the lack of role models (Tembo 1984).

6. *Purdah* is a system of screening women (especially Muslims and Hindus) from strangers. It often involves the wearing of veils in public or the seclusion of women within their homes during the day. Girls enter *purdah* at marriage, generally around puberty.

7. The apparent contradiction arises from the low time-intensity of childcare. Mothers' work is often fully compatible with childcare, but the use of foster care can relieve mothers of the need to care for their babies.

8. Each additional older person increases by 26 percent the likelihood that a child will be in school, whereas being in the middle category of cattle ownership reduces the level of education attained by children enrolled in school by half a year.

9. The rate at which women participate in the labor force is highest for women aged 15–25 (Amon-Nikoi 1978).

10. Eshiwani (1982) reports that female students at the University of Nairobi commented several times, "Mathematics and science make you ugly."

11. The efficacy of school-based vocational programs is dubious for both sexes. For girls, the training they receive is often irrelevant to the lives they lead; for boys, the inferior quality of the training is the more salient issue, although its relevance can also be doubtful.

12. Of course, this is not the only explanation for this fall in female labor supply. Another is that the rise in women's education has meant an increase in their nonmarket productivity in relation to productivity in the available (and probably quite limited) labor market opportunities for better-educated women.

13. See Dixon (1982) and UNECA (1984) for evidence on women in the agricultural sector.

14. Research on secondary school characteristics includes quality (Akande 1987; Eshiwani 1982; Weis 1981); teacher attitudes (Amara 1987; Boit 1986; Wondimagegnehu and Tiku 1988); and single-sex schools (Amuge 1987; Boit 1986; Lockheed and Komenan 1988; Wheldon and Smith 1986).

15. For example, the government of the Gambia released 2,000 teachers in 1988.

References

Abraha, Seged, Assefa Beyene, Tesfaye Dubale, Bruce Fuller, Susan Halloway, and Elizabeth King. 1991. "What Factors Shape Girls' School Performance? Evidence from Ethiopia." *International Journal of Educational Development* 11:107–18.

Adams, M. N., and S. E. Kruppenbad. 1987. "Gender and Access in the African School." *International Review of Education* 33:457–63.

Adjebeng-Asem, S. 1988. "Women and Technology." Paper presented at the African Studies Association Meeting, Chicago, Ill., November.

African Development Bank. 1986. *Education Sector Policy Paper.* Abidjan.

Akande, B. E. 1987. "Rural-Urban Comparison of Female Educational Aspirations in Southwestern Nigeria." *Comparative Education* 23:75–83.

Amara, J. M. 1987. "Indigenous Technology of Sierra Leone and the Science Education of Girls." *International Journal of Science Education* 9:317–24.

Amon-Nikoi, G., 1978. "Women and Work in Africa." In U. G. Damachi and V. P. Diejomaoh, eds., *Human Resources and African Development.* New York: Praeger.

Amuge, I. M. 1987. "Gender Differences in Academic and Post-School Experience among Tanzania Secondary School Students." Ed.D. diss. State University of New York, Albany.

Assie, N. 1983. "Educational Selection and Social Inequality in Africa." Ph.D. diss. University of Chicago, Chicago, Ill.

Bali, S. K., P. J. D. Drenth, H. van der Flier, and W. C. E. Young. 1984. *Contribution of Aptitude Tests to the Prediction of School Performance in Kenya: A Longitudinal Study.* Lisse, The Netherlands: Swets and Zeitlinger.

Barr, Rebecca, and Robert Dreeben. 1983. *How Schools Work.* Chicago, Ill.: University of Chicago Press.

Bedri, N. S., and L. G. Burchinal. 1985. "Educational Attainment as an Indicator of the Status of Women in the Sudan." *Ahfad Journal* 2:30–38.

Biazen, Ambesu, and B. Junge. 1988. "Problems in Primary School Participation and Performance in Bahir Dar Awraja." Report prepared for UNICEF and Ministry of Education, Addis Ababa.

Biraimah, K. L. 1987. "Class, Gender and Life Chances: A Nigerian University Case Study." *Comparative Education Review* 31:570–82.

Bledsoe, Caroline. 1988. "The Politics of Polygyny in Mende Education and Child Fosterage Transactions." In B. D. Miller, ed., *Gender Hierarchies.* Chicago, Ill.: University of Chicago Press.

Boit, M. K. 1986. "The Relationship of Teacher Behavior to Student Achievement in High and Low Achievement High Schools in Nairobi, Kenya." Ph.D. diss. University of Oregon at Eugene.

Bowman, Mary Jean, and C. A. Anderson. 1980. "The Participation of Women in Education in the Third World." *Comparative Education Review* 24(2):S13–S32.

Callaway, B. J. 1984. "Ambiguous Consequences of the Socialization and Seclusion of Hausa Women." *Journal of Modern African Studies* 22:429–50.

Chamie, Mary. 1983. *National, Institutional and Household Factors Affecting Young Girls' School Attendance in Developing Societies.* Washington, D.C.: International Center for Research on Women and U.S. Agency for International Development.

Chernichovsky, Dov. 1985. "Socioeconomic and Demographic Aspects of School Enrollment and Attendance in Rural Botswana." *Economic Development and Cultural Change* 33:319–32.

Chinapah, V. 1983. *Participation and Performance in Primary Schooling.* Studies in Comparative and International Education 8. University of Stockholm, Institute of International Education.

Chishimba, M. M. 1984. "Language Policy and Education in Zambia." *International Education Journal* 1:151–80.

Csapo, Marg. 1981. "Religious, Social and Economic Factors Hindering the Education of Girls in Northern Nigeria." *Comparative Education* 17:311–19.

Damiba, A. 1982. "Educational Inequalities in Upper Volta." In Mark Blaug and others, eds., *Inequalities in Educational Development*. Paris: International Institute for Educational Planning.

Denzer, L. 1988. "Colonial Education for Women in Nigeria, 1861–1945." Paper delivered at the Women and Education in Africa Symposium, University of Wisconsin, Madison, November.

de Souza, A. R. 1982. "The New School Policy to Reduce Inequality in the People's Republic of Benin." In Mark Blaug and others, eds., *Inequalities in Educational Development*. Paris: International Institute for Educational Planning.

Dixon, Ruth. 1982. "Women in Agriculture: Counting the Labor Force in Developing Countries." *Population and Development Review* 8:539–66.

Dreeben, Robert, and Rebecca Barr. 1988. "The Formation and Instruction of Ability Groups." *American Journal of Education* 97:34–64.

Eshiwani, G. S. 1982. *A Study of Women's Access to Higher Education with a Special Reference to Science and Math Education*. Working Paper 5003. Nairobi: Kenyatta University College, Bureau of Educational Research.

Fapohunda, E. R. 1978. "Women at Work in Nigeria: Factors Affecting Modern Sector Employment." In U. G. Damachi and V. P. Diejomaoh, eds., *Human Resources and African Development*. New York: Praeger.

Gambetta, D. 1987. *Were They Pushed or Did They Jump?* Cambridge, U.K.: Cambridge University Press.

Garenne, M., and E. van de Walle. 1988. "Polygyny and Fertility among the Sereer of Senegal." Paper presented at the University of Chicago, Spring.

Harding, J. 1985. "Girls and Women in Secondary and Higher Education: Science for Only a Few." *Prospects* 15:553–64.

Heyneman, Stephen. 1975. "Influences on Academic Achievement in Uganda: A 'Coleman Report' from a Non-Industrial Society." Ph.D. diss. University of Chicago, Chicago, Ill.

Kelly, Gail P. 1988. "Perspectives on Women and Education in the Third World." Paper presented at the Women and Education in Africa Symposium, University of Wisconsin, Madison, November.

Knowles, J. 1988. "Non-Formal Education Review: Agriculture." Paper presented at the Women and Education in Africa Symposium, University of Wisconsin at Madison, November.

Kossoudji, Sherrie, and Eva Mueller. 1983. "The Economic and Demographic Status of Female-Headed Households in Rural Botswana." *Economic Development and Cultural Change* 34(4):831–59.

Lockheed, Marlaine E., and Andre Komenan. 1988. "School Effects on Student Achievement in Nigeria and Swaziland." Policy Research Working Paper 71. World Bank, Population and Human Resources Department, Education and Employment Division, Washington, D.C.

Mann, D. 1986. "Can We Help Dropouts? Thinking about the Undoable." In G. Natriello, ed., *School Dropouts: Patterns and Policies.* New York: Teachers College Press.

McSweeney, Brenda Gail, and Marion Freedman. 1980. "Lack of Time as an Obstacle to Women's Education: The Case of Upper Volta." *Comparative Education Review* 24:S124–S139.

Metra Consulting. 1983. *Handbook of National Development Plans.* Vols. 1 and 2. London: Graham and Trotman.

Morgan, W. R., and J. M. Armer. 1988. "Islamic and Western Educational Accommodation in a West African Society: A Cohort Comparison Analysis." *American Sociological Review* 53:634–39.

Newman, J. S. 1984. *Women of the World: Sub-Saharan Africa.* Washington, D.C.: U.S. Department of Commerce.

Nkinyangi, J. 1980. "Socioeconomic Determinants of Repetition and Early Withdrawal at the Primary School Level and Their Implications for Educational Planning in Kenya." Ph.D. diss. Stanford University, Stanford, Calif.

———. 1982. "Access to Primary Education in Kenya: The Contradictions of Public Policy." *Comparative Education Review* 26:199–217.

Orubuloye, O. 1987. "Values and Costs of Daughters and Sons to Yoruba Mothers and Fathers." In C. Oppong, ed., *Sex Roles, Population and Development in West Africa.* London: Heinemann.

Robertson, C. C. 1977. "The Nature and Effects of Differential Access to Education in Ga Society." *Africa* 47:208–19.

———. 1984. "Formal or Nonformal Education? Entrepreneurial Women in Ghana." *Comparative Education Review* 28:639–58.

———. 1986. "Women's Education and Class Formation in Africa, 1950–1980." In C. Robertson and I. Berger, eds., *Women and Class in Africa.* New York: Africana Publishing Co.

Robertson, C., and I. Berger, eds. 1986. *Women and Class in Africa.* New York: Africana Publishing Co.

Smith, J. E., and P. R. Kunz. 1976. "Polygyny and Fertility in Nineteenth Century America." *Population Studies* 30:465–80.

Stromquist, Nelly P. 1987. "School-Related Determinants of Female Primary School Participation and Achievement in Developing Countries: An Annotated Bibliography." EDT Discussion Paper 83. World Bank, Education and Training Department, Washington, D.C.

Tembo, L. P. 1984. *Men and Women in School Textbooks: A National Survey of Sex Biases in Zambian Textbooks in Primary and Junior Secondary Schools and Their Implications for Education in Zambia.* Lusaka: UNESCO.

Tibenderana, P. K. 1988. "The Irony of Indirect Rule in Sokoto Empire, Nigeria, 1903–1944." *African Studies Review* 31:67–92.

Tripp, A. M. 1988. "Women and the Changing Urban Household Economy in Tanzania." Northwestern University, Evanston, Ill.

UNECA (United Nations Economic Commission for Africa). 1984. "The Role of Women in the Solution of the Food Crisis in Africa." Arusha, Tanzania.

UNESCO (United Nations Educational, Scientific, and Cultural Organization). 1983. *Trends and Projections of Enrollment by Level of Education and by Age: 1960–2000 (as Assessed in 1982)*. Paris.

——. 1987. *Statistical Yearbook*. Paris.

——. 1990. *Statistical Yearbook*. Paris.

Weis, L. 1981. "Schooling and Patterns of Access in Ghana." *Canadian Journal of African Studies* 15(2):311–22.

Wheldon, A. E., and A. C. Smith. 1986. "Gender-Based Differences in O-Level Choice and Performance in Swaziland." *Bulletin of the Swaziland Institute for Educational Research* 7:78–91.

Wondimagegnehu, A., and K. Tiku. 1988. "Participation of Ethiopian Women in Education." Ministry of Education, Addis Ababa.

Wood, M. M., W. W. Swan, and N. J. Wood. 1986. "Supply and Demand Factors Influencing the Educational Dropout Rate in Africa and Asia." *International Education* 15:37–44.

World Bank. 1988. *Education in Sub-Saharan Africa: Policies for Adjustment, Revitalization and Expansion*. Washington, D.C.

——. 1989. *World Development Report 1989*. New York: Oxford University Press.

Wrzesinska, Alicja. 1980. "A Young African Girl, Her School and Her Family Environment." *Africa* 35:357–85.

4

Middle East and North Africa

Nagat El-Sanabary

The Middle East and North Africa region encompasses affluent oil exporters such as Kuwait and Saudi Arabia and lower-middle-income countries such as Egypt and Morocco. The countries of the region are predominantly Muslim, but Tunisia and Turkey have comparatively liberal laws on women and family matters, whereas Saudi Arabia follows a much stricter interpretation of Islamic laws. Public and private life has been shaped by Arab culture dating back thousands of years, by Islam, by Ottoman Turkish rule, by European influences that in the case of Egypt go back to Napoleon's invasion in 1789, and by Christian missionary activity in the nineteenth and early twentieth centuries. The region's economic and cultural diversity is reflected in its education systems and attitudes toward education.

Female literacy and educational attainment have been lower in the Middle East and North Africa than in Latin America and East Asia. Although Islam supports the education of women and although laws in almost all Arab states mandate equal educational opportunities for both sexes, the Arab value system is stern regarding women's sexual conduct. Family honor depends on the conformity of women to a "modesty code," and once a woman's honor has been lost, it cannot be regained. The result of this value system is sexual segregation, strict parental surveillance, veiling, early marriage, and rigid sex roles—practices that may have an impact on education. Nevertheless, because of variations in how the Islamic code is interpreted from country to country, reinforced by differences in the level of economic development, the size and growth rate of the population, and exposure to Western influences, educational status diverges widely in the region. National illiteracy rates for women in the 1980s ranged from about 30 percent to well over 70 percent. Primary school enrollment is nearly universal in Tunisia and Turkey, but more than a third of school-age girls do not attend primary school in Morocco and Saudi Arabia.

The education systems in these countries developed at different times. Whereas public education for girls in Egypt dates from the mid-nineteenth century, public education for girls in Saudi Arabia began only in 1960. Yet in Egypt a fourth of all girls of primary school age are not in school. Saudi Arabia's newer system, in contrast, has expanded quickly and appears headed toward universal enrollment. Overall, enrollment rates at the primary level have made impressive gains in the region, from less than half of the total school-age population in 1960 to about three-quarters in 1987; in the same period the female share of primary enrollment rose from 41 to 45 percent. But schools for males are more numerous and of better quality than schools for females. And despite recent gains, the gender gap in education is wider in this region than in many other parts of the developing world, South Asia excepted, as measured by female enrollment rates, literacy rates, and years of schooling.

This chapter focuses on seven Middle Eastern and North African countries: Egypt, Jordan, Kuwait, Morocco, Saudi Arabia, Tunisia, and Turkey. All are Arab except Turkey, which bridges Europe, Asia, and the Middle East and is a member of the OECD. Predominantly Muslim, the seven countries have a shared history of more than five centuries. Geographically, Egypt, Morocco, and Tunisia are in North Africa, Jordan and Turkey in northwestern Asia, and Kuwait and Saudi Arabia on the Arabian Peninsula. Politically, Jordan, Morocco, and Saudi Arabia are monarchies, Kuwait is a semimonarchy, and Egypt, Tunisia, and Turkey are republics. Kuwait and Saudi Arabia are members of the Gulf Cooperating Council and of the Organization of Petroleum Exporting Countries (OPEC).

Economic and Demographic Overview

Middle Eastern and North African countries exhibit extreme economic diversity. The seven countries included in this review had GNP per capita in 1987 that ranged from a high of $14,610 in Kuwait to a low of $610 in Morocco (table 4-1). Life expectancy, another indicator of development, varies widely as well, from a low of sixty-one years in Morocco and Egypt to a high of seventy-three years in Kuwait. Although Saudi Arabia is a high-income country, its people have an average life expectancy of only sixty-three years, which is in the range commonly found among lower-middle-income countries.

The countries also differ demographically. Egypt and Turkey have populations that exceed 50 million, whereas Kuwait has a population of less than 2 million (see table 4-1). Kuwait and Saudi Arabia are

Table 4-1. *GNP Per Capita and Population, Selected Countries in the Middle East and North Africa, 1980–87*

Group and country	GNP per capita, 1987 (dollars)	Population mid-1987 (millions)	Population growth rate 1980–87 (percent)
Middle-income			
Morocco	610	23.3	2.7
Egypt	680	50.1	2.7
Tunisia	1,180	7.6	2.6
Turkey	1,210	52.6	2.3
Jordan	1,560	3.8	3.9
High-income oil exporters			
Saudi Arabia	6,200	12.6	4.3
Kuwait	14,610	1.9	4.5

Source: World Bank 1989.

among the countries with the world's highest population growth rates. Egypt's population, which in 1987 was just over 50 million, is expected to reach 62 million by the year 2000 and 86 million by 2025 (World Bank 1992). Because of the generally high birthrates and low life expectancies, the Middle East and North Africa is a youthful region. About 40 percent of the people in Egypt, Kuwait, Morocco, and Tunisia are under fifteen years of age. In Jordan and Saudi Arabia 48 and 45 percent of the population, respectively, fall within this age group.

This demographic profile has far-reaching implications for the challenge of expanding education in general and female education in particular. The size of the population and its growth rate determine the effort required to reach the target age groups, at the same time that economic constraints limit what countries can spend on expanding their education systems. Ironically, as table 4-1 makes clear, two of the three most populous states in the region are also the poorest; they lack the resources to educate their large and growing numbers of school-age children. In Egypt, for example, a population of about 50 million and an income per capita of $680 (in 1987) combine to make universal primary education, especially for girls, an elusive goal, despite efforts to satisfy the growing demand; moreover, the quality of education leaves much to be desired. Morocco is also handicapped by being a relatively populous country of about 23 million with a GNP per capita of $610 in 1987. Kuwait, with a population of just 1.9 million and a GNP per capita of $14,610 in 1987 has, as noted, made remarkable progress. Saudi Arabia, with a much larger population than Kuwait, has also made significant progress but is taking much longer to reach the level and quality of education achieved in Kuwait.

Educational Status

A review of the burgeoning literature on Middle Eastern and North African women reveals a dearth of research on women's education. Reflecting the academic background of researchers, most of whom are sociologists and anthropologists, the focus has been on women's status and roles, on their participation in the modern and traditional sectors of the labor market, and on family, fertility, and related topics. Most of this research has been carried out by non–Middle Easterners. The limited research on female education has been conceptual or theoretical, except for a few recent empirical studies.

The data available on these countries show that illiteracy is much more prevalent among females than among males (table 4-2). In Tunisia in 1984 the illiteracy rate was 50 percent higher for women than for men. The most recent data available, which cover a wide span of years, suggest that Kuwaiti females have the lowest illiteracy rates and Egyptian and Moroccan women have the highest illiteracy rates. But national figures mask intracountry differences in literacy and educational attainment, such as those between urban and rural areas. What limited data exist indicate much higher illiteracy levels for both men and women in rural areas.

School Enrollments

Girls are less likely than boys to enter primary school and, if enrolled, are less likely to complete the cycle or to continue on to secondary school (Kaneko 1987). Nevertheless, female enrollment at all levels has

Table 4-2. *Illiteracy Rates, by Gender, Selected Countries in the Middle East and North Africa, Various Years*
(percent)

		Male		Female	
Group and country	Year	Total	Rural	Total	Rural
Egypt	1976	46.4	55.5	77.6	86.9
Jordan	1979	19.9	—	49.5	—
Kuwait	1985	21.8	—	31.2	—
Morocco	1971	66.4	78.1	90.2	98.7
Saudi Arabia	1982	28.9	—	69.2	—
Tunisia	1984	39.5	—	59.4	—
Turkey	1985	12.4	—	35.7	—

— Not available.

Note: The reference population includes all those fifteen years and older except in the case of rural Egypt, where it includes those ten years and older.

Source: UNESCO, *Statistical Yearbook,* 1990.

increased substantially in the region since the 1960s, at the same time that, as shown by the overall participation rates of the school-age population, educational opportunities have broadened (table 4-3). At the primary level, Jordan, Tunisia, and Turkey have achieved universal enrollment for both boys and girls. Morocco and Saudi Arabia, however, continue to fall short of this goal, especially for girls. In Morocco 85 percent of boys but only 56 percent of girls were enrolled in primary school in 1987; in Saudi Arabia the figures were 78 and 65 percent, respectively. In Egypt universal primary education has been achieved for boys, but only 79 percent of girls were enrolled in primary school in 1987. Achieving universal access in Saudi Arabia is probably just a matter of time, given that public education for girls began only in 1960. In contrast, although female education in Egypt dates from the second half of the nineteenth century, gender disparities in primary education persist.

At the secondary level, an increase in the female enrollment rate in Kuwait, from 1 percent in 1950 to 80 percent in 1987, has put that country far ahead of the others in the region. Kuwait appears to have been successful in enforcing compulsory education at the primary and lower secondary levels. Despite its lower ranking at the primary level, Egypt had a female enrollment rate at the secondary level of 58 percent, compared with only 34–35 percent in Saudi Arabia, Tunisia, and Turkey. Jordan, like Kuwait, has been relatively advanced in its female enrollment rates not just for secondary education but for all levels.

At the tertiary level, Jordan led the other countries with enrollment rates of 42 percent for males and 33 percent for females. Egypt was second at 29 percent for males and 15 percent for females, followed by Kuwait and Saudi Arabia. Morocco, Tunisia, and Turkey each had a female enrollment rate of less than 6 percent. Women pursuing a higher education tend to select traditionally female fields of study—the humanities and social sciences. As in other Islamic countries, however, women are highly represented in medicine, and in Egypt and Turkey they are also well represented in the traditionally male field of engineering.

Annual growth rates, given in table 4-4, indicate relatively greater improvements for girls than for boys in all countries at the primary and secondary levels and in Egypt, Morocco, Saudi Arabia, Tunisia, and Turkey at the tertiary level as well. In Kuwait, although the average annual growth rate of enrollment in higher education is lower for girls than for boys, female students were a majority in both 1975 and 1985. As a result of the recent growth in female enrollments, the gender gap in educational attainment is narrower among the younger age groups than among older segments of the population.

Table 4-3. *Gross Enrollment Rates at the Primary, Secondary,*
and Tertiary Levels, Selected Countries in the Middle East
and North Africa, 1950–87
(percentage of relevant population)

Country and year	Primary Male	Primary Female	Secondary Male	Secondary Female	Tertiary Male	Tertiary Female
Egypt						
1950	52	30	27	7	7.8[a]	1.6[a]
1968	85	55	40	20	10.8[b]	4.0[b]
1975	89	60	55	31	18.5	8.3
1987	100	79	79	58	28.6	14.8
Jordan						
1950	71	25	7	1	—	—
1968	100	85	54	24	1.0[c]	0.3[c]
1980	105	102	79	73	28.9	24.2
1983	98	99	80	78	41.5	33.2
Kuwait						
1950	92	45	4	1	*	*
1968	100	85	71	61	0.9[c]	2.5[c]
1975	99	85	71	61	7.1	11.2
1987	95	92	85	80	11.9	21.0
Morocco						
1950	31	11	1	1	0.8[a]	0.1[a]
1968	72	36	18	6	2.0[b]	0.4[b]
1975	78	45	21	12	5.2	1.2
1987	85	56	43	30	11.9	5.7
Saudi Arabia						
1950	4	—	0.2	*	0.2[a]	—
1968	44	18	12	2	1.0[c]	0.1[c]
1980	75	50	36	23	8.8	5.0
1986	78	65	52	35	12.0[c]	9.3[c]
Tunisia						
1950	51	19	11	5	—	—
1968	100	83	29	11	—	—
1975	116	78	28	15	6.3	2.1
1987	126	107	46	34	7.2	4.0
Turkey						
1950	56	36	7	3	4.5[a]	1.1[a]
1968	93	61	34	14	4.4[c]	2.0[c]
1980	103	92	40	19	14.8	3.1
1987	121	113	57	34	11.8[d]	5.8[d]

(Notes continue on the following page.)

Notes to Table 4-3

— Not available.

* Nonexistent.

Note: The net enrollment rates are actually lower than those shown. The gross enrollment rates exceeding 100 are the result of the enrollment of overage students.

a. 1960.

b. 1970.

c. 1969.

d. 1984.

Source: Data for the primary and secondary levels are from UNESCO, *Statistical Yearbook,* 1970 and 1990. Data for the tertiary level are from UNESCO, *Statistical Yearbook,* 1971, 1972, and 1990.

Several writers have stressed the important effect of national economic development on girls' education, giving illustrations from Kuwait (El-Sanabary 1973, 1978, 1985; Meleis, El-Sanabary, and Beeson 1979) and from Bahrain and Libya (Chamie 1983). The data in tables 4-3 and 4-4 corroborate their findings, showing the remarkable progress made by the wealthier countries of Jordan, Kuwait, and Saudi Arabia in reducing the gender gap and extending education to large segments of the school-age population. Despite their much more conservative social climate, these countries have spent generously on education, expanding indigenous and expatriate staff and the supply of textbooks. Within a short time they have caught up with and even surpassed, at least in the percentage of females attending postprimary education, other Middle Eastern countries with much longer histories of girls' education. The most recent enrollment rates put Saudi Arabia ahead of the more liberal Tunisia and Turkey. The poorer Middle Eastern and North African countries have been unable to provide the schools, teachers, equipment, and materials needed to educate a considerable segment of their populations, despite compulsory education

Table 4-4. *Average Annual Growth Rates of Total and Female Enrollment, Selected Countries in the Middle East and North Africa, 1970–85*
(percent)

Group and country	Primary		Secondary		Tertiary	
	Total	Female	Total	Female	Total	Female
Egypt	3.4	4.3	6.5	8.2	9.1	10.0
Jordan	4.5	5.0	8.6	11.1	18.2	16.1
Kuwait	5.9	6.7	8.5	9.2	15.6	13.7
Morocco	4.5	5.4	9.7	12.2	16.8	21.4
Saudi Arabia	8.0	10.4	13.6	18.9	18.9	32.3
Tunisia	2.2	3.1	6.0	8.7	9.8	13.8
Turkey	1.9	2.6	5.5	7.0	7.1	11.1

Source: UNESCO, *Statistical Yearbook,* 1989.

laws and free schools; the two countries with the lowest GNP per capita, Egypt and Morocco, have had the greatest difficulty in expanding educational opportunities and reducing gender disparities. Insufficient educational facilities limit children's access to education, and participation rates reflect this scarcity.

Gender Disparities

Notwithstanding the increases in female enrollments, gender disparities persist throughout the education system (table 4-5). For example, although Tunisia was second only to Turkey in extending primary education to girls, the gender gap was still wide in 1987, at 19 percentage points. Egypt, which had the third highest female enrollment rate at the tertiary level after Jordan and Kuwait, had the widest gender gap, at 14 percentage points. Except in Jordan, the gender gap was lower at the tertiary level than at either the primary or secondary level.

The lower educational attainment of girls and women has been a result of low enrollments combined with high attrition and repetition of grades. A growing body of literature shows that girls are more likely than boys to drop out of school before they complete the cycle, especially in rural areas. Research on Egypt, Morocco, Tunisia, and several other countries documents this pattern.[1] The reverse is true of Kuwait and Saudi Arabia, where girls in primary and secondary school have had consistently lower dropout and repetition rates than boys. This pattern has led their governments and education planners to conclude that the internal efficiency of girls' education is higher than that of males (Arab Bureau of Education in the Gulf States 1983; Saudi Arabia 1985).

Table 4-5. *The Gender Gap in Gross Enrollment Rates, Selected Countries in the Middle East and North Africa, 1987*
(percentage points)

	Primary		Secondary		Tertiary	
Rank	Country	Gap	Country	Gap	Country	Gap
1	Jordan	−1	Jordan	2	Kuwait	−9.1
2	Kuwait	3	Kuwait	5	Saudi Arabia	2.7
3	Turkey	8	Tunisia	12	Tunisia	3.2
4	Saudi Arabia	13	Morocco	13	Turkey	6.0
5	Tunisia	19	Saudi Arabia	17	Morocco	6.2
6	Egypt	21	Egypt	21	Jordan	8.3
7	Morocco	29	Turkey	23	Egypt	13.8

Source: Computed from table 4-3

Generally, secondary education in Middle Eastern and North African countries is of three types: general academic, teacher training, and vocational or technical. The latter is divided further into industrial, commercial, agricultural, nursing, and domestic sciences. Table 4-6 provides statistics on the distribution of female secondary school enrollment among the three main types of programs.

Between 1975 and 1985 a remarkable increase occurred in female secondary education enrollment in all seven countries, leading to changes in its composition. Despite the shifts, most female as well as male secondary school students are enrolled in college-preparatory academic programs; the shares range from 75 percent of female secondary students in Egypt to more than 98 percent in Kuwait and Saudi Arabia. The predominance of girls in this type of program is a result of its prestige. Only those with the highest grades are admitted from the intermediate secondary graduating classes; it is considered the appropriate education for bright, hard-working, ambitious girls. The proportion of girls who enter the scientific track in preparation for college is relatively high. Not all those who enter secondary school complete the cycle, however, and not all who complete it achieve the grades required for college admission.

A large share of the girls enrolled in vocational education study domestic sciences. About 50 percent of female secondary school enrollment in Turkey is in this field. Enrollment in secondary teacher

Table 4-6. *Enrollment of Girls, by Type of Secondary Education, Selected Countries in the Middle East and North Africa, 1975 and 1986–87*
(percentage of total secondary enrollment)

Country	Year	General education	Teacher education	Vocational education
Egypt	1975	81.1	1.9	17.0
	1987	74.8	3.7	21.5
Jordan	1975	97.0	0.0	3.0
	1987	91.9	0.0	8.1
Kuwait	1975	100.0	0.0	0.0
	1987	100.0	0.0	0.0
Morocco	1975	95.8	1.2	3.0
	1987	98.9	0.0	0.9
Saudi Arabia	1975	93.9	6.1	0.3
	1986	97.7	2.3	0.0
Tunisia	1975	73.5	0.9	26.5
	1987	83.4	1.5	15.6
Turkey	1975	78.7	4.5	16.5
	1987	81.1	0.3	18.6

Source: UNESCO, *Statistical Yearbook,* 1990.

training has declined in Jordan, Kuwait, and Morocco because the training of primary school teachers has been upgraded to the junior college level.

The issue of girls' limited access to vocational and technical education in Arab countries has been addressed at numerous regional conferences and at two special UNESCO conferences, the first in Algeria in 1964 (UNESCO 1964) and the second in Kuwait in 1969 (UNESCO 1969). The concerns expressed at those conferences persist, and the recommendations are still valid. Participants at the 1969 conference attributed the situation to dominant attitudes concerning the nature and aptitudes of women and the types of work suitable for them (El-Ghannam 1970). Sex-role stereotypes limit the supply of vocational education for girls, and the low status of vocational education depresses the demand for existing programs. The attitude that a woman's place is in the home prevails, obviating the need for job-related vocational and technical education. At the same time, the stigma attached to vocational education as a repository for the untalented discourages those who may need it from enrolling.

These attitudes are strongest in Kuwait and Saudi Arabia. Female access to vocational education in both of these countries is negligible; it is generally limited to sewing and tailoring schools and nursing institutes. Because of their unique situation, Kuwait and Saudi Arabia are not included in the following discussion. It should be noted, however, that in recent years Saudi Arabia has faced mounting pressure from female secondary school graduates who wish to enter colleges and universities. In response, officials have been considering offering vocational education to prepare women for work in factories patterned after the sweatshops of the West, so that women can use their "nimble little fingers" in traditional textile and garment industries.

A series of surveys carried out by the UNESCO National Commission in various countries, including Jordan and Turkey, formed the basis of a study on gender differences in secondary school curricula in 1981. The surveys found that many of the differences reflected perceived social norms rather than individual abilities or interests. This situation was the main hurdle facing girls in education. Although both boys and girls in Jordan took the same courses, girls tended to become typists or secretaries, whereas boys looked for jobs in management or continued on to the university or to polytechnic institutes. The new comprehensive schools that were introduced experimentally to integrate general academic and vocational subjects had not avoided these gender disparities. In boys' schools a wide range of traditional male vocational subjects was offered; in contrast, the girls' school in Amman offered traditional female subjects—dressmaking, art, ceramics, childcare, and hairdressing. The girls studied all these subjects in the first year and specialized in the last two years (UNESCO 1983).

Other types of vocational training followed gender lines as well. In trade schools that were not part of the formal secondary cycle in Jordan, boys learned traditional subjects, whereas girls learned home economics along with twenty-four hours of "practical" subjects, including beauty culture, dressmaking, and ceramics (Cameron and others 1983). In the vocational schools run by the United Nations Relief and Work Agency, similar curriculum stereotypes prevailed.

Inadequate vocational education places women at a disadvantage in the job market. Several researchers have found that in most of these countries many women have had to settle for low-paying, low-status jobs because they lacked the skills needed to get other work (Hammam 1981; Hatem 1983; Rihani 1983).

The concentration of girls in general secondary education is reflected in their distribution among the various academic disciplines at the postsecondary level. They tend to enter traditionally female fields—the humanities, social sciences, and education (table 4-7). Nonetheless, because cultural values encourage women to enter occupations that serve other women and because Muslims are averse to the treatment of female patients by male doctors, women are well represented in medicine in all seven countries. Also, because they have good access to mathematics and science courses at the secondary level in many Middle Eastern countries, women are better represented in

Table 4-7. *Female Enrollment in Higher Education, Overall and in Selected Fields of Study and Selected Countries in the Middle East and North Africa, 1987*
(percentage of total enrollment)

Country	Total	Education and teacher training	Commerce and business administration	Home economics	Natural science	Medicine and health-related sciences	Engineering
Egypt	34	46	31	79	40	39	13
Jordan	50	73	39	—	46	52	16
Kuwait	55	76	60	—	54	66	31
Morocco	33	28	51	—	28	33	12
Saudi Arabia[a]	39	52	—	—	37	42	17
Tunisia	37	30	41	43	38	54	12
Turkey	33	45	30	97	45	40	17

— Not available.

a. 1985 data.

Source: UNESCO, *Statistical Yearbook*, 1990.

engineering and natural sciences in these countries than they are in many Western nations.

Education Policy

The extent of development of an education system is revealed by the history, range, and type of its institutions and their distribution, as well as by the literacy rate and educational attainment of the adult population. Some Middle Eastern countries have well-developed education systems that go back more than a century; others have less developed and more recent ones. Generally, the more developed and diversified the education system, the better are the educational opportunities for girls and women. Oil has transformed this relationship, however, giving the wealthy states an edge over the poor ones. The oil-rich countries may not offer as much educational diversity as the better-developed systems do, but they are catching up quickly.

The old concept of education as a prelude to government employment, inherited from the colonial era, has had a depressing effect on the supply of girls' educational facilities. Despite laws making education compulsory and proclamations about the right of all citizens to an education, governments designed education for job preparation and accorded a lower priority to educating females because most of them did not enter the labor force. In the 1970s this concept was replaced by a new and more sophisticated one: manpower planning as an approach to education. Governments, with the help of education planners and international consultants, shifted their attention to preparing young men for mid-level and high-level jobs required for industrialization and modernization. The result was an emphasis on secondary and higher education and the relative neglect of mass primary education. Governments also emphasized vocational and technical education for boys, whereas girls had to content themselves with home economics classes that prepared them for domestic responsibilities.

The education policies of Middle Eastern and North African countries can be categorized as either general or gender-specific (Klein 1987). General policies apply to all children equally; all countries in the region have easily identifiable general education policies. Gender-specific policies may be directed toward gender differentiation or toward gender equity, depending on their intention and on how they affect the education of girls and women. Where such policies exist in this region, they are directed toward differentiation rather than equity. To date, no Middle Eastern or North African country has issued policies designed specifically to promote gender equity, such as the affirmative action policies of the United States and the United Kingdom. Where gender-specific policies are not explicit, however, they are often implicit in educational practices.

Compulsory Education

Legislation mandating compulsory education has not guaranteed that girls will have equal access to education. The countries that enacted such legislation earliest were Egypt (in 1923) and Turkey (in 1924). Although both countries set target dates for achieving universal primary education—1970 in Egypt and 1972 in Turkey—Egypt kept extending the date and has yet to approach the goal, whereas Turkey made a national commitment to enforce compulsory education laws on social and political grounds. The Turkish government saw primary education as fundamental to democracy and as a key channel for promoting modernization (Szyliowicz 1973).

In the 1960s and 1970s, many economists and institutions, including the World Bank, believed that primary education was not as important in promoting development as higher levels of education (see Harbison and Myers 1964; World Bank 1974). Reflecting this viewpoint, Szyliowicz (1973) criticized the Turkish policy because of its massive requirements for fiscal and human resources and because of a fear that it would lead to further deterioration in educational quality. Yet Turkey succeeded in reducing illiteracy rates (to 12 percent for males and 36 percent for females in 1985) and in raising the educational level of its people. Not so Egypt, which continues to suffer from high illiteracy rates among both men and women, especially in rural areas, according to survey estimates. Hartley and Swanson (1986) note that compulsory education laws were not enforced in Egyptian schools and that they were "probably unenforceable" because of inadequate facilities.

Compulsory education laws are ineffectual unless enforced and supported by adequate finances and facilities. Otherwise, they only serve as a shield against allegations of discrimination. If it is to raise the educational standard of girls and women, Egypt must firmly commit itself to expanding girls' access to basic primary education, to improving the quality of that education, and to reducing dropout and grade repetition. These goals cannot be accomplished without political support (El-Ghannam 1970, quoted in Chamie 1983; Silliman 1987).

Open Admissions

All seven of these countries have liberal open admission policies, especially for general secondary schools and most institutions of higher learning. Entrance is based on student scores in highly competitive national examinations. Although in theory these policies apply regardless of gender, class, or other characteristics, they do not guarantee equity in practice because educational motivation and achievement are strongly influenced by students' socioeconomic status.

Furthermore, an open admission policy cannot compensate for the lack of girls' schools in small towns and remote rural areas.

An open admission policy does not apply to all types of education. Gender-specific policies restrict or prohibit, explicitly or implicitly, female access to certain types of secondary vocational and technical schooling and to certain fields of higher education. These policies are based on a belief in innate gender differences and on prevailing notions about appropriate male and female educational and occupational spheres. Among the seven countries, Saudi Arabia has the most explicit gender-specific differentiation policies, and it is the only Islamic country that has completely separate systems of male and female education. Nevertheless, it continues to expand women's curriculum choices in higher education.

Free Education

All seven countries provide free education to everyone from the primary through the tertiary, and even graduate, levels. Moreover, some provide scholarships and low-cost dormitory facilities at the university level. In principle, this policy should ensure access to those from the lower socioeconomic groups, but free education is not enough, especially at the primary level. Parents of millions of children, mostly female, still cannot afford the other direct and indirect costs of schooling: clothing and shoes, books and school supplies, and fees for private tutors, now a necessity in most education systems because of crowded classrooms and declining educational quality. Schooling also has opportunity costs—that is, the income and other benefits of productive or learning activities at home that are forgone in favor of school attendance.

Free or publicly subsidized postprimary education (especially at the university level) can run counter to the expansion of primary education. Furthermore, it favors the urban bourgeoisie and helps perpetuate the elitist orientation of education (Coombs 1985; Psacharopoulos 1977; Psacharopoulos and Woodhall 1985; Todaro 1985).

Emphasis on Academic Education

The policy of free and open admissions, as well as an emphasis on certification and degrees leading to jobs in the modern sector, have created a dysfunctional imbalance in Middle Eastern and North African education systems that has had important implications for female education. Two manifestations of this imbalance are the emphasis on general rather than vocational and technical education and the emphasis on higher education at the expense of basic primary education.

At the same time, access to higher education has opened new opportunities for women, as documented by statistics and research showing
the advanced position of Middle Eastern women in higher education
compared with those in other developing countries.[2] Moreover, an
examination of the data on the number of students in higher education per 100,000 inhabitants in 1987 reveals that, in relation to their
respective populations, Jordan and Kuwait had more women in higher
education than either Japan or the United Kingdom (table 4-8).

Much of this success in expanding higher education was achieved
through costly subsidies and at the expense of basic primary education. The spread of higher education has created an elite group of
women as well as men and has widened the gap between them and
illiterate females (El-Sanabary 1973, 1985).

Cultural and Religious Influences

The body of literature developed over the past fifteen years documents changes in the position of women in various Islamic countries,
primarily as a result of the spread of modern education. Nonetheless,
misconceptions about Middle Eastern and Muslim women persist because of a lack of appreciation of the complex socioeconomic forces

Table 4-8. *Enrollment in Higher Education, Selected Countries,
1975, 1980, and 1987*
(per 100,000 inhabitants)

Country	Male			Female		
	1975	1980	1987	1975	1980	1987
Middle East and North Africa						
Egypt	1,821	2,372	2,485	808	1,103	1,086
Jordan	594	1,313	1,877	313	1,183	2,096
Kuwait	635	739	1,110	1,009	1,330	1,758
Morocco	426	892	1,214	97	267	607
Saudi Arabia	555	882	1,237	154	403	917
Tunisia	536	696	714	191	297	434
Turkey	1,348	805	1,322	269	246	700
Other countries						
France	2,101	—	2,394	1,845	—	2,395
Germany, Fed. Rep.	2,168	2,447	3,273	1,241	1,566	2,123
Japan	2,773	2,820	2,636	1,284	1,333	1,507
United Kingdom	1,716	1,924	2,099	920	1,056	1,735
U.S.S.R.	2,045	—	1,772	1,803	—	1,876

— Not available.
Note: Data for Jordan are for 1985; data for Saudi Arabia are for 1986.
Source: UNESCO, *Statistical Yearbook,* 1990.

that affect women's status in the region. Unfortunately, empirical evidence about the effects of cultural traditions and values on the education of females in Islamic countries is scarce, except for a few attitudinal studies on Egypt, Jordan, Morocco, and Tunisia.

The strongest indictment of Islam as the cause of the gender disparities in education in Muslim countries comes from Finn, Dulberg, and Reis (1979), who conclude that "in no major portion of the world is the noneducation of females so much a purposeful part of religious and social custom as it is in the Middle East," and that "education is contrary to the social pressure for Muslim women to become wives and mothers." Smock and Youssef (1977) echo this viewpoint. It is true that the record of Muslim countries on women's education compared with the record of non-Muslim countries has been generally wanting. Contrary to the Western stereotype, however, no inherent bias against educating girls and women exists in these countries.[3] In support of female education, Muslims quote the saying of the Prophet: "The search for knowledge is the duty of every Muslim, man or woman." Within Islamic culture, however, certain attitudes and traditions inhibit female education. Muslims have a strong concern for the modesty and safety of girls and women; a desire to guard their honor is evident in their seclusion and veiling. Abu Zahra (1970), Antoun (1968), Mernissi (1987), and Saadawi (1985) provide insight into the workings of this system and the limitations it imposes on the private and public roles of women. It is Arab cultural traditions, rather than Islam itself, that have constrained girls' education (Othman 1964). Evidence of these traditions includes opposition to coeducation and to the presence of male teachers in girls' schools, resistance to sending girls to schools away from home, and pressures on girls to marry at an early age.

Prevailing sex-role stereotypes and the division of labor in the home and marketplace also put a lower value on educating girls than on educating boys. Socialization starts at a very early age and continues during the early years of schooling and beyond (Safilios-Rothschild 1986). From the moment of birth, sons are regarded more highly than daughters, although attitudes vary across classes and communities. Very little research is available on the dynamics of this process, however. Saadawi (1985), writing about Egypt, and Mernissi (1987), writing about Morocco, have detailed the sharp distinction between male and female socialization from a feminist perspective and have discussed the negative effects on girls' self-esteem and aspirations. In addition, Patai (1973) has argued that the Arab world has no childrearing practices, only boy- and girl-rearing practices. Middle Eastern girls are socialized into accepting that marriage and raising a family is their ultimate goal. Schools reinforce gender roles. The prevailing attitude is that a woman should stay home to care for her family while her male guardian—husband, father, brother, or older son—supports her. This division of responsibility obviates the need for women to be educated or to join the labor force to earn a living. Perhaps as a result of this dependence, Middle Eastern women are accorded a lower social and economic status than are males.

Fear of the greater independence of thought and action that women gain through education was a concern in Egypt in the 1950s and 1960s and in Saudi Arabia in the 1980s. The assertiveness, self-esteem, and belief in gender equality that education may foster in women threaten those who espouse a traditional belief in male superiority. According to Nelson (1968), "the dilemma for both men and women is how to reconcile the man's self-image as dominant authority to the woman's emerging self-image as an equal."

Recently, significant if somewhat contradictory changes have taken place in these attitudes toward women in all Middle Eastern and North African countries. Although observers fear that the emergence of so-called Islamic fundamentalism signals a reversal of women's progress and a return to the home, the impact of this trend on women's status, role, and education has yet to be ascertained. Veiled girls and women are able to participate as students even on coeducational campuses (El-Guindi 1981). To many Middle Easterners, veiling has been a way of reconciling the public and private spheres of women. As Egyptian and other Middle Eastern women venture into the public spheres of education and employment, they have found ingenious ways to bridge the two worlds and accommodate new opportunities within traditional cultural and Islamic values.

The persistence of traditional attitudes and values calls for caution when arguing for reforms in women's education and employment. Care must be taken in the use of phrases such as liberation of women, equality of men and women, economic independence, and reduction of fertility because they have negative connotations, especially among conservative parents and educators. Phrases such as providing equality of educational opportunities, enhancing the welfare of the family, and acquiring income-generating skills that contribute to family welfare are less threatening and more likely to enlist support. Policymakers, educators, and parents are unlikely to challenge a woman's basic right to education. Anything that threatens family stability or the welfare of children, however, including a reduction in fertility, is likely to be seen as cultural encroachment by the West.

Family Influence

As the basic social unit, the family has ultimate authority over its members, especially the young and the females. Decisions regarding education, career, marriage, and even childrearing are a family affair. Parents' attitudes, expectations, and the support they provide for their daughters' educational and occupational aspirations depend on the family's socioeconomic status and specific characteristics. Whether parents demand education for their children is determined not only by their attitudes and values but also by their assessment of the cost and the outcome of educational choices. Under certain circumstances, parents may feel that the anticipated returns on their investment in a daughter's education do not justify the expected cost, and they will prefer income-generating activities or marriage.

Family Income

A family's socioeconomic status influences a daughter's education directly through financial and moral support for schooling and indirectly through a set of variables that includes the daughter's physical, cognitive, and psychological development as well as her own motivation, aspirations, and expectations. Girls and women from middle-income and upper-income families are more likely than those from low-income families to enter school and progress all the way to the university level.

Wealthy families are able to enroll their daughters in public or private schools, at home or abroad. Before Saudi Arabia opened its first public girls' school in 1960, many well-off families sent their daughters to public and private schools in Egypt and Lebanon. These families were also the first to take advantage of university education for women when it became available at home (El-Sanabary 1988). Throughout the Middle East and North Africa, girls and women are a majority of the students in private schools and colleges, proof that well-off families place a high value on their daughters' education and will support them in expensive institutions. Egyptian parents working as professionals in the oil-rich Gulf states are able to place their children in private schools and provide them with extensive tutoring for the British general competency examination (GCE) required for admission to college. Many of these children are able to bypass the secondary education cycle by succeeding on this examination and entering an Egyptian university or the American University of Cairo right after the intermediate education level.

In contrast, many working-class families cannot even afford to send their children to free public schools. They find the cost of such necessities as books, supplies, clothes, and transportation too high; moreover, they often need their children at home to care for siblings. In urban slums and rural areas, parents' demand that daughters engage in domestic and farm labor is a significant barrier to female education.

Daughters from a working-class background are more likely to enroll in vocational education, nursing, and teacher training institutes than in general academic programs at the secondary level or in professional programs at the tertiary level (El-Sanabary 1983; Howard-Merriam 1979). Nonacademic secondary schools provide access to paid jobs. Professional higher education, although prestigious, takes longer and is costly, even when heavily subsidized. Female students in engineering, medicine, and other professional programs are likely to come from wealthy families (El-Sanabary 1985; Howard-Merriam 1979, 1981; Moore 1980; Papanek 1985). For example, Egyptian engineers tend to have an "elite social origin," and female engineers come from an even wealthier family background than do men (Moore 1980).[4]

Rural Residence

About half the population of Middle Eastern and North African countries lives in rural areas—53 percent in Morocco and Turkey, 52 percent in Egypt—and some countries have sizable nomadic groups. Girls and women who live in rural areas or belong to nomadic groups are educationally handicapped by their gender, place of residence, and class. Their enrollment rates are consistently lower than those of urban populations.[5] The concentration of schools in the more affluent urban areas, cultural traditionalism among rural inhabitants, and the perception that formal education is irrelevant to agricultural activities place rural children at a disadvantage compared with urban children.

Girls who live in a rural community with no school may either commute daily to a school in a neighboring town or live away from home. The daily commute to school (either on foot or by undependable and often primitive transportation) may be costly and risky and so is not always an option for young village girls. Boarding near the school may not be an option either because rooms can be expensive and because social norms may keep young girls from living away from home.

The lower participation rates of girls in rural areas reflect both low rates of enrollment and high rates of attrition. In Morocco attrition and repetition occur in all primary grades but especially in the fifth (and final) grade. Youssef's (1978) research indicates that among Moroccan students who completed the primary level, only 10 percent did so without repeating a grade, 26 percent repeated once, and 42 percent repeated twice. Dropping out is also a serious problem in Morocco; the rate was estimated at 21 percent for boys and 28 percent for girls during the first year of primary school, and half of the rural children who entered primary school never completed the cycle. Similarly, Hartley and Swanson (1986) found that attrition rates were much higher in rural than in urban areas and among girls than among boys in Egypt.

Parents' Education

How much education a girl's parents have is probably the most important factor in determining her educational opportunities. Education tends to generate its own demand. Educated people want and appreciate education for their children and often push them to acquire at least as much education as they themselves have. Schooling norms become a tradition, and the social demand for education perpetuates itself from generation to generation (Psacharopoulos 1977). Educated parents are also more likely to have access to resources and information. A study of a sample of about 500 students at Kuwait University found that the majority came from families in which both parents knew at least how to read and write; only 14 percent had illiterate fathers and 28 percent had illiterate mothers (Al-Thaquib 1975). Cochrane, Mehra, and Osheba (1986) found that, holding income constant, parental education had the most influence on educational aspirations for children in both rural and urban areas in Egypt. The higher the educational attainment of the parents, the greater their aspirations for their children, and this effect was larger for daughters' than for sons' education (table 4-9). In rural families this intergenerational effect could imply an increase in education for daughters, which argues strongly for raising the level of education among girls in the present generation. Another study, this one in Jordan, found that the level of education attained by fathers was systematically associated with the schooling of daughters (Stuart 1981).

In one of the largest surveys of Egyptian students and their families, in the southern and western parts of Cairo, researchers found that

Table 4-9. *Effect of Parents' Education on Educational Aspirations for Daughters and Sons, Urban and Rural Egypt, 1980*
(regression coefficients)

Area	Father's aspirations		Mother's aspirations	
	For daughters	*For sons*	*For daughters*	*For sons*
Urban	0.22[a]	0.10[a]	0.11[a]	0.05
Rural	0.48[a]	0.22[a]	2.13[a]	0.98[b]

Note: The regression coefficients indicate the additional years of schooling parents would have wanted for a son or daughter if they themselves had one more year of schooling.

a. Statistical significance at 1 percent level.

b. Statistical significance at 5 percent level.

Source: Cochrane, Mehra, and Osheba 1986.

parents placed a high value on their daughters' education and made economic sacrifices to enable them to continue their studies. Most of the parents, almost 95 percent, intended to allow their daughters to pursue an education, and 84 percent of those wanted them to have a university education to prepare for prestigious jobs (Khattab 1984). For others, educating their daughters was compensation for their own lack of schooling. In many families the tradition of education was a deciding factor. Among the parents of limited means, 82 percent considered the cost of private tutors a burden on the family budget but were still willing to provide them to improve the scores of their daughters on the national examinations and to increase their chances of being admitted to a university. The girls also had high aspirations for their own education; most wanted to become doctors or engineers, the two most prestigious occupations.

In an Egyptian fertility survey, parents were asked what level of education they desired for their children (Egypt 1983).[6] Overall, three-fourths wanted a university education for their sons and more than half wanted the same for their daughters. The regional differences were very sharp, however (Cochrane, Mehra, and Osheba 1986). People in urban areas generally held high aspirations for both sons and daughters, but in rural upper Egypt interest in a daughter's education was dramatically lower. In a study of two rural communities in Egypt and Tunisia, parents strongly emphasized that education would lead their daughters to an office job and an easier life (Larson 1988). Similarly, a study of a sample of 100 nomadic, urban, and rural women in Saudi Arabia found that the majority of the urban women interviewed wanted their daughters to complete their education up to the university level (cited in Allaghi and Almana 1984). This finding was true even for recently settled illiterate women, although some of them did not understand the differences between the various levels of schooling.

Poverty continues to stand in the way of many families' aspirations for their children. Khattab (1984) noted that in Egypt lack of financial resources influenced parents to enroll their daughters in vocational education so that they could work after graduation and help support their families. More than half the forty-six respondents in this group indicated financial need as the reason their daughters did not pursue higher education, whereas early marriage was reported in only six cases.

A mother's education has a strong influence on her daughters' education. Educated mothers can help their children with their schoolwork, especially during the primary years. They also provide positive reinforcement of their children's educational and occupational achievement. Their standards and expectations for their daughters are different from those of uneducated mothers, and their daughters usually have greater confidence in their abilities to pursue an education (Bach and others 1985). Al-Thumali (1984) found that in Saudi Arabia the better educated a mother was, the greater her influence on her daughters' academic plans. A study of Arab university students in Egypt, Kuwait, and Lebanon found that daughters of educated mothers held less stereotypical sex-role attitudes than did daughters of uneducated mothers. A mother's work experience also had a positive effect on the attitudes of her sons and daughters (Lorfing and Abu Nasr 1985).

Basson (1981, 1982) reports that even within the same family, attitudes may differ toward girls' education. In Jordan many girls drop out of school because they are needed to help with domestic tasks or because villagers see twelve years of education as irrelevant to marriage. Often girls continue their schooling under harsh family circumstances. Although one daughter is taken out of school to help at home, another daughter in the same family may be sent to a teachers' college and her marriage delayed several years. Like her unmarried brothers, she is expected to contribute cash income to the household. The decision could depend on the daughter's birth order, school performance, or attitude toward learning; a highly motivated daughter may be difficult to dissuade from attending school. A family may also expect her education to result in such tangible benefits as a job or better marriage prospects.

Family Size

Because family size is associated with other factors, including a family's income and parents' (especially mother's) education and occupation, evidence of how it affects girls' education is scarce and inconclusive. It has been suggested, however, that the smaller the family, the greater the chance that daughters will enter school and remain there. Small families, even those of modest means, may not have to choose whether to educate a daughter or a son. A study of parents' aspirations for their children found that larger families with children under thirteen years of age had lower aspirations for the education of their children, especially their daughters, than did smaller families (Cochrane, Mehra, and Osheba 1986). In another study, also in Egypt, the number of children in the family affected how much praise a child received at home and how self-confident the child felt (Bach and others 1985). These findings are consistent with those of Rosen (1961), who argues that in a smaller family parents are able to spend more time with each child, thus enhancing their children's verbal and cognitive development and consequently their educational attainments (cited in Bach and others 1985).

Despite the positive effects of small family size on schooling, this factor may be insignificant in wealthy families or in poor families if elderly family members can relieve a girl from domestic responsibilities. In affluent Kuwait, among a large sample of students at Kuwait University, 67 percent came from families with seven or more members and 20 percent from families with four to six members (Al-Thaquib 1975). The same link has been established by research in Taiwan (China) and in Botswana (Chamie 1983).

Women's Participation in the Labor Force

One of the main functions of education is to prepare young people for their adult roles. Women's roles in the family and in the paid labor force have important implications for their education. The pattern of female participation in the work force is reflected in the goals and orientation of women's education. Both policymakers and parents base their decisions, in part, on the perceived links between education and employment.

Despite the growing numbers of Middle Eastern and North African women who work outside the home in formal and nonformal occupations, women's rates of participation in the paid labor force are low compared with rates in other countries. For example, in 1975 the percentage of economically active females in the modern sector ranged from 3 percent in Jordan to 8 percent in Morocco. Moreover, women are often concentrated in traditionally female fields of employment, such as education, medicine, and social welfare (Azzam 1979; Hammam 1986; Youssef 1974, 1976–77). In practice, women have played and continue to play a vital role in the agricultural and nontraditional work force, either as unpaid family workers or as small-scale business owners (Basson 1981; Hammam 1986; Hatem 1983; Larson 1988). Large variations exist in the region both in the types of positions open to women and in attitudes toward their employment. Conditions range from the quite open and often mixed workplaces in Egypt to the strictly gender-segregated workplaces in Saudi Arabia.[7] Traditional attitudes continue to prevail in most of these countries, favoring occupations with minimal intermingling of the sexes.

Although the potential for women to participate in the labor force influences the family's decision regarding education options for daughters, no systematic study has tried to measure the magnitude of this effect or to identify which families are likely to respond to labor market opportunities for women. In Saudi Arabia, by law, women's employment is limited to teaching, social welfare, and medicine. This severely restricts the educational choices open to women. This extreme situation does not apply in the other six countries. Moreover, although this restriction shapes the professional choices of Saudi women who acquire a higher education, it may or may not affect the educational attainment of those who do not continue beyond secondary school.

School Factors

Although school inputs—including type of school, curricula, textbooks, and teachers—influence girls' and women's school enrollment and performance, their impacts have not been systematically tested. Empirical evidence exists for the effect of distance to school, but very little is available on other school factors. Most studies examine the effect of a given school characteristic in isolation (through simple tabulations), thus preventing an assessment of the importance of these characteristics in relation to each other and to family or community factors.

School Location

As pointed out earlier, the availability of a school in the local community increases girls' enrollment. Cochrane, Mehra, and Osheba (1986) found that, in rural areas of Egypt the distance to a secondary school is negatively associated both with the aspirations of parents for their children's education and with the probability of a child's attending secondary school. Interviews with parents in Egypt, Morocco, and Tunisia indicated a reluctance to send their daughters to distant schools because of the moral or physical risks involved (Allman 1978, 1979; Basson 1981). This reluctance applies whether the girl would commute or live in boarding facilities. Some reluctance is also due to the fact that daughters may be needed at home to help with domestic or farm work.

School Type and Physical Characteristics

Because of prevailing social and religious values, Islamic countries oppose coeducation, especially at the secondary level. Parents and policymakers are concerned about the behavior of adolescent girls and boys in a mixed environment. Attitudes and policies vary, however, among countries and socioeconomic groups. Saudi Arabia prohibits coeducation beyond kindergarten, but in Tunisia and Turkey coeducation is prevalent at all levels. In the other four countries, the general pattern is single-sex schools at the secondary level and both coeducational and single-sex schools at the primary and tertiary levels. Coeducational private schools, in which female students outnumber males, are found in all these countries. Coeducational schools usually have both female and male teachers and administrators, whereas single-sex schools usually have teachers and administrators of the same gender as the students. None of the seven countries has women teachers in boys' intermediate or secondary schools, but several countries allow men to teach in girls' schools.

How does the prevalence of single-sex schools affect female access to education and the quality and outcome of their educational experience? After reviewing several studies on coeducation in primary schooling in developing countries, Chamie (1983) concluded that the negative impact which was detected results in part from the problems faced by governments in providing separate schools and in recruiting female teachers for girls' schools. In areas where education authorities have to provide separate but equal facilities for males and females, particularly in sparsely populated areas and villages, girls' schools or schools with more than a few primary grades are often lacking. Attempts to solve this problem by adopting coeducation may be counterproductive. The reluctance of some Arab governments to ratify the UNESCO Convention against Discrimination in Education may have stemmed from the inclusion of a clause urging member states "to adopt the practice of coeducation in first and second level education as one means of ensuring equality of access to education" (El-Sanabary 1973).

Single-sex schools are not necessarily discriminatory, according to UNESCO (1966), "so long as the same number of places is offered to pupils of each sex, and the conditions under which instruction is given are equal." In many countries in the region, this is a costly proposition. Only in Kuwait and Saudi Arabia has this option been implemented on a large scale. In Kuwait almost as many girls as boys attend secondary school, and more girls than boys go on to get a higher education. In Saudi Arabia much progress has been made in narrowing the gender gap. The success of Kuwait and Saudi Arabia stems from their oil wealth, which makes it possible to absorb the costs imposed by cultural values and gender segregation. It is probably fair to say that the issue in most countries is not whether schools are single-sex or coeducational but whether an adequate number of schools exists at all.

Many girls' schools in the poorer countries of the region not only are in inferior physical condition but also lack specialized educational and recreational facilities such as libraries, laboratories, boarding facilities, and cafeterias. Well-supervised boarding facilities, for example, are important in attracting girls from remote areas. As part of its massive effort to make primary education universal in the early 1970s, the government of Turkey set up regional boarding facilities for children from sparsely populated areas. This measure can be expected to be effective with girls in secondary schools and colleges, although not with younger girls. Boarding facilities are essential at teacher training and nursing institutes.

Single-sex schools frequently offer a narrower range of curriculum options. The offerings, which usually vary from school to school, depend in large part on the availability of trained teachers of the same gender as the students. Because girls and boys compete on the same national examinations, the possibility of curriculum choice along gender lines is reduced. Western research has documented that girls in single-sex schools are less likely than girls in coeducational schools to make stereotypical career choices because of the emphasis on competition and excellence in all subjects and because of identification with strong role models such as female mathematics and science teachers and female principals.

In Middle Eastern and North African countries, girls who choose science subjects have an equal or better than equal chance of success in these subjects compared with boys. Girls have consistently achieved higher examination scores than boys, especially on the General Secondary Education Examination, in several Arab countries, including Jordan, Kuwait, and Saudi Arabia. A study of two rural secondary schools in Jordan recounted that 56 percent of the girls and 46 percent of the boys passed the General Secondary Education Examination—results that paralleled the scores for the whole country in 1983 (Layne 1984). In Saudi Arabia a survey of 1,992 students, 222 teachers, and 36 principals documented that girls outperformed boys academically in both science and literary subjects (Endargeeri 1986). Similar findings come from Kuwait, where girls achieved significantly better results than boys in all science subjects but worse results in mathematics (Al-Methen and Wilkenson 1988). Hypotheses offered to explain this outcome are (a) that girls spend more time studying than boys, who have more personal freedom; (b) that girls need to excel on these examinations to gain access to universities; and (c) that girls who make it to secondary schools are a more select group than boys—that is, on average, they come from better-off families and have greater ability than the male students.

As in other areas of research on women's education in Islamic countries, little hard data exist on the effects of coeducation and single-sex schools on achievement. A study of the effect of single-sex schools on fear of success and sex-role orientation among a sample of 626 Jordanian community college students found no difference in motivation between males and females. The students in coeducational institutions, however, revealed more stereotyped attitudes (Al-Nhar 1986).

Because the effects of single-sex schools on curriculum choice and achievement appear to be positive, no valid reason exists to question their academic viability. Instead, the challenge is to ensure quality in both girls' and boys' schools.

Stereotypes in School Textbooks

Much has been written about sex-role stereotypes in school textbooks and their effect on educational and occupational aspirations and choices. Two studies on this subject, one in Arab countries (Abu Nasr, Lorfing, and Mikati 1983) and another in Egypt only (Mohamed 1985), corroborated the many research findings but with a slight variation.[8] In Arabic textbooks the most important roles cited for females were mother and little girl; the role of wife was mentioned less often and mostly in Saudi Arabian textbooks. Women in other roles (such as widow, older daughter, fighter, fantasy woman, princess, historical figure, slave, witch, aunt, cousin, and neighbor) figured in less than 10 percent of all portrayals. Working women were engaged in traditional feminine occupations—teaching, nursing, pediatrics, dressmaking, administration of girls' schools, textile factory work, domestic help, and agricultural work. References to working women were most frequent (22 percent of all references to females) in the former People's Democratic Republic of Yemen, where they were presented as shouldering the dual burden of domestic and agricultural work. In Egypt and Tunisia women as workers made up 16 percent and 11 percent, respectively, of the references. Although the Tunisian textbooks referred to mothers engaged in income-generating activities because of pressing economic need, the division of labor was clear: mothers were baking cakes at home for their sons to sell in the market.

The textbooks stressed such desirable feminine traits as weakness, sensitivity, submissiveness, dependency, and self-sacrifice. Women were seen to derive their identity and status from conformity to gender-based role expectations as caring mother, dutiful wife, and obedient daughter. Mohamed (1985) concluded from a study of Arabic elementary reading textbooks that they did not reflect the changing roles of women in Egyptian society, nor were women present in equal proportion to their numbers in the population (they were only 20 percent of the characters portrayed in these books). Such textbooks perpetuate the predominant sex-role stereotypes and may limit girls' educational and occupational aspirations and choices.

Women Teachers

Where schools are segregated by gender, the availability and quality of female teachers crucially affect female enrollment, achievement, and attainment. Despite their predominance in teacher training institutes and teachers' colleges in the countries studied, women are a minority of the teaching force in this region, especially beyond the primary level (table 4-10). The number of female primary and secondary school teachers grew substantially between 1975 and 1987, more than tripling at the primary level in Morocco, Saudi Arabia, and Tunisia and more than doubling at the primary level in Egypt, Jordan, and Kuwait. Turkey, which by 1987 had achieved universal primary enrollment, showed but a modest increase in female teachers.

Despite this progress, only in Jordan and Kuwait were women a majority of primary school teachers, and only in Kuwait were they more than 50 percent of secondary teachers, with Jordan a close second at 49 percent. Women were only about one-third of all secondary teachers in the remaining five countries in 1987.

The same factors that have depressed women's access to schooling have restricted their access to and persistence in a teaching career. These factors vary from one country to another and from one area to another in the same country. They include cultural attitudes, financial constraints, increasing devaluation of the teaching profession (especially at the primary level), difficulty in recruiting and retaining female teachers in rural and sparsely populated areas, lack of mobility of women because of family responsibilities or cultural considerations, and added difficulties when they are married. Despite the importance of female teachers for the quantitative and qualitative development of girls' education, no research has addressed the factors that influence supply or the problems that these teachers and their schools encounter because of special needs and circumstances.

In most Middle Eastern and North African countries, the marked educational expansion over the past few decades has not been

Table 4-10. *Percentage of Female Teachers at Primary and Secondary Levels, Selected Countries in the Middle East and North Africa, 1987*
(percent)

Country	Primary	Secondary
Egypt	49	34[a]
Jordan	67	49[b]
Kuwait	69	52
Morocco	35	29
Saudi Arabia	46	43
Tunisia	42	30
Turkey	42	37
All countries	50	39

a. 1986 data.
b. 1988 data.
Source: UNESCO, *Statistical Yearbook,* 1990.

matched by sustained initiatives to train teachers and administrators. Most countries have teacher shortages, especially in mathematics and science, foreign languages, and even native languages. The result is overcrowded classrooms and high pupil-teacher ratios, a reliance on male teachers in girls' schools in some countries, or even classes with no teachers. The nature and intensity of the problem vary from country to country. North African and Arabian Gulf states suffer greatly from shortages of indigenous teachers. In Morocco, for example, replacing European teachers with Moroccans, especially at the upper secondary level, has been a challenge since independence. In 1977–78, the ratio of native women teachers to all women teachers was less than one-third at the secondary level and two-thirds at the intermediate level (Cameron and others 1983).

Heavy reliance on expatriate teachers is also a problem in the oil-exporting Gulf states such as Kuwait and Saudi Arabia (El-Sanabary 1988; Meleis, El-Sanabary, and Beeson 1979). In 1979–80 in Saudi Arabia only 15 percent of all female teachers in intermediate and upper secondary schools were Saudis. These figures were expected to rise to 46 percent and 42 percent, respectively, by 1984–85, but whether this happened is not known (Saudi Arabia 1980). Saudization of primary teaching staff in girls' schools was realized by the mid-1980s, except in some rural areas where the output of local teacher training institutes has been insufficient to meet local needs and recruiting urban women as rural teachers has been difficult. At the intermediate and upper secondary levels, Saudi female teachers are in short supply because the teachers' colleges do not produce enough graduates to meet the demand, especially for foreign language and science teachers. At the same time, thousands of women graduate from colleges and universities with specializations that do not match existing needs. Reliance on expatriate teachers who do not understand local cultural traditions may hurt educational quality because of communication problems between teachers and students or because of the tendency of expatriates to compromise educational quality for the sake of their own work security (Birks and Rimmer 1984).

The need to juggle the double burden of work and domestic responsibilities accounts for the reported high rate of absenteeism and dropout (in Jordan and Saudi Arabia, for example) and the reduced productivity among female teachers. Rumaihi (1986) quotes a Saudi government report issued in 1981 as saying that an average of three women a day, both Saudi nationals and contract teachers, left their jobs in primary education. Where childcare is unavailable or inadequate, most women quit to look after their children.

Little has been done to address this problem, and the measures that have been taken may be creating new and serious problems. Before the

1950s only unmarried women could become teachers in Egypt. The government eventually abolished that policy and also issued maternity benefits. In Jordan, because of the high absenteeism of married teachers for maternity leave and other family reasons and because of the difficulty of finding substitutes, especially in remote areas, the Ministry of Education in 1965 prohibited the hiring of married women as teachers and pressured those already teaching to resign (Al-Tall 1979). This measure only exacerbated teacher shortages, and the regulation was canceled in 1967. Solving a serious problem by discriminatory measures worsens the teacher shortage, violates the human rights of married teachers, and discourages girls from enrolling in teacher training programs.

Most countries provide maternity leave and other benefits for childbirth and childrearing. Egypt, for example, allows a working mother up to six years of leave (no more than two years at one time) for childcare, with no loss of seniority and other benefits. What proportion of teachers in Egypt take advantage of these benefits and what provisions the government makes for substitute teachers are unknown. In Saudi Arabia absenteeism among female teachers and dropping out among women in teacher training programs are common, but no satisfactory solutions have been found. The Saudi government gives female teachers a six-week maternity leave that may be combined with a six-month sick leave on the recommendation of a physician. It also permits female teachers to resign for marriage or childrearing without giving a six-month notice, as is required of all other employees. This policy wastes the slender supply of female teachers and aggravates the continuing reliance on foreigners. Several Saudi writers have suggested more equitable solutions such as part-time teaching, job-sharing, and expansion of on-site childcare. Some women advocate a longer maternity leave, similar to that in effect in Egypt (El-Sanabary 1987).

Recent education studies have highlighted the importance of teacher-student interaction to pupil motivation, achievement, and attainment. Teachers often perpetuate sex-role stereotypes directly and indirectly through what they teach and through their behavior, their interactions with pupils, and their assumptions about the different skills and abilities of girls and boys (Whyte 1986). Female teachers may inspire girls to high achievement and accomplishment or direct them toward conformity with prevailing domestic ideals. Having qualified female teachers is important but not sufficient; they must also understand sex-role stereotypes and their potential effects. Female teachers, if adequately trained, can identify girls at risk of dropping out and provide the special care and encouragement needed to keep them in school.

Female Administrators

Female administrators play a central role in girls' schools in all Middle Eastern and North African countries, except in Tunisia, where they are very few. Through efficient management and leadership as well as support of female teachers and students, they can help improve the quality of girls' education. Unfortunately, many are unprepared to handle the absenteeism, dropping out, and lack of motivation that affect female students and teachers. With proper training and support, including being sensitized to these problems through printed materials and in-service training, female administrators would be better able to deal with these problems, thereby reducing attrition and improving educational quality.

Female school administrators, like their male counterparts, receive little if any preservice training, they are often overworked and underpaid, and they lack adequate resources. Many are less qualified academically than their male colleagues. In Jordan, for example, female principals in the mid-1970s were more likely than men to be graduates of secondary schools or teacher training institutes and less likely to have a college degree. These disparities reflect the different percentages of men and women who continue beyond secondary education and the different qualifications of teachers who are promoted to administrative posts. As with teachers, female principals participate less in in-service programs than do their male counterparts, who are more likely to learn of these programs and take advantage of them because of men's networks and greater access to resources.

Other School Factors

No firm evidence is available on other school-related factors that might affect the state of women's education. Most schools in rural areas lack basic instructional materials, even a chalkboard and chalk. Textbooks are unavailable, inefficiently distributed among students, or misused. In Egypt, where textbooks are distributed annually to students free of charge, many ultimately end up as wrapping paper in grocery stores. Audiovisual materials are unheard of, except in some schools in wealthy countries such as Kuwait and Saudi Arabia. Through external assistance, ironically, modern educational technology such as computers is being introduced on a limited scale in some rural schools. Such technology is not accessible or feasible for most schools, however. What are needed are simple, inexpensive, and readily available aids such as radios, posters, films, and instructional toys that can be produced cheaply and locally.

In the classroom, the emphasis on rote learning and theoretical constructs with no relevance to the realities of students' lives detracts from the appeal of attending school. This educational approach targets the hardworking and highly motivated students, ignores individual differences, and disregards children who need special assistance and support. Those most likely to suffer are girls who are poorly motivated and malnourished or who have other demands on their time. The crowded classrooms in most countries and the poor qualifications of many teachers, however, may leave no alternative to memorizing facts to be recalled on poorly formulated examinations.

Another deterrent to effective education is automatic promotion, which permits students to move up to the next grade without having acquired basic skills. Some countries have adopted this policy to reduce repetition at the primary level. Schooling under these circumstances becomes an exercise in futility, and discouraged children are then withdrawn from school. Most of the countries that have this policy also have a serious student attrition problem.

Lack of educational guidance and counseling services in the schools often leads to attrition or premature specialization. As UNESCO (1983) notes, guidance is frequently lacking or is provided too late to influence students' attitudes as well as their educational and career choices. Consequently, students and their parents make decisions on the basis of prevailing perceptions of women's roles and limited knowledge of educational and career options. The result may be loss of human talent and resources. Furthermore, female students at risk of dropping out go undetected and are permanently lost to the system.

Concluding Remarks

Despite the considerable progress by Middle Eastern and North African countries in improving female access to schools and educational attainment, serious problems remain and call for expedient solutions. The studies reviewed in this chapter illuminate the issues concerning female education and its socioeconomic context. They highlight the effects of economic development and income distribution, demographic patterns, education policies, religious and cultural values, sex-role stereotypes, the division of labor in the home and marketplace, socioeconomic and educational background of parents, and the availability and quality of schools and their physical characteristics and instructional programs. This research, however, does not weigh the relative significance of the various determinants or analyze them with scientific rigor.

Most governments in this region recognize the enormous educational problems, including gender disparities, and have undertaken various reforms. But they face tough decisions because of inadequate resources. Ironically, they often follow Western models that have proved unsuited to local needs and circumstances, sometimes with unintended results. For instance, the adoption of automatic promotion policies, as noted earlier, has led to deterioration of achievement; and the extension of compulsory education to eight years before achieving universal access to the six-year cycle has meant more education for some and less or none for others, mostly girls.

Very few of the education reforms, if any, are specifically directed to girls and women. Progress in female education has mostly been a by-product of these reforms, and the results have been mixed. The reforms have included expansion of educational facilities in rural areas, albeit slowly; diversification of school curricula and increased access to technical and vocational education (more so in some countries than others); school reorganization, including emphasis on basic primary education and the introduction of some comprehensive high schools that teach marketable skills; improvements in teaching methods and curriculum; upgrading training for primary school teachers from the secondary to the junior college level; and providing in-service training for teachers and administrators. Much more still needs to be done to enhance gender equity in education to benefit not only women but the whole society.

Education reform models and patterns must evolve from local circumstances and needs. Each country will have to clarify its goals and policies for female education and set priorities for educational objectives. Poor countries will need extensive external financial assistance to achieve these objectives, and richer countries may need help in identifying problems and mapping out solutions. Regional and international cooperation can be effective in encouraging and assisting Middle Eastern and North African countries to narrow the gender gap in education.

Notes

1. See Cochran (1986) and Hartley and Swanson (1986) for Egypt; Massialas and Jarrar (1983) and Youssef (1978) for Morocco; and Chamie (1983) and Deble (1980) for several other Middle Eastern countries.

2. Cochrane, Mehra, and Osheba (1986) note that in the Egyptian education system, higher education accounted for 17 percent of total school enrollment, compared with an average of about 4 percent for developing countries. The relatively high proportion of Middle Eastern women in higher education has also been pointed out by El-Sanabary (1973); Meleis, El-Sanabary, and Beeson (1979); and Youssef (1974, 1978).

3. A similar view is expressed by Marshall (1984): "Muslim women have been less involved in traditional agricultural and trading activities and have significantly lower rates of literacy, educational achievement, and nonagricultural labor force participation than women in other developing areas at similar stages of industrialization. This divergence has commonly been explained by

the religiocultural influence of Islam, which presumably mitigates the impact of social changes precipitated by the development process. While Islam has certainly affected the lifestyles of adherents of both sexes, this constant cultural factor is insufficient explanation for the considerable range of variation in national levels of female participation within the Muslim region."

4. In Egypt 65 percent of female engineers under the age of thirty-five came from the urban bourgeoisie and aristocracy (the top 11 percent of the country's population), compared with 41 percent of their male counterparts (Moore 1980).

5. The rural-urban disparities were noted by Youssef (1976–77) for Morocco; Szyliowicz (1973) for Turkey; El-Sanabary (1973) for Algeria, Libya, and Syria; and Massialas and Jarrar (1983) for the Arab countries in general.

6. This fertility survey has provided much of the data for the published research about parental effects on female education in Egypt.

7. For an overview of the employment of Arab women see Azzam, Abu Nasr, and Lorfing (1985, chapter 1).

8. The Arab regional study was conducted for UNESCO by researchers from the Institute of Women's Studies in Arab Countries, located in Lebanon. The researchers analyzed a sample of seventy-nine Arabic readers—fifty-two from Lebanon and the rest from Egypt, Kuwait, Qatar, Saudi Arabia, Tunisia, and the former People's Democratic Republic of Yemen. All were primary-level textbooks except for a number of intermediate-level textbooks in the Lebanese sample.

References

Abu Nasr, Julinda, I. Lorfing, and J. Mikati. 1983. *Identification and Elimination of Sex Stereotypes in and from School Textbooks: Some Suggestions for Action in the Arab World*. Paris: UNESCO.

Abu Zahra, N. 1970. "On the Modesty of Arab Muslim Villages: A Reply." *American Anthropologist* (Lebanon) 72.

Allaghi, Farida, and Aisha Almana. 1984. "Survey of Research on Women in the Arab Gulf Region." In UNESCO, *Social Science Research and Women in the Arab Countries*. London: Francis Pinter.

Allman, J., ed. 1978. *Women's Status and Fertility in the Muslim World*. New York: Praeger.

———. 1979. *Social Mobility, Education and Development in Tunisia*. Leiden, The Netherlands: E. J. Brill.

Al-Methen, A. E., and W. J. Wilkenson. 1988. "In Support of a Sociological Explanation of Sex Differences in Science and Mathematics Achievement: Evidence from a Kuwaiti Study of Secondary School Certificate Examinations." *Research in Science and Technological Education* 6(1):91–101.

Al-Nhar, Taisier. 1986. "Coeducational versus Single-Sex Schooling, Sex-Role Orientation and Fear of Success: Results from Jordan." Ph.D. diss. University of Pittsburgh, Pittsburgh, Pa.

Al-Tall, A. Y. 1979. *Education in Jordan*. Islamabad: National Book Foundation.

Al-Thaquib, F. T. 1975. "The Attitude of Kuwaitis toward Women in Contemporary Society." In *Studies of the Status of Women in Kuwait and the Arab Gulf*.

Proceedings of the Regional Conference on Women in Contemporary Society, Kuwait, April 1975. Kuwait: Women's Cultural and Social Organization,

Al-Thumali, S. A. 1984. "Family, Peer, and School Influences on Saudi Arabian High School Seniors' Undergraduate College Plans and Academic Majors." Ed.D. diss. University of Houston, Houston, Tex.

Antoun, Richard. 1968. "On the Modesty of Women in Arab Moslem Villages: A Study in the Accommodation of Tradition." *American Anthropologist* (Lebanon) 70(4).

Arab Bureau of Education in the Gulf States. 1983. *A Study of Education Attrition in the Arab Gulf States.* Riyadh.

Azzam, Henry T. 1979. "The Participation of Arab Women in the Labour Force: Development Factors and Policies." World Employment Programme Research, Population and Labour Policies Programme, Working Paper 80. Geneva: International Labour Office.

Azzam, H., J. Abu Nasr, and I. Lorfing. 1985. "An Overview of Arab Women in Population, Employment and Economic Development." In Julinda Abu Nasr, N. Khoury, and H. Azzam, eds., *Women, Employment and Development in the Arab World.* Berlin: Mouton.

Bach, Rebecca, Saah Gadallah, H. A. S. Khattab, and John Gulick. 1985. "Mother's Influence on Daughters' Orientations toward Education: An Egyptian Case Study." *Comparative Education Review* 29(3).

Basson, Priscilla. 1981. "Women and Traditional Food Technologies: Changes in Rural Jordan." *Ecology of Food and Nutrition* 11 (May).

————. 1982. "Domestic Productivity in Male and Female Headed Households of Rural Jordan." *Ecology of Food and Nutrition* 12:75–78.

Birks, J. S., and J. A. Rimmer. 1984. "Developing Education Systems in the Oil States of Arabia: Conflicts of Purpose and Focus." University of Durham Occasional Papers Series 21, Manpower and Migration Series 3. Durham, U.K.: Center for Middle Eastern and Islamic Studies.

Cameron, John, Robert Cowan, Martin McLean, and Brian Holmes. 1983. *International Handbook of Educational Systems.* Section B. *North Africa and the Middle East.* Chichester, U.K.: John Wiley and Sons.

Chamie, Mary. 1983. *National, Institutional and Household Factors Affecting Young Girls' School Attendance in Developing Societies.* Washington, D.C.: International Center for Research on Women and U.S. Agency for International Development.

Cochran, Judith. 1986. *Education in Egypt.* London: Croom Helm.

Cochrane, Susan H. 1979. *Fertility and Education: What Do We Really Know?* Baltimore, Md.: Johns Hopkins University Press.

Cochrane, Susan H., Kalpana Mehra, and Ibrahimaha T. Osheba. 1986. "The Educational Participation of Egyptian Children." EDT Discussion Paper 45. World Bank, Education and Training Department, Washington, D.C.

Coombs, Philip H. 1985. *The World Crisis in Education: The View from the Eighties.* New York: Oxford University Press.

Deble, Isabell. 1980. *The School Education of Girls: An International Comparative Study on School Wastage Among Girls and Boys at the First and Second Levels of Education.* Paris: UNESCO.

Egypt, Central Agency for Public Mobilisation and Statistics, and World Fertility Survey. International Statistics Institute. 1983. *Egyptian Fertility Survey 1980.* Vol. 3. *Socio-Economic Differentials and Comparative Data from Husbands and Wives.* Cairo.

El-Ghannam, Mohammad. 1970. *Education in the Arab Region Viewed from the 1980 Marrakesh Conference.* Educational Studies and Documents. Paris: UNESCO.

El-Guindi, Fadwa. 1981. "Veiling Infitah with Muslim Ethics: Egypt's Contemporary Islamic Movement." *Social Problems* 28(4).

El-Sanabary, Nagat. 1973. "A Comparative Study of the Disparities of Education Opportunities for Girls in Arab Countries." Ph.D. diss. University of California at Berkeley.

———. 1978. "Female Education and Manpower Needs of Arab Countries." In *Issues in Human Resource Development in Arab Countries.* Kuwait, National Ministry of Culture. In Arabic.

———. 1983. "Access of Girls and Women to Technical and Vocational Education in Arab Countries." In Nagat El-Sanabary, ed., *Women and Work in the Third World: The Impact of Industrialization and Global Economic Interdependence.* University of California at Berkeley, Center for the Study, Education and Advancement of Women.

———. 1985. "Continuity and Changes in Women's Education in Arab Countries." In Elizabeth W. Fernea, ed., *Women and the Family in the Middle East.* Austin: University of Texas Press.

———. 1987. "Women's Education and Work for Children and Development." Paper prepared for the Conference on Childhood and Development, Riyadh. Ministry of Planning, Riyadh.

———. 1988. "Educating the Second Sex: Saudi Arabia's Educational Policy for Women and Its Implication." Paper presented at the Annual Conference of the Comparative and International Education Society, Western Regional Conference, Sacramento.

Endargeeri, M. S. 1986. "The Impact of Selected Social and Familial Factors on the Academic Achievement of Female Students in Saudi Arabia." Ed.D. diss. University of Southern California.

Finn, Jeremy D., Loretta Dulberg, and Janet Reis. 1979. "Sex Differences in Educational Attainment: A Cross-National Perspective." *Harvard Education Review* 49 (4):477–503.

Hallouda, A. M., S. Z. Amin, S. Cochrane, and S. M. Farid. 1983. *The Egyptian Fertility Survey 1980: Socio-Economic Differentials and Comparative Data from Husbands and Wives.* Cairo: Central Agency for Public Mobilisation and Statistics.

Hammam, Mona. 1981. "Labor Migration and the Sexual Division of Labor." *MERIP Reports* 95 (March–April).

————. 1986. "Capitalist Development, Family Division of Labor, and Migration in the Middle East." In Eleanor Leacock and Helen I. Safa, eds., *Women's Work: Development and the Division of Labor by Gender.* Boston, Mass.: Bergin and Garvey.

Harbison, Frederick, and Charles A. Myers. 1964. *Education, Manpower and Economic Growth: Strategies of Human Resource Development.* New York: McGraw-Hill.

Hartley, Michael J., and Eric V. Swanson. 1986. "Retention of Basic Skills among Dropouts from Egyptian Primary Schools." EDT Discussion Paper 40. World Bank, Education and Training Department, Washington, D.C.

Hatem, M. 1983. "Women and Work in the Middle East: The Regional Impact of Migration to the Oil-Producing States." In Nagat El-Sanabary, ed., *Women and Work in the Third World: The Impact of Industrialization and Global Economic Interdependence.* Berkeley: University of California at Berkeley, Center for the Study, Education and Advancement of Women.

Howard-Merriam, Kathleen. 1979. "Women, Education, and the Professions in Egypt." *Comparative Education Review* 23(2).

————. 1981. "Egypt's Other Political Elite." *Western Political Quarterly* 34.

Kaneko, Motohisa. 1987. "The Educational Composition of the World's Population: A Database." 2d ed. EDT Discussion Paper 29. World Bank, Education and Training Department, Washington, D.C.

Khattab, H. A. S. 1984. "Female Education in Egypt: Changing Attitudes over 100 Years." In Freda Hussain, ed., *Muslim Women.* New York: St. Martin's Press.

Klein, Susan S. 1987. "The Role of Public Policy in the Education of Girls and Women." *Educational Evaluation and Policy Analysis* 9(3):219–30.

Larson, B. K. 1988. "Women's Work and Status: Rural Egypt and Tunisia Compared." Paper presented at the Middle East Studies Association Meeting, Los Angeles, California, November 5, 1988.

Layne, Linda. 1984. "Educational and Social Hierarchy in Rural Jordan." Paper presented at the Annual Meeting of the American Anthropological Association, Chicago.

Lorfing, Linda, and J. Abu Nasr. 1985. "Sex-Role Orientation of Arab University Students." In Julinda Abu Nasr, N. Khoury, and H. Azzam, eds., *Women, Employment and Development in the Arab World.* Berlin: Mouton.

Marshall, Susan E. 1984. "Politics and Female Status in North Africa: A Reconsideration of Development Theory." *Economic Development and Cultural Change* 32(3):499–524.

Massialas, Byron G., and S. Jarrar. 1983. *Education in the Arab World.* Praeger Special Studies. New York: Praeger.

Meleis, Afaf Ibrahim, N. El-Sanabary, and D. Beeson. 1979. "Women, Modernization, and Education in Kuwait." *Comparative Education Review* (February):115–24.

Mernissi, Fatima. 1987. *Beyond the Veil: Male-Female Dynamics in Modern Muslim Society.* Rev. ed. Bloomington: Indiana University Press.

Mohamed, F. E. 1985. "Sex-Role Stereotyping in Arabic Elementary Reading Textbooks in Egypt." Ph.D. diss. University of Pittsburgh, Pittsburgh, Pa.

Moore, Clement H. 1980. *Images of Development: Egyptian Engineers in Search of Industry.* Cambridge, Mass.: MIT Press.

Nelson, Cynthia. 1968. "Changing Roles of Men and Women: Illustrations from Egypt." *Anthropological Quarterly* 41(2).

Othman, Ali. 1964. *Observations on the Cultural Attitudes toward the Education of Women in Arab Society, Considerations for Planning.* Sirs el-Liyyan, Egypt: UNESCO, Arab States Training Center for Education for Community Development (ASFEC). In Arabic.

Papanek, Hanna. 1985. "Class and Gender in Education-Employment Linkages." *Comparative Education Review* (August):317–46.

Patai, Raphael. 1973. *The Arab Mind.* New York: Charles Scribner and Sons.

Psacharopoulos, George. 1977. "The Perverse Effects of Public Subsidization of Education." *Comparative Education Review* 21(1):69–90.

Psacharopoulos, George, and Maureen Woodhall. 1985. *Education for Development: An Analysis of Investment Choices.* New York: Oxford University Press.

Rihani, May. 1983. "Women and Work in Morocco." In Nagat El-Sanabary, ed., *Women and Work in the Third World: The Impact of Industrialization and Global Economic Interdependence.* University of California at Berkeley, Center for the Study, Education and Advancement of Women.

Rosen, B. C. 1961. "Family Structure and Achievement Motivation." *American Sociological Review* 26 (August):574–85.

Rumaihi, Muhammaad. 1986. *Beyond Oil: Unity and Development in the Gulf.* London: Al Saqi Books.

Saadawi, Nawal. 1985. "Growing Up Female in Egypt." In Elizabeth Warnock Fernea, ed., *Women and the Family in the Middle East.* Austin: University of Texas Press.

Safilios-Rothschild, Constantina. 1986. "Sex Differences in Early Socialization and Upbringing and Their Consequences for Educational Choices and Outcomes." In OECD, *Girls and Women in Education: A Cross-National Study of Sex Inequalities in Upbringing and in Schools and Colleges.* Paris.

Saudi Arabia, Ministry of Planning. 1980. *The Third Development Plan, 1980–1985.* Riyadh.

————. 1985. *The Fourth Development Plan, 1985–1990.* Riyadh.

Silliman, J. M. 1987. "Basic Education for Women: The Promise Fulfilled? A Comparative Analysis of Five Countries (Nepal, Egypt, Indonesia, Tanzania, Peru)." Ed.D. diss. Columbia University Teachers College, New York.

Smock, Audrey Chapman, and N. H. Youssef. 1977. "Egypt: From Seclusion to Limited Participation." In Janet Zollinger Giele and Audrey Chapman Smock, eds., *Women: Roles and Status in Eight Countries.* New York: John Wiley and Sons.

Stuart, Madeleine F. 1981. "Developing Labor Resources in the Arab World: Labor Activity Effects from School Attendance and Socio-Economic Background among Women in the East Jordan Valley." Ph.D. diss. University of Southern California, Los Angeles.

Szyliowicz, Joseph S. 1973. *Education and Modernization in the Middle East.* Ithaca, N.Y.: Cornell University Press.

Todaro, Michael P. 1985. "Education and Development." In *Economic Development in the Third World.* 3d ed. London: Longman.

UNESCO (United Nations Educational, Scientific, and Cultural Organization). 1964. *Access of Girls to School Education in the Arab States.* General background document prepared by the UNESCO Secretariat for the Meeting of the Experts on the Access of Girls to School Education in the Arab States, Algiers, April 6–16. UNESCO/ED/FAR/3. Paris.

———. 1966. *Access of Girls to Secondary Education.* Paris.

———. 1969. *Access of Girls to Technical and Vocational Education in Arab Countries.* Working document submitted by the UNESCO Secretariat for the Meeting of the Experts on the Access of Girls and Women to Technical and Vocational Education in Arab Countries, Kuwait, November 1–7. ETF/AR/3. Paris.

———. 1983. *Equality of Educational Opportunity for Girls and Women.* Paris.

———. Various years. *Statistical Yearbook.* Paris.

Whyte, Judith. 1986. "The Development of Sex Stereotyped Attitudes among Girls and Boys: Different Models of Their Origin and Their Educational Implications." In OECD, *Girls and Women in Education: A Cross-National Study of Sex Inequalities in Upbringing and in Schools and Colleges.* Paris.

World Bank. 1974. *Education.* Sector Working Paper. Washington, D.C.

———. 1989. *World Development Report 1989.* New York: Oxford University Press.

———. 1992. *World Development Report 1992.* New York: Oxford University Press.

Youssef, Nadia H. 1974. *Women and Work in Developing Societies.* Population Monograph Series 15. Berkeley: University of California.

———. 1976–77. "Education and Female Modernism in the Muslim World." *Journal of International Affairs* 30(2):191–209.

———. 1978. "Women and Their Professional Future: Assessment of Training Needs and Training Programs in Morocco." U.S. Agency for International Development, Office of Women in Development, Washington, D.C.

5
Latin America and the Caribbean
Ines Bustillo

Women in Latin America do not suffer the same educational disadvantages compared with men that women in other developing regions face. But gender inequities remain in a few countries where women bear the brunt of pervasive poverty and in some rural areas where indigenous Indian populations are not integrated into the education system because of poverty or a language barrier. In Haiti, one of the poorest countries in the region, with a GNP per capita of $360 in 1987, illiteracy rates were close to 63 percent for men and 68 percent for women. In Bolivia, with a large, poor Indian population and a GNP per capita of $580 in 1987, 29 percent of men and 49 percent of women were illiterate. But in Argentina, which underwent early industrialization and educational expansion and which had a GNP per capita of $2,390 in 1987, fewer than 6 percent of the population was illiterate, with no significant difference between men and women.

Although women trail men at least slightly in ability to read in most Latin American countries, illiteracy tells more about past than about present gender disparities in education. School enrollment and achievement rates for women broken down by age group are better measures of the current situation. Except in Haiti and Bolivia, girls in this region are as likely as boys to attend primary school and more likely than them to continue on to secondary school, even though they may be found more often in lower-quality schools with a more limited curriculum. Moreover, girls demonstrate higher achievement levels than boys.

The biggest influence on women's education has been the remarkable expansion of education systems throughout Latin America since 1960. The gross primary school enrollment of girls climbed from 71 percent in that year to 104.1 percent in 1985.[1] Education has been a priority in the region, and since 1960 public spending on this sector has risen as a share of GNP in many countries. A second influence is increasing urbanization, since school accessibility and quality tend to be higher in urban than in rural areas. In Argentina, Chile, Uruguay, and Venezuela about 85 percent of the population reside in cities. Latin America has one of the highest rural-to-urban migration rates in the world, and in many countries more women than men migrate to the cities (IDB 1980–81). A third factor stimulating the education of women is the increase in employment opportunities open to them, which is reflected in their growing participation in the labor force. The service sector, which is more likely than other sectors of the economy to hire women, is expanding as fast as the industrial sector, which hires mostly men. A similar situation exists in East Asia, whereas in Sub-Saharan Africa, in contrast, the industrial sector is growing faster than the service sector, and women's wage-earning opportunities are therefore fewer.

But these factors alone cannot account for the high level of education among Latin American women. Other developing regions have undergone rapid educational expansion, urbanization, and growth in the female work force in the past several decades without the gender gap in education shrinking as much as it has in Latin America. An additional factor may be that many of the region's indigenous Indian cultures had certain egalitarian attitudes toward women; Peruvian women during the Inca period, for example, engaged in agricultural and other productive work on equal terms with men. Some of these social patterns persist in today's peasant communities. In fact, although more females than males are illiterate in Peru, the gap is narrower in rural agricultural areas than elsewhere in the country (Gill 1990). Similarly, in the rural Bahia area of Brazil, 30 percent of males but only 21 percent of females have had no primary education. It may also be that the Christian missionary influences accompanying colonial rule in the region constricted women's freedom less than Moslem or Confucian influences did in other parts of the world.

Latin America's progress in expanding women's education and eliminating the gender gap in most places should not leave policymakers complacent. Additional measures are needed to raise literacy and educational levels further for both women and men and to eliminate the inequities still faced by women in some countries and by the rural poor throughout the region.

This chapter reviews the literature on the factors influencing the educational attainment and achievement of girls and women in Latin America and assesses the policies designed to improve their educational status. Three questions are central:

- What are the effects of the general expansion of education on the schooling of girls and women?
- What are the effects of supply factors, such as school attributes, and of demand factors, such as family socioeconomic characteristics, on the educational attainment and achievement of girls and women?
- Which policies are likely to be most successful in addressing the educational needs of girls and women?

Any comprehensive study of educational status and policy in Latin America faces several difficulties. First, data for some countries are limited, so cross-country comparisons are often incomplete. Second, research has tended to focus on the determinants of enrollment in primary school and to neglect performance as well as issues in education beyond the primary level. Finally, most studies have considered males and females together, so their conclusions and policy recommendations are general rather than specific to women's education.

Economic and Demographic Overview

The population of Latin America exceeded 400 million in 1987 and was 70 percent urban, reflecting heavy migration to the cities, in part by women searching for better economic opportunities. Fertility rates have declined substantially in all Latin American countries in recent decades, yet current and projected rates remain high in Bolivia, Ecuador, Guatemala, and Honduras, among others. In Chile, Cuba, and Uruguay, however, total fertility rates compare favorably with those in industrial nations (table 5-1).

One of the most important changes in the status of women in Latin America is their growing presence in the labor force. Between 1950 and 1980 the percentage of women of working age in paid employment rose from 18 to 26 percent, a faster increase than for men, and it is projected to exceed 27 percent in 2000 (IDB 1987). Female employment continues to increase in the service sector, which provided jobs to more than half of working women in 1950 and to more than 65 percent in 1980. In contrast, the participation of women in the industrial sector declined from 23 percent in 1950 to less than 20 percent in 1980.

A growing share of Latin American households is headed by women; estimates range from 15 percent to more than 40 percent for the region as a whole. Those living in female-headed households make up an increasing part of the low-income population. They have less access to basic urban services, enjoy fewer opportunities to improve their ability to earn an income, and fall more often below the poverty line (White and others 1986).

Table 5-1. *GNP and Population, Latin America and the Caribbean,*
Selected Countries, 1987

Country	GNP per capita (dollars)	Total fertility rate	Population (millions)
Haiti	360	4.7	6.1
Bolivia	580	6.1	6.7
Dominican Rep.	730	3.8	6.7
Honduras	810	5.6	4.7
Nicaragua	830	5.5	3.5
El Salvador	860	4.9	4.9
Guatemala	950	5.8	8.4
Paraguay	990	4.6	3.9
Ecuador	1,040	4.3	9.9
Colombia	1,240	3.2	29.5
Chile	1,310	2.7	12.5
Peru	1,470	4.1	20.2
Costa Rica	1,610	3.3	2.6
Mexico	1,830	3.6	81.9
Brazil	2,020	3.5	141.4
Uruguay	2,190	2.6	3.0
Panama	2,240	3.1	2.3
Argentina	2,390	3.0	31.1
Venezuela	3,230	3.8	18.3
Cuba	—	1.8	10.7

—Not available.
Sources: World Bank 1989; Inter-American Development Bank 1988.

Educational Status

Since 1960 education systems in Latin America have undergone a striking expansion. Both the supply of schools and the demand for educational services have increased. Between 1960 and 1980 the average annual rates of growth in enrollment were 4.4 percent for primary education, 9.2 percent for secondary education, and 11.4 percent for higher education. And between 1980 and 1988 enrollments continued to grow at an average annual rate of 1.5, 3.6, and 4.6 percent, respectively, for the three levels of schooling (table 5-2).

The timing and nature of this educational expansion have differed from country to country. Some patterns emerge, however, making it possible to group countries according to general similarities in their educational achievements and development history.[2]

Group I includes Argentina, Chile, Costa Rica, and Uruguay, all of which had an illiteracy rate of about 10 percent in 1980 and a GNP per capita that was above average for the region. Modernization of their economies and education systems took place early. By 1960

Table 5-2. *Average Annual Growth Rates of Enrollment, by Level of Education, Latin America and the Caribbean, 1960–88*
(percent)

	Primary		Secondary		Tertiary	
Period	Total	Females	Total	Females	Total	Females
1960–70	5.5	5.6	9.5	9.6	11.1	13.0
1970–80	3.2	3.2	8.9	9.4	11.6	13.8
1980–88	1.5	1.2	3.6	4.0	4.6	5.5

Source: UNESCO, *Statistical Yearbook,* 1989, 1990.

illiteracy rates in Argentina and Uruguay were already less than 10 percent. Today most children in these four countries attend primary school, and many complete secondary and even tertiary schooling as well. Compared with averages for the region, women in these countries have high levels of educational attainment and low rates of illiteracy.

Group II includes Brazil, Colombia, Ecuador, Mexico, Peru, and Venezuela, countries with illiteracy rates between 10 and 20 percent in 1980. Although expansion of the education systems in these countries occurred later than in the group I countries, it proceeded swiftly as part of a growth process that emphasized rapid industrialization. The education structures of these countries have been described as undergoing a "mutation" in that the number of people enrolled at the tertiary level swelled at the same time that many others did not even complete primary school (ECLAC 1988). Women as well as men have exhibited this mutation pattern.

Group III includes Bolivia, El Salvador, Guatemala, Haiti, and Honduras. In 1980 these countries had illiteracy rates of more than 20 percent and GNPs per capita that were among the lowest in Latin America. Haiti is the extreme case, with more than half its population illiterate and the lowest GNP per capita in the region. Compared with regional averages, these countries are less urbanized, women participate less in the labor force, and a higher percentage of the labor force is in agriculture. Levels of educational attainment reflect the low or uneven extent of economic development.

Group IV comprises Cuba and Nicaragua. Despite their undeveloped economies, these two countries have emphasized preschool and basic education for both girls and boys and have conducted national literacy campaigns. Nicaragua's illiteracy rate was more than 40 percent in 1971, the last year for which data are available. Without recent data it is not possible to assess the country's educational efforts. In Cuba less than 2 percent of the population between the ages of ten and forty-nine is illiterate, reflecting the success of the literacy campaign begun in the 1960s.

In general, a close relationship exists between a country's economic development and the educational profile of its population. Earlier industrialization and higher income per capita are associated with lower illiteracy and higher educational attainment. Conversely, less economic development is associated with less educational attainment. Countries that have experienced rapid but uneven development have made substantial progress in secondary and higher education but lag behind in primary education, as evidenced by continued widespread illiteracy among the young and the rural population.

Female-Male Differences

Although deficiencies still exist, as a whole Latin American countries have markedly improved the education of their populations in the past three decades. Women have benefited from these dramatic improvements; the figures for educational attainment in the region as a whole, presented in table 5-3, show small gender differences. The gains made by women are outgrowths of the general expansion in education and of socioeconomic change rather than of gender-specific education policies.[3] This does not mean, however, that governments have been unaware of the need to ensure that development benefits women as much as men. They have assigned priority to women's issues in broad plans and programs, but they have rarely defined gender-specific strategies and policies for implementation, whether in education or in other sectors. Even education projects undertaken by international development agencies have given little consideration to strategies directed to women (Stromquist 1986).

At the regional level, interest in improving the status of women has been expressed in many forums. Four conferences in the 1980s explored ways to integrate women into the economic and social development of Latin America; they were held in Macuto, Venezuela, in 1979, Mexico City in 1983, Havana in 1984, and Guatemala City in 1988. In the early 1980s the Project on Education for Latin America and the Caribbean, along with follow-up meetings and workshops, proposed measures to address the situation of girls and women. Recommenda-

Table 5-3. *Adult Population by Highest Educational Level and Gender, Latin America and the Caribbean, about 1980*
(percent)

Gender	None	Primary	Secondary	Tertiary
Males	20.2	46.5	28.0	5.4
Females	24.3	43.5	27.9	4.2

Source: Kaneko 1987.

tions made to governments to improve female education have encompassed coeducation, revision of textbooks and educational curricula, and adult education programs emphasizing women in rural areas.[4] Often, however, implementation of these recommendations has been hampered by institutional and financial constraints.

Despite the growth in educational opportunities in Latin America, not all women have benefited as fully as men have. Educational attainment, for women as for men, is strongly linked to GNP per capita and economic development, yet gender also makes a difference—most notably but not only in higher education. Table 5-4 shows that except in the Dominican Republic and Uruguay, illiteracy rates in about 1980 were higher for women than for men in all countries for which data are available. Those countries with the lowest illiteracy rates—Argentina, Chile, Costa Rica, Cuba, and Uruguay—were also among

Table 5-4. *Illiteracy Rates by Gender, Latin America and the Caribbean, Various Years*
(percent)

		Male		Female	
Country	Year	Total	Rural	Total	Rural
Argentina	1980	5.7	14.2	6.4	15.1
Bolivia	1976	24.2	37.3	48.6	68.5
Brazil	1985	20.9	44.7	23.4	48.0
Chile	1982	8.5	20.9	9.2	23.2
Colombia	1981	13.6	—	16.1	—
Costa Rica	1984	7.3	—	7.4	—
Cuba	1981	1.7	—	2.1	—
Dominican Rep.	1981	31.8	—	30.9	—
Ecuador	1982	12.8	21.7	19.4	33.1
El Salvador	1980	26.9	39.0	33.2	45.5
Guatemala	1973	46.4	59.9	61.5	77.6
Haiti	1982	62.7	—	67.5	—
Honduras	1974	41.1	52.1	44.9	56.8
Mexico	1980	13.8	—	20.1	—
Nicaragua	1971	42.0	63.8	42.9	67.0
Panama	1980	13.7	23.6	15.1	28.9
Paraguay	1982	9.7	—	15.2	—
Peru	1981	9.9	—	26.1	—
Uruguay	1985	5.6	11.1	4.5	7.4
Venezuela	1981	13.5	—	17.0	—

—Not available.

Note: The reference population includes those 15 years and older except for Cuba (ages 10–49), El Salvador (10 years and older), and the Dominican Republic (5 years and older).

Sources: CELADE 1987; UNESCO, *Statistical Yearbook,* 1986.

Table 5-5. Rates of Enrollment in Primary, Secondary, and Tertiary Education about 1987, and Annual Growth Rates since 1960, Latin America and the Caribbean

(percent)

Country	Primary Total Enrollment rate	Primary Total Growth rate	Primary Female Enrollment rate	Primary Female Growth rate	Secondary Total Enrollment rate	Secondary Total Growth rate	Secondary Female Enrollment rate	Secondary Female Growth rate	Tertiary Total Enrollment rate	Tertiary Total Growth rate	Tertiary Female Enrollment rate	Tertiary Female Growth rate
Argentina	110	0.45	110	0.41	74	4.86	75	4.71	40.8	10.16	44.1	18.98
Bolivia	91	1.56	85	2.59	37	8.75	34	8.89	17.3[a]	14.64	10.7[a]	21.88
Brazil	99	0.16	97	0.16	37[a]	19.87	42[a]	23.08	10.9[b]	20.76	11.2	42.39
Chile	102	−0.24	103	−0.14	68[a]	6.79	69	6.94	17.8	11.99	16.0	15.41
Colombia	114	1.78	115	1.83	56	13.58	56	15.15	13.9	26.58	13.4	79.01
Costa Rica	98	0.08	97	0.08	41	3.53	45	4.23	22.1[a]	13.86	25.1[a]	18.60
Cuba	104	−0.20	100	−0.34	86[a]	19.05	90[a]	17.79	22.6	24.20	26.0	31.96
Dominican Rep.	101	0.11	103	0.19	74[a]	22.03	84[a]	25.52	10.0[c]	44.62	8.9	43.39
Ecuador	117	1.52	116	1.73	56	13.58	53	15.93	36.5	48.29	27.5	109.47
El Salvador	79	−0.05	81	0.19	27[d]	5.39	26	5.93	17.7	55.89	14.8	133.33
Guatemala	76	2.55	70	2.47	20[a]	11.54	19[a]	10.77	4.3[c]	11.25	2.0	20.99
Haiti	83	2.98	80	3.35	19[a]	13.89	16	25.93	1.2[e]	8.00	0.6	18.52
Honduras	106	2.16	108	2.27	32[d]	11.11	36	15.34	9.5	28.28	7.2	62.96
Mexico	118	1.97	116	2.02	53	14.14	53	20.83	15.7	18.66	12.1	46.09
Nicaragua	99	1.85	104	2.13	43	19.05	48	25.93	8.4	22.22	9.2	81.48
Panama	107	0.42	105	0.43	60	3.96	63	3.59	25.9[e]	18.52	30.2	23.58
Paraguay	103	0.19	101	0.45	29	6.06	29	6.06	8.8	10.47	7.6	5.09
Peru	122	1.55	120	2.30	65[c]	9.67	57	12.54	21.5	15.72	15.6	16.93
Uruguay	110	−0.07	109	0.14	72[a]	3.50	76[a]	3.85	47.2	18.15	50.8	25.24
Venezuela	107	0.26	107	0.26	54[a]	5.82	49	4.94	26.5	19.12	25.5	30.03

a. 1986. b. 1988. c. 1975. d. 1984. e. 1985.

Source: UNESCO, Statistical Yearbook, 1975, 1989, 1990.

those with the smallest gender differences, a reflection of the cumulative effect of changes in education policy over several decades. Two of the countries with the largest gender differences—Bolivia and Guatemala—are among those with the highest overall illiteracy rates. The gender gap in illiteracy is widest in countries with large indigenous populations and low per capita incomes.

Rural-Urban Differences

Rural women are at a greater disadvantage educationally than other Latin American women, with a few exceptions already noted. In Bolivia, Brazil, and Nicaragua, the female illiteracy rate is about 20 percentage points higher in rural than in urban areas (see table 5-3). Among the countries for which data are available, those that industrialized early (Argentina, Chile, and Uruguay) tend to have narrower differentials between rural and urban women than most others in the region. Rural-urban differences are especially evident in areas with large indigenous populations, with the exception of Peru and Bahia in Brazil. For linguistic, cultural, and economic reasons, widespread education for rural women remains a challenge.

As with literacy rates, so with educational attainment, a person's place of residence makes a significant difference for both women and men. Among the countries for which data are available, this is especially true for Bolivia, Guatemala, and Haiti. In Haiti, for example, nearly 25 percent of the women in urban areas have finished secondary school, compared with less than 2 percent in rural areas.

Primary Education

Most Latin American countries have achieved universal or nearly universal primary education for all children (table 5-5). The exceptions are some of the lower-income countries—Bolivia, El Salvador, Guatemala, and Haiti. In El Salvador the enrollment rate of girls was slightly higher than that of boys in 1987, a result of some growth in the enrollment rate of girls but not of boys since 1960. In Bolivia, Guatemala, and Haiti the enrollment rate of boys was somewhat higher than that of girls in 1987. But in Bolivia and Haiti the gap is narrowing; the average annual growth of enrollment has been significantly greater for girls than for boys. In Guatemala, in contrast, if the trend in the annual growth rate between 1960 and 1987 continues, the gender gap in favor of boys is likely to widen.

In the more populous countries of the region, the gross enrollment rates at the primary level suggest equity in education. But in all countries rural children are less likely than urban children to be enrolled in school. Moreover, repetition of grades, attrition, and late entry into school are especially pervasive among children from rural areas or lower socioeconomic groups.

In the majority of countries the survival rate—that is, the rate at which students continue in school given the successful completion of the previous grade—is slightly higher for girls than for boys. This could reflect either a lower opportunity cost of sending girls to primary school or better school performance by girls, making them less likely to drop out for academic reasons. According to UNESCO (1980) estimates, the average survival rate up to the fourth grade was 73 percent or less for Latin America as a whole. Yet in some countries one-fourth of the children were lost between the first and second year of school, and this figure ran as high as one-half in rural areas. In six countries in 1984, less than 40 percent of a cohort reached the fifth grade (often the final year of the primary cycle). Rates differ widely among countries of the region, however. Besides Cuba at 99 percent, the highest rates of survival through primary school are found in the four Group I countries: Uruguay, 96 percent; Chile, 84 percent; Costa Rica, 79 percent; and Argentina, 71 percent. Group III countries— those with low levels of economic development—had the lowest percentages of each cohort reaching the fifth grade.

Repeating grades contributes to low rates of primary school completion. Repetition rates are high in the region; they reached 20 percent in Brazil in the late 1980s (table 5-6). Repetition is much more common in the first grade than in other grades, often exceeding 25 percent. The limited available data suggest that girls are less likely to repeat a grade than boys are. In poor and rural areas children start school when they are older, attend school less often, and repeat grades and drop out of school more than children in urban areas do. Retention rates are more than twice as high in urban as in rural areas. In Paraguay, for example, 48 percent of first graders in urban areas completed grade six, according to one study, compared with only 15 percent in rural areas (Winkler 1980).[5] Although the trends in repetition and dropout rates have been downward, the figures have remained high.

Secondary Education

Latin American countries have among the highest enrollment rates in secondary education in the developing world. Moreover, as in no other region, the picture that emerges is a favorable one for girls. In thirteen of the twenty countries included in table 5-5, the gross enrollment rate of girls is at least equal to, if not greater than, the rate for boys. Girls lag far behind boys only in Peru and Venezuela. In Peru the trend in

Table 5-6. *Grade Repetition at the Primary Level, Latin America and the Caribbean, about 1987*
(percent)

Country	Total	Females
Brazil	20	—
Chile	7	6
Colombia	17	17
Costa Rica	10	9
Cuba	8	—
Dominican Rep.	17	—
Ecuador	6	6
El Salvador	8	7
Guatemala	4	—
Haiti	9	9
Honduras	15	15
Mexico	10	—
Nicaragua	15	14
Panama	11	9
Paraguay	9	8
Peru	19	19
Uruguay	10	8
Venezuela	9	—

Note: Data for Argentina and Bolivia were not available.
Source: UNESCO, *Statistical Yearbook*, 1990.

the annual growth rate suggests that girls will catch up with boys within a few years. In Venezuela the gap is likely to worsen.

At the secondary as at the primary level, enrollment rates are linked to the GNP per capita of a country and to when its education system expanded. With some exceptions, secondary school enrollment rates are highest for the countries in group I, where expansion took place early.

The distribution of women in secondary education is heavily weighted toward general education as opposed to teacher training or vocational and technical programs (table 5-7). A comparison of enrollment distributions in 1970 and 1987, however, shows interesting patterns. For example, the percentage of female students in teacher training programs at the secondary school level declined steeply in Colombia, Cuba, Ecuador, Mexico, Panama, Paraguay, and Venezuela. In Cuba and Ecuador this decline was accompanied by a large shift to vocational and technical education; in the other five countries the share of women enrolled in general education courses rose.

Higher Education

Women are not as well represented at the tertiary level as at the secondary level. Nevertheless, in only six countries is the rate at which

Table 5-7. *Distribution of Female Secondary Enrollment by Type of Education, Latin America and the Caribbean, 1970 and Most Recent Year*
(percent)

	1970			Most recent year[a]		
Country	General	Teacher training	Vocational and technical	General	Teacher training	Vocational and technical
Argentina	48	0	52	51	0	49
Brazil	74	14	12	—	—	—
Chile	71	0	29	83	0	17
Colombia	62	13	25	76	4	20
Costa Rica	93	0	7	78	0	22
Cuba	82[b]	10[b]	8[b]	69	4	27
Ecuador	80	7	13	62	1	37
El Salvador	64	0	36	28	1	71
Guatemala	71	15	14	64	20	17
Honduras	75	9	16	64	8	28
Mexico	74[b]	6[b]	20[b]	84	0	16
Nicaragua	87	6	7	71	8	21
Panama	62	4	34	72	1	27
Paraguay	83	11	5	94	0	6
Peru	82	0	18	96	0	4
Uruguay	83	0	17	92	0	8
Venezuela	66	4	31	95	0	5

Note: Rows may not add to 100 percent because of rounding. Data for Bolivia, Dominican Republic, and Haiti were not available.

a. The most recent year for which data are available ranges from 1980 through 1988.
b. 1975.

Source: UNESCO, *Statistical Yearbook,* 1975, 1990.

women participate in higher education less than 10 percent, and in seven countries it exceeds the men's enrollment rate (see table 5-5). Ecuador has the largest gender gap; 28 percent of women in the appropriate age group are enrolled in tertiary institutions, compared with more than 40 percent of men. In Argentina and Uruguay, where the total enrollment rate at this level is greater than it is in most industrial countries, a higher share of women than men is enrolled. Indeed, in most Latin American countries, great progress in female education is evident from the annual growth in women's tertiary enrollment rates since 1960.

Although women are a greater presence in most fields of study than they used to be, they are still concentrated in traditionally female areas such as education and health sciences. Table 5-8 gives an overall picture of women in higher education in 1975 and 1982. In most countries they accounted for at least 35 percent of enrollment in the arts in both years but for less than 35 percent of enrollment in the sciences. A

Table 5-8. *Distribution of Countries by Percentage of Women in Tertiary Education by Broad Field of Study, Latin America and the Caribbean, 1975 and 1982*

Field	Less than 35 percent		35–50 percent		More than 50 percent	
	1975	1982	1975	1982	1975	1982
Arts	Peru	Guatemala	Uruguay	Paraguay	Brazil[a]	Uruguay
	Guatemala	Haiti	Dominican Rep.[a]	Ecuador	Panama	Panama
	Honduras		Ecuador	Mexico	Argentina	Nicaragua
	Haiti		Paraguay	Honduras	Chile	Chile
			Colombia	El Salvador		Colombia
			Honduras	Peru		Argentina
			Mexico			
Sciences	Dominican Rep.[a]	Colombia	Paraguay	Uruguay		
	El Salvador	Honduras	Uruguay	Panama		
	Brazil[a]	Chile	Argentina	Paraguay		
	Chile	Haiti	Panama	Argentina		
	Peru	Peru		Nicaragua[a]		
	Colombia	El Salvador				
	Honduras	Mexico				
	Mexico	Ecuador				
	Ecuador	Guatemala				
	Haiti					
	Guatemala					

Note: Arts include education and social sciences; sciences include natural and medical sciences and agriculture. The countries are classified within each broad field of study by descending order of percentage of women. Data are for 1975 and 1982 or nearest available years.
a. Data are available for only one of the two years.
Source: UNESCO, *Statistical Yearbook,* 1985.

more detailed breakdown shows that education, a predominantly female field in the 1970s, had an even heavier concentration of women in the 1980s.

Women have made considerable progress in the social sciences. In three of the twelve countries for which data were available—Colombia, Panama, and Uruguay—they constituted more than half the students. The medical sciences, too, have attracted many women; by 1982 women accounted for more than half the enrollment in this field in ten Latin American countries. The natural sciences and agriculture have drawn fewer women, although in many countries the trend has been for more women to enter these fields as well.

Often more telling than the share of women in a broad field is information about the specific courses of study they pursue. In the medical sciences women were concentrated in nursing rather than medicine. And in education they were usually preparing for positions in primary school systems rather than in the more prestigious and better-paid secondary and tertiary systems. This concentration of women in certain fields, and in specific areas within those fields, holds true for all countries in the region.

Primary Education: Determinants and Initiatives

Most studies of the determinants of attainment and achievement in primary school fall into two categories: those that focus on the availability and quality of education—the supply side—and those that focus on the needs and desires of students and their families—the demand side. Teachers, textbooks, curricula, and other school-related factors affect the supply of education. Family characteristics, such as parents' income and education, and the cost of schooling to parents affect the demand for education.[6]

Although earlier research on the determinants of school participation emphasized such factors as the availability of schools, the distance to school, and the costs of education, more recent research has examined the characteristics of the decisionmaking unit. Few studies, however, use this framework to identify school-related factors that explain gender differences in enrollment or attainment. And even fewer studies systematically analyze the differing returns from investing in girls' and in boys' education. Of the studies summarized in table 5-9, only Bowman and Goldblatt (1984), Irwin and others (1978), King and Bellew (1989), and Schiefelbein and Farrell (1980) estimate separate equations for males and females to allow for gender differences in the determinants of attainment and achievement. The studies by Armitage and others (1986), Birdsall (1985), Klees (1979), Psacharopoulos and Arriagada (1989), Tienda (1979), and Wolfe and Behrman (1984) treat gender as an explanatory variable—one that is sometimes found to be statistically significant. These authors assume the marginal effects of factors to be the same for both sexes. Three of them conclude that girls had a higher attainment level than boys even after controlling for various individual characteristics, but they can only guess at the explanations behind the gender effect. The rest of the studies listed in table 5-9 do not differentiate between males and females.

School-Related Factors

One question that has received considerable attention is how the school itself influences the achievement of its students, after controlling for family characteristics. Simmons and Alexander (1978) reviewed the research and suggested that school-related factors, independent of family characteristics, had only a small effect on achievement in developing countries. In a later study Heyneman and Loxley (1983) contradicted these findings. They examined the impact of school factors and family characteristics on student achievement in science in twenty-nine countries and found that for the nine Latin American countries in their study, school factors explained a significant part of the variance in what students learned. For example, they attributed more than 80 percent of the variance in achievement in Brazil and Colombia to the quality of the school.

In a recent comprehensive review of the literature on school factors and achievement, Fuller (1987) concluded that "much of the empirical work 'suggests' that the school institution exerts a greater influence on achievement within developing countries compared to industrialized nations, after accounting for the effect of pupil background" (pp. 255–56). The evidence indicates that the more developed a society is, the smaller the effect of school factors on achievement, given family characteristics. Yet even in Chile, one of the more advanced Latin American countries, Schiefelbein, Farrell, and Sepulveda-Stuardo (1983) found school factors to be of great importance, with effects larger than those of family characteristics.

Evidence also suggests that children who are economically and socially disadvantaged are more likely than other children to benefit from an increase in the availability and quality of schools. Birdsall (1985) reports that in Brazil rural children as well as urban children from low-income and poorly educated households benefited substantially from improvements in educational inputs. Using household data from the 1970 census, she estimated high elasticities of demand with respect to the availability and quality of schools in both urban and rural areas.[7] The percentage change in years of schooling associated with a given change in the availability and quality of schools was

Table 5-9. Summary of Studies of Determinants of Educational Achievement and Attainment

Author and date	Country	Outcome measured	Main conclusions
Armitage and others (1986)	Brazil	Comprehensive exam	Textbooks and other instructional materials and teacher upgrading have positive effects.
Birdsall (1985)	Brazil	Years of schooling	In urban areas the positive effect of school inputs is greater for children from poorer and less-educated families. In rural areas the effect is greater for children from higher-income families.
Bowman and Goldblatt (1984)	Mexico	School attainment	Work demands on children delay schooling and lower attainment. The negative effect of low income is greater for girls than for boys.
Clark (1981)	Guatemala	School attendance	Income-earning and housekeeping activities reduce school attendance.
Filp and Schiefelbein (1982)	Argentina, Bolivia, Chile, Colombia	Language and mathematics tests	Preschool education narrows the gap in achievement, with rural children benefiting the most.
Heyneman and Loxley (1983)	Argentina, Bolivia, Brazil, Colombia, El Salvador, Mexico, Paraguay, Peru	Science achievement; reading and mathematics achievement	School and teacher quality are the predominant influences on student learning.
Irwin and others (1978)	Guatemala	School attendance	Parents' perceptions of their children's intellectual development determine schooling decisions, especially for girls.
Jamison and others (1981)	Nicaragua	Mathematics achievement	Textbooks and radio-based instructional programs have significant effects on achievement.

King and Bellew (1988)	Peru	School attainment	The influence of family characteristics has lessened over time. The impact of parents' education differs for sons' and daughters' schooling. School inputs, such as textbooks and desks, raise schooling levels, especially for girls.
Klees (1979)	Mexico	Language and mathematics achievement	The use of television in secondary schools has a significant positive effect.
Psacharopoulos and Arriagada (1989)	Brazil	School participation, attainment, and dropout	Household resources and the demand for child labor have positive and negative effects, respectively. Parents' occupation is the strongest predictor of grade attainment. Boys are less likely to enroll in school, attain less schooling, and drop out more than do girls.
Schiefelbein and Farrell (1980)	Chile	School attainment and achievement	No evidence of systematic discrimination in education against women was found, but women score significantly lower than men on university admission tests.
Tienda (1979)	Peru	Labor force participation	Rural children are more than twice as likely to be working than urban children. Social background is the strongest predictor of this for younger children; age and school enrollment are more important for teenagers.
Wolfe and Behrman (1984)	Nicaragua	School attainment	Rural boys receive less schooling than rural girls. Family income and parental schooling—particularly maternal schooling—have a significant impact on child schooling.

virtually the same for rural and urban eight-to-eleven-year-olds (1.09 and 1.08, respectively). In contrast, rural children ages twelve to fifteen were more responsive to a change in the schools than urban children from comparable households (0.95 and 0.18, respectively). For urban children, moreover, as the income and education of their parents rose, differences associated with the availability and quality of schools diminished. The implication, Birdsall submits, is that improvements in school supply benefit children from poor households most. The effects are similar for boys and girls. A dummy variable for gender was significant (at the 5 percent level) only for urban eight-to-eleven-year-olds: being female increased by 0.13 the number of completed years of schooling.

Researchers have also tried to determine which specific school inputs are most effective in raising attainment and achievement. Latin American experience suggests that simple changes in school inputs can be quite beneficial in reducing repetition and dropout rates and also in improving school performance. Most relevant are the availability and content of textbooks and instructional materials and, to a lesser extent, the characteristics of teachers.

Textbooks and Instructional Materials. Although the robustness of the results differ, most studies find that textbooks have a significant positive effect on children's achievement (see Fuller 1987 for a review of these studies).[8] Some of them conclude that textbooks matter most to students from low-income families, to rural students, and to female students. For example, Brazilian children whose parents had no schooling were almost three times as likely to complete primary school if they had two or more textbooks than if they had none. Among children whose parents had a primary school education, 73 percent of those with at least two textbooks completed primary school, compared with 61 percent of those with no books.

Research on Nicaraguan children suggests that textbooks can compensate students for the disadvantage of being in a rural school. Jamison and others (1981) examined whether the availability of textbooks improved the mathematical skills of a sample of urban and rural first graders. They found that textbooks had a significant positive effect on achievement, their availability increasing average test scores for the entire sample by about 3.5 correct items. On another exam administered before and after textbooks were made available, the urban control group averaged 4.5 more correct answers on the second than on the first exam, whereas the rural group averaged an additional 6.1 correct answers. The authors conclude that textbooks not only improved school quality but also reduced the gap in achievement between urban and rural schools. As in Birdsall's (1985) study, the evidence confirms that improvements in school-related inputs can benefit poor rural children.[9]

Research on Brazil by Armitage and others (1986) supports the conclusion that textbooks are important in educating children. The authors found that the use of textbooks in rural Brazil in 1983 had a positive and significant effect (7–8 points) on achievement test scores. Their analysis shows that providing textbooks, writing materials, and drinking water as well as improving the teachers' own primary school education and subsequent training seem to be the most cost-effective means of increasing achievement. Investing in furniture and buildings was much less cost-effective.

These same authors also considered whether textbooks affected boys' and girls' achievement differently, using data on second and fourth graders in 1981 and 1983. Being male had a negative effect, but the effect was significant only for second graders in 1983, and it was small. The differences became highly significant, however, when broken down by performance in Portuguese and mathematics; girls consistently did better than boys in Portuguese and worse in mathematics.

King and Bellew (1989) found textbooks to have a positive and statistically significant influence on the educational attainment of girls in Peru. Reading or mathematics books, or both, raised the years of schooling by nearly half a year for both girls and boys. Separate analyses by birth cohort, using five-year intervals extending from 1925 to 1966, yielded significant estimates for the impact of textbooks on attainment for each of the six cohorts included; textbooks increased years of schooling for both sexes in the younger cohorts, those born in 1955–59 or later. For example, having books for every student increased schooling by 0.69 years for the 1940–44 female birth cohort and by 1.14 years for the 1955–59 female birth cohort. These cohort regressions also indicated that access to textbooks had a larger effect on females than males; for example, the impact of textbooks on the 1955-59 male cohort was only 0.92 years of schooling. The greater impact of textbooks on females could mean that "because there was less interest [within the family] in the education of girls, the quality of the learning process was more important in determining how many years of schooling girls attained" (King and Bellew 1989, p. 23).

Several studies conclude that textbooks are an agent for transmitting gender stereotypes in Latin America (see, for example, Braslavsky 1984). The books portray women as housewives and mothers, passive and with no power to make decisions. When working women are shown, they hold jobs traditionally associated with female nurturing (teaching, nursing, and domestic service).

Although ample evidence indicates that textbooks, by devaluing the roles and status of women, strengthen the negative stereotype of females in society, little research has probed the impact of those stereotypes on girls' attainment and achievement. If information absorbed at a young age shapes attitudes and aspirations, then such textbooks probably affect future performance at the secondary and postsecondary levels. Removing traditional gender stereotypes from textbooks and other instructional materials, as Mexico has done, and providing strong role models in their place may motivate girls to higher educational achievement.

Another concern is how relevant the educational content of curricula, as well as textbooks, is to girls from rural areas and indigenous cultures. The education that such girls receive through formal schooling may bear little relation to their future employment opportunities and personal lives. Making curricula in rural areas more relevant to rural girls would increase the returns to their schooling.

Teachers' Education and Attitudes. Evidence for good teaching as a factor in students' achievement is not as conclusive as it is for textbooks and instructional materials. In a review of nineteen studies, Schiefelbein (1987) notes that only eight of them reported a positive correlation between teachers' education and students' achievement. The greatest differences emerged when comparing teachers with some professional training and those with none; increments in the length of training seemed to produce decreasing marginal returns in student achievement. Moreover, only four of twelve studies found teaching experience to be statistically significant. Despite this, Schiefelbein suggests that upgrading teachers' skills in stages through training in good schools or participation in discussion groups (as opposed to having them attend traditional classes on selected topics) may have a positive effect on how much their students learn.

A study of rural Brazil (Armitage and others 1986) looked at four indicators of teacher quality: teachers' basic cognitive skills (measured by years of schooling), in-service training, motivation to teach (measured by salary as a percentage of the regional minimum wage), and years of experience. Of the four, teachers' schooling had the most consistently positive and significant impact on student achievement, but the impact was small: one additional year of schooling for the teacher raised students' achievement only slightly. Nevertheless, the authors consider this finding important, given that teachers in rural areas generally have few years of schooling themselves. For example, 30 percent of the teachers in the sample from northeast Brazil had four years or less of formal education. Upgrading the quality of teaching through in-service training programs also seems promising; preliminary estimates indicated a large positive impact, measured as a 6-point gain in achievement among a sample of second graders in 1983.

The other two indicators of teacher quality yielded mixed results. Although teachers' salaries were positively related to student achievement, the effect was small, and the authors caution against relying only on increasing the salaries of current teachers to improve achievement. The length of teaching experience proved insignificant.

Calculations of cost-effectiveness in the Brazil study suggest that the payoff in student achievement for each dollar spent on teacher education is higher if teachers' primary rather than secondary schooling is emphasized. Having prospective teachers complete four years of primary school or improve their skills through in-service training is more cost-effective than raising their formal education to include three years of secondary school.

Finally, the authors point out that certain aspects of teachers' attitudes may affect the performance of girls and boys differently. Female as well as male teachers hold stereotyped attitudes about girls' ability in mathematics, for example, and they use teaching techniques that are likely to depress girls' achievement in this area.

Other Supply Factors. Among other school-related factors that may affect education are radio instruction, furniture, the number of teachers per student, and the number of grades in primary school, to name but a few. Jamison and others (1981) determined that radio-based instructional programs had significant positive effects on achievement. In a Nicaraguan experiment instruction by radio increased students' exam scores by 14.9 correct items, compared with an increase of 3.5 correct items following the introduction of textbooks. The authors attribute the better results from radio instruction to the fact that such lessons are uniformly administered, unlike "the more inconsistent application of the textbook treatment (in the hands of teachers with relatively low levels of education)" (p. 565). More important, the use of either textbooks or radio can reduce rural-urban differences in school quality.

King and Bellew (1989) assessed the effects of availability of furniture, the number of teachers in a school, and the number of grades offered on primary schooling in Peru. The results for all birth cohorts combined indicate that providing each student with a desk and chair, while keeping other factors constant, raised school attainment among males by about 0.4 years and among females by about 0.2 years (the latter is not statistically significant). As for increasing the number of teachers in a school, the largest effect occurred in going from one to three teachers; further increases, for a given number of grades in a school, did not make a significant difference to attainment. Finally, each additional grade offered in a school increased boys' schooling by about 0.8 years and girls' by about 0.5 years. The authors interpret this gender difference to mean that demand for schooling is weaker for girls than for boys. The positive effect of offering additional grades in a primary school was greater for younger than for older cohorts. For females born between 1950 and 1954, for example, adding one more grade would have increased attainment by about half a year, whereas for those born in the 1960s the gain would have been 1.1 years. Thus, improvements in the availability of classes would have increased the attainment of younger cohorts.

Family-Related Factors

Most of the studies of factors affecting the demand for education have examined the impact on student attainment and achievement of family influences, such as parents' education and income and the work demands placed on children. The evidence suggests that parents' education and their ability to pay have strong, positive effects on their children's educational attainment. Work constraints have a negative effect, which seems to be greater for boys than for girls in Latin America.

Parents' Education. Studies of Nicaragua by Wolfe and Behrman (1984), of Peru by King and Bellew (1989), and of Brazil by Birdsall (1985) suggest a strong relationship between parents' education and children's schooling. Wolfe and Behrman's estimates show a significant correlation between the two, with diminishing returns after eight or nine years of parents' education, which is where the maximum effect occurred. The mother's level of education had a greater impact on her children's schooling than did that of the male in the household. Every additional year of a mother's schooling increased her child's schooling by 0.12 grades; an additional year of education for the male in the household had only about one-third the impact.[10]

King and Bellew (1989) determined that the schooling levels of both parents had a positive and statistically significant effect on the educational attainment of Peruvian children, both boys and girls. The father's education had twice as large an impact on a son's schooling as did the mother's education, but both parents' education had the same impact (strong and positive) on a daughter's schooling. The authors calculated that the elasticity of a son's schooling with respect to the father's education, evaluated at the mean level of fathers' education in the sample, is more than twice the elasticity with respect to the mother's education (0.19 and 0.09, respectively). For a daughter's schooling, these two elasticity measures are about equal (0.19 and 0.21, respectively). The explanation offered for these results is that an educated mother partly counterbalanced the father's preference for sending sons rather than daughters to school.

When King and Bellew (1989) analyzed the effect of parents' schooling in each of six cohort regressions, they again found positive and statistically significant effects. The impact of parents' schooling was larger, however, for older cohorts than for younger ones for both genders. For females born between 1950 and 1954, for example, the elasticities with respect to mother's and father's education, at their mean values, were 0.19 and 0.22; for females born between 1960 and 1966, these same elasticities were only 0.11 and 0.13. According to the authors, these findings reflect the increased availability and quality of schools or the higher returns associated with education in more recent years.

Birdsall (1985) also estimated a significant relationship in Brazil between parents' education and their children's years of schooling. Elasticities calculated at the mean values from Birdsall's reported results indicate that a mother's education generally had a stronger impact than a father's on the years of schooling completed by their children. This held true especially in the cities. For urban children ages eight to eleven, the elasticity measures were 1.12 for mother's education and 0.11 for father's, whereas in rural areas the elasticities were 0.14 and 0.11, respectively.

In a study in rural Guatemala of the link between children's school attainment, family characteristics, and preschool cognitive test performance, Irwin and others (1978) found that early intellectual ability influenced how long girls stayed in school. In addition, parents' perceptions of the intellectual ability of their children had a positive influence on both school enrollment and years of completed schooling.

Family Income. Parents' ability to pay for education also appears to be positively related to their children's schooling attainment. Wolfe and Behrman (1984) reported for Nicaragua that higher earnings, as statistically predicted, for the woman in the household as well as higher household income from other sources (generally representing the earnings of the male in the household) were both significantly associated with greater educational attainment by the children. For the national sample, the elasticity with respect to woman's income, evaluated at its mean level, was 0.83. With respect to household income from other sources, children's schooling was more responsive in the central metropolis than in the less urban areas and rural areas of the country.

Evidence from Peru confirms the importance of family income to children's schooling. King and Bellew (1989) used parents' occupation as a proxy for income to examine this relationship. Children of farmers had fewer years of schooling than children of parents with white-collar jobs had. For example, if a mother had a white-collar job, her sons were in school 0.6 years longer, and her daughters 1.1 years longer, than children with mothers working in the farm sector. If a father had a white-collar job instead of working in the farm sector, his sons and daughters were in school 1.1 and 1.4 years longer, respectively. Children of mothers who were not in the labor force tended to have more years of schooling than did children of mothers in farm-related occupations, presumably because nonfarm mothers who were not employed were likely to have higher family incomes than mothers from farm families. In another study, Farrell and Schiefelbein (1985) report that all the children of upper-class fathers in Chile had completed primary school, compared with 70 percent of the children of middle-class fathers, 48 percent of children whose fathers were urban laborers, and only 18 percent of children whose fathers were rural laborers.

In a study of Mexico, Bowman and Goldblatt (1984) indicated that low family income was more detrimental to the schooling of girls than of boys. Visible returns to schooling, which the authors measured by the proportion of white-collar fathers with high incomes, were not a significant factor in girls' educational attainment but were important for that of boys. This weaker income effect for girls implies that a given increase in the income of poor households would fail to raise girls' schooling by as much as it would raise boys' schooling.

Demand for Children's Labor. In many parts of Latin America, children are required to contribute to their family's income, and this need to work can affect their educational attainment. The effect of work on schooling seems to differ for boys and girls. Moreover, the demand for children's labor is generally higher in rural than in urban areas and is most pressing among low-income households. In Tienda's (1979) study of the economic activity of children in Peru, rural children enrolled in school were nearly six times more likely to work than urban children. One explanation may be that rural children can more easily combine school and work because of the seasonal nature of many agricultural tasks. Frequent absences from school also probably facilitate combining the two. Although Tienda found children's employment to be negatively associated with school enrollment, the net effect was more important for teenagers than for six-to-thirteen-year-olds. Also, gender was an important determinant of participation in the labor force only among teenagers. Tienda reports no difference in the probability that boys or girls between the ages of six to thirteen will be economically active, but fourteen-to-eighteen-year-old males had a higher rate of participation in the labor force than did females of the same age.

The link between low school enrollment and work constraints for Guatemalan children was explored by Clark (1981) in a time-use survey. She found that a high percentage of children of primary school age were not attending school. For some children, especially for older boys, income-earning activities and household chores explained this. But work constraints did not explain all the findings. Some parents assigned a low value to the expected return from investing in schooling and therefore chose not to send their children to school.[11]

A lower opportunity cost for girls' schooling could explain why girls sometimes receive more schooling than boys. Wolfe and Behrman (1984) found this gender difference in rural Nicaragua but not in Managua, and they attributed it to the higher opportunity cost of male schooling in rural areas, since farm tasks generally require a boy's physical strength. This same study also explored the effect on boys' schooling of mothers who expressed a desire for male children.[12] In the country as a whole, the sons of such mothers—unlike other boys—did not have significantly less schooling than girls did. And in Managua the sons of such mothers got considerably more schooling than other children did. The authors concluded that a mother's preference for a son compensated "for a systematic tendency for boys to otherwise be slightly less schooled than girls" and may also have reflected the evidence that the expected returns on male schooling were greater than those for girls.

Schiefelbein and Farrell (1980), finding similar gender differences in Chile, attribute them to the fact that forgone earnings were higher for older boys than for girls and that, consequently, low-income families were more likely to withdraw sons than daughters from school. Similar findings also emerge in an analysis of the education of Brazilian children by Psacharopoulos and Arriagada (1989); boys are less likely to enroll in school, tend to have lower attainment levels, and have a significantly higher probability of dropping out of school than girls. The authors suggest that these findings could be the result of a higher opportunity cost because of a greater labor demand for boys than for girls.

Policy Initiatives

Many strategies for improving the educational status of Latin American children have been suggested, and some have been implemented. Among the school-related strategies not yet mentioned in this chapter are changes to the school calendar, preschool education, outreach to parents, revision of promotion procedures, and provision of school lunches and transportation.[13] Some of these programs seem to be relatively successful in improving the educational attainment and achievement of girls.

In Argentina, Bolivia, Costa Rica, Cuba, Guatemala, and Uruguay, the school calendar has been revised to enable children to help with agricultural work and to allow for extreme weather conditions. These changes have been effective in improving girls' attendance (Schiefelbein 1987). Whether similar adjustments to the school day and the school year would benefit girls who mainly engage in housework remains to be tested.

Preschool education and other early stimulation for poor children can also prove effective. Filp and Schiefelbein (1982) report that in Argentina, Chile, and Colombia rural children of lower socioeconomic status reaped the greatest benefits from preschool education. The participation of such children in preschool programs appears to have had a positive effect on their entry into the first grade at the appropriate age in Argentina and Chile and on their promotion to the second grade in Argentina and Colombia.[14] Negligible effects were found, however, for Bolivian children.

For peasant and indigenous children whose transition from home to school may be difficult, early childhood intervention seems promising. In a review of such programs in Latin America, Halpern (1986) concluded that "it is the early childhood teacher's tendency to recognize and respond to individual children's learning needs that, if adopted in primary schools in Latin America, might have the most far-reaching consequences for children's primary school careers" (p. 215).

Family-oriented strategies for improving educational status have also been tried with some success, even though many of the family characteristics that determine the demand for education are difficult to modify in the short run. Two possibilities are worth exploring further. First, programs to train parents and encourage their participation in the school system have been found effective in improving children's school experience. In Chile, for example, parents' involvement in the actual construction and management of schools increased their interest in their children's education (Schiefelbein and others 1978). They also became more aware of their children's intellectual ability, and this stimulated their children to greater achievement. Second, programs to reduce the amount of time girls are expected to devote to housework can be useful. Clark (1981) and Chamie (1983) have recommended providing community day-care facilities for preschool siblings so that girls would have time to attend school.

In summary, both school inputs and family influences have a strong impact on the attainment and achievement of children at the primary level. Even in Argentina and Chile, countries that have higher incomes per capita and more balanced education systems than most other Latin American countries, school inputs seem to have been the predominant influence on students' education. Evidence from some countries suggests that improvements in school factors can have a significant impact especially on poor and rural children. Even simple changes in school inputs, such as providing more textbooks and adjusting the school calendar, have proved effective in raising the level of education.

But expansion of schools and improvements in their quality are not enough to close the gap in primary school attainment between rural residents and the more advantaged urban groups. These measures must be complemented with policies that change parents' attitudes toward their children's education, as well as with efforts to ease the constraints imposed by the need for children to work inside and outside the home.

Secondary and Higher Education: Determinants and Policies

The number of secondary schools and institutions of higher education has grown dramatically in recent decades throughout most of Latin America. For example, in 1958 Venezuela had six universities and one pedagogic institute; by 1984 it had nineteen universities, seven pedagogic institutes, and forty-six other institutions of higher education (Psacharopoulos and Steier 1988). Much of this growth occurred in the private sector.[15] In 1955 only 14 percent of those enrolled in postprimary education in Latin America were in private schools; by 1965 this figure had reached 20 percent and by 1975, 34 percent. The growth in public education at the secondary and tertiary levels was also extraordinary, with enrollments in the region jumping from 350,000 in 1955 to more than 2 million in 1975.

The growth of postprimary institutions and enrollments was concentrated in urban areas. In many countries rural secondary schools are scarce, and in some countries universities exist only in the capital city. As a result, the greater availability of secondary schools and universities has mainly satisfied the demand for education of urban residents, including women. Various studies have looked at the educational advantage that urban residents have over rural residents in the region as a whole.[16] For example, King and Bellew (1989) showed that in Peru being an urban resident at age thirteen added about one year to completed schooling.

Family Socioeconomic Characteristics

Socioeconomic status is a good predictor of secondary and postsecondary schooling in Latin America. According to Schiefelbein (1987), graduates from high school tended to come from the upper 25 percent of the socioeconomic distribution of each cohort. Farrell and Schiefelbein (1985) estimated that the distribution of students finishing secondary school was 77 percent for upper-class children, 49 percent for middle-class children, 21 percent for children of urban workers, and 4 percent for children of agricultural workers.

The selection processes for entry into secondary and higher institutions have tended to discriminate against students from lower socioeconomic groups. Entry into the high-quality public universities tends to be restricted primarily to graduates of good high schools, which are usually private. In Brazil and Colombia the use of university entrance examinations to determine admission has prompted many families to invest in good, costly private high schools as a way for their children to gain access to good, free public universities (Schiefelbein 1987). As a result, students from upper-income families have been the ones to attend public universities, rather than the less affluent students who would have the most to gain from access to free education.

Discrimination in the education system resulting from socioeconomic factors also affects women. A 1982 study of five metropolitan areas—Bogotá, Caracas, Lima-Callao, Panama City, and San José—showed that the proportion of women with thirteen years or more of schooling was much larger among high-income groups than among other socioeconomic groups. In Caracas, for example, 47.7 percent of women between the ages of twenty-five and thirty-four in the highest income group had thirteen or more years of education, compared with 1.7 percent of women in the lowest income group (Braslavsky 1984). Of those women enrolled in higher education in Venezuela in the past few decades, the majority had the means to attend private institutions charging fees (UNESCO 1981).

Labor Market Factors

Even where gender equality seems to prevail in education, women find themselves at a disadvantage in entering the labor market, as suggested by studies of Chile and Uruguay. The education systems of these two countries are among the best developed and most efficient in the region. The expansion of educational opportunities for women took place earlier than in most other Latin American countries, and today women have adequate access to most, if not all, semiprofessional and professional occupations.[17] Nevertheless, gender disparities arise in the transition between the formal school system and the labor market.

In their longitudinal study of a cohort of young Chilean adults, Schiefelbein and Farrell (1980) found that the first noticeable educational difference between men and women showed up in their performance on the university admissions test, with women scoring significantly lower than men. The authors attribute this result to "anticipatory socialization" among women. Because women chose traditionally female fields of study, which required lower test scores for university admission, they were under less pressure to perform well on the exam. The study also revealed that the length of time spent in school was more important for women than for men in getting a job. In a subsequent study Schiefelbein and Farrell (1984) reinforced this finding by noting that the labor market for women seemed to function more traditionally than the labor market for men, a situation that explained why educational attainment was more important and occupational aspirations less important for women than for men.[18]

The evidence from Uruguay is similar. Although women have equal access to universities and even enjoy a bias in their favor, a higher percentage of men than women graduate. Piotti's (1988) explanation for women's lower survival rate is that women who got married or had a baby dropped out of school or took more years to complete their degrees. Women in Uruguay also found themselves at a disadvantage in the labor market; and, as in Chile, educational attainment proved to be more important for women than for men in similar occupations.

Policy Initiatives

As at the primary level, so at the secondary and tertiary levels the broadening of women's opportunities has been a consequence of the general expansion of both the education systems and the economies in Latin America. In almost all these countries, however, the gap between men's and women's educational attainment has been wider at the tertiary level than at lower levels. It has been most persistent in those countries where industrialization and urbanization started late.

Various strategies have been proposed to increase the educational access, achievement, and attainment of disadvantaged groups in Latin America. Few of them, however, have focused specifically on women. The Organization of American States (oas 1985) has set two general goals for enhancing women's education in the region: to address the needs of rural women; and to encourage women to enter diverse, and typically male-dominated, fields of study.

To realize the first goal, the oas recommended increasing the availability of secondary schools.[19] This would lower the cost of secondary education to women. But even tuition-free education is not sufficient to ensure access to low-income groups. Other expenses, such as the cost of textbooks and travel, may be prohibitive. Another limiting factor is forgone family income; thus, measures such as scholarships, subsidized student loans, or funds to cover the forgone income are needed as well. Whatever the financing scheme, it should be used to support secondary education, since at this level lack of access for socioeconomic reasons is a serious obstacle.[20] In addition, strategies are needed that will modify attitudes toward the education of women. Among low-income and rural groups in Latin America, women's opportunities are restricted to marriage, childbearing, and housework. Consequently, neither parents nor daughters see the benefits of additional years of formal schooling.

To encourage women's interest in diverse fields of study, the OAS suggested establishing public and private fellowship programs for women in new fields of study which hold promise of providing future employment and good wages. It also recommended setting up employment agencies for women to increase their equal access to job markets, as well as strengthening organizations of female workers and female professionals.

Findings and Guidelines for Action

In recent decades Latin America's supply of schools and demand for educational services have expanded substantially. As a result, the educational attainment of girls and women has improved throughout the region, although with differences in gains both among and within countries.

The educational profile of Latin Americans in general and of Latin American women in particular is closely related to a country's income per capita and the history of its educational expansion. Countries whose economies and education systems were modernized early have lower illiteracy rates, higher levels of educational attainment, and greater equality in education for men and women. Countries with more recent economic growth and educational expansion show a strong increase in enrollments at the secondary and tertiary levels of education, yet illiteracy rates among younger people in rural areas often remain high. In these countries women still average fewer years of schooling than men, especially at the postsecondary level. Finally, countries with low incomes per capita have higher illiteracy rates, lower educational attainment, and a wider gender gap above the primary level.

Although the gender gap in primary schooling has narrowed greatly or even closed in most Latin American countries, a wide gap remains between urban and rural residents. In countries with large rural and indigenous populations, vast groups of women are illiterate. Full primary education for rural children has not yet been achieved. Moreover, the advantages of secondary and postsecondary education generally accrue only to urban women from middle and upper socio-economic groups.

The review of the empirical literature on women's education undertaken in this chapter suggests these findings and guidelines for action:

- Both school-related factors and family characteristics have a strong impact on the educational attainment and achievement of children. The impact of changes in school inputs is greater among children from low-income and rural backgrounds.
- The primary school inputs that have a positive impact on girls' attainment and achievement include textbooks and instructional materials, teachers' education and attitudes, and other supply factors such as complete schools (that is, schools that offer all the grades in the primary cycle). Among the school-related policies to be recommended are more widespread use of textbooks, removal of traditional gender stereotypes in teaching materials, revisions to school curricula to make them more relevant to the lifestyles of rural children, implementation of teaching techniques to foster girls' achievement, and preschool and early intervention programs for rural children.
- Parents' income and years of schooling have a strong and positive impact on children's education. There is some evidence that the mother's influence may make a bigger difference to daughters than to sons; this counterbalances the weaker demand for daughters' than for sons' schooling linked to the father's education.
- The links between children's work and their schooling are uncertain. The lower opportunity cost of girls' schooling in some parts of Latin America may explain in part why girls receive more education than boys. To the extent that work conflicts with schooling, adapting the school calendar to agricultural tasks and providing day-care facilities for preschool siblings are ways of reducing the conflict and decreasing the opportunity cost of education.
- At the secondary and postsecondary levels, selection processes within the education systems discriminate against students from lower socioeconomic backgrounds. Women in institutions of higher education are concentrated in fields of study associated with traditionally female roles in society. Policies suggested for addressing these two issues are to provide scholarships to low-income students and to establish fellowship programs to attract women to fields of study traditionally dominated by men.
- Even where equality in the education of men and women has been achieved, women remain at a disadvantage in entering the labor market. Educational attainment is found to be more important for women than for men when seeking similar employment.
- Finally, any future successes in improving the educational levels of less-advantaged girls and women in Latin America will depend not only on the design of education policies and strategies that address the specific needs of females but also on a firm commitment and concerted effort by educators, government officials, and interna-

tional organizations to provide more and better education for all Latin American women.

Notes

1. See chapter 1, note 2 for an explanation of how the method of calculating gross enrollment rates can result in rates exceeding 100 percent.

2. Not all countries in Latin America are included in these groupings, and only a few Caribbean countries are included.

3. For a review of women as a target of public policy in Latin America, including education policy, see ECLAC (1988).

4. See, for example, the resolutions from the Second and Third Regional Conferences on the Integration of Women into the Economic and Social Development of Latin America in Macuto, Venezuela, in 1979 and in Mexico City in 1983 (ECLAC 1988).

5. Winkler (1980) also reports that the reading achievement of urban pupils was double that of rural pupils.

6. For a model of schooling choice using this framework, see Birdsall (1985).

7. As a measure of the availability of schooling, Birdsall (1985) used the sum of the incomes of all schoolteachers in an area divided by the number of children ages seven to thirteen in that area. As a measure of the quality of the schools, she used the mean number of years of education of all teachers in the area.

8. The studies cited in this section are not strictly comparable because they use different outcome variables for measuring achievement. Most of the studies found some correlation between textbooks and educational attainment. But Muelle-Lopez (1984), working in Ecuador, did not find a strong positive relationship between the availability of textbooks and the level of education.

9. In Nicaragua combining textbooks with radio instruction has proved effective in teaching rural children. Television programs such as "Plaza Sesamo" have been quite effective too.

10. The authors state that it is unclear to what extent the larger coefficients for women's schooling reflected preferences, inherited characteristics, or household productivity.

11. Bowman and Goldblatt (1984) provide evidence that children's work also explained the presence of overage students in Mexican schools. In their study overage refers to students in the first grade who were at least ten years old when they started school.

12. This preference was indicated by a positive response to the question, "If you had four daughters and no son, would you have another baby in hopes of having a son?"

13. For a description of these strategies see, for example, Braslavsky (1984), Schiefelbein (1987), and Schiefelbein and others (1978). Interesting experiments have also been conducted in nonformal education, but they are outside the scope of this study.

14. Chile had a policy of automatic promotion.

15. Levy (1985) notes that Cuba and Uruguay, where private universities have not opened, are exceptions.

16. See, for example, Fernandez (1986), Klees (1979), and Velasquez (1987).

17. In Chile by 1920 about half of primary students and 43 percent of secondary students were female (Schiefelbein and Farrell 1980). In Uruguay women already represented half of secondary students by about 1920 (Piotti 1988).

18. The authors also report that, for women, educational attainment was more important than educational achievement in determining the level of the first job. For both men and women, although more so for men, educational quality had a strong direct effect on occupational attainment.

19. Other researchers have proposed ways, such as using tele-education, to improve student performance in regions with little access to schools. Mexico's use of television at the secondary level, *Telesecundaria*, has had a positive effect on student achievement. For an evaluation of Mexico's experience, see Klees (1979).

20. The various means of financing education in Latin America, and their efficiency and equity implications, have been much debated. For a comprehensive review of the main issues, see IDB (1978), Schiefelbein (1987), and Woodhall (1983). Financing schemes can be a source of discrimination against women; see Jiménez and Tan (1987).

References

Armitage, Jane, João Batista Ferreira Gomes Neto, Ralph W. Harbison, Donald B. Holsinger, and Raimundo Helio Leite. 1986. "School Quality and Achievement in Rural Brazil." EDT Discussion Paper 25. World Bank, Education and Training Department, Washington, D.C.

Birdsall, Nancy. 1985. "Public Inputs and Child Schooling in Brazil." *Journal of Development Economics* 18:67–86.

Bowman, Mary Jean, and P. Goldblatt. 1984. "School Attainments in a Development Perspective: Transition Patterns in Mexico." Working Paper Series 84-6. University of Chicago, Chicago, Ill.

Braslavsky, Cecilia. 1984. *Mujer y Educación: Desigualdades Educativas en America Latina y el Caribe*. Oficina Regional de Educación para América Latina y el Caribe, Santiago.

CELADE (Centro Latinoamericano de Demografía). 1987. *Boletin Demografico* (Santiago) 20(39).

Chamie, Mary. 1983. *National, Institutional and Household Factors Affecting Young Girls' School Attendance in Developing Societies*. Washington, D.C.: International Center for Research on Women and U.S. Agency for International Development.

Clark, Carol. 1981. "Children's Economic Activities and Primary School Attendance in Rural Guatemala." Paper presented at the annual meeting of the Society for Research in Child Development, Boston, Mass.

ECLAC (Economic Commission for Latin America and the Caribbean). 1988. *The Decade for Women in Latin America and the Caribbean*. Santiago.

Farrell, Joseph, and Ernesto Schiefelbein. 1985. "Education and Status Attainment in Chile: A Comparative Challenge to the Wisconsin Model of Status Attainment." *Comparative Education Review*, 29(4):490–506.

Fernandez, H. 1986. "Women's Educational Situation in Peru." INIDE, Lima.

Filp, J., and E. Schiefelbein. 1982. "Efecto de la Educación Preescolar en el Rendimiento de Primer Grado de Primaria: El Estudio UMBRAL en Argentina, Bolivia, Colombia y Chile" [The Effect of Pre-School Education on Achievement in First Grade in Primary School: The UMBRAL Study in Argentina, Bolivia, Colombia, and Chile]. *Revista Latinoamericana de Estudios Educativos* 12(1):9–42.

Fuller, Bruce. 1987. "What School Factors Raise Achievement in the Third World?" *Review of Educational Research* 57(3):255–92.

Gill, Indermit. 1990. "Does the Structure of Production Affect Demand for Schooling in Peru?" Population and Human Resources Department Working Paper. World Bank, Washington, D.C.

Halpern, Robert. 1986. "Effects of Early Childhood Intervention on Primary School Progress in Latin America." *Comparative Education Review* 30(2):193–215.

Heyneman, Stephen P., and William A. Loxley. 1983. "The Effect of Primary-School Quality on Academic Achievement across Twenty-nine High- and Low-Income Countries." *American Journal of Sociology* 88(6):1162–94.

IDB (Inter-American Development Bank). 1980–81. *Economic and Social Progress in Latin America*. Washington, D.C.

———. 1987. *Economic and Social Progress in Latin America*. Washington, D.C.

———. 1988. *The Financing of Education in Latin America*. Washington, D.C.

Irwin, M., and others. 1978. "The Relationship of Prior Ability and Family Characteristics to School Attendance and School Achievement in Rural Guatemala." *Child Development* 49:415–27.

Jamison, Dean, B. Searle, K. Galda, and S. Heyneman. 1981. "Improving Elementary Mathematics Education in Nicaragua: An Experimental Study of the Impact of Textbooks and Radio on Achievement." *Journal of Educational Psychology* 73(4):556–67.

Jiménez, Emmanuel, and J. P. Tan. 1987. "Selecting the Brightest for Post-Secondary Education in Colombia: The Impact of Equity." EDT Discussion Paper 61. World Bank, Education and Training Department, Washington, D.C.

Kaneko, Motohisa. 1987. "The Educational Composition of the World's Population: A Database." 2d ed. EDT Discussion Paper 29. World Bank, Education and Training Department, Washington, D.C.

King, Elizabeth M., and Rosemary Bellew. 1989. "Gains in the Education of Peruvian Women, 1940 to 1980." Policy Research Working Paper 472. World Bank, Population and Human Resources Department, Education and Employment Division and Women in Development Division, Washington, D.C.

Klees, Steven. 1979. "Television as an Educational Medium: The Case of Mexican Secondary Education." *Comparative Education Review* 23:82–100.

Levy, Daniel C. 1985. "Latin America's Private Universities: How Successful Are They?" *Comparative Education Review* 29(4):440–59.

Muelle-Lopez, L. 1984. "La Eficiencia Interna del Sistema de Educación Basica: Estado del Arte en América Latina" [The Internal Efficiency of The Basic Education System: State of the Art in Latin America]. *La Educación* 28:162–93.

OAS (Organization of American States). 1985. "Status of Women in the Americas at the End of the Decade of Women (1976–1985)." Series Studies 14. Washington, D.C.

Piotti, D. 1988. "Mujer Joven y Educación en el Uruguay" [Young Women and Education in Uruguay]. Paper presented at the Seminario Taller de Politicas sobre la Mujer Joven en Latinoamerica, Montevideo.

Psacharopoulos, George, and Ana-Maria Arriagada. 1989. "The Determinants of Early Age Human Capital Formation: Evidence from Brazil." *Economic Development and Cultural Change* 37(4):683–708.

Psacharopoulos, George, and Francis Steier. 1988. "Education and the Labor Market in Venezuela, 1975–1984." *Economics of Education Review* 7(3):321-32.

Schiefelbein, Ernesto. 1987. "Education Costs and Financing Policies in Latin America." EDT Discussion Paper 60. World Bank, Education and Training Department, Washington, D.C.

Schiefelbein, Ernesto, and Joseph Farrell. 1980. "Women, Schooling, and Work in Chile: Evidence from a Longitudinal Study." *Comparative Education Review* 24(2):S224–S263.

————. 1984. "Education and Occupational Attainment in Chile: The Effects of Educational Quality, Attainment, and Achievement." *American Journal of Education* 92(2):125–62.

Schiefelbein, Ernesto, Joseph P. Farrell, and Manuel Sepulveda-Stuardo. 1983. *The Influence of School Resources in Chile: Their Effect on Educational Achievement and Occupational Attainment.* World Bank Staff Working Paper 530. Washington, D.C.

Schiefelbein, Ernesto, and others. 1978. "Financial Implications of Changes in Basic Education Policies." In IDB, *The Financing of Education in Latin America.* Washington, D.C.

Simmons, John, and Leigh Alexander. 1978. "The Determinants of School Achievement in Developing Countries: A Review of the Research." *Economic Development and Cultural Change* 26 (2):341-57.

Stromquist, Nelly P. 1986. "Empowering Women through Knowledge: Policies and Practices in International Cooperation in Basic Education." Stanford University, School of Education, Stanford, Calif.

————. 1987. "School-Related Determinants of Female Primary School Participation and Achievement in Developing Countries: An Annotated Bibliography." EDT Discussion Paper 83. World Bank, Education and Training Department, Washington, D.C.

Tienda, Marta. 1979. "Economic Activity of Children in Peru: Labor Force Behavior in Rural and Urban Contexts." *Rural Sociology* 44(2):370–91.

UNESCO (United Nations Educational, Scientific, and Cultural Organization). 1980. "Comparative Analysis of Male and Female Enrollment and Illiteracy." Paris.

————. 1981. "El Acceso de la Mujer Venezolana a la Ensenanza y la Formación Cientifica y a las Carreras Correspondientes."

————. 1989. "Trends and Projections of Enrolment by Level of Education and by Age, 1960–2025 (as assessed in 1989)." Paris.

————. Various years. *Statistical Yearbook*. Paris.

Uruguay, Ministerio de Educación y Cultura. 1988. "La Ideologia Patriarcal: el Rol de la Educación." Instituto de la Mujer, Montevideo.

Velasquez, M. 1987. "Does Foreign Education Benefit Rural Women? The Case of Mexico." Colegio de México, Mexico City.

White, K., M. Otero, M. Lycette, and M. Buvinic. 1986. *Integrating Women into Development Programs: A Guide for Implementation for Latin America and the Caribbean*. Washington, D.C.: International Center for Research on Women.

Winkler, Donald. 1980. "The Distribution of Educational Resources in Paraguay: Implication for Equality of Opportunity." *Comparative Education Review* 24(1):73–86.

Wolfe, Barbara, and Jere R. Behrman. 1984. "Who Is Schooled in Developing Countries? The Roles of Income, Parental Schooling, Sex, Residence and Family Size." *Economics of Education Review* 3(3):231–45.

Woodhall, Maureen. 1983. *Student Loans as a Means of Financing Higher Education: Lessons from International Experience*. World Bank Staff Working Paper 599. Washington, D.C.

World Bank. 1989. *World Development Report 1989*. New York: Oxford University Press.

6

South Asia

Shahrukh R. Khan

South Asia is the region, along with Sub-Saharan Africa, in which girls' education lags behind boys' education most dramatically. At the primary level all South Asian countries except Sri Lanka have sharply lower enrollment rates for girls than for boys, with the difference in 1987 ranging from 15 percentage points in Bhutan to more than 50 percentage points in Nepal. Overall, primary school enrollments in these countries grew significantly between 1960 and 1987, increasing from 51 to 78 percent. But the growth has been less spectacular than in other regions, and public spending on education has been comparatively low. At the secondary and tertiary levels South Asia has the largest gender gap of any developing region, despite steep increases in female enrollments in the past several decades.

South Asian countries have one of the world's richest mixes of religious and cultural influences. India is overwhelmingly Hindu (about 80 percent) with Muslim, Buddhist, and Christian minorities. Pakistan and Bangladesh are predominantly Muslim; Bhutan, Tibet, and Burma are predominantly Buddhist; and Nepal is predominantly Hindu. Sri Lanka is part Buddhist and part Hindu. The "jewel in the crown" of the British empire until independence, these countries inherited education systems patterned after Britain's and set up by the colonialists to train bureaucratic functionaries. But in the past several decades schools have taken on more of a blend of British and American characteristics. All the countries have tried to introduce reforms to attune their education systems better to indigenous cultures.

Grinding poverty is the biggest barrier to education in South Asia, making the direct costs of schooling and the opportunity costs of forgone child labor too expensive for many families. These countries are among the poorest in the world, suffer some of the highest infant mortality rates, and are less urbanized than many other developing countries. Educational levels are drastically lower in rural areas than in cities, in part because of greater poverty and in part because of less access to schools.

Poverty may be the most pervasive barrier to the education of South Asian girls and women, but it is not the only one. Cultural factors such as the customs of early marriage and dowries, as well as concern for girls' physical and moral welfare, also limit their schooling. Moreover, Islam and Hinduism both place some restrictions on girls' education because they call for widespread segregation of the sexes, veiling, and the seclusion of women (*purdah*), although adherence to these practices varies considerably throughout the region. Cultural practices can be altered, however, by economic conditions. In the rural south of India, for example, families educate daughters to increase their chances of marrying white-collar husbands who might prove helpful should famine strike. In contrast, poor families in Nepal use their limited resources to educate one son through part or all of secondary school to equip him for a white-collar job.

This chapter looks at the state of women's education in South Asia, at the extent of the gender gap, and at the policies and programs designed to increase female schooling. In addition, it reviews available studies to identify the family, community, and school factors that influence decisions about schooling in the region. Higher education is treated separately because, much more than other levels of education, it is characterized by limited access, admissions restrictions, and high private and social costs, all of which put it out of the reach of the vast majority of South Asians. In addition, higher education is more directly related to labor market factors than are primary and secondary education.

A variety of materials are included in this review: general studies based on secondary materials, village studies, analyses using purposively selected samples, and analyses using well-designed probability samples. Some of the information gleaned is representative of an entire country; other information is of more specific relevance. Table 6-1 summarizes the kinds of data underlying each study.[1] Even when using data generated from sample surveys, few analyses go beyond one-way cross-tabulations. These studies generate hypotheses rather than firm conclusions that can guide decisions about resource allocation.

Economic and Social Conditions

The amount of resources a country or a family can devote to female education is strongly related to the country's general economic and social development. All five of the countries covered in this chapter fall in the low-income group, with GNP per capita ranging from $160 to $400 in 1987 (table 6-2). Economic growth rates in the 1980s were fairly robust: gross domestic product (GDP) rose faster in these countries than in the middle-income and high-income country groups. But except in Pakistan, GDP growth in the region was slower than the average for low-income countries.

Urbanization, which economists view as part of the structural change that accompanies economic development, varies widely among these countries. Pakistan is the most urbanized; about a third of its population lives in cities. Least urbanized is Nepal, where fewer than 10 percent of the population live in cities. In all of South Asia urbanization lags far behind the averages for middle-income and high-income countries.

Infant mortality and life expectancy are significantly linked to literacy, as discussed in chapter 1. Sri Lanka far outstrips the other four countries in literacy, with 80 percent of the rural population and 90 percent of the urban population able to read as of 1981. Its infant mortality and life expectancy rates are more favorable even than those of the average middle-income country. Literacy rates in the other four countries are less than 20 percent in rural areas and, except for India, less than 40 percent in cities. As expected, infant mortality is much higher and life expectancy sharply lower in these four countries than in Sri Lanka. More surprising is the fact that female life expectancy is the same as or lower than male life expectancy in South Asia, including Bhutan but excluding Sri Lanka. This occurs nowhere else in the world and is a measure of the harsh conditions that women in this region face.

Nutrition is another variable with links to education and literacy, as also set forth in chapter 1. Literacy provides access to knowledge about good nutrition; conversely, improved nutrition may foster more schooling. In none of these countries in 1987 was the average daily calorie intake (an indicator of nutrition) far below the 2,500 calories needed by a 150-pound adult male engaged in moderate activity. Activity levels in these countries are more likely to be strenuous than moderate, however, so the number of calories needed for good nutrition is probably much higher than this minimum.

Population growth also influences a country's ability to expand access to education for girls and women. Except for Sri Lanka, these countries have experienced population growth rates since 1965 that match or exceed the average for low-income countries as a whole (see table 6-2). Only India and Sri Lanka succeeded in slowing population growth in the 1980s. Nepal's average annual population growth rate for the 1980–87 period actually exceeded that for the 1965–80 period.

(Text continues on page 218.)

Table 6-1. *Summary of Studies Reviewed*

Country	Author	Data	Method	Focus
Bangladesh	Ahmed and Hasan (1984)	Sample survey (1984) of four village primary schools	Cross-tabulations	Impact of socioeconomic status on enrollments
	Chaudhury (1977)	Sample survey (1974) of middle-class working women (582) and nonworking women (548)	Nonparametric statistics, cross-tabulations	Determinants of female labor force participation
	FREPD (1981)	Stratified random sample including 2,480 rural households	Nonparametric statistics, cross-tabulations	Determinants of school dropout and nonparticipation
	Miyan (1979)	Survey (1979) of various populations (parents, employers, institutions) partly based on probability sampling	Nonparametric statistics, cross-tabulations	Determinants of women pursuing technical education, with particular emphasis on parental attitudes
	Qadir (1986)	Purposively selected sample of various populations in eight villages	Nonparametric statistics, cross-tabulations	Assessment of the success of drive to boost child enrollment; identification of parental and community views on what would work better
	Sattar (1981)	Survey of eleven schools from ten randomly selected villages in ten dispersed administrative areas	Nonparametric statistics, cross-tabulations	Assessment of a project referred to as Shawnivar to see if educational performance was better than national average

India				
	Caldwell, Caldwell, and Reddy (1985)	Survey (1981–82) of one large and eight smaller hamlets in rural Karnataka; sample included 364 couples and 1,294 surviving children	Cross-tabulations	Parental attitudes toward female schooling and differential causes of dropout by gender
	Gould (1983)	Sample survey (1974–76) of 551 Parsi households in Gujarat, including urban and rural populations	Cross-tabulations	Sex discrimination in educational attainment among one of the allegedly most "progressive" communities in the subcontinent
	Rosenzweig and Evenson (1977)	1961 population census	Regression	Analysis, including determinants of female child schooling
	Rosenzweig (1980)	Third-round sample (1975) of a three-year national survey of 4,000 rural households	Regression	Analysis, including determinants of female child schooling
	Sambamoorthi (1984)	Probability sample survey of a small regional labor market	Regression	Analysis of female labor market discrimination using earning functions
	Seetharamu and Ushadevi (1985)	Probability sample survey in rural Karnataka	Cross-tabulations	Determinants of low female educational attainment
	Tara (1981)	Probability sample survey of villages in Tamhur district	Cross-tabulations	Determinants of high female dropouts and low female enrollments

(Table continues on the following page.)

Table 6-1 (*continued*)

Country	Author	Data	Method	Focus
India (continued)				
	Tilak (1980)	Sample survey of 100 members of the West Godavari district in Andhra Pradesh	Regression	Estimation of earning equations to identify female labor market discrimination
Nepal	Ashby (1985)	Systematic random sample of 302 farm households in Kahur Palanchark district	Regression	Causes of low female educational attainment, including effect of family composition and size
	Jamison and Lockheed (1987)	Sample survey data covering 795 households (15 percent sample size) from twenty-eight randomly selected villages in each of six panchayats in two selected districts, Bara and Rautahat	Regression	Determinants of adult attitudes and child schooling, including gender as independent variable
	UNICEF (1978)	Survey of headmasters (38), male and female teachers (31, 51), parents (168), district education officers (9), and panchayat members (26)	Cross-tabulations	Evaluation of impact of a female teacher program on female enrollments

Country	Study	Sample	Method	Topic
Pakistan	Hussain and others (1987)	Stratified three-stage random sample of several populations, including employees and students	Regression and cross-tabulations	Gender differentials of various higher educational and employment issues
	Irfan (1985)	National population labor force and migration survey (1979); sample included 1,208 girls from farm households and 133 girls from nonfarm households	Regression and cross-tabulations	Determinants of rural child schooling
	King and others (1986)	Areas purposely selected and households selected using a multistage clustered sample; sample of 1,400 from village, urban poor, and urban middle-class districts	Range of multivariate analyses	Intergenerational transfer of gender differentials in schooling
	Shah and Eastmond (1977)	Sample survey including 416 villages	Cross-tabulations	Determinants of dropouts and low educational attainment, including factors affecting females
Sri Lanka	Rice and Wilber (1979)	Urban and rural household interviews in three purposively selected areas	Cross-tabulations	Impact of childcare needs and other social factors on female education

Table 6-2. *GNP Per Capita, GDP Growth, and Population Growth,
South Asia*

Country and group	GNP per capita, 1987 (dollars)	Average annual GDP growth rate (percent)		Annual average population growth rate (percent)	
		1965–80	1980–87	1965–80	1980–87
Bangladesh	160	2.4	3.8	2.8	2.8
India	300	3.7	4.6	2.3	2.1
Nepal	160	1.9	4.7	2.4	2.7
Pakistan	350	5.1	6.6	3.1	3.1
Sri Lanka	400	4.0	4.6	1.8	1.5
Income group					
Low	290	5.4	6.1	2.3	2.0
Lower-middle	1,200	5.7	2.1	2.5	2.3
Upper-middle	2,710	6.7	3.4	2.1	1.9
High	14,430	0.8	2.8	0.9	0.7

Source: World Bank 1989.

Despite several decades of economic growth and despite the great
need as reflected in low literacy rates, each of these countries dedi-
cated less than 11 percent of its total budget to education in the
mid-1980s (table 6-3). As a share of GNP, education expenditures represented 3.3 percent for India in 1985 and a low 2.1 percent for
Pakistan in 1987.[2] Bangladesh spent more than 10 percent of its budget on education, but this was only 2.2 percent of its GNP. Low-income
countries, on average, allocate 13 percent of their government budgets, or 3.3 percent of their GNP, to education. Although public spending on education in the mid-1980s was about the same in India as in
Sri Lanka, girls benefited less in India, judging from the much larger
gender gap in enrollments in that country.

Educational Status

The gender gap in education in South Asian countries is remarkably
wide even at the primary level (table 6-4). Despite higher annual
growth rates for girls than for boys between 1960 and 1986, girls'
enrollment rates lag far behind. In Bangladesh fewer than one-half of
girls between the ages of seven and twelve were in primary school in
1986, compared with more than two-thirds of boys in this age group.
In Pakistan fewer than one-third of girls were enrolled, compared with
more than one-half of boys. And in India, although universal primary
education has been achieved for boys, this is not true for girls.

The absolute gap at the secondary level is actually smaller than it is
at the primary level; this is explained by the much lower overall enrollment rates for secondary education. If the pattern at the primary level

Table 6-3. *Public Spending on Education in South Asia, Selected Years, 1975–87*
(percent)

Country and year	Share of GNP	Share of total government expenditure
Bangladesh		
1975	1.1	13.6
1980	1.5	8.2
1986	2.2	10.5
India		
1975	2.8	8.6
1980	2.8	10.0
1985	3.3	9.4
Nepal		
1975	1.5	11.5
1980	1.8	12.4
1985	2.8	10.8
Pakistan		
1975	2.2	5.2
1980	2.0	5.0
1987	2.1	6.2
Sri Lanka		
1975	2.8	10.1
1980	2.0	8.8
1986	3.6	9.4

Source: UNESCO, *Statistical Yearbook,* 1989.

is any indication of what might occur at the secondary level, rising demand for more schooling is likely to widen the gender gap as a larger share of boys than girls continues on from primary school. But if the annual growth rates for girls since 1960—which were much higher than the rates for boys—prevail, the gender gap may not expand as much as it has at the primary level.

In both primary and secondary schooling, Sri Lanka was an exception in the region. It had achieved universal primary education for both boys and girls by 1980. Enrollment at the secondary level was comparable to what is found in industrial countries, and the reported enrollment rate for girls exceeded the rate for boys.

As in other measures of educational status, so in years of schooling women lag far behind men, and rural women are at the greatest disadvantage (table 6-5). In Pakistan about 1980, nearly 90 percent of adult women did not complete a single grade in school, compared with 66 percent of adult men. Bangladesh and India had only a

Table 6-4. *Total and Female Gross Enrollment Rates and Annual Growth Rates at Primary and Secondary Levels, South Asia, 1960–86*
(percent)

	Primary		Secondary	
Country	Gross enrollment rate, 1986	Average annual growth rate, 1960–86	Gross enrollment rate, 1986	Average annual growth rate, 1960–86
Total				
Bangladesh	59.8	0.3	17.7	6.5
India	98.0	2.0	39.0	5.5
Nepal	82.2[a]	2.5	26.1[a]	12.1
Pakistan	43.6	2.9	18.2	3.3
Sri Lanka	103.6	0.1	66.3	2.6
Females				
Bangladesh	49.5	2.2	11.2	35.3
India	81.0	3.3	27.0	10.2
Nepal	50.0	60.2	12.5	33.1
Pakistan	31.9	7.6	10.5	9.2
Sri Lanka	102.3	0.3	69.7	4.5

a. 1985 data.
Source: UNESCO, *Statistical Yearbook*, 1989, 1990.

slightly better record. Nepal and especially Sri Lanka show the best results. In Nepal adult females were more likely than males to have some schooling.

Table 6-5 also reveals how widely educational levels vary within each country for both women and men. In Bangladesh 86 percent of rural women had no schooling, compared with 68 percent of urban women. The disparity, measured in percentage points, was even larger between rural and urban men: 62 percent compared with 40 percent. Yet the percentage of rural men with no schooling was still lower than the percentage of urban women with no schooling. This is not true in Nepal and Pakistan, where urban women appear to acquire at least as much schooling as rural men. (Data are not available for India.) These urban-rural discrepancies in educational attainment underscore the need to target education programs to rural girls, an approach that is bound to yield large gains for shrinking the gender gap.

As educational opportunities have expanded, South Asia's literacy levels, although still very low except in Sri Lanka, have improved (see figure 6-1). The female literacy rate rose in rural Nepal from 2.7 percent in 1971 to 7.8 percent in 1981, and in rural Pakistan from 4.2 percent in 1972 to 7.3 percent in 1981. Nevertheless, the literacy rates of urban women in both countries were still more than four times as high as the rates of rural women in 1981. Rural women in Bangladesh and

Table 6-5. *Distribution of Adult Population by Highest Education Level,*
Gender, and Urban or Rural Residence, South Asia, about 1980
(percent)

Country and level of schooling completed	Females			Males		
	Total	Urban	Rural	Total	Urban	Rural
Bangladesh						
No schooling	83.2	68.2	85.5	57.5	39.7	61.7
Primary	12.0	15.6	11.5	21.1	20.1	21.3
Secondary	4.4	14.5	2.9	19.1	32.1	15.9
Tertiary	0.3	1.8	0.1	2.4	8.0	1.1
India						
No schooling	83.2	—	—	57.6	—	—
Primary	7.9	—	—	15.6	—	—
Secondary	7.6	—	—	22.4	—	—
Tertiary	1.2	—	—	4.3	—	—
Nepal						
No schooling	36.4	27.8	39.0	41.2	24.9	43.8
Primary	41.6	24.5	46.6	26.3	16.3	27.9
Secondary	17.1	32.3	12.7	25.0	34.4	23.5
Tertiary	4.9	15.3	1.9	7.6	24.4	4.8
Pakistan						
No schooling	89.1	71.2	96.0	65.8	44.5	75.3
Primary	5.2	11.5	2.8	12.8	14.9	11.8
Secondary	4.8	14.3	1.2	18.1	31.9	11.9
Tertiary	0.9	2.9	0.1	3.3	8.6	1.0
Sri Lanka						
No schooling	20.1	10.4	22.8	8.3	5.2	9.5
Primary	45.6	39.4	47.3	51.2	39.9	55.6
Secondary	33.5	48.3	29.3	39.0	51.6	34.0
Tertiary	0.9	1.9	0.6	1.5	3.4	1.0

—Not available.
Note: Includes population aged 25–64.
Source: United Nations 1988.

India also improved their literacy status during the 1970s, yet in 1981 the literacy rate of urban women was still double the rate for rural women in Bangladesh and triple the rate for rural women in India.

Women in South Asia are underrepresented in institutions of higher education, as they are in primary and secondary schools (table 6-6). In Bangladesh and Pakistan in the 1980s they accounted for fewer than one-fifth of postsecondary students; in Nepal for about one-fifth; and in India for about 30 percent. In Sri Lanka, once again the front-runner, almost 41 percent of all those enrolled in programs of higher education in 1986 were women. The patterns of specialization among

Figure 6-1. *Female Literacy Rates, South Asia, 1970s and 1981*

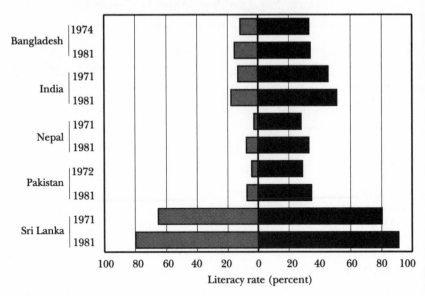

■ Rural   ■ Urban
Source: UNESCO 1987.

female students are similar in these countries. In Sri Lanka women constituted the large majority of students in education and a smaller majority in business administration. Women were a sizable share of all students in medicine and other health-related fields in both Sri Lanka and Nepal.

Factors Affecting Primary and Secondary Education

Many factors account for the large gender gap in education in South Asian countries. Although most of the studies reviewed here do not explicitly apply a conceptual framework, the analytical model presented in chapter 1 captures the implicit behavioral framework that underlies them.[3] It is assumed that households (or families) act as rational welfare-maximizing agents, with the limit on family welfare set by family resources. In the context of South Asia, viewing the family as pooling the resources of its members and sharing consumption and investment decisions seems reasonable.

Family and Community Influences

Most studies point to poverty as the main reason that families either fail to enroll their children in, or withdraw them prematurely from,

Table 6-6. Female Enrollment in Tertiary Education, Overall and in Selected Fields of Study, South Asia, 1980s
(percentage of total enrollment)

Country	Total	Education and teacher training	Commerce and business administration	Home economics	Natural science	Medicine and health-related sciences	Engineering
Bangladesh (1988)	17.2	9.7	13.9	100.0	16.5	26.2	3.9
India (1987)	29.9	47.0	21.8	0.0[a]	32.4	32.8	8.7
Nepal (1980)	21.6	30.1	11.9	0.0[a]	12.2	44.4	2.4
Pakistan (1986)	18.3	43.5	14.9	100.0	22.8	33.7	2.2
Sri Lanka (1986)	40.8	64.3	55.5	100.0	43.2	44.4	19.0

a. Enrollment reported was nil.

Source: UNESCO, Statistical Yearbook, 1987.

primary school.[4] This suggests that families find both the direct and the opportunity costs of schooling difficult to bear. Related to poverty is the demand that children help care for siblings and do household and farm work—a demand that falls much more heavily on girls than boys.[5] Jamison and Lockheed (1987) cite studies showing that the demand for girls' labor in Nepal exceeds the demand for boys' labor by about 50 percent. Papanek (1985) indicates that in Bangladesh the rate of participation in the labor force for the youngest group of girls included in the study (ten-to-fourteen-year-olds) was the highest of any female age group, whereas the rate for boys of that age was the lowest of any male age group. According to Rosenzweig (1980), women's and girls' (but not boys') labor in India is interchangeable, so a 10 percent rise in female wages reduces girls' school attendance by about 5 percent. Participation in the paid labor force, however, is only a partial measure of the labor demand for girls. Most girls who are employed work as unpaid labor.

Understanding the sources of the demands for girls' labor can lead to strategies for increasing girls' opportunities to attend school. Tara (1981), noting that taking care of siblings usurps much of a young girl's time, recommends the development of some form of community daycare. Labor-saving technologies, in principle, can also make time for schooling. Seetharamu and Ushadevi (1985) suggest that providing a safe and reliable water supply be made a priority because fetching water can occupy up to four hours of a girl's day. These recommendations, although not directly concerned with education policy, nevertheless address factors that influence a family's schooling decisions.

Cultural Norms. Families may lack interest in or be openly hostile to the formal education of their daughters for other reasons related to social and religious norms in general and to marriage prospects in particular. Singhal (1984) cites a study conducted by the National Center for Education Research and Training in India, which found that domestic work, marriage, betrothal, and parental indifference account for 55 percent of the total wastage—caused by repeating grades and dropping out—in girls' education at the upper primary level. Clason (1975–76) reports that poor rural parents in Nepal view female education as immoral; a similar attitude is reported by UNESCO (1975). In culturally conservative environments, adolescent girls may be viewed as morally suspect if they continue going to school. Early marriage and the importance of preserving a girl's good reputation lead to widespread withdrawal of girls from school at puberty, especially if they attend coeducational institutions.[6]

Table 6-7 gives the age of marriage for both females and males in four South Asian countries in the early 1970s. The legal minimum age

Table 6-7. Age at Marriage, Ever-Married Women and Men, South Asia, 1970s and 1981
(years)

Country, year, and percentage ever married	Men	Women
Bangladesh, 1974		
25 percent	14	21
50 percent	15	24
75 percent	17	27
Mean singulate age at marriage, 1981	16.7	23.9
India, 1971		
25 percent	14	19
50 percent	17	22
75 percent	19	26
Mean singulate age at marriage, 1981	18.7	23.4
Pakistan, 1973[a]		
25 percent	17	22
50 percent	19	25
75 percent	22	29
Mean singulate age at marriage, 1981	17.9	21.5
Sri Lanka, 1971		
25 percent	20	25
50 percent	23	28
75 percent	27	32
Mean singulate age at marriage, 1981	24.4	27.9

a. Sample excludes tribal areas and the Malakand Division in the North-West Frontier Province.

Source: Data compiled and made available by the Inter-university Consortium for Political and Social Research (U.S. Department of Commerce, Bureau of the Census 1983).

of marriage for females was either fifteen or sixteen. In Bangladesh 75 percent of ever-married females had married by the age of seventeen; in India the corresponding age was nineteen and in Pakistan it was twenty-two. But among ever-married females in Sri Lanka, only 25 percent had married by the age of twenty and only 50 percent by the age of twenty-three. In all of South Asia women in urban areas tended to marry later than women in rural areas. Data for 1981 indicate that single men in these countries married from 3.5 to 7.2 years later than single women did, so marriage may not have deterred male education as much as it did female education.

Almost all South Asian cultures are conservative, but the manner in which Islam and Hinduism have been practiced leads to an especially restrictive environment for girls' and women's schooling. According to Gunawardena (1987), progress in education among the Muslims in Sri

Lanka has lagged behind progress among the Sinhalese, Tamils, and Burgers. The importance of cultural conservatism in discouraging female education can be overstated, however. Chamie (1983) challenges the conventional view that Islam contributes to low enrollment among girls by citing the high rates in Libya and Bahrain. Rosenzweig's results (1980, table 4) imply that being Muslim was not a significant barrier to female enrollment in India. Sarkar (1986) found mixed evidence and concludes that the hypothesis that Muslims are opposed to educating both males and females does not hold. These results suggest that no single factor is adequate to explain gender differentials in schooling.

In India the Hindu caste system indirectly constrains the educational opportunities of low-caste children despite constitutional guarantees of equality. To increase the equity of access to educational services and to the job market, the government has instituted quotas for those from the lower castes in education and in public service jobs. But the reforms have not been as effective as intended. Teachers may unconsciously treat low-caste children differently from other children or have reduced expectations for them.

Disentangling the effects of cultural norms from other factors that influence educational attainment can be difficult. In an empirical study on female education in Asia, King and others (1986) sought to ascertain how much of the gender gap in enrollment results from cultural norms as reflected in parents' attitudes and how much results from the individual characteristics of their children. To do this, the authors computed a family-specific discrimination index. Looking at families with both sons and daughters, they found that if daughters were treated similarly to sons, their educational attainment would rise by 65 percent in middle-class urban Lahore (Pakistan), by 129 percent in lower-class urban Lahore, and by 224 percent in rural Punjab.

The link between mothers' attitudes and their daughters' education has also been studied. Smock (1981), citing a village survey in Pakistan, found that only 10 percent of the village women supported the notion of equality of opportunity for women. N. M. Shah (1986) recounts the results of another survey in Pakistan: among households in the sample that owned no assets, 51 percent of the urban mothers and 58 percent of the rural mothers believed that religious education (equivalent to about one year of formal schooling) was enough for their daughters.

Family opposition to secondary education for girls is much greater than it is to primary education because the direct costs are higher and the girls are already of marriageable age. Unexpectedly, a study on Bangladesh found little difference in parental attitudes toward the continuation of daughters' or sons' education at the primary level (FREPD 1981). But 91 percent of the heads of household wanted their sons to go on to the lower secondary level, whereas only 61 percent wanted their daughters to do so.

In a study on Nepal, Ashby (1985) points out that poor families develop a strategy of educating one son in the family at least through the upper secondary level so that he can obtain a white-collar job. Ashby's results also indicate that having additional women and young girls in the pool of family labor significantly increases the amount of schooling that male children receive. Caldwell, Caldwell, and Reddy (1985) report that in rural south India the situation is sometimes the opposite. Growing pressure on land, technological change, and a trend toward hiring individual laborers rather than entire families have produced excess labor in families. As a result, girls are allowed and even encouraged to go to school, since a girl with at least some education is a better match for a white-collar husband, who may help his wife's family in the event of famine or at least would not be a liability. This suggests, as noted earlier, that changing economic conditions can alter deep-seated cultural practices.[7]

Parents' expectations about a daughter's marriage and the concomitant effects these have on her education differ dramatically by income group. Middle-class families may view some education as promoting a good marriage for daughters by enabling them to manage a household more efficiently.[8] Because marriages are often perceived as an alliance of families, educating a daughter may confer positive benefits on the family if it raises the probability of her marrying into a better-off family. Lower-middle-class families, in contrast, have reason to regard their daughters' education as costly. Women in South Asia are usually expected to marry men with more education than they have. In cultures in which dowries are customary, securing a more highly educated husband for an educated woman would require a larger dowry— another "hidden" cost of educating females.[9] Seetharamu and Ushadevi (1985) recommend an antidowry campaign in the media and a policy linking a dowry subsidy to the educational attainment of girls.

The expectation that poor rural families will require their sons' wives to work at home discourages some parents from enrolling their daughters in school lest they become less desirable as housewives. Education is perceived as undermining girls' traditional attitudes and reducing their willingness to engage in physical labor, according to Desai (1987) and Seetharamu and Ushadevi (1985) for India, and Shrestha (1986) for Nepal. Smock (1981) reports the results of an attitude survey in Pakistan: education was perceived as making females self-centered, defiant of parental authority, and uninterested in household affairs.

Many studies have reported that rural families perceive the formal curriculum as useless (see UNESCO 1980). In one village survey in Bangladesh, parents were asked what they considered to be a useful education for girls; most of them wanted to see childcare, cooking, and handicrafts in the curriculum (Khatun 1979). This is consistent with the role anticipated for girls when they marry. In fact, such training may make girls more eligible brides and so more likely to marry into an economically and socially powerful family. Furthermore, if the returns from a family's investment in a daughter's formal education accrue to another household, the family has little incentive to make such an investment.[10]

Income and Education. A family's income appears to be related positively to the education of girls. A higher income enables the family to bear both the direct and indirect costs of education. Rosenzweig (1980), using multivariate analysis and the appropriate separate equations by gender, found land size and nonearned income to be positively and significantly associated with rural female enrollments in India. Ahmed and Hasan (1984), using data from a sample survey in Bangladesh, calculated simple two-way cross-tabulations to show that girls' education varies positively with their family's income and landholdings.

Parents who are themselves educated may have a more enlightened attitude about female education or provide a more stimulating environment for education than other parents. Islam (1982) reports a high correlation in Bangladesh between girls' enrollment and the proportion of adult household members who are educated. This evidence is corroborated by Ahmed and Hasan (1984): 91 percent of the children from the most educated families in their sample survey, defined as those in which the head of household has at least eight years of education (4 percent of the families sampled), were enrolled in school, whereas only 12 percent of the boys and 7 percent of the girls from illiterate families were in school. For Pakistan, N. M. Shah (1986) cites a study indicating that about two-thirds of illiterate rural women wanted only religious education for their daughters. But of those rural women with up to six years of schooling, about two-thirds wanted their daughters to complete secondary school and 17 percent wanted them to obtain a college education.

Drawing on a large 1979 data set for Pakistan, Irfan (1985) also explored this intergenerational effect of education. Cross-tabulations demonstrated that for all income groups, the education of the head of the household was positively linked to the enrollment rate for ten-to-fourteen-year-old girls in the family. In a multivariate analysis, Irfan used enrollment rates as the dependent variable in separate regressions by gender to explore the relative effects of supply and demand factors. On the supply side, the existence of a middle (upper primary) school or a high school in the community proved to be a significant influence on enrollment in nonfarm but not in farm households. On the demand side, the income of parents was a significant influence for both types of households. For farm households landownership was important, whereas for nonfarm households the education of the household head was important. For all households the literacy rate in the village in the last census (1972) also proved an important determinant. That education generates education is evident not only from the significance of the variable representing the years of schooling of the head of the household but also from the independent influence of the general level of literacy in the village.

This finding is confirmed by computing elasticities at means from equations estimating the determinants of education (King and others 1986).[11] In a cross-section of families in Pakistan, the father's education had a significant impact and was among the most powerful influences on the education of both sons and daughters. Although the elasticities are approximately equal for the sexes in middle-income urban families in Lahore (0.30 and 0.29 for sons and daughters, respectively), they are much higher for daughters than for sons in lower-income urban families in Lahore (0.32 and 0.18, respectively) and in rural Punjab families (0.32 and 0.12, respectively).[12] This indicates that an educated father may play a more important role in the schooling of daughters than of sons in lower-income urban families as well as in rural families. The mother's schooling was not as influential as the father's; its elasticity was significant only for females belonging to middle-income urban families in Lahore (0.14). Although the conservatism of a lower-income urban family or a rural family may be gauged by male attitudes (or by the educational level of the father or another male as a proxy), the social attitudes of middle- and upper-income families may well be determined by the educational level of the mother.

School Factors

Location, physical facilities, teachers, examination policies, hours of instruction, and curriculum are among the school-related factors that can contribute to gender differentials in enrollments. These supply factors, like the demand factors, often have a different impact on parents' decisions about educating girls than on their decisions about educating boys.

Distance to School. In the studies reviewed in this chapter that estimate school demand functions, school location—specified as the distance to the nearest school—is often used as a measure of school supply and thus of the cost of attendance. Distance to school implies expenses for travel, board, and lodging; if these costs are prohibitive, parents may send their children to stay with relatives who live closer to the school, or they may simply give up. The hypothesis is that when other factors are held constant, female enrollments should be inversely related to distance; that is, the shorter the distance to school, the greater the likelihood that girls will attend. Many researchers have reported that long distances to school are a barrier to female education.[13]

Yet even a short distance may seem long to some parents. A review by UNESCO-ROEAP (1984) contends that supply is not the issue in India because 90 percent of the children have access to a primary school or to a primary section in a secondary school within a kilometer of their homes. Similarly, Islam (1982) argues on the basis of evidence for Bangladesh that increasing the number of schools will not necessarily foster larger enrollments; she cites a survey that interviewed 208 female dropouts, 84 percent of whom lived within a mile of the school. In another study on Bangladesh, however, Ahmed and Hasan (1984) report that enrollment is negatively associated with distance because parents may be unwilling to allow girls to cross a major road or a river on the way to school. Given the rugged terrain in Nepal, the remoteness of schools can be an important reason for low female enrollment, according to Clason (1975–76). Yet Jamison and Lockheed (1987) did not find distance to be an important determinant of school participation in Nepal. They admitted, however, that the extent of school availability for the sample they were using was atypical for the country as a whole; also, they did not estimate separate equations by gender and thus statistically constrained the effect to be identical for males and females. Distance can be an even greater deterrent to girls' secondary than primary education because one secondary school must often serve several villages (UNESCO 1975).

As more public schools are provided in South Asia, distances to school will continue to decline and the supply of school places will no longer be as significant a constraint. This is, in fact, one of the lessons of the Bangladesh Rural Advancement Committee (BRAC) school program, which attributes part of its success in attracting and retaining girls to the proximity of schools to home (Lovell and Fatema 1989).[14]

Physical Facilities. But other school factors besides supply impose constraints on female enrollment. One of these is a lack of basic amenities, which may discourage girls' attendance more than boys'. Qasem (1983) found that 71 percent of the rural schools and 53 percent of the urban schools in Bangladesh had no latrines, and Ahmed and Hasan (1984) found that families have withdrawn girls from schools lacking latrines. Many Pakistani parents feel uncomfortable about enrolling girls in schools that do not have high, solid boundary walls to ensure privacy (Anderson 1988).

A cultural concern for the privacy of girls is one reason for single-sex schools. Studies from several South Asian countries indicate that parents are concerned about a lack of separate schools for girls.[15] Parents desire segregation by sex even at the primary level. The absence of such segregation at the secondary level is likely to be a serious barrier to continued female education. Testing for the effects of separate school facilities, boundary walls, and latrines on female enrollments at puberty would be of great value in guiding policy. As Anderson (1988) has pointed out, however, coeducation is a reality in Pakistan at the primary level, and the expense of setting up segregated schools with separate administrations is unwarranted.[16] Islam (1982) recounts that after the nationalization of schools in Bangladesh, the education administration strongly discouraged segregated schools, and the statistics imply a downward trend in the number of such institutions.

Female Teachers. The same cultural forces that create the need for single-sex schools also result in broad support for employing women to teach girls.[17] Since the early 1970s the government of Nepal, in conjunction with several international donors, has undertaken an extensive program to provide girls and women with equal access to education. The key strategy in this program has been to recruit and train female teachers from various regions, including remote areas, where they could then serve as teachers. An evaluation of the program midway through implementation showed it was having some success in encouraging girls to enroll and remain in school (UNICEF 1978).

Pakistan has also experimented with training local female teachers. An example is a *mohalla* (home) school project in Baldia, a large squatter settlement (UNESCO 1980). In addition to training women in the community with a high school education to be teachers, the project has emphasized cost-cutting by holding classes in homes and by not requiring uniforms or shoes. At least initially, the project met with great success; at the time this report was written, sixty-four schools and 1,600 students were involved. The good results were attributed to the hard work of the two-member project team in gaining the support and participation of the local communities.

But the wisdom of recruiting female teachers locally is not universally accepted. A monitoring study by Qadir (1986) in Bangladesh found that, although local women were able to communicate with and gain acceptance by villagers, local teachers (including women) were chronically absent because of their household chores. In addition, they were primarily concerned with earning extra income from private tutoring and were reported to show favoritism toward the students they tutored.[18] Well-connected teachers continually pestered the local administration for a transfer to town schools. Perhaps for these reasons, villagers said they opposed the use of local teachers. Attracting and retaining female teachers from outside the village poses a different set of problems, however, since they must relocate, gain local acceptance, and clear the difficult hurdle of finding suitable accommodations.[19]

Other Barriers and Incentives. Another school issue is the rigid examination policy, which may affect girls more adversely than boys (see Chamie 1983). Because girls are under more pressure to engage in household and farm work, they are absent from school more often than boys. When they fail examinations, the family perceives that its educational investment has soured and withdraws them.[20]

Entering school late, repeating a grade, and withdrawing at puberty contribute to low levels of attainment (Ahmad and others 1978). UNESCO-ROEAP (1984) suggests compulsory enrollment at the prescribed age to ensure more years of schooling. Forced withdrawal of girls from school by their parents may become more difficult the longer the student has been in school. This hypothesis is worth testing.

In its campaign to increase the enrollment of girls, India has experimented with a host of school-related incentives which, in effect, are intended to reduce the direct cost of education.[21] These policies include providing girls with attendance scholarships, free textbooks, school supplies, uniforms, and meals. Seetharamu and Ushadevi (1985) suggest that many Indian parents are not aware of these incentives and therefore have not taken advantage of the program. Bangladesh has experimented with free uniforms for girls in primary school and with scholarships for girls in secondary school to defray part of the direct costs.[22] Qadir (1986) reports that both rural and urban households in Bangladesh felt that giving girls a midday meal would help raise enrollment.

Bangladesh's Shawniwar village movement in the 1970s, although not focused exclusively on increasing female education, included that goal among its objectives. It emphasized the importance of local participation to create demand for various social services, including education. Sattar (1981) has evaluated this program and views it as very successful. The share of girls in total enrollment in the Shawniwar villages was 44 percent at the primary level, significantly higher than the national average of 38 percent. In addition, village opinion leaders reported that the average enrollment of primary and secondary female students in the Shawniwar villages increased by more than 50 percent after the movement began.

Local participation, apparently the key to the Shawniwar movement's success, is emphasized in another study on Bangladesh. In a survey to evaluate Bangladesh's drive for universal primary education, Qadir (1986) notes that villagers were suspicious of corruption in the way contracts were issued for building schools and other social facilities. The villagers were willing, and believed they were able, to participate in building such facilities themselves.[23]

Two experimental projects have highlighted the special importance of flexible school hours for encouraging female enrollment. If school hours do not conflict with the times when girls are needed for domestic chores, the opportunity cost to the family of sending them to school is reduced or eliminated. Naik (1982) reports that in a village school project near Pune in Maharashtra state in India, the key feature was that classes were held from 7:00 to 9:00 in the evening, after household chores and dinner were finished. Parents supported the project and the community provided teachers with rent-free accommodations. The teachers were local primary school graduates with some secondary education; they were intensively trained for one week after every six-week period. Learning was carried out in small groups, with peer teaching heavily encouraged. Within one year, 75 percent of the children in the school could read fairly well, write a little, and do the expected arithmetic. The dropout rate was much lower than the average for formal schooling. Although marriage or betrothal still proved to be one of the main reasons for dropping out, 8 percent of the girls who left the program did so to enter a regular school.

Junge and Sharestha (1984) have reported on a similar project aimed at low-caste girls in Nepal. Classes were held from 7:30 to 9:30 in the morning—before household chores began. Like the Indian project, this one recruited and trained local teachers. Students started reading by using cards to learn whole words, chosen from their own life experience, rather than by memorizing the alphabet; they were expected to read at the third- or fourth-class level after one year. Some girls did drop out of the project, but generally to take advantage of short-term opportunities to earn cash, and the overall retention rate was excellent. There was concern, however, that upper-caste Brahmins might oppose the subsequent enrollment of these girls in the local public schools.

Curriculum content is another issue that may affect female schooling. Kalia (1980) notes that as early as 1965 the government of India, having nationalized the preparation and approval of textbooks in 1955, proposed to create a curriculum conducive to gender equality. Kalia's analysis of the content of forty-one Indian textbooks (in Hindi and English) used in four states and Delhi revealed that males were the exclusive leading actors in 75 percent of the lessons, with females taking precedence in only 7 percent of the lessons. She found only seven biographical sketches of women but forty-seven of men. Women, she concludes, were still being prepared for a role requiring only servitude and support.

Singhal (1984) also cites evidence from India confirming the existence of extensive sex stereotyping in Hindi textbooks.[24] In contrast, Gunawardena (1987) points to a textbook survey showing that non-stereotyped sex roles outnumbered stereotyped roles in Sinhala and Tamil textbooks but that the opposite was strongly true for English textbooks. The governments of South Asia cannot talk plausibly in their policy documents about eliminating gender differentials in schooling if textbooks provided by the state continue to offer girls and women little motivation to obtain an education.

Better information needs to be collected on supply constraints to female education other than school availability and distance, on which much of the research has focused. Data on the influence of special amenities such as latrines and boundary walls could help ferret out other important supply-related barriers to girls' school attendance. Policymakers would benefit from knowing how much these and other factors, such as single-sex schools and female teachers, contribute to the enrollment and retention of female students. In the same vein, it is important to gauge the marginal impact of efforts to reduce the direct cost of schooling to poor families. Parents may welcome such incentives, but systematic evidence about their success in increasing female enrollments is lacking. Similarly, the impact of flexible school hours needs to be investigated more rigorously.

Factors Affecting Tertiary Education

Very few women in South Asian countries (except in Sri Lanka) continue their studies beyond the secondary level. There is ample evidence that parents prefer sons rather than daughters to continue their education.[25] Khatun's (1979) study of a village in Bangladesh found that 75 percent of the parents desired higher education for boys but only 25 percent desired it for girls. Such attitudes have also been documented for rural Sri Lanka; Smock (1981) reports on a 1973 study in which 60 percent of the respondents whose children were currently in school wanted their sons to get a college education but none had the same aspirations for their daughters. Rice and Wilber (1979) found in one of the areas they surveyed in Sri Lanka that 73 percent of the women wanted their sons to have a university education, whereas 77 percent wanted their daughters to be "knowledgeable" but not university graduates.

Motivations for Higher Education

Low-income parents, who were the respondents in the studies cited in the preceding paragraph, find the direct cost of higher education even more difficult to bear than the cost of primary or secondary education. Attitudes toward higher education differ, however, among the urban middle and upper classes. According to Jahan and Papanek (1979), the recognition that young Muslim men who came of age in Bangladesh after it separated from Pakistan preferred educated wives gave the initial impetus to the higher education of women in that country. As the cost of living rises, young middle-class women understand that they may be expected to earn income for the family into which they marry. Like other levels of schooling, higher education may have a marriage-related investment motivation, although the nature of this motivation may be changing because of the potential role of the young women as income-earners as well as good wives and mothers.

In a carefully conducted survey of several populations in Bangladesh that included young university graduates, 75 percent of the women stated that their main motivation for pursuing higher education was to meet the increased cost of living (Miyan 1979; see also Papanek 1985). In another survey in Bangladesh, this one of working and nonworking women, almost 80 percent of the women who worked did so for economic reasons (Chaudhury 1977).[26] The husbands of working women were significantly less educated and had lower incomes than the husbands of nonworking women. Another finding was that fewer working than nonworking women had educated fathers and more had a rural background. Chakrabarti (1977) mentions the increasing number of matrimonial advertisements in India seeking working women as brides. The growing enrollment of married women (22 percent of female students) at the University of Dhaka (Islam 1982) may also indicate economic pressure on single-income families.

A survey by UNESCO's International Institute for Educational Planning of several populations in Pakistan, including employed college graduates as well as college students, revealed that the women and men came from different socioeconomic backgrounds (Hussain and others 1987). Cross-tabulations show that, among those employed, a smaller share of women than men came from low-income families (7 and 14 percent, respectively) and a larger share of women than men came from upper-income families (43 and 34 percent, respectively). Among the female students, 32 percent had parents with higher degrees, compared with 17 percent among the college-educated female employees. Given the age differences between the students and the employees in the sample, this finding was interpreted to suggest that more women from well-educated families were continuing on to higher education than had done so previously. Similar findings from a study cited by Islam (1982) indicate that the majority of the University of Dhaka's female students come from well-educated and wealthy families. More middle- and upper-class Pakistani women may be attending college because a college degree is now necessary for a good marital match. Singhal (1984) expresses this same view for India.

Cultural Barriers

Economic motivations may in time erode the cultural barriers to higher education for women, but for now cultural factors remain impediments. Desai (1987) believes that falling female enrollments in medicine in India result from the more expensive dowries required to marry a highly educated daughter to a highly educated man. Anxieties and reservations about female participation in higher education exist in Bangladesh, where more women are entering the labor market. Miyan (1979) mentions parental concern about the "free mixing" of sexes in coeducational schools, although parents seem less concerned about married women working with men. Parents, and even the women themselves, have supported the idea of establishing separate women's polytechnic institutions. Of the parents surveyed, 74 percent said they would seriously consider sending their daughters to such a school should one become available. Besides alleviating "moral" concerns, a women's institution would circumvent the stiff male competition that women face in trying to gain admission to coeducational schools.

Another obstacle to female participation in higher education may be the lack of accommodations. Since institutions of higher education tend to be concentrated in a few main cities, either commuting long-distance or residing away from home is often necessary. Islam (1982) and Miyan (1979) observed that the absence of secure accommodations deterred young women living outside the metropolitan area from pursuing a higher education. Rice and Wilber (1979) found that the lack of accommodations restricted the enrollment of women in Sri Lanka's Kundasale School of Agriculture to 20 percent of the total.

Labor Market Discrimination

The direct cost to families of educating daughters may be greater than that of educating sons because sons are better able to contribute to their own support while studying. Islam (1982) conjectures that parents are reluctant to let an unmarried daughter support herself, whereas sons routinely do so. Even if parents are not an obstacle, the functioning of the labor market may prevent female students from becoming self-supporting. Women may not be hired or, if hired, may receive lower wages than men for the same work. Labor market discrimination can discourage women in a second way: by reducing their potential future income, it may dampen their aspirations for careers and hence their motivation for higher education.

For all levels of education, but especially for higher education because of the much greater direct and indirect costs, the behavioral model of household choice can be complemented by the human capital model to analyze and understand gender differentials. The human capital model views incremental spending on higher education as an investment in the individual for which a return accrues later in the form of incremental earnings. The theory is that each increment of education leads to an incremental increase in productivity, which is rewarded in the job market by greater earnings. If males earn more on average than females with the same education, the human capital model would predict a lower investment in (or lower demand for) education for females than for males. King and others (1986) have combined insights from the household choice model with this insight from the human capital model.

Using the human capital model, Tilak (1980) found that the mean earnings of women in India were up to six times lower than those of men for the same level of productivity. Using the same model, Sambamoorthi (1984) concluded that discrimination accounted for 21 percent of the male-female wage differential. Raj (1982) used Indian census data to show that women were in lower posts than men despite equal or better qualifications, that they tended to be concentrated in a narrow range of occupations, and that male-female wage differentials widened with age. Raj also reports subtle sex discrimination in selecting people to attend conferences and serve on committees; he adds that women tended to receive lukewarm job recommendations. Rice and Wilber (1979) point out that the repeal of Sri Lankan legislation allowing employers to pay women less than men in the late 1970s failed to stem this practice.

A 1977–78 Indian survey showed that, among those with a higher education, women were at a great disadvantage in finding jobs: unemployment rates were 44.8 and 35.9 percent for women in rural and urban areas, respectively, compared with 19.7 and 9.3 percent for men in rural and urban areas, respectively (Singhal 1984). Gunawardena (1987), using data for Sri Lanka, reports an unemployment rate among those with a higher education of 23.8 percent for women compared with 6.5 percent for men. The same study indicates that in 1985, 23.6 percent of university teachers were women, even though in 1984 women accounted for 42.2 percent of total university enrollment. In Pakistan, however, the 1980 population census (Pakistan, Population Census Organization, 1984) showed an unemployment rate of 2.5 percent for highly educated females compared with 3.2 percent for all females.

Although Gunawardena (1987) found that the number of women in the category "professional and related occupations" in Sri Lanka equaled the number of men, women were virtually absent in administrative and managerial positions, which are included in this category. According to the Pakistan Labour Force Survey for 1986–87 (Pakistan, Federal Bureau of Statistics, 1987), women made up about 17 percent of the professional and technical work force but only 3 percent of the administrative and managerial work force. About 5 percent of all working women were in the professional and technical category; fewer than 1 percent were in the administrative and managerial category.

Not all the findings or perceptions about the participation of educated women in the labor force are negative. In an opinion survey of middle-class educated women of childbearing age conducted in Bangladesh by Chaudhury (1977), only 22 percent of the working women felt that there was sex discrimination with regard to salary or promotion, even though 67 percent cited low salary as their reason for job dissatisfaction. Forty-eight percent of the women saw no discrimination in hiring, but Chaudhury suggests that this figure is low because women were not in positions for which men would compete.

Miyan (1979) notes that although the Bangladesh government has imposed mandatory quotas for the employment of women in the public sector, these quotas were not being filled, primarily because qualified candidates could not be found. But in Sri Lanka, according to Rice and Wilber (1979), quotas limited the number of educated women being hired; once met, the quotas set a ceiling on the number of women hired instead of serving as an instrument of affirmative action.

The extent of discrimination may sometimes decline as women progress to higher professional positions. Tilak (1980) found some negative discrimination coefficients at higher professional levels (for example, for doctors) in India; women were earning more than men, and their higher earnings could not be attributed to greater productivity. The explanation could be that, as in other conservative cultures, most women are allowed to see only female physicians. A cross-tabulation of the mean earnings of highly educated employees by gender and occupation in a UNESCO survey conducted in Pakistan demonstrated that women were earning significantly more than men in the scientific and medical fields, significantly less in engineering and technology, and the same in teaching (Hussain and others 1987).

Such positive evidence, although encouraging, is scant compared with the bulk of evidence suggesting strong labor market discrimination, which in turn can deter women from pursuing higher education. Also, no evidence has yet surfaced that men are willing to accept any significant change in their domestic role. Even if they encourage women to enter the labor market, men continue to expect women to shoulder most of the work load at home (Raj 1982 for India). The pressure of domestic responsibilities constricts the careers of professional women because they prefer convenient locations, flexible work hours, and longer vacations to higher positions (Desai 1987).

Conclusions

This chapter has identified many factors that have discouraged girls and women in South Asia from going to school. Although it does not set forth the best way of allocating scarce resources for education at the national and local levels, it does offer a starting point for rigorous research on those factors that seem most detrimental to female schooling and for which the greatest leverage for influencing policy exists.

Useful research directed toward policy initiatives must estimate the increase in enrollment likely to result from a given amount of spending on specific projects—such as providing lunches, free textbooks, or uniforms—or on broader programs, such as conducting media campaigns or arranging for childcare. These estimates require extensive data bases that include information on various exogenous price variables and on detailed family, school, and community characteristics. Because cultural norms are important in female enrollments, researchers may need to develop indexes (an index of conservatism, for example) to capture the effect of these variables. This approach would permit a more accurate approximation of other effects in multivariate comparative studies, either across countries or across different ethnic groups within one country or region.[27]

Raising enrollments is not simply a matter of expending resources on schools. Family and community factors also affect female schooling. To some extent effective media campaigns can reduce cultural constraints. Economic changes can also modify deep-rooted cultural traditions. In Bangladesh, for example, the need for a second income among the middle class is making it more acceptable for women to seek higher education and participate in the labor force. In south India, because of changing conditions in the agricultural labor market, one evolving famine-fighting strategy is to increase girls' education so that they can find a husband in the urban sector. In Pakistan some employers countered militant trade unionism by seeking out educated women, who were cheaper to hire and more docile than male union members. Although segregation in the workplace was attempted, some contact between the sexes was inevitable despite cultural barriers.[28] Education itself appears to have a snowballing effect in that girls' educational access and attainment are positively related to the general level of literacy in their villages as well as to the educational attainment of adults, especially fathers, in their households.

A reorganization of existing resources, or policy changes that require no new resources, may accomplish as much as, if not more than, large and expensive programs. A massive and expensive campaign in Bangladesh to achieve universal primary enrollment was not rated a success despite the large infusion of funds for materials and infrastructure (Qadir 1986). Among the projects covered in this survey, those found to be successful in raising female enrollment were low in cost, and all entailed some measure of local participation. Although involving local residents is not a new idea in the development literature, it has not been tried extensively. In all the education projects that have stressed local participation, women in the community with at least a primary education were trained as instructors. Although training is undoubtedly indispensable, it is not necessarily only those with formal training who have something to contribute to the local school. Among the main reasons cited for children's dropping out of school is the parents' perception that the curriculum is irrelevant and that their children lack interest in it. Drawing on village women to teach handicrafts or domestic skills in the schools could provide side income to those women, improve community involvement in the schools, and pave the way for girls to gain access to formal schooling. Some of the successful projects featured flexibility in school hours, which blurred the distinction between formal and informal schooling. In the late 1970s Sri Lanka's Ministry of Education gave all rural school principals the authority to implement a more flexible school holiday schedule in keeping with the demand for child labor in agriculture (Rice and Wilber 1979).

None of these initiatives required large government outlays. Rather, they relied on an awareness of the actual determinants, positive and negative, of parents' decisions about educating their daughters. Accurate and incisive research on how this decisionmaking process works is of great relevance to policymakers as they search for affordable means to shrink the wide gender gap in education that persists in much of South Asia.

Notes

1. Material on Sri Lanka is scarce; three separate data-base searches produced few current published or unpublished works. This is unfortunate because Sri Lanka is the clear front-runner in educational progress in South Asia. A review of studies attempting to explain why this is so would be useful,

although the explanation is implicit in the recounting of the deterrents to female education in other South Asian countries.

2. India and Pakistan trailed the region in education spending as a percentage of the national budget in 1987. But they led the region in military spending. Although the two are not necessarily inversely related, this relationship roughly holds for East Asia. Sri Lanka's stellar social development appears to have been hampered by political turmoil in 1987; this partly explains its rising defense expenditures and shrinking support for education.

3. The seminal works on this topic are Becker and Lewis (1973) and de Tray (1974). Birdsall (1980), Rosenzweig (1980), and Rosenzweig and Evenson (1977) have contributed useful expositions and estimations of such a model. Of special relevance is King and others (1986), in which the model is extended to explain and subsequently test the intergenerational transmission of gender differentials.

4. See, for example, Islam (1982) and Qasem (1983) for Bangladesh; Tara (1981) for India; UNESCO (1980) for Nepal; and Anderson (1988) and Shah and Eastmond (1977) for Pakistan.

5. For additional evidence on this issue see Chamie (1983).

6. See Papanek (1985) and Qasem (1983) for Bangladesh; Caldwell, Caldwell, and Reddy (1985) for India; and Anderson (1988) for Pakistan.

7. One can also argue that some cultural practices evolve as a result of economic imperatives.

8. See, for example, Ahmad and others (1978) for Bangladesh and Junge and Sharestha (1984) for Nepal. Also, a change in norms in the upper-income groups may eventually filter down, possibly in conjunction with economic changes. A country study of India in UNESCO (1980) reports that even poor villagers view female education as a means of enhancing security and marriage prospects. This is not the opinion expressed by most authors, however.

9. See Lavador (1986) for Bangladesh, Desai (1987) and Seetharamu and Ushadevi (1985) for India, and Shrestha (1986) for Nepal. The most frequent references to this phenomenon are for India.

10. Such a view is reported by Qasem (1983) for Bangladesh (in a study based on two purposively selected villages), Junge and Sharestha (1984) for Nepal, and N. M. Shah (1986) for Pakistan.

11. Elasticities at means indicate what the percentage change in schooling from its mean level would be, given a unit percentage change in a particular factor from its average value. These are calculated from the regression coefficients.

12. All the elasticity coefficients are significantly different from zero at the 10 percent level.

13. See Caldwell, Caldwell, and Reddy (1985) for India, UNESCO (1980) for Nepal, and N. M. Shah (1986) for Pakistan.

14. The BRAC established experimental primary schools in twenty-two villages in 1985 in response to requests from rural people to bring schools closer to them.

15. See, for example, FREPD (1981) and UNESCO (1980) for Bangladesh, the latter source also for India, and N. M. Shah (1986) for Pakistan.

16. See Nayar (1985) on this issue for Pakistan.

17. Among the school-related factors discussed here, the employment of female teachers is probably the one on which there is the greatest consensus in the literature. See, for example, UNESCO (1980).

18. This is also a problem in Pakistan. One solution may be to legalize tutoring but allow teachers to tutor only students from other than their own schools.

19. The Indian government has tried special allowances to attract rural female teachers and has provided accommodations for them (UNESCO 1980). No report on the success of this effort was available.

20. UNESCO-ROEAP (1984) points this out for India. This does not indicate that girls are poorer performers; Khan, Siddiqui, and Hussain (1986) provide overwhelming evidence that girls in Pakistan have consistently been outperforming boys at the secondary level.

21. These policies started with the Second Five-Year Plan and continued until the Fifth Five-Year Plan. The current policy is universal elementary education. It is argued that this policy will necessarily focus more on females, since their enrollment rates are lower. An evaluation study of the special program for girls' education, undertaken by the Programme Evaluation Organization of the Planning Commission, concluded that where the special programs were well planned and implemented, they did have considerable impact on female enrollments (UNESCO 1980).

22. See Qadir (1986) on the distribution of free uniforms, a policy reported to have been discontinued. Several organizations are involved in the scholarship program, including the Bangladesh Association for Community Education. USAID has disbursed more than 20,000 scholarships.

23. See also UNESCO (1980) on low-cost schools built with community participation.

24. See Smock (1981) for evidence of sex stereotyping in the curriculum in Pakistan. An interesting example is the reference to Fatima Jinnah only as the sister of the founder of the nation, never as a prominent politician in her own right.

25. For additional evidence on this issue see, for example, Islam (1982), who points out that families in Bangladesh are even willing to mortgage a piece of land for a son's education if need be. Junge and Sharestha (1984) note a similar preference for educating sons in Nepal.

26. Chaudhury (1977) performed nonparametric tests but not at disaggregated levels of education. The women surveyed ranged in education from completion of pre–high school to receipt of bachelor's and advanced degrees.

27. See King and others (1986) for an empirical technique that avoids explicit use of such an index.

28. Weiss (1983) recounts the experience in the pharmaceutical industry in the Punjab province of Pakistan.

References

Ahmad, P., and others. 1978. *Women for Women: Women and Education*. Dhaka: Bangladesh Books.

Ahmed, K. S., and M. Y. Hasan. 1984. *A Case Study on Enrolment and Attendance of Primary School-Aged Children by Socioeconomic Grouping for the UPE/IDA Schools.*

University of Dhaka, Foundation for Research on Educational Planning and Development.

Anderson, Mary B. 1988. "On Girls' Access to Primary Education in Pakistan." *Bridges Forum,* January 3–8.

Ashby, Jacqueline A. 1985. "Equity and Discrimination Among Children: Schooling Decisions in Rural Nepal." *Comparative Education Review* 29:68–79.

Becker, Gary S., and H. Gregg Lewis. 1973. "On the Interaction between Quantity and Quality of Children." *Journal of Political Economy* 81(2):S279–S288.

Birdsall, Nancy. 1980. "A Cost of Siblings: Child Schooling in Urban Colombia." *Research in Population Economics* 2:115–50.

Caldwell, John C., P. Caldwell, and P. H. Reddy. 1985. "Educational Transition in Rural South India." *Population and Development Review* 11:29–51.

Chakrabarti, A. K. 1977. "The Causes of Women's Unemployment in India." *Economic Affairs* 22:177–83.

Chamie, Mary. 1983. *National, Institutional and Household Factors Affecting Young Girls' School Attendance in Developing Countries.* Washington, D.C.: International Center for Research on Women and U.S. Agency for International Development.

Chaudhury, R. H. 1977. "Married Women in Non-Agricultural Occupations in a Metropolitan Urban Area of Bangladesh–Some Issues and Problems." *Bangladesh Development Studies* 5:153–200.

Clason, Carla. 1975–76. "Women and Development: Three Experimental Projects." *Literacy Discussion* 6(4):77–95.

Desai, Neera. 1987. "Establishing Gender Justice through Education: A Case of Women's Education in India, 1951–1987." Women's University, Bombay, India.

de Tray, Dennis N. 1974. "Child Quality and the Demand for Children." In Theodore W. Schultz, ed., *Economics of the Family.* Chicago, Ill.: University of Chicago Press.

FREPD (Foundation for Research on Educational Planning and Development). 1981. *The Study on the Situation of Children in Bangladesh.* Dhaka.

Gould, Ketayun. 1983. "Sex Inequalities in the Dual System of Education: The Parsis of Gujarat." *Economic and Political Weekly* (September):1668–76.

Gunawardena, Chandra. 1987. "Women in Higher Education in Sri Lanka." *Higher Education Review* 19:8–23.

Hussain, Tahir, Bikas C. Sanyal, Mohammad H. Abbasi, and Shahrukh R. Khan. 1987. *Higher Education and Employment Opportunities in Pakistan.* International Institute for Educational Planning. Paris: UNESCO.

Irfan, Mohammed. 1985. "Poverty, Class Structure and Household Demographic Behavior in Rural Pakistan." Pakistan Institute of Development Economics (PIDE) Research Report. Islamabad.

Islam, Shamima. 1982. *Women's Education in Bangladesh: Needs and Issues.* University of Dhaka, Foundation for Research on Educational Planning and Development.

Jahan, Rounaq, and Hanna Papanek, eds. 1979. *Women and Development: Perspectives from Southeast Asia.* Dhaka: Bangladesh Institute of Law and International Affairs.

Jamison, Dean T., and Marlaine E. Lockheed. 1987. "Participation in Schooling: Determinants and Learning Outcomes in Nepal." *Economic Development and Cultural Change* 35(2):279–306.

Junge, Barbara, and Shashi M. Sharestha. 1984. "Another Barrier Broken: Teaching Village Girls to Read in Nepal." *Reading Teacher* (May):846–52.

Kalia, Narendra Nath. 1980. "Images of Men and Women in Indian Textbooks." *Comparative Education Review* (June):209–23.

Khan, S. R., R. Siddiqui, and F. Hussain. 1986. "Analysis of School Level Drop-Out Rates and Output in Pakistan." Pakistan Institute of Development Economics Research Report 149. Islamabad.

Khatun, Sharifa. 1979. "Women's Education in a Rural Community in Bangladesh." In Rounaq Jahan and Hanna Papanek, eds., *Women and Development: Perspectives from Southeast Asia.* Dhaka: Bangladesh Institute of Law and International Affairs.

King, Elizabeth M., Jane R. Peterson, Sri Moertiningsih Adioetomo, Lita J. Domingo, and Sabiha Hassan Syed. 1986. *Change in the Status of Women across Generations in Asia.* Santa Monica, Calif.: Rand Corporation.

Lavador, Seremidad. 1986. "Women in Development: Issues and Strategies in Education." Prepared for International Labour Office. Geneva.

Lovell, Catherine H., and Kaniz Fatema. 1989. *The BRAC* [nonformal primary education program in Bangladesh]. New York: UNICEF.

Miyan, M. Alimullah. 1979. *Report on Job Market Survey for Women in Dacca.* Dhaka: Danida Mission, Royal Danish Embassy.

Naik, Chitra. 1982. "An Action Research Project on Universal Primary Education–the Plan and Process." In Gail P. Kelly and Carolyn M. Elliott, eds., *Women's Education in the Third World: Comparative Perspectives.* Albany: State University of New York.

Nayar, Usha. 1985. "Women in Educational Administration in the Third World." Presented at a conference on the Professional Preparation and Development of Educational Administrators in Commonwealth Developing Areas, held in Barbados, August 26–30.

Pakistan, Federal Bureau of Statistics, Statistics Division. 1987. *Labour Force Survey, 1986–87.* Karachi.

Pakistan, Population Census Organization. 1984. *1981 Census Report of Pakistan.* Islamabad.

Papanek, Hanna. 1985. "Class and Gender in Education-Employment Linkages." *Comparative Education Review* (August):317–46.

Qadir, S. A. 1986. *School Enrolment Drives and Enrolment of Children in Class 1.* Dhaka: Bangladesh Institute of Development Studies, Human Resource Division.

Qasem, K. A., ed. 1983. *Attitude of Parents towards Schooling of Children.* Dhaka: Foundation for Research on Educational Planning and Development.

Raj, M. K. 1982. "Women, Work and Science in India." In Gail P. Kelly and Carolyn M. Elliot, eds., *Women's Education in the Third World: Comparative Perspectives*. Albany: State University of New York.

Rice, Carol, and Jane E. Wilber. 1979. *Childcare Needs of Low Income Women in Rural and Urban Sri Lanka*. League of Women Voters, Overseas Education Fund, in collaboration with the Sri Lanka Federation of University Women.

Rosenzweig, Mark R. 1980. "Household and Non-household Activities of Youths: Issues of Modelling, Data and Estimation Strategies." Working Paper 90. Population and Labour Policies Programme, World Employment Programme Research. United Nations and International Labour Office, New York.

Rosenzweig, Mark R., and Robert E. Evenson. 1977. "Fertility, Schooling, and the Economic Contribution of Children in Rural India: An Econometric Analysis." *Econometrica* 45:1065–79.

Sambamoorthi, Usha. 1984. "Labor Market Discrimination against Women in India." Working Paper 58. Women in Development. Michigan State University, East Lansing.

Sarkar, B. N. 1986. "Enrolment and Primary Education Force in Rural India." *Margin* (April):72–89.

Sattar, Ellen. 1981. *Primary Education, Mass Literacy, Family Planning and Women's Programme in Ten Intensive Shawnirvar Thanas of Bangladesh*. Vol. 1. Dhaka: Bangladesh Association for Community Education.

Seetharamu, A. S., and M. D. Ushadevi. 1985. *Education in Rural Areas: Constraints and Prospects*. New Delhi: Ashish Publishing House.

Shah, Nasra M. 1986. *Pakistani Women: A Socioeconomic and Demographic Profile*. Honolulu: East-West Population Institute.

Shah, S. U., and J. N. Eastmond. 1977. *Primary Education in Pakistan*. Islamabad: Bureau of Educational Planning and Management.

Shrestha, Pushpa. 1986. "Participation of Women in Higher Education in Nepal." *Economic Journal of Nepal* 9:30–34.

Singhal, Sushila. 1984. "The Development of Educated Women in India: Reflections of a Social Psychologist." *Comparative Education* 20:355–70.

Smock, Audry Chapman. 1981. *Women's Education in Developing Countries: Opportunities and Outcomes*. New York: Praeger.

Tara, S. Nayana. 1981. *Education in Rural Environments*. New Delhi: Ashish Publishing House.

Tilak, J. B. G. 1980. "Inequality by Sex in Human Capital Formation, Labour Market Discrimination, and Returns to Education." *Margin* 12:57–80.

United Nations. 1988. *Women's Indicators and Statistics (WISTAT)—User's Guide*. New York.

UNESCO (United Nations Educational, Scientific, and Cultural Organization). 1975. *Women, Education and Equality*. Paris.

———. Various years. *Statistical Yearbook*. Paris.

UNESCO-ROEAP 1984. *The Drop-out Problem in Primary Education: Some Case Studies*. Bangkok: Regional Office for Education in Asia and the Pacific.

UNICEF (United Nations Children's Fund). 1978. *Equal Access of Women to Education Programmes in Nepal.* Center for Educational Research, Innovation and Development.

Weiss, Anita M. 1983. "Women and Factory Work in Punjab, Pakistan." In Nagat El-Sanabary, ed., *Women and Work in the Third World: The Impact of Industrialization and Global Economic Interdependence.* University of California at Berkeley, Center for the Study, Education and Advancement of Women.

World Bank. 1989. *World Development Report 1989.* New York: Oxford University Press.

7
East Asia
Jandhyala B. G. Tilak

Developing East Asia, comprising about a dozen large and small countries (Japan excluded) and a few tiny Pacific islands, enjoys the fastest
economic growth rate and the highest level of education of any developing region. The two achievements are linked; economic growth is
affected by, and in turn affects, the rapid expansion of education. The
region has achieved almost universal primary school enrollment. Two-
thirds of the population is literate, with adult literacy rates in the early
1980s ranging from 66 percent in China to 88 percent in Thailand.
The gender gap in education is less pronounced than in most of the
developing world, and women comprise a larger share of the labor
force than in any other developing region.

East Asia as used in this chapter includes Cambodia, China, Hong
Kong, Indonesia, the Republic of Korea (hereafter referred to as Korea), the Democratic Republic of Korea, the Lao People's Democratic
Republic (PDR), Malaysia, Mongolia, the Philippines, Singapore, Taiwan (China), Thailand, and Viet Nam. Together these economies account for more than 30 percent of the world's population and 11
percent of its area. In part because of lack of data for some countries,
such as Cambodia and the Democratic Republic of Korea, this chapter
focuses on the newly industrializing economies (NIES), known as the
"four little tigers" of the East—Hong Kong, Korea, Singapore, and
Taiwan (China)—which are the most developed areas in the region
after Japan; two other industrializing countries—Malaysia and Thailand; and four poorer countries—China, Indonesia, the Philippines,
and Viet Nam. These economies vary enormously in geographic size
and population. They also differ significantly in economic development, despite the overall high level, with GNP per capita that ranged in
1987 from $290 in China to $8,070 in Hong Kong.

Although these countries are at various stages of development, they share certain characteristics. Some were prosperous and industrially advanced long ago. "The fame of their wealth earned for this region the appellation of the 'gorgeous East' and inspired the quest that led to the discovery of the New World and created the preconditions for the Industrial Revolution in Europe" (Huq 1965, p. 5). Except for China and Thailand, the countries experienced colonial rule for periods of varying length under France, Japan, the Netherlands, Spain, the United Kingdom, or the United States. They became independent during the 1940s and 1950s, except for Singapore, which attained independence from the United Kingdom in 1965, and Hong Kong. In addition to a colonial legacy, the countries share a cultural heritage that encompasses indigenous cultures and religions as well as Buddhism, Confucianism, Islam, Christianity, and to a lesser extent Taoism and Hinduism. Religion is important in most of the region, and traditions remain strong within a modern, technologically developing world. At the same time, each economy has its own "unique historical and cultural background, and its own social, political and economic institutions to inspire and guide its development goals" (Huq 1965, p. 5).

Economic Background

In recent years the overcrowded, resource-poor East Asian economies have succeeded so well on the economic front that other developing nations often look to them for lessons (Tang and Worley 1988). Many economies of the region are now classified by the World Bank as middle-income (World Bank 1989).

Table 7-1 shows the impressive growth of the East Asian economies in the past three decades. Whereas the average increase in GNP per capita was 2.6 percent a year during 1965–87 for the middle-income group as a whole, most countries in this region had growth rates of more than 4 percent a year. The highest annual growth rate was 7.2 percent in Singapore, followed by 6.6 percent in Taiwan (China) and 6.4 percent in Korea. Even China, a low-income country, made rapid progress; its GNP per capita grew at the annual rate of 5.2 percent during this period.

These economies also differ in their degree of urbanization. Hong Kong and Singapore are almost totally urbanized, but more than 75 percent of the population in China, the Lao PDR, Thailand, and Viet Nam live in rural areas. In Indonesia, Malaysia, the Philippines, and Thailand (the only countries for which data on poverty are available) 30–40 percent of the rural population live below the poverty line. Income inequality is high in most of these countries.

Table 7-1. *GNP Per Capita and Population, East Asia, 1965–87*

	GNP per capita		Population	
Economy	1987 (dollars)	Growth rate, 1965–87 (percent)	1987 (millions)	Growth rate, 1980–87 (percent)
China	290	5.2	68.5	1.2
Indonesia	450	4.5	171.4	2.1
Philippines	590	1.7	58.4	2.5
Thailand	850	3.9	53.6	2.0
Malaysia	1,810	4.1	16.5	2.7
Korea, Rep. of	2,690	6.4	42.1	1.4
Taiwan (China)[a]	3,048	6.6	18.9	2.7
Singapore	7,940	7.2	2.6	1.1
Hong Kong	8,070[b]	6.2	5.6	1.6
Viet Nam	—	—	65.0	2.6

—Not available.

Note: All growth rates in tables in this chapter are annual unless otherwise stated.

a. Figures refer to the most recent period for which data are available.

b. GDP data.

Sources: World Bank 1989; the data on Taiwan (China) in tables in this chapter are from various sources, including Kurian 1982, Tang and Worley 1988, and national statistical bases.

The general belief is that the higher the level of economic development—as measured, say, by GNP per capita—the higher the level of female participation in schooling. In a study that covered many countries, Schultz (1987) confirmed this, finding larger income elasticities of education for females than for males: "Female enrollments tend to increase more rapidly with income per adult than do male enrollment rates. . . . The rise in income and the decline in relative price of schooling that appear to occur at the onset of modern economic growth contribute reinforcing gains to the educational attainment of women that exceed those achieved by men" (pp. 450–51). The level of higher education for females does not necessarily correspond closely, however, to the country's level of economic development. As Kelly (1984) concluded,

Women's access to education and the disparity between male and female enrollments at all levels of schooling cannot be predicted by the level or pace of a nation's economic development. Sex inequality in education is not a problem that will go away once a nation has increased its Gross National Product and built an industrial infrastructure." (p. 83)[1]

These two views are not necessarily inconsistent. GNP per capita may not be the best measure of the level of economic development. For example, high rates of economic growth may require more women to participate in the economy, a condition that leads to an increase in education for girls and women.

With total employment in the region growing more than 3 percent a year (except in Indonesia and Korea during 1960–84), women have been participating more and more in the labor force. In 1985 they constituted 31 percent of all workers in Indonesia and 47 percent in Viet Nam, with the figures for the other economies falling between these extremes. These levels were higher than the overall averages for lower- and upper-middle-income countries, although in this region as in the rest of the world women were still a smaller share of the labor force than men. Labor force participation rates remain much lower for women than for men (table 7-2); the rates for women in 1985 varied between 24 percent in Indonesia and the Philippines and 52 percent in China, whereas for men they varied between 49 percent in the Philippines and 84 percent in Taiwan (China). The rate of unemployment, except in China and the Philippines, was generally lower among women than among men. Discrimination against women was quite marked, however, in a few countries for which data are available, a point discussed later in this chapter.

The economic development of the East Asian countries has improved the status of women dramatically. On the whole, gender inequalities are not as marked as in some neighboring South Asian

Table 7-2. *Women's Rate of Participation in the Labor Force, East Asia, 1965 and Most Recent Available Data*
(percent)

	1965		Most recent available data (about 1985)	
Economy	*Female*	*Male*	*Female*	*Male*
China	44	60	52	64
Hong Kong	25	51	38	64
Indonesia	22	55	24	53
Korea, Rep. of	20	48	28	53
Lao PDR	52	58	45	53
Malaysia	20	47	28	51
Philippines	25	49	24	49
Singapore	15	49	33	63
Taiwan (China)[a]	—	—	42	84
Thailand	47	52	48	56
Viet Nam	46	54	44	52

—Not available.
a. Latest data available are for 1975.
Source: World Bank 1988b, 1989.

countries. But the patriarchal society in China, the matrilineal society in Thailand, and the fading Islamic practice of seclusion (*purdah*) in Indonesia result in significant differences in the status of women across East Asia.[2]

Educational Status

The rapid economic and technological growth of the East Asian economies stems in part from the rapid expansion of their education systems, leading to a fast-growing reservoir of workers with more than a primary education. Economic and technological growth, in turn, has had a profound influence on the education sector. Educational levels attained in the Philippines, for example, are in certain respects comparable to those found in the developed world. Here again, however, the factors behind educational expansion vary from country to country in the region. With a GNP per capita of $590 in 1987, the Philippines has made strong advances in educating girls and women not so much because of economic growth as because of long-standing education policies. Even before World War II, and especially afterward, the country implemented a massive expansion of its education system. Moreover, in this most Western of Asian countries, there are no serious cultural constraints to schooling for girls.

Despite impressive gains in education, literacy rates are uneven in the region, and they are substantially lower for women than for men, except in the Philippines (table 7-3). The problem is most acute in China, where nearly half the women are illiterate. Yet this is still much

Table 7-3. *Literacy Rates of Adults Fifteen and Older, East Asia, Various Years*
(percent)

Economy	Year	Female	Male
China	1982	51.1	79.2
Hong Kong	1971	64.1	90.1
Indonesia	1980	57.7	77.5
Korea, Rep. of	1970	81.0	94.4
Lao PDR[a]	1985	75.8	92.0
Malaysia	1980	59.7	79.6
Philippines	1980	82.8	83.9
Singapore	1980	74.0	91.6
Taiwan (China)	1975	75.6	92.2
Thailand	1980	84.0	92.3
Viet Nam	1979	78.3	90.5

Note: Percentages are for adults between the ages of fifteen and forty-five.
Source: UNESCO, *Statistical Yearbook*, 1987.

Table 7-4. Composition of the Labor Force by Highest Educational Level, East Asia, 1980s

| | | Highest school level (percentage of labor force) | | | | | | |
| | | | Primary | | Secondary | | | |
Economy	Year	No schooling	Incomplete	Complete	Incomplete	Complete	Tertiary	Mean years of school
China	1988	7.2	14.5	18.1	19.8	7.4	13.8	5.6
Hong Kong	1988	8.1	11.7	17.5	19.9	33.9	8.8	9.1
Indonesia	1988	16.6	28.2	34.5	9.0	9.6	1.3	5.0
Korea, Rep. of	1980	14.7	1.1	33.2	18.5	23.4	9.1	8.0
Malaysia	1986	13.2	26.8	12.0	27.7	15.8	5.1	7.0
Philippines	1980	7.8	21.3	27.4	15.1	12.7	15.7	7.0
Singapore	1980	21.9	3.0	46.4	18.4	6.3	4.0	6.0
Taiwan (China)	1988	8.3	5.4	23.6	12.3	35.4	13.2	4.0
Thailand	1980	10.1	64.2	7.0	11.2	4.1	3.4	4.6

Source: Psacharopoulos and Arriagada 1992.

lower than the 70–80 percent illiteracy rates in neighboring South Asian countries. Overall, more than half the adult women in East Asia are literate, and in Korea, the Philippines, and Thailand four out of five women can read. Throughout the region illiteracy is higher in rural than in urban areas.

The level of educational achievement also varies considerably across the region (see Postlethwaite and Thomas 1980; Thomas and Postlethwaite 1983). Data on the composition of the labor force by completed schooling make these differences clear (table 7-4). Workers in the Philippines and Taiwan (China) are much better educated than those in China and Indonesia. In mean years of schooling of the labor force, which serves as a summary statistic of educational development, Hong Kong and Taiwan (China) are most advanced and China, Indonesia, and Thailand are least advanced among the East Asian economies for which data are available (see Oshima 1988).

Enrollments

Although disparities exist, all the economies in the region have made great strides forward in education. China, Hong Kong, Korea, the Philippines, Singapore, and Viet Nam achieved universal primary education more than two decades ago, whereas many countries in South Asia are still struggling to reach this target. The repetition rates at the primary and secondary levels are on the whole very low for both girls and boys—the result in part of automatic promotion policies in primary education (Levy 1971; UNESCO-ROEAP 1984). In general, whether a result or a cause, when gender equity is achieved in enrollment, gender differences in repetition rates are less. If girls are held back in school because the burden of household chores prevents them from attending classes as regularly as boys do, then girls benefit from automatic promotion policies.

In nearly all East Asian countries, universal or nearly universal primary education for both boys and girls was achieved by 1987 (table 7-5). Indonesia made the most progress; the gross enrollment rate rose by 37 percentage points for girls and 27 percentage points for boys in about a decade. The striking exception to progress in the region was Korea, where gross enrollment rates for both boys and girls fell from 107 to 94 percent, possibly as a result of a declining pool of overage children not yet in school. But the Korean picture was brighter at the postprimary levels.

The region as a whole made great strides in raising overall enrollment rates at the secondary level, with notable improvements in the figures for girls relative to boys. The largest increases occurred in Korea; at the end of a decade or so of change, girls had narrowed the

Table 7-5. *Gross Enrollment Rates by Level of Education and by Gender, East Asia, Various Years*
(percent of relevant population)

Economy	Year	Primary Female	Primary Male	Secondary Female	Secondary Male	Tertiary Female	Tertiary Male
China	1975	114	130	38	54	0.4	0.7
	1987	124	132	37	50	1.2	2.3
Hong Kong	1975	117	122	47	51	5.3	14.7
	1987	105	106	76	71	9.3[a]	16.8[a]
Indonesia	1975	78	94	15	25	—	—
	1987	115	121	42	53	4.2[a]	8.9[a]
Korea, Rep. of	1975	107	107	48	64	5.9	14.6
	1987	94	94	86	91	22.2	48.6
Lao PDR	1980	86	102	14	21	0.3	0.6
	1987	98	101	22	31	1.2	2.0
Malaysia	1975	89	92	39	48	1.6	4.0
	1987	102	100	57	56	6.2	7.1
Mongolia	1975	104	111	84	77	8.6	8.2
	1986	103	104	96	88	26.0	17.4
Philippines	1980	113	113	69	61	28.5	26.8
	1987	110	105	68	67	—	—
Singapore	1975	107	113	52	51	7.3	10.7
	1987	111	118	69	67	10.2	13.3[b]
Thailand	1975	80	87	23	28	2.7	4.0
	1980	97	99	28	30	—	—
Viet Nam	1975	108	106	41	38	1.6	2.6
	1985	99	105	40	43	1.0[c]	3.8[c]

—Not available.

Note: Gross enrollment rates are defined as the ratio (expressed in percent) of all students enrolled in say, the primary level to the population in the relevant age group. These rates can exceed 100 percent due to a large number of underage or overage students. Data for Taiwan (China) are from another source and are given in table 7-1.

a. 1984.
b. 1983.
c. 1980.

Source: UNESCO, *Statistical Yearbook,* 1987, 1990.

16-percentage-point gap in 1975 to just 5 percentage points in 1987. The gender gap was greatest in China, Indonesia, and the Lao PDR. Mongolia also had a large gender gap in secondary school enrollment, but with girls outnumbering boys.

At the tertiary level only five of the eleven economies had double-digit gross enrollment rates. In two of them, Mongolia and the Philippines, women outnumbered men in institutions of higher learning. In the other three, as in the countries with much lower tertiary enrollments, women lagged behind men. Korea and Mongolia show the biggest rise in tertiary enrollment for the period covered. In Korea the gender gap widened greatly in favor of men, but in Mongolia women experienced a much greater increase in enrollment than men did.

High rates of enrollment do not necessarily correspond to high levels of public spending on education in East Asia (table 7-6). Some economies that spend comparatively little, including Hong Kong and the Philippines, have made remarkable progress in education in general and in female education in particular.[3] Other economies that have devoted higher shares of their GNP and government budget to education have not made as much progress. Malaysia invested 7.8 percent of its GNP in education in 1986 yet had a secondary school enrollment rate of only 57 percent. Korea and Singapore invested 3.9 and 3.8 percent, respectively, in 1987, yet they had secondary school enrollment rates of 88 and 68 percent. The Philippines expanded its education system remarkably, given a meager investment of just 2.0 percent of GNP. The implication is that the level of public spending on education only partly explains the expansion of education. The willingness of households and the nongovernment sector to invest in education is also an important component.

Gender Differences

Despite significant progress in extending educational opportunities to more and more East Asian girls and women, being female is still a disadvantage, as statistics on literacy rates, already cited, make clear. The distribution of males and females by level of education is another

Table 7-6. *Public Investment in Education, East Asia, Various Years*

Economy	Year	Percentage of GNP	Percentage of budget
China	1987	2.4	8.1[a]
Hong Kong	1984	2.8	18.7
Indonesia	1981	2.0	9.3
Korea, Rep. of	1987	3.9	26.6
Lao PDR	1986	—	6.6
Malaysia	1986	7.8	16.9
Philippines	1987	2.0	7.0[b]
Singapore	1987	3.8	11.5
Taiwan (China)	1979	4.1	5.6[c]
Thailand	1987	3.6	17.9

—Not available.
Note: Data are not available for Mongolia and Viet Nam.
a. 1983.
b. 1984.
c. 1982.
Source: UNESCO, *Statistical Yearbook*, 1987, 1990.

measure of this gender gap. Table 7-7 shows this distribution for adult males and females in the early 1980s (in 1970 for Malaysia). In every country of the region for which data are available, the share of women with no formal schooling was larger than the share of men. The largest discrepancy was in China; in 1982 nearly two-thirds of adult women had no formal schooling, compared with about one-fourth of adult men. Even in the NIES, except in Singapore, the percentage of adults with no schooling was at least twice as high for women as for men.

These statistics do not fully reflect recent gains, however. The enrollment rates in table 7-5 suggest that by the 1980s most of these economies had significantly reduced, if not eliminated, the gender imbalances in primary education. In fact, such imbalances had mostly disappeared by the 1970s. Primary education is now universal or nearly universal for girls and boys in almost all countries of the region.[4]

Table 7-7. *Distribution of Adult Population by Highest Educational Level and by Gender, East Asia, Various Years*
(percent)

Economy	Year	Population	No schooling	Primary[a]	Secondary[b]	Tertiary
China	1982	Females	62.3	23.6	13.6	0.5
		Males	27.6	41.3	29.2	1.5
Hong Kong	1981	Females	35.9	34.8	24.3	5.0
		Males	10.3	44.4	40.0	9.0
Indonesia	1980	Females	53.9	39.5	6.3	0.4
		Males	27.8	57.6	13.0	1.2
Korea, Rep. of	1980	Females	26.9	39.4	29.6	4.0
		Males	12.0	29.3	44.7	14.1
Malaysia[c]	1970	Females	51.0	38.2	10.8	—[d]
		Males	35.9	46.9	17.0	—[d]
Philippines	1980	Females	13.3	55.1	16.6	15.1
		Males	10.3	53.1	21.2	15.3
Singapore	1980	Females	54.3	31.2	12.5	2.0
		Males	33.5	46.1	16.6	4.8
Taiwan	1980	Females	22.8	36.5	34.0	6.8
(China)[e]		Males	9.3	34.7	43.2	12.7
Thailand	1980	Females	26.3	67.0	4.3	2.4
		Males	14.4	72.6	9.5	3.4

Note: Population is age twenty-five and older, except where noted.
a. Includes incomplete and complete.
b. Includes "entered."
c. Includes population of all ages.
d. Included in secondary enrollment.
e. Includes population age fifteen and older.
Sources: For Taiwan (China), Kaneko 1987; for others, UNESCO, *Statistical Yearbook*, 1987.

Because the populations of these countries are divided almost evenly between males and females, equality in education would exist if half of all students were female. In the mid-1980s almost half the children in primary schools were girls, and this ratio held for secondary schools in much of the region as well. Korea, for example, made significant progress in equalizing enrollments at the secondary level, with female enrollment rising from 41 to 47 percent of total enrollment between 1975 and 1987.

Growth rates, given in table 7-8, tell the story of how fast female and male enrollments have been rising in the region. The negative rates for primary education in Hong Kong, Korea, and Singapore reflect declines in their population growth rates and thus in the youngest school-age cohorts. In the countries with positive growth rates, girls' enrollment in primary school rose about as fast as, if not faster than, boys' enrollment. Beyond the primary level, enrollments grew much faster for females than for males. Exceptions are the Philippines, where, prior to 1980, male enrollment at the tertiary level had lagged behind female enrollment, as well as China and Viet Nam.[5]

And yet, despite the significant progress recounted here, gender differences in education persist, most notably in the distribution of students by gender and field of study at the secondary and higher levels. For example, girls gravitate toward those fields traditionally dominated by women: nutrition, nursing, and teacher training. In the Philippines more than 90 percent of the students in each of these fields have been women; males have been prevalent in engineering, law, agriculture, and technology (Borcelle 1985; Neher 1982).

Table 7-8. *Average Annual Growth Rates of Female and Male School Enrollment, East Asia, 1970–85*
(percent)

Economy	Primary		Secondary		Tertiary	
	Females	*Males*	*Females*	*Males*	*Females*	*Males*
China	1.6	1.6	4.4	4.7	26.5	28.7
Hong Kong	−2.1	−2.1	6.3	3.9	9.0	7.2
Indonesia	5.1	4.4	11.0	8.4	12.4	9.7
Korea, Rep. of	−1.0	−1.1	8.0	5.3	15.8	13.5
Lao PDR	6.6	4.3	17.9	12.8	23.6	17.0
Malaysia	2.0	2.1	6.4	4.1	17.0	11.2
Mongolia	2.1	2.1	5.7	5.1	14.1	10.1
Philippines	1.7	1.6	4.6	4.0	7.5	7.9
Singapore	−1.8	−1.8	2.1	1.6	10.3	6.4
Thailand	2.0	1.8	7.0	5.4	18.8	16.8
Viet Nam	1.0	0.8	5.1	3.9	−1.9	−1.4

Source: Computed from UNESCO, *Statistical Yearbook,* 1989.

Table 7-9 confirms that the overwhelming majority of female secondary students in all East Asian countries were enrolled in the general education stream in the 1980s and that, except in the Lao PDR and Malaysia, very few were enrolled in teacher training institutes. The fraction of girls who chose to attend vocational and technical schools at the secondary level varied much more, from about 2 percent in Malaysia to almost 25 percent in Indonesia. These figures may not accurately capture the vocational orientation of female secondary school students, however, because general secondary schools in some countries offer selected vocational and technical courses alongside the traditional academic subjects.

At the tertiary level two fields of study dominate as the choice of female students in nearly all the East Asian countries: education and business administration (table 7-10). Contrary to a commonly held belief, very few women in higher education specialize in home economics, except in Korea. Engineering does not attract many women except in Singapore, where they accounted for 17 percent of the engineering students in 1983. Among male students the pattern is very different. Except in Indonesia, Malaysia, and Viet Nam, only a small fraction are in education and teacher training. Engineering is the primary field of study for men in all countries except Indonesia.

Table 7-9. *Distribution of Female Secondary Enrollment by Type of Education, about 1975 and Most Recent Year Available*
(percent)

	1975			Most recent year[a]		
Economy	General	Teacher training	Vocational and technical	General	Teacher training	Vocational and technical
China	98.3	1.1	1.5	92.4	0.9	6.5
Hong Kong	91.9	0.0	7.7	90.5	0.0	9.4
Indonesia	73.5	2.0	24.5	86.8	2.4	9.6
Korea, Rep. of	84.0	0.0	16.0	83.7	0.0	16.3
Lao PDR	88.7[b]	8.8[b]	2.0[b]	87.6	9.9	2.6
Malaysia	97.7[c]	0.0[c]	2.2[c]	97.7	0.0	2.3
Mongolia	94.4	0.3	4.7	93.8	0.3	5.6
Singapore	92.3	0.0	7.1	93.5	0.0	6.7
Thailand	80.7	3.5	15.7	84.1	0.5	—
Viet Nam	96.9[b]	0.5[b]	2.7[b]	—	—	—

—Not available.

Note: Rows may not add to 100 percent because of rounding.

a. The most recent year for which data are available is usually early to mid-1980s.

b. 1976.

c. 1980.

Source: UNESCO, *Statistical Yearbook,* 1987, 1991.

Table 7-10. *Distribution of Students in Higher Education by Field of Study and Gender, East Asia, 1980s*

Economy	Education and teacher training	Commerce and business administration	Home economics	Natural science	Medicine and health-related sciences	Engineering
Hong Kong, 1984						
Females	14.3	38.3	0.0	2.3	3.0	2.1
Males	4.4	17.9	0.0	4.5	3.3	42.9
Indonesia, 1984						
Females	28.4	17.3	0.5	2.6	2.5	5.7
Males	22.1	12.3	0.1	2.0	2.5	13.8
Korea, Rep. of, 1986						
Females	21.7	8.7	9.6	3.1	8.7	2.1
Males	6.5	21.1	0.2	3.8	4.0	23.0
Malaysia, 1985						
Females	36.8	16.4	0.2	6.2	3.3	4.0
Males	17.1	14.5	0.2	7.2	3.0	19.5
Philippines, 1985						
Females	20.1	44.5	0.9	1.0	9.0	4.3
Males	8.6	17.7	0.0	0.6	3.2	30.0
Singapore, 1983						
Females	25.4	18.8	0.0	10.3	2.5	17.4
Males	7.0	6.8	0.0	4.2	3.7	62.6
Viet Nam, 1980						
Females	44.9	13.0	0.0	1.9	6.8	6.7
Males	34.5	12.0	0.0	2.3	11.0	10.8

Note: Rows do not add to 100 percent because of the omission of the category "Other fields."

Source: UNESCO, *Statistical Yearbook,* 1987.

Women's educational choices are both influenced by and influence women's occupational prospects (see Sutherland 1988). When educational options and occupations correspond closely, gender differences may be sharp. In the Philippines, for example, 95 percent of the teachers in primary and secondary schools were women, and nearly three-fourths of those in education and teacher training courses at the tertiary level were women. This gender bias was also evident in postschool training. Lazo (1984) reports that women usually learned the garment trade, embroidery, clerical work, food and nutrition, and food preservation and processing. Men mostly trained to be supervisors or instructors or they studied such fields as electricity, automotive mechanics, and radio and television mechanics.

The concentration of women in a few areas of study and training has several causes. Girls are pushed by social pressures into fields that lead to low-paying jobs. They choose subjects that complement both market and nonmarket activities since, unlike men, they foresee periods of specialization in the household as wives and mothers (Ram 1982). The lack of access to professional jobs also influences women's choices. One study reports that in Indonesia, Korea, and Thailand barely 3 percent of the female labor force was in professional occupations; in Malaysia and Taiwan (China) the figure was only about 5 percent (Kurian 1982). Comparisons over time may indicate, as Don (1984) has argued in the case of Malaysian secondary education, that the use of educational facilities by women has tended to complement the use by men—that is, female enrollment decreased when male enrollment in economically advantageous programs rose. Such patterns are not unusual.[6] More important, however, is that these patterns seem to be "resistant to changes even under conditions where equalization between men and women has been a prime goal in educational reforms" (Harnqvist 1987, p. 358), as it has been in developing East Asia.

Some people argue that occupational segregation by gender may not be totally disadvantageous to women but may in fact contribute to an increase in female enrollment. A greater demand for teachers, for example, may induce more women to enroll in teacher training courses. The Islamic tradition of gender segregation may, as McGrath (1976) argues, help promote the employment of women as teachers or physicians because only women are allowed to teach or to treat women. In the long run, however, this pattern may not be to women's advantage.

Labor Market Factors

Conditions in the labor market also influence a family's educational decisions significantly. Gender-based disparities in the workplace can determine the educational level and choice of subject for sons and daughters. At least four factors in the labor market are important in this context: wage structure, employment and unemployment levels, rates of participation in the labor force, and rates of return on education. Very few studies that seek to explain schooling choices estimate the feedback effect of these labor market conditions, however.

Wage Discrimination

According to human capital theory, the wage structure and especially expected changes in wages play a dominant role in shaping decisions about investing in education. Wage structures everywhere in the world tend to favor men.[7] The East Asian economies are no exception. Table 7-11 presents data on nonagricultural wages, not specified by years of schooling, for three East Asian economies. In 1985–86 women in Korea earned less than half what men earned; in Singapore, about two-thirds; and in Hong Kong, three-fourths. In a detailed examination in the Philippines, Arcelo and Sanyal (1987) found that men had higher wages in all fields except in those regarded as female, such as food, nutrition, dietetics, and also, surprisingly, law and certain liberal arts. In some industries in Malaysia, wages were three times as high for men as for women (Sundaram and Leng 1985).[8]

These male-female wage ratios reinforce parents' traditional bias against educating their daughters, and they discourage the daughters themselves. According to a study on Malaysia (Wang 1982), boys expected their salaries to be higher than did girls. The less a group perceives further education as contributing to earnings, the less it tends to continue in school.[9] Differentials in "full" earnings, which include benefits, would be a more appropriate measure of the gap in earnings between men and women. Although many modern government sectors pay equal wages to men and women for the same job, men may enjoy greater fringe benefits, such as cost of living and housing allowances, as they do in Malaysia (Wang 1982).

Employment and Unemployment

The link between education and female participation in the labor force is well documented. Frequent estimates have been made of the effect of education on the probability of being employed (see Shields 1987). Individual survey data from Indonesia (Corner 1987;

Table 7-11. *Wage Discrimination in Hong Kong, Korea, and Singapore, Nonagricultural Sector*

Economy	Year	Earnings (local currency) Female	Male	Coefficient of discrimination[a]
Hong Kong	1982	66.70	87.90	0.3178
(wages per day)	1986	98.10	129.80	0.3231
Korea, Rep. of	1977	47.40	107.60	1.2700
(earnings per month)	1986	208.90	426.90	1.0436
Singapore	1980	1.68	2.67	0.5893
(earnings per hour)	1985	2.78	4.04	0.4532

a. The coefficient of discrimination, as defined by Becker (1957), is $(W_m/W_f) - 1$, where W_m and W_f refer to male and female wages, respectively. A lower coefficient indicates greater equality.

Source: Based on United Nations 1985.

Nagib 1986) and the Philippines (Encarnacion 1974; Harman 1970) show a clear and positive relation between females' average years of schooling and their participation in the labor force. The ways in which the rate of labor force participation influences education have rarely been examined, however. Becker (1964, p. 51) argues that "women spend less time in the labor force than men, and therefore, have less incentive to invest in market skills."[10] In other words, a lower rate of participation in the labor force by women can lead to less education.

A strong employment picture may reduce school enrollment because the opportunity cost of education rises, or it may stimulate enrollment because the future returns to education (in the form of better jobs) increase. Women's demand for schooling may be directly tied to their perceptions about their employment opportunities and future earnings. According to Wang (1982), Malaysian women thought that employment conditions were unfavorable and that they would get jobs that paid less than men with the same education would get. Their perceptions were well founded. The range of jobs available to women was restricted by discriminatory hiring practices, inadequate information about employment opportunities, society's expectations for women, and the "male monopoly of the labor market" (Madden 1975). Compared with women, men expected that a wider range of better-paying jobs would be open to them. The perceptions of parents and husbands regarding employment probabilities for women also significantly influence decisions about women's education. A worsening employment situation may have serious adverse effects on enrollments, more so for females than for males. When unemployment becomes widespread, a popular opinion is that "women should withdraw into their homes and leave the available posts for men"; men are seen as the principal breadwinners, women as earners of supplementary income or "pin money" (Sutherland 1988, p. 486). Given such attitudes, women have little incentive to pursue a career. In China the Communist party has stated in its theoretical publication that women's productive role should be only "secondary and supportive" (Hooper 1984, p. 327).

Employment conditions are quite good in those East Asian economies that have experienced rapid technological advances. As noted earlier, the annual rate of growth in employment exceeded 3 percent in most of the region during 1960–84, Indonesia and Korea being the exceptions. Although education-specific data on unemployment rates by gender are not available, women as a whole experienced lower rates of unemployment than men in Hong Kong, Korea, Singapore, and Thailand (table 7-12). The opposite was true in the Philippines; nev-

Table 7-12. *Unemployment in the Labor Force, East Asia*

Economy	Year	Females	Males
China[a]	1983	1.1	0.7
	1986	1.0	0.6
Hong Kong[b]	1977	4.2	4.4
	1986	2.5	3.0
Korea, Rep. of[b]	1977	2.4	4.6
	1986	2.1	4.9
Philippines[b]	1977	8.6	2.6
	1985	8.2	4.8
Singapore[b]	1977	1.6	2.3
	1986	5.5	7.0
Taiwan (China)	1968	11.9	5.3
Thailand[b]	1977	0.8	1.2
	1980	0.7	1.0

a. Official estimates.
b. Based on labor force surveys.
Sources: Taiwan (China), Visaria and Pal 1980, p. 90; others, United Nations 1985.

ertheless, unemployment was increasing more slowly for women than for men (see also Encarnacion, Tagunicar, and Tidalgo 1976).[11]

These overall trends in employment were inversely related to current enrollment in higher education. The very low female unemployment rates in China and Thailand were positively associated with comparatively low female enrollment rates in secondary and higher education, and the high female unemployment rate in the Philippines was associated with a very high female enrollment rate in higher education. These facts lend some support to the argument that opportunity cost is an important factor in schooling decisions. Although tertiary education is largely private in the Philippines, private schooling tends to be quite affordable, being generally even less costly than public education.

Unequal Rates of Return to Education

Another aspect of the human capital theory is that the rate of return, which reflects both the costs and benefits of education, provides "signals of direction" for additional demand for education. T. Paul Schultz, in chapter 2 of this volume, presents estimates of the rates of return to education by gender.[12] Because of differences in estimation methods, the rates of return across countries are not directly comparable. But the estimates are useful for comparing rates of return between men and women within a country. In Indonesia, Korea, Taiwan (China), and Thailand, the rates of return were higher to women's education than to men's. In Malaysia investing in secondary education yielded a higher rate of return to women than to men, whereas investing in higher education returned more to men than to women, although the differences were not large. In Singapore rates of return to all levels of education were marginally higher for men than for women. On the whole, then, women's education in East Asian economies yielded returns that were higher than or about equal to the returns to men's education.[13] In these economies, however, with few exceptions, female enrollment rates in secondary and tertiary education were still lower than male enrollment rates. Thus, rates of return alone fail to explain female enrollment rates in East Asia.[14] They do strongly suggest, however, that most East Asian economies underinvest in women's education.

School Characteristics

School supply and other related factors have an important impact on educational attainment. Schools that have inadequate resources or that fail to provide relevant curricula lead to low enrollment, poor attendance, and underachievement by students. Heyneman and Loxley (1983) in a study of twenty-nine countries and Fuller (1986) in a review of about sixty empirical studies found that school characteristics were more significantly linked to levels of educational achievement than were socioeconomic characteristics of the family.

Availability of Schools

The availability of school facilities is important in determining levels of participation by both boys and girls. It may be more important for girls, however; parents may not mind sending their sons to a neighboring village for school but may hesitate to send their daughters. As Kelly (1984, p. 86) observes, "the greatest single indicator of whether or not a girl will attend school may well be whether schooling is made both available and accessible." A study on Indonesia concludes that "when educational facilities are available and accessible (in proximity and cost), daughters are likely to be given equal opportunity with sons" (Scott 1985, p. 13). Opening more schools after independence in Malaysia boosted female enrollment significantly (Hirschman 1979). As mentioned earlier, the Philippines' achievements in female education are attributable in part to the great expansion of the school system over the past fifty years.

Closely related to the supply of schools is the distance to schools. "Among the most problematic factors for girls are the costs of travel to school (in time of hazards), a matter of both logistics and cultural norms" (Bowman and Anderson 1982, p. 25). Physical accessibility is

important to improving enrollments—if a school is within the community and within easy walking distance, enrollment is likely to be
high for both boys and girls—and it may be critical to the enrollment
of girls. In a study of 400 households in twenty-two rural villages in
Thailand, Cochrane and Jamison (1982) found that the distance to
school negatively and significantly affected participation by both boys
and girls. Surprisingly, however, the impact on girls' participation was
less. In the Philippines the effect was as expected; when a school was
provided within the village or at a "short distance," enrollment was
estimated to increase by 3 percent for girls but by only 1 percent for
boys (King and Lillard 1987). King and Lillard also report positive
effects in Malaysia from having a school in the community where
children live.[15]

Schools with only lower primary grades may not attract as many
students as would a complete primary school. This factor may be more
important in decisions regarding schooling for girls than for boys
because to complete the primary level a child would have to travel
some distance to school. As Johnstone (1976, p. 234) notes, "parents
perceiving the non-availability of complete primary level schooling
are more prone to withdraw their children (or not to send them at all)
than are parents who live in regions or areas where complete primary
schools exist." De Tray (1988) found that Malaysian children living in
communities without a secondary school had lower rates of enrollment in primary school than did children living in communities with
a secondary school, and this effect was larger for girls than for boys.
Distance to the secondary school did not appear to affect girls and
boys differently, but the lack of convenient transportation affected
girls' enrollment more adversely than it did boys' enrollment.

Type of School

Both the type and the quality of schools also influence parents' decisions about their daughters' education. In a traditional or religious
environment, for example, religious schools may be more effective
than other schools in enrolling female children. The Islamic schools
in Malaysia assure parents that traditional social values will be taught
so that their daughters will make better wives and better Muslims (Don
1984). Female students compose a large majority in these schools,
indicating that religious schools are more important for girls than for
boys.

One relevant consideration is whether a school is coeducational (see
Lee and Lockheed 1990). Many traditional middle-class parents prefer
to place their daughters in the protective environment of a girls'
school. Free mixing of boys and girls in coeducational schools is re-

garded as morally unhealthy for girls. Empirical research confirms that this attitude exists: single-sex schools are considered more prestigious for social as well as educational reasons (Smock 1981). Jiménez and Lockheed (1988) found that even after controlling for such factors as socioeconomic family background and school resources, girls in Thailand achieved more in girls' schools than in coeducational schools, whereas boys did better in coeducational schools. A variety of factors contributed to this advantage for girls, including a more supportive atmosphere in girls' schools (see also Jiménez, Lockheed, and Wattanawaha 1988). In East Asia, however, such schools are few in number. In Malaysia, for example, coeducational schools greatly outnumber single-sex schools (Don 1984).

Female Teachers

Traditional middle-class families, especially Muslim ones, prefer that their daughters be taught by female teachers. A shortage of female teachers may be an important educational constraint in these societies. The number of female teachers is a function of how many women enroll in teacher training courses in secondary and higher education. China and the Lao PDR rank lowest in the share of primary school teachers who are women (table 7-13). In 1987 only about two-

Table 7-13. Women as Share of Teachers by Level of Education, East Asia, 1980s
(percent)

Economy	Year	Primary	Secondary	Tertiary
China	1987	41	29	28
Hong Kong	1987	74	49	24[a]
Indonesia	1987	49	33	18[a]
Korea, Rep. of	1987	46	31	15[b]
Laos PDR	1987	35	35[c]	22[c]
Malaysia	1987	53	49	22[c]
Mongolia	1986	—	—	39
Philippines	1984	95	95	53[b]
Singapore	1987	71	52[b]	21[d]
Thailand	1980	49	—	56[e]
Viet Nam	1985	70	57[e]	22[b]

—Not available.
a. 1984.
b. 1980.
c. 1985.
d. 1983.
e. 1976.
Source: UNESCO, Statistical Yearbook, 1990.

fifths of the primary school teachers in China and just over one-third of those in the Lao PDR were women. At the secondary level these two countries are joined by Indonesia and Korea in having many fewer female than male teachers. In the Philippines, where the share of female teachers corresponds closely to the share of female students in total school enrollment, male teachers are in the minority. The evidence suggests that patterns of female enrollment in East Asia are associated with the share of teachers who are women, but no micro-level studies focused on students rather than schools have analyzed whether the presence of female teachers encourages girls' enrollment. Because this factor is often cited as a potential force in raising girls' education beyond present levels, a more rigorous examination of this correlation is needed.

Direct Costs

Several direct school expenses, including fees, books, clothing (uniforms), hostels, and transport, have been found to be higher for girls than for boys in many countries. Chernichovsky and Meesook (1985) have estimated that fees and other school expenditures in Indonesia were Rp. 190 (rupiah) for primary school and Rp. 1,090 for junior high school for girls, compared with Rp. 132 and Rp. 862, respectively, for boys. At the senior high school level, however, expenditures were much less for girls than for boys—Rp. 841 and Rp. 1,425, respectively. The explanation may be that boys are more likely to be enrolled in courses such as science laboratories that entail extra capital expenditures.

In the household calculus of the total costs and benefits of education, higher direct costs at the lower school levels for girls than for boys may be a substantial barrier to the education of girls from poor families (see also Deble 1980). The expansion of public education in many countries has paid rich dividends in raising girls' enrollment in primary school. Reforms contributing to this expansion include abolishing the fee in lower primary grades in Indonesia in 1976 and making primary education free in Malaysia and other countries. The large-scale textbook program in Indonesia, as well as the textbook loan scheme, supplementary feeding programs, and scholarships for the needy at the secondary level in Malaysia, are also seen as significant factors in boosting women's schooling.

The Philippines guaranteed equal rights to education as early as 1901, and Thailand enacted policies for compulsory education in 1921. As expected, policies designed to achieve universal primary education in the East Asian countries reduced the significant gap in education that had previously existed (see UNESCO 1980b). In Indonesia special government efforts to direct more resources to primary educa-

tion and a massive program to build more schools increased enrollment in primary education remarkably. China provides an excellent
example of what can be accomplished through effective policies of
decentralization and local financing of primary education. Furthermore, in China's Gansu province, allowing girls to take younger siblings to school with them has enabled many to attend school who
would otherwise have had to remain at home (World Bank 1988a).

Governments have directed other assistance to female students. In
Korea, for example, a larger number of women than men in colleges
and universities receive scholarships: 58 percent of the scholarships
went to women in 1980, compared with 38 percent in 1975 (Korean
Council for University Education 1988). These financial aid policies
may be partly responsible for Korea's significant improvement in enrolling women in institutions of higher education.

Cultural Factors

In most developing societies, families place a lower value on educating
their daughters than on educating their sons. In East Asia this preference seems less strong than elsewhere and is declining. As McGrath
(1976, p. 37) puts it, "Most obstacles to full equality in education exist
only in people's minds, in the insubstantial, diaphanous forms of
prejudice, traditional beliefs, and cultural stereotypes." In a study on
Taiwan (China), Greenhalgh (1985) presents evidence of gender discrimination in education. The highly patriarchal traditional family
system was reflected in parental discrimination against daughters.
Girls had to renounce education for themselves and work to finance
their brothers' education. The data indicate that in families with a
larger number of daughters, the number of years of schooling of sons
is also higher.[16] Taiwanese families' investments in postschool training
and apprenticeship show a marked discrimination against daughters.
Parents viewed their daughters' education as a stopgap between childhood and marriage and as a means of improving their marriageability.
In Malaysia as well, education seems to have been considered primarily a way for girls to increase their desirability as marriage partners
(Weekes-Vagliani 1980). Parents tried to equalize schooling among
their sons but not among all their children including daughters. In
another study King and others (1986) estimated that if daughters were
treated like sons, female schooling levels would rise by 150 percent in
rural Java (Indonesia) and by 30 percent in the Philippines, where
discrimination was less severe.

One reason for parental bias against educating girls is that by the
time daughters are employed, they may be married, so parents do not
reap the benefits of their daughters' increased earnings. Education, by

its very nature, has a long gestation period. In Thailand, however, where women take care of their parents in old age, parents wanted to provide as much education to their daughters as to their sons (Safilios-Rothschild 1980).

Religion and Ethnic Origin

Religion is generally believed to be a dominant influence on a family's decisions about educating daughters.[17] Religious ideas and teachings exert a powerful influence in shaping society's values in general and its views on female education in particular. In the Philippines "religion and linked cultural patterns provide the major origins of division" by gender (Smock 1981, pp. 17–18).

Although most religions do not explicitly discourage female education, in practice some religions have done so. Certain religions, such as Theravada Buddhism, are regarded as fostering technological change (Niehoff 1964), whereas others, such as Islam and Confucianism, are believed to hinder progress. Islam has discouraged female education, given its view of the proper place of women (Kelly 1984).[18] Among the economies in East Asia other than China, the two Muslim countries—Indonesia and Malaysia—have had the lowest rates of female literacy and the highest gender gap in literacy. In Islamic societies, as Dasgupta (1988, p. 130) observes, "even if literacy is regarded as a good thing for men, the same may not apply to women. Female literacy may be thought, at best, to be unimportant. Some may even be persuaded that it is undesirable, for literacy could have the effect of making women *less* fit for the role they are traditionally expected to perform." But the Muslim states in East Asia differ from Muslim states elsewhere in Asia and in the rest of the world. Muslim women in East Asia do not practice seclusion (*purdah*) and by and large are not constrained by rigid gender segregation (see Whyte and Whyte 1978).

Some Islamic states have made progress in educating females comparable to that in industrial countries. In Malaysia, for example, although the relatively conservative Sunni Muslims were in the majority in 1985, women constituted 44 percent of total enrollment in higher education, a rate comparable to that in some European countries. But religious education has played a significant role in the development of women's education in Malaysia. Girls predominated in Islamic schools because most parents preferred to send their daughters to schools that segregate boys and girls. Parents also felt that girls in religious schools were less likely to go astray and would make better wives (see Don 1984). The Islamic schools in Indonesia have not had a similar effect on women's enrollment, however, probably because they have become "more and more like secular schools" (Thomas 1988).

Ethnicity—which is linked to culture, values, and social position— appears to be an important determinant of educational participation in many countries. In Malaysia significant differences in educational levels are evident between Malay and Chinese women. Studies of Kuala Lumpur in the early 1980s found that 2.3 percent of working Chinese women had a postsecondary education, whereas among Malay women the share was three times as high. Indeed, a greater share of Malay women in the work force have a secondary or higher education than do Malay men (see Mazumdar 1981; Weekes-Vagliani 1980). Controlling for family socioeconomic characteristics, de Tray (1988) found that Chinese and Indians in Malaysia tended to have lower enrollment rates than Malays, but this inequity seemed to have been less for girls than for boys. King and Lillard (1987), also controlling for other socioeconomic characteristics, found that the enrollment rates of Malay women improved much more than those of Chinese women as a result of the education reforms begun in the early 1970s. The ratio of Malay to Chinese enrollment rates at the secondary level increased from 0.6 for cohorts born before 1952 to 1.3 for cohorts born after 1964; at the tertiary level, this ratio rose from 0.8 to 1.2.

Marital Status

Several studies have argued that marriage, which is almost universal for women in East Asia, discourages women from continuing their education.[19] Systematic differences have been found between the educational levels of married and unmarried women. Single women have more education than married women.[20] This implies that the lower the legal age of marriage, the lower is the level of enrollment of females, particularly in secondary and higher education. The scanty evidence is not decisive, however. As Bowman and Anderson (1982, p. 19) have observed, "There is no simple trade-off between marriage and schooling, for in most countries the proportions married plus those in school add up to much less than 100 percent. Rather, it appears that there are common causes for both early marriage and low school attendance."

In Hong Kong women marry late, work before marriage, and help their parents financially. As a result, parents attach the same importance to their daughters' education as to their sons' (Salaff 1976). Of the six economies in the region for which data are available, the minimum legal age at which women may marry is fifteen in Thailand, sixteen in Indonesia and Korea, eighteen in Taiwan (China) and Malaysia (Kurian 1982), and twenty in China. Enrollment rates for women in secondary and higher education have been much lower in Thailand than in Malaysia but have been higher in Korea. In China, which has the highest legal age for marriage, enrollment in secondary and higher education has been among the lowest in the region. Thus, the relationship between the minimum age of marriage and participation in secondary and higher education has not been consistent.

The direction of causality in this relationship is also unclear. Actual or desired level of educational attainment may postpone marriage. Women who have more education marry later, so marriage does not substantially affect their education or participation in the labor force (Montgomery and Sulak 1989). King and others (1986) examined the effect of the level of completed schooling on age at marriage and labor force participation in Indonesia and the Philippines. They found that among poor urban and rural families in Java, education increased the chances that women would enter the labor market and that they would marry later.

Even though education is associated with higher socioeconomic status and other direct benefits, East Asian men do not necessarily prefer to marry better-educated women. A survey of university students in China found that only 28 percent of the male students preferred to marry university graduates (Hooper 1984, pp. 331–32). The others feared that women with university degrees would lose the "traditional feminine virtues of gentleness and devotion." Hooper concluded that in China "higher education might well be detrimental to a young woman's marriage prospects."

Dowry practices also have implications for female education. The dowry is an important cultural factor with economic consequences. Huge dowries force poor parents to postpone their daughters' marriages and spend resources that might otherwise be available for educating them. To the extent that women's education is viewed as an asset, however, it may supplement or even replace a dowry. For many parents, providing daughters with a higher education is at least a partial substitute for paying a dowry to the bridegroom. In several societies women's earnings before marriage also become part of the dowry.

Household Characteristics

Although culture and the economy have a critical role in determining educational levels, the family (and household) bears the ultimate responsibility for educating its children. In the literature, several factors together describe the socioeconomic status of a household: family education and wealth, parents' own education, and family size.

Family Income. Among the many factors that influence parents' decisions about educating their daughters, the family's economic status, as

Table 7-14. Distribution of Reasons for Not Attending School, Indonesia
(percent)

| | Ages 7–12 | | | | Ages 13–15 | | | | Ages 16–18 | | | |
| | Java | | Outer Islands | | Java | | Outer Islands | | Java | | Outer Islands | |
Reason	Male	Female	Male	Female	Male	Female	Male	Female	Male	Female	Male	Female
Had sufficient schooling	1.9	8.4	0.0	5.3	5.0	4.9	5.6	7.8	3.9	10.0	10.7	9.0
No funds	48.1	49.1	49.3	43.9	51.5	47.7	56.9	55.8	55.9	49.8	53.4	55.9
Too difficult	12.5	20.4	16.4	17.9	13.1	12.4	14.5	11.6	11.8	11.7	11.3	8.3
School too far away	9.6	2.4	0.0	0.0	7.0	8.4	4.5	1.1	5.8	5.5	2.8	1.5
Other	27.9	19.8	34.2	33.0	23.4	26.6	18.6	23.7	22.7	23.0	21.8	25.3

Note: Columns may not add to 100 percent because of rounding.
Source: Chernichovsky and Meesook 1985, p. 16.

measured by income and assets, is critical. Several studies have confirmed this for East Asia. Cochrane and Jamison (1982) observed that parental landholding, an important indicator of wealth in rural society, was the most important predictor of female (but not male) educational attainment. In rural Malaysia the low socioeconomic status of Chinese families was an important barrier to education for females but not for males (see Safilios-Rothschild 1980). De Tray (1988) found that in Peninsular Malaysia family income had three times as much influence on the probability that twelve-to-eighteen-year-old girls would be enrolled in school as on the probability that boys of the same age would be in school. Chernichovsky and Meesook (1985) concluded that in Indonesia, although school enrollments were lower for females than for males in every income group, females from better-off and urban families had higher enrollment rates than those from other segments of the population. In one survey, direct responses from Indonesian parents about why their children were not in school also indicated the importance of income as a determinant of school investments (table 7-14). Economic hardship ("no funds") was the single most frequent reason given for not sending children to school; its importance appears to be the same for daughters as for sons.

A low family income may force girls to abandon school because the opportunity cost of sending a child to school is perceived as being higher for a daughter than for a son. Girls may earn wages in the labor market or help in household work so that their mothers can take up wage labor.[21] This also enables their brothers to go to school. The higher opportunity cost of educating women, combined with the narrower range of economic opportunities open to them as adults, account for the low participation by women in secondary and higher education in poor countries such as Indonesia.

Parents' Education and Occupation. Parents' education and occupation are particularly important to the education of daughters. Parental education generally influences female participation in schooling positively. Well-educated parents perceive the intrinsic and monetary benefits of schooling more clearly than less-educated parents do. Parents who have themselves benefited from the link between education and earnings tend to send their children to school. Working mothers may be especially motivated to send their daughters to school.

A study on Indonesia found that, in families where the head of household had a university education, the gender difference in their children's enrollment rates was narrower than it was for the general population. Moreover, in some age groups (or at some levels of education), females had higher enrollment rates than males did (Chernichovsky and Meesook 1985). King and others (1986) noted that the mother's education was an important determinant of children's schooling in Indonesian and Philippine households. Among the Malays in Malaysia, King and Lillard (1987) found that a mother's education had a strong, positive effect on her daughters' but not on her sons' schooling, whereas a father's education generally did not affect his children's schooling. In the Philippines, in contrast, the authors found a positive link between the educational attainment of both parents and their children's schooling. Smith and Cheung (1982) concluded that the gender difference in educational participation varied significantly with the father's education. In Taiwan (China), among the several determinants of female educational attainment that Hermalin, Seltzer, and Lin (1982) examined, the father's education turned out to be the most dominant. In their study on Thailand, Cochrane and Jamison (1982) ascertained that fathers' (but not mothers') educational aspirations for their daughters were important in determining daughters' schooling but that this was not true for sons.

The occupations of parents have generally proved to be a significant factor in their children's educational attainment, particularly for girls. Hermalin, Seltzer, and Lin (1982) found that after parental education, the most important variable influencing female educational attainment in Taiwan (China) was parental occupation: the higher that parents' occupations ranked, the greater the probability that their daughters would go to school.[22] This is similar to results obtained for Indonesia by King and others (1986), who concluded that females whose fathers had white-collar jobs tended to have significantly more schooling than those whose fathers had blue-collar jobs. In both Indonesia and the Philippines, children of farmers had much less schooling than others.

Family Size. Among the factors that might influence girls' educational participation, family size has attracted wide attention among researchers.[23] Children in large families receive less individual attention and other resources from the parents than children in small families do. Furthermore, large families may not be able to afford to send all their children to school. Given both a preference for boys' education and higher school costs for girls, the daughters in large families are less likely to be sent to school than the sons. Also, girls' household work is a greater burden in a large family. Research findings appear to indicate a persistently negative correlation between family size and children's educational performance as well: children from small families tended to perform better in school than did those from large families, in part because they had more financial resources and received greater parental encouragement (E. M. King 1987).

Aggregate patterns, however, do not clearly support the general hunch that family size and female educational participation are inversely related. Of the countries for which data on household size are available, the Philippines has the largest average family size, 5.9; yet its female enrollment rate in higher education is also the highest in the region. Indonesia, with an average household size of 4.8, one of the lowest in the region, has the second lowest level of female enrollment in secondary and higher education. Household size in Malaysia is also a low 4.8, but its female enrollment rates are not particularly high in comparison with other countries. Thailand, however, which has low female enrollment rates in secondary and higher education, has a mean household size of 5.7, the second highest in the region.

The results of investigations at the family level are similarly mixed. Studies of Taiwan (China)—for example, Hermalin, Seltzer, and Lin (1982)—and of Indonesia and the Philippines (King and others 1986) conclude that family size was not significantly related to the educational levels of siblings in general or of daughters in particular. But in rural Thailand the presence of young children in the household reduced the participation of both boys and girls in school, especially at the upper primary level (Cochrane and Jamison 1982; see Jamison and Lockheed 1987 for similar results for Nepal).

Urban Residence

Educational attainment is biased against rural children; rural-urban differences are well documented in the literature. These differences are glaring for women. For example, female literacy rates in China are 47 percent in rural areas and 74 percent in urban areas. The differences are smaller in other countries but still significant: in Indonesia, 52 percent of rural women and 76 percent of urban women can read, and in Malaysia 52 percent of rural women and 74 percent of urban women can read.

Schultz (1987) found in his cross-country study that urbanization was not a significant variable in explaining the differences in enrollment rates at the primary level for either boys or girls but that it became an important factor at the secondary level and was more important for female than for male enrollment. Smith and Cheung (1982) found that in the Philippines urban-educated parents made more favorable decisions regarding their daughters' education than did those (especially fathers) with a rural background.

Country-level data do not unanimously support an urban-rural difference in the propensity to educate females. Hong Kong and Singapore, which are almost entirely urban, have lower female enrollment rates for both secondary and higher education than do many other economies. The Philippines, with only a third of its population in urban areas, has much higher enrollment rates than less rural countries. China and Indonesia, however, have both low levels of urbanization and low female enrollment ratios.

Conclusions

On the whole, educational opportunities for women in East Asia are good in comparison with other developing regions. Literacy and school enrollment among girls and women are fairly high and are in some respects comparable to levels in industrial countries. The East Asian economies differ significantly, however, in their social, economic, political, demographic, and educational characteristics. China, Indonesia, and Malaysia lag behind the rest of the region in educational attainment, whereas not only Korea but also the Philippines are far ahead.

Variations in social, economic, cultural, political, and historical conditions explain to some extent the differences in levels of female education among East Asian countries. Whether pedagogical factors such as textbooks, curricula, and teaching methods are relevant cannot be determined from the available research, which usually has not estimated equations separately for males and females but has included gender only as a dummy variable, while assuming that all other factors affect the education of both sexes equally.

This review of the East Asian experience leads to several conclusions:

- The educational experiences of most of the economies in the region suggest that colonial legacies in education can be overcome easily and education expanded quickly, and that gender equality in education is achievable.
- The experience of the Philippines clearly suggests that economic development is not a prerequisite for expanding education for women. Education and economic policies and programs that are carefully planned and implemented can enhance female schooling to a remarkable extent.
- Social customs, such as early or late marriage, do not systematically affect whether girls and women enroll in school. Ultimately, the decision on how much to educate girls rests with the family—the value it places on female education and its willingness to bear the costs of schooling.
- Demographic factors, such as household size, are not necessarily related to female enrollment.
- Although the literature places much of the blame for the low enrollment of girls on cultural factors, including religion, the facts do not

strongly support this. Evidence from Indonesia and Malaysia suggests that religion, including Islam, need not stand in the way of ensuring equality of educational opportunities for girls and women. The gender gap in education in these two countries is not much greater than in other countries. No religion—be it Christianity, Islam, Buddhism, or Confucianism—has been a great obstacle to narrowing the gender gap in education.

These conclusions are reassuring. Although by tradition women have been subject to discrimination at home, at school, and in the labor market, the situation is not immutable. Rather, traditions have been responsive to changes induced by economic development and government policy. Meaningful public policies have paid rich dividends in improving women's educational attainment in this region. Ensuring free and universal primary education, improving school quality to increase promotion and survival rates, and establishing single-sex schools are among the policies and programs that have succeeded in East Asia. Few well-designed and well-executed education policies and programs fail. Efforts to reduce parents' direct costs for schooling, such as programs that provide textbooks, scholarships, and meals, have had a very significant effect on female enrollment. Offered the appropriate incentives, girls and women enter schools and attain educational levels close to those achieved by boys and men.

Notes

1. See also Bowman and Anderson (1982), Deble (1980), and Smock (1981).

2. See several papers in Ward (1963) for descriptions of the changing roles of women in South and Southeast Asia.

3. In the Philippines a substantial number of students is enrolled in private universities and colleges, a fact that may mean that a lower share of the government budget is needed for education.

4. Even though the net enrollment rates (that is, the gross enrollment rates adjusted for overage and underage children) in the early and mid-1980s were generally lower than the gross enrollment rates and were less than 100 percent, education at the primary level was more or less universal in developing East Asia.

5. In 1980 there were 1,559,000 females and 733,000 males enrolled in secondary schools in the Philippines. In 1985 female and male enrollments were about equal.

6. See Moore (1987) for documentation of these patterns in male and female enrollment for a large number of countries. See also UNESCO (1980a, 1985).

7. Although discrimination does not entirely account for differences in gross earnings unadjusted for differences in productivity-related factors, the term is used here in the broad sense that these differences reflect "cumulative

discrimination" (Madden 1975). See also the discussion in Tilak (1987). That gender itself is an important determinant of earnings is well documented (see, for example Blaug 1974 on Thailand).

8. See also Singh (1987) and Yue (1987) on Malaysia and Tonguthai (1987) on Thailand and the Philippines.

9. Rarely does wage discrimination force women to get more education so that they may earn wages equal to men's; for Chile, see Schiefelbein and Farrell (1982). For India, Rosenzweig and Evenson (1977) found that male wages and enrollment levels were negatively related, whereas female wages and enrollment levels were positively related.

10. Mincer (1962, p. 68) also observes that "in view of the expected smaller rate of participation in the labor market, education of women is more strongly focused on the 'consumption' sphere, and returns are more non-pecuniary than for males." See also Mincer and Polacheck (1974).

11. Arcelo and Sanyal (1987) show that the rate of unemployment was higher among graduates of private institutions of higher learning than among graduates of public institutions of higher learning. In both cases, women had higher unemployment rates than men.

12. In chapter 2 Schultz also discusses the problems involved in gender-based comparisons of conventionally estimated rates of return to education.

13. If allowance is made for nonmarket work, as Woodhall (1973) rightly argues should be done, the rates of return to women's education are likely to be much higher than those to men's. In addition, Tilak (1987) has shown that greater participation by women in the labor force would substantially increase the rates of return to their education.

14. This result is not altogether surprising. The rates of return to education rarely explain differences in enrollment in education across different countries. See, for example, Tilak (1982) for a wider cross-country study.

15. Compare chapter 6 on South Asia, where the author points out that enrollment may be low even when schools are located nearby.

16. Rosenzweig (1975) argues, in contrast, that a predominance of males in a family would be to the advantage of females.

17. See U. King (1987) for an analysis of the ways in which the main religions have generally given a lesser and sometimes extremely limited role to women in education.

18. For another view of the link between female education and Islam, see chapter 4 on the Middle East and North Africa.

19. See Safilios-Rothschild (1979) for a comprehensive review of the literature.

20. See Weekes-Vagliani (1980) for details on Malaysia.

21. See de Tray (1979) for evidence on children's economic contributions in Malaysia.

22. This occupational hierarchy places white-collar workers at the top and blue-collar skilled workers next, followed by unskilled labor and farm workers.

23. It is also possible that parental education influences family size. Considerable research is available on the effects of education on demographic factors such as fertility rates and population growth. See, for example, Hermalin (1974) on Taiwan (China), and Goldstein (1972) on Thailand.

References

Arcelo, Arcelo A., and Bikas C. Sanyal. 1987. *Employment Opportunities and Career Opportunities after Graduation: The Philippine Experience.* IIEP/UNESCO study. Manila: Fund for Assistance to Private Education.

Becker, Gary S. 1964. *Human Capital: A Theoretical and Empirical Analysis with Special Reference to Education.* New York: Columbia University Press (2d ed. National Bureau of Economic Research, 1975).

Blaug, Mark. 1974. "An Economic Analysis of Personal Earnings in Thailand." *Economic Development and Cultural Change* 23(1):1–32. (Reprinted in Mark Blaug, *The Economics of Education and the Education of an Economist,* Aldershot, U.K.: Edward Elgar, 1987.)

Borcelle, Germaine. 1985. *Jobs for Women: A Plea for Equality of Opportunity, Technical Education, Vocational Training and Employment.* Paris: UNESCO.

Bowman, Mary Jean, and C. A. Anderson. 1982. "The Participation of Women in Education in the Third World." In Gail P. Kelly and Carolyn M. Elliott, eds., *Women's Education in the Third World: Comparative Perspectives.* Albany: State University of New York Press.

Chernichovsky, Dov, and Oey A. Meesook. 1985. *School Enrollment in Indonesia.* World Bank Staff Working Paper 746. Washington, D.C.

Cochrane, Susan H., and Dean T. Jamison. 1982. "Educational Attainment and Achievement in Rural Thailand." In Anita A. Summers, ed., *Productivity Assessment in Education.* New Directions for Testing and Measurement 15. San Francisco, Calif.: Jossey-Bass,

Corner, Lorraine. 1987. "Female Labor Force Participation and Earnings in Indonesia." In United Nations Economic and Social Commission for Asia and the Pacific, *Women's Participation in Asia and the Pacific.* Bangkok.

Dasgupta, A. K. 1988. *Growth, Development and Welfare: An Essay on Levels of Living.* Oxford, U.K.: Basil Blackwell.

Deble, Isabell. 1980. *The School Education of Girls: An International Comparative Study on School Wastage among Girls and Boys at the First and Second Levels of Education.* Paris: UNESCO.

de Tray, Dennis. 1979. "Children's Economic Contributions in Peninsular Malaysia." Rand Note. Rand Corporation, Santa Monica, Calif.

——. 1988. "Government Policy, Household Behavior, and the Distribution of Schooling: A Case Study of Malaysia." In T. Paul Schultz, ed., *Research in Population Economics: A Research Annual,* vol. 5. Greenwich, Conn.: JAI Press.

Don, F. H. 1984. "Educational Opportunities for Girls in Malaysian Secondary Schools." In Sandra Acker, ed., *Women in Education: World Yearbook of Education 1984.* London: Kogan Page.

Encarnación, Jr., José. 1974. "Fertility and Labour Force Participation: Philippines 1968." Working Paper 2. Population and Employment Research Project, World Employment Programme. International Labour Office, Geneva.

Encarnación, Jr., José, Gerardo A. Tagunicar, and Rosa Linda Tidalgo. 1976. "Unemployment and Underemployment." In *Philippine Economic Problems in Perspective.* Manila: University of the Philippines, Institute of Economic Development and Research.

Fuller, Bruce. 1986. *Raising School Quality in Developing Countries: What Investments Boost Learning?* World Bank Discussion Paper 2. Washington, D.C.

Goldstein, Sidney. 1972. "The Influence of Labor Force Participation and Education on Fertility in Thailand." *Population Studies* 26:419–36.

Greenhalgh, Susan. 1985. "Sexual Stratification: The Other Side of 'Growth with Equity' in East Asia." *Population and Development Review* 2(2):265–314.

Harman, A. J. 1970. "Fertility and Economic Behavior of Families in the Philippines." Rand Corporation, Santa Monica, Calif.

Harnqvist, K. 1987. "Social Demand Models." In George Psacharopoulos, ed., *Economics of Education: Research and Studies.* Oxford, U.K.: Pergamon Press.

Hermalin, Albert. 1974. "Empirical Research in Taiwan on Factors Underlying Differences in Fertility." *Studies in Family Planning* 5 (October):314–24.

Hermalin, Albert, J. A. Seltzer, and C-H Lin. 1982. "Transition in the Effect of Family Size and Female Education Attainment: The Case of Taiwan." *Comparative Education Review* 26 (June):254–70.

Heyneman, Stephen P., and William A. Loxley. 1983. "The Effect of Primary-School Quality on Academic Achievement across Twenty-nine High- and Low-Income Countries." *American Journal of Sociology* 88(6):1162–94.

Hirschman, Charles. 1979. "Political Independence and Educational Opportunity in Peninsular Malaysia." *Sociology of Education* 52: 67–83.

Hooper, Beverly. 1984. "China's Modernization: Are Young Women Going to Lose Out?" *Modern China* 10 (July):317–43.

Huq, M. S. 1965. *Education and Development Strategy in South and Southeast Asia.* Honolulu: East-West Center Press.

Jamison, Dean T., and Marlaine E. Lockheed. 1987. "Participation in Schooling: Determinants and Learning Outcomes in Nepal." *Economic Development and Cultural Change* 35(2):279–306.

Jiménez, Emmanuel, and Marlaine E. Lockheed. 1988. "The Relative Effectiveness of Single-Sex and Coeducational Schools in Thailand." Policy Research Working Paper 29. World Bank, Population and Human Resources Department, Education and Employment Division, Washington, D.C.

Jiménez, Emmanuel, Marlaine E. Lockheed, and Nongnuch Wattanawaha. 1988. "The Relative Efficiency of Private and Public Schools: The Case of Thailand." *World Bank Economic Review* 2(2):139–64.

Johnstone, J. A. 1976. "The Location and Distribution of Primary Schools in the Asian Region." *Bulletin of the UNESCO Regional Office for Education in Asia* 17 (June).

Kaneko, Motohisa. 1987. "The Educational Composition of the World's Population: A Database." EDT Discussion Paper 29. 2d ed. World Bank, Education and Training Department, Washington, D.C.

Kelly, Gail P. 1984. "Women's Access to Education in the Third World: Myths and Realities." In Sandra Acker, ed., *Women and Education: World Yearbook of Education 1984.* London: Kogan Page.

King, Elizabeth M. 1987. "The Effect of Family Size on Family Welfare: What Do We Know?" In D. Gale Johnson and Ronald D. Lee, eds., *Population*

Growth and Economic Development: Issues and Evidence. Madison: University of Wisconsin Press.

King, Elizabeth M., and Lee A. Lillard. 1987. "Education Policy and Schooling Attainment in Malaysia and the Philippines." *Economics of Education Review* 6:167–81.

King, Elizabeth M., Jane R. Peterson, Sri Moertiningsih Adioetomo, Lita J. Domingo, and Sabiha Hassan Syed. 1986. *Change in the Status of Women Across Generations in Asia.* Santa Monica, Calif.: Rand Corporation.

King, Ursula. 1987. "World Religions, Women and Education." In Patricia Broadfoot and Margaret B. Sutherland, eds., "Sex Differences in Education," *Comparative Education* 23 (special number 10):35–49.

Korean Council for University Education. 1988. *Equity, Quality and Cost in Higher Education.* Bangkok: UNESCO Principal Regional Office for Asia and the Pacific.

Kurian, George T. 1982. *Encyclopedia of the Third World.* New York: Facts on File, Inc.

Lazo, Lucy S. 1984. "Work and Training Opportunities for Women in the Philippines." Islamabad: ILO-APSDEP.

Lee, Valerie E., and Marlaine E. Lockheed. 1990. "The Effects of Single-Sex Schooling on Student Achievement and Attitudes in Nigeria." *Comparative Education Review* 34(2):209–32.

Levy, M. B. 1971. "Determinants of Primary School Dropouts in Developing Countries." *Comparative Education Review* 15 (February):44–58.

Lockheed, Marlaine E., Stephen C. Vail, and Bruce Fuller. 1986. "How Textbooks Affect Achievement in Developing Countries: Evidence from Thailand." *Educational Evaluation and Policy Analysis* 8(4):379–92.

McGrath, P. L. 1976. *The Unfinished Assignment: Equal Education for Women.* Worldwatch Paper 7. Washington, D.C.: Worldwatch Institute.

Madden, J. F. 1975. "Discrimination—A Manifestation of Male Market Power?" In Cynthia B. Lloyd, ed., *Sex, Discrimination and Division of Labor.* New York: Columbia University Press.

Mazumdar, Dipak. 1981. *Urban Labor Market and Income Distribution: A Study of Malaysia.* New York: Oxford University Press.

Mincer, Jacob. 1962. "On-the-Job Training: Costs, Returns, and Some Implications." *Journal of Political Economy* 8(2), pt. 2 supplement: S76–S108.

Mincer, Jacob, and S. Polachek. 1974. "Family Investments in Human Capital: Earnings of Women." *Journal of Political Economy* 18(1):3–24.

Montgomery, Mark R., and D. S. Sulak. 1989. "Female First Marriage in East and Southeast Asia: A Kiefer-Neumann Model." *Journal of Development Economics* 120:33–52.

Moore, K. M. 1987. "Women's Access and Opportunity in Higher Education: Toward the Twenty-first Century." In Patricia Broadfoot and Margaret B. Sutherland, eds., "Sex Differences in Education," *Comparative Education* 23 (special number 10):23–24.

Nagib, Laila. 1986. *Factors Relating to Female Work Force Participation in Three Central Javanese Communities.* Jakarta: National Institute of Economic and Social Research, Indonesian Institute of Science.

Neher, C. D. 1982. "Sex Roles in the Philippines: The Ambiguous Cebuana." In Penny Van Esterik, ed., *Women of Southeast Asia.* Occasional Paper 9. Northern Illinois University, Center for Southeast Asian Studies, De Kalb.

Niehoff, A. H. 1964. "Theravada Buddhism: A Vehicle for Technical Change." *Human Organization* 23:108–12.

Oshima, Harry T. 1988. "Human Resources in East Asia's Secular Growth." In Anthony M. Tang and James S. Worley, eds., "Why Does Overcrowded, Resource-Poor East Asia Succeed—Lessons for LDCs?" *Economic Development and Cultural Change* 36 (April)(supplement):S103-S122.

Postlethwaite, T. N., and R. M. Thomas, eds. 1980. *Schooling in the ASEAN Region: Primary and Secondary Education in Indonesia, Malaysia, the Philippines, Singapore, and Thailand.* Oxford, U.K.: Pergamon Press.

Psacharopoulos, George, and Ana-Maria Arriagada. 1986. "The Educational Composition of the Labour Force: An International Comparison." *International Labour Review* 135(5):561–74.

Ram, Rati. 1982. "Sex Differences in the Labor Market Outcomes of Education." In Gail P. Kelly and Carolyn M. Elliott, eds., *Women's Education in the Third World: Comparative Perspectives.* Albany: State University of New York Press.

Rosenzweig, Mark R. 1975. "Child Investment and Women." In Cynthia B. Lloyd, ed., *Sex, Discrimination and Division of Labor.* New York: Columbia University Press.

Rosenzweig, Mark R., and Robert E. Evenson. 1977. "Fertility, Schooling, and Economic Contribution of Children in Rural India." *Econometrica* 45(5):1065–79.

Safilios-Rothschild, Constantina. 1979. *Sex Role Socialization and Sex Discrimination: A Synthesis and Critique of the Literature.* Washington D.C.: Department of Health, Education, and Welfare, National Institute of Education.

———. 1980. "The Role of the Family: A Neglected Aspect of Poverty." In Peter T. Knight, ed., *Implementing Programs of Human Development.* World Bank Staff Working Paper 403. Washington, D.C.

Salaff, J. W. 1976. "The Status of Unmarried Hong Kong Women and the Social Factors Contributing to Their Delayed Marriage." *Population Studies* 30:13–34.

Schiefelbein, Ernesto, and Joseph P. Farrell. 1982. "Women, Schooling, and Work in Chile: Evidence from a Longitudinal Study." In Gail P. Kelly and Carolyn M. Elliott, eds., *Women's Education in the Third World: Comparative Perspectives.* Albany: State University of New York Press.

Schultz, T. Paul. 1987. "School Expenditures and Enrollments, 1960–1980: The Effects of Income, Prices, and Population Growth." In D. Gale Johnson and Ronald D. Lee, eds., *Population Growth and Economic Development: Issues and Evidence.* Madison: University of Wisconsin Press.

Scott, Gloria L. 1985. "Indonesian Women and Development." World Bank, Population and Human Resources Department, Women in Development Division, Washington, D.C.

Shields, N. G. 1987. "Female Labor Force Participation and Education: Developing Countries." In Torsten Husen and T. Neville Postlethwaite, eds., *The International Encyclopedia of Education: Research and Studies*. Oxford, U.K.: Pergamon Press.

Singh, J. S. 1987. "The World of Work." In A. A. Aziz, C. S. Buan, L. K. Hock, and B. C. Sanyal, eds., *University Education and Employment in Malaysia*. IIEP Research Report 66. Paris: International Institute for Educational Planning.

Smith, Peter C., and Paul P. Cheung. 1982. "Social Origins and Sex Differential Schooling in the Philippines." In Gail P. Kelly and Carolyn M. Elliott, eds., *Women's Education in the Third World: Comparative Perspectives*. Albany: State University of New York Press.

Smock, Audrey Chapman. 1981. *Women's Education in Developing Countries: Opportunities and Outcomes*. New York: Praeger.

Sundaram, J. K., and T. P. Leng. 1985. "Not the Better Half: Malaysian Women and Development Planning." In Noeleen Heyser, ed., *Missing Women: Development Planning in Asia and the Pacific*. Kuala Lumpur: Asian and Pacific Development Centre.

Sutherland, Margaret. 1988. "Women in Higher Education: Effects of Crises and Change." *Higher Education*, special issue on women, Sheila Slaughter, ed., 17:479-90.

Tang, A. M., and J. S. Worley, eds. 1988. "Why Does Overcrowded, Resource-Poor East Asia Succeed—Lessons for the LDCs?" *Economic Development and Cultural Change* 36 (April)(supplement).

Thomas, R. M. 1988. "The Islamic Revival and Indonesian Education." *Asian Survey* 28 (September):897-915.

Thomas, R. M., and T. N. Postlethwaite, eds. 1983. *Schooling in East Asia: Forces of Change: Formal and Nonformal Education in Japan, the Republic of China, the People's Republic of China, South Korea, North Korea, Hong Kong, and Macau*. Oxford, U.K.: Pergamon Press.

Tilak, Jandhlaya B. G. 1982. "Educational Planning and International Economic Order." *Comparative Education* 18(2):107-21.

———. 1987. *Economics of Inequality in Education*. New Delhi: Sage Publications.

Tonguthai, Pawader. 1987. "Women and Work in Thailand and the Philippines." In *Women's Economic Participation in Asia and the Pacific*. Bangkok: Economic and Social Commission for Asia and the Pacific.

United Nations Department of International Economic and Social Affairs. 1985. *Statistical Yearbook 1985*. New York.

UNESCO (United Nations Educational, Scientific, and Cultural Organization). 1980a. *Comparative Analysis of Male and Female Enrollment and Illiteracy*. Current Surveys and Research in Statistics. Paris.

———. 1980b. "Wastage in Primary and General Secondary Education: A Statistical Study of Trends and Patterns in Repetition and Drop-Out." Current Studies and Research in Statistics. Paris.

————. 1985. *Female Participation in Higher Education: Enrollment Trends, 1975–1982.* Current Surveys and Research in Statistics. Paris.

————. 1987. *Statistical Yearbook.* Paris.

————. 1989. *Trends and Projections of Enrolment by Level of Education and by Age, 1960–2025.* Paris.

————. 1990. *Statistical Yearbook.* Paris.

————. 1991. *Statistical Yearbook.* Paris.

UNESCO-ROEAP. 1984. *The Drop-Out Problem in Primary Education: Some Case Studies.* Bangkok: UNESCO Regional Office for Education in Asia and the Pacific.

Visaria, Pravin, and Shyamalendu Pal. 1980. *Poverty and Living Standards in Asia: An Overview of the Main Results and Lessons of Selected Household Surveys.* Living Standards Measurement Study Working Paper 2. Washington, D.C.: World Bank.

Wang, B.-L. C. 1982. "Sex and Ethnic Differences in Educational Investment in Malaysia: The Effect of Reward Structure." In Gail P. Kelly and Carolyn M. Elliott, eds., *Women's Education in the Third World: Comparative Perspectives.* Albany: State University of New York Press.

Ward, B. F., ed. 1963. *Women in the New Asia.* Paris: UNESCO.

Weekes-Vagliani, Winifred, in collaboration with Bernard Grossat. 1980. *Women and Development: At the Right Time for the Right Reasons.* Paris: OECD.

Whyte, Robert O., and Pauline Whyte. 1978. "Rural Asian Women: Status and Environment." Research Notes and Discussion Paper 9. Singapore: Institute of Southeast Asian Studies.

Woodhall, Maureen. 1973. "Investment in Women: A Reappraisal of the Concept of Human Capital." In Evelyn Bromhead, ed., "The Education of Women." *International Review of Education* 19 (special issue):9–29.

World Bank. 1988a. *China: Growth and Development in Gansu Province.* World Bank Country Study. Washington, D.C.

————. 1988b. *Social Indicators of Development 1988.* Baltimore, Md.: Johns Hopkins University Press.

————. 1989. *World Development Report 1989.* New York: Oxford University Press.

Yue, C. S. 1987. "Women's Economic Participation in Malaysia." In *Women's Economic Participation in Asia and the Pacific.* Bangkok: United Nations Economic and Social Commission for Asia and the Pacific.

8

Educating Women: Lessons from Experience

Rosemary T. Bellew and Elizabeth M. King

Expanding education, especially basic education, has been a policy objective in developing countries for the past three decades. The reasons for this are clear. Basic education is often considered a right which governments have a responsibility to guarantee to each generation. And the benefits of education are by now well established. Education improves the quality of life. It promotes health, expands access to paid employment, increases productivity in market and nonmarket work, and facilitates social and political participation.

The evidence is also convincing that these benefits are especially large for women. Educated women have smaller families, fewer of their children die in infancy, and the children who survive are healthier and better educated. Moreover, educated women are better prepared to enter the paid labor force, which is critical to the welfare of the many female-headed households in developing countries.[1] It is not surprising, then, that countries where school enrollment among girls and women has been comparatively high enjoy greater economic productivity, lower fertility, lower infant and maternal mortality, and longer life expectancy than countries where female enrollment rates have not been as high (Schultz 1989; chapter 1 of this volume).

The previous chapters indicate, however, that many parents and societies underinvest in girls' education. How can public policy change this? Making primary schooling compulsory and free has not been sufficient. Direct intervention has proved necessary, and it has sometimes succeeded. Past research provides few hard and fast rules to guide governments in their efforts, but it does suggest that where enrollment in primary school is low, efforts should be directed toward expanding access to primary education rather than to secondary or higher education. Not only are the rates of return highest at the primary level, but, even under the best of circumstances, it takes five to eight years of schooling to acquire the reading and math skills essential for operational literacy and numeracy (Lockheed, Verspoor, and associates 1991). Governments would therefore be wise to invest in basic education in both formal and nonformal school settings. Where all boys and girls are enrolled in primary school—as in many Latin American and East Asian countries—interventions should be directed at reducing gender differentials in enrollment and attainment at the secondary and tertiary levels.

Beyond these broad guidelines, little can be said with certainty about the most cost-effective measures for boosting girls' schooling. Motivated by the challenge to provide more specific guidelines, we set out to identify and assess the approaches taken by governments, nongovernmental organizations (NGOs), donor agencies, and communities to raise girls' and women's participation in education programs. This chapter discusses these approaches and examines the conditions under which they seem to succeed or fail. The survey, summarized in table 8-1, is by no means exhaustive; it includes only interventions for which some performance data are available. Yet even when data are available, most initiatives have not been evaluated rigorously enough to permit strong conclusions about their effectiveness. At this time, striving to advance women's education often means proceeding with best guesses, guided by what has worked well under similar circumstances or by what theoretically might work. Experimentation and careful monitoring are essential. No simple or uniform prescriptions are possible. How governments, communities, and donors approach the challenge of closing the gender gap in education must depend on the specific context, including the existing supply of schools, the quality of education, prevailing cultural and social norms, families' incomes and productive activities, and women's opportunities for paid work.

Expanding Access to Schools

Students cannot attend school when places are in short supply or when schools are located far from home. Recognizing this, planners have worked out various low-cost strategies for expanding access and increasing proximity. These efforts have included experimenting with multigrade classrooms, double shifts, feeder and satellite schools at the primary level (see box 8-1), radio education and correspondence courses at the postprimary levels, and literacy programs for adults. Educational opportunities for females have also been increased by eliminating discriminatory admissions practices and by instituting quotas that reserve places for them in education programs.

Box 8-1. *Not Too Far to Walk: Bhutan's Extended Classrooms*

The land is rugged. Rivers flow down from tall mountains to densely forested valleys. Villages are remote and widely scattered. School facilities are scarce, overcrowded, and shabby. Teachers are in short supply.

If children go to school at all, they must walk long distances or find boarding accommodations near one of Bhutan's 147 primary schools. Because Bhutan has never had a formal census, enrollment rates are estimates, but they suggest that the overall enrollment rate for primary school is 35 percent and that of those enrolled only 35 percent are girls.

To increase female participation in primary school, the government of Bhutan is providing multigrade education from the preprimary level through class III using an extended classroom model (ECR). ECRs, or lower primary schools, are clustered around Development Service Center schools (DSCs), which have boarding facilities for children in classes IV–VI. Children who successfully pass class III feed into the DSCs. The government recruits and pays for teachers in communities that can provide ECR facilities and ensure a minimum of 100 students. Bhutan believes that ECRs will increase the enrollment of girls in primary school by avoiding the need for boarding schools at the lower grades. Providing dormitories at the upper primary levels will motivate parents to keep their daughters in school by alleviating their fears about young girls' traveling long distances and by guaranteeing that children who complete primary school will have the opportunity to continue their education.

These supply-side strategies to expand access are necessary to increase girls' enrollment, but they are not always sufficient. When the demand for girls' education is low, parents will not send their daughters to school even if one is available. Experiences in Egypt, Mali, and the former Arab Republic of Yemen illustrate this.

Egypt, in its efforts to expand primary education to rural children, built 400 new primary schools in rural areas between 1981 and 1987. The increased availability of spaces permitted more children to attend. The share of school-age girls enrolled in school increased from 56 to 74 percent; boys' enrollment increased from 94 to 100 percent. An evaluation of this initiative concluded that the existing demand for girls' education had been met and that additional school construction at the original sites would do little to attract those girls still not in school (Robinson, Makary, and Rugh 1987).

A similar situation occurred in the Koulikoro region of Mali, where small multigrade schools are common, when a program to expand

(Text continues on page 291.)

Table 8-1. Summary of Interventions to Raise Female Enrollment

Intervention	Country	Description and funding agency (if known)	Year started
Increase supply of school places	Bhutan	Built "extended" primary school classrooms in rural areas	1988
	Egypt	Built primary schools in rural areas	1981
	Mali	Built and renovated school buildings	1989[a]
	Yemen, Arab Rep.	Established vocational centers for women	1987
Support culturally appropriate school facilities	Bangladesh	Built primary schools and teacher training centers	1985
	Kenya	Secularized curricula in Koranic schools to attract more students	1985
	Mali	Provided Koranic schools with pedagogic support	1989[a]
	Pakistan	Secularized curricula in mosque schools	1979
	Pakistan	Provided sanitation and water facilities in schools and built boundary walls (Sind)	1990[a]
Recruit female teachers	Nepal	Trained rural females with secondary education as schoolteachers; trained others to qualify	1971
	Pakistan	Recruited female teachers in rural areas and trained them there; provided residences for female teachers	1984
	Somalia	Established incentive systems for teachers	1975
	Yemen, Arab Rep.	Built separate urban institutes to train women as primary teachers, and rural pilot institutes to attract rural women	1987
Reduce cost of uniforms	Bangladesh	Distributed free uniforms to primary girls	1981
	Pakistan	Abolished required uniforms in rural areas	1990[a]

Provide scholarships	Bangladesh	Offered scholarships to girls in secondary schools	1982
	Guatemala ⎫	Offered scholarships to girls in primary school	1987
	India ⎬		n.d.
	Nepal ⎭		Early 1980s
Establish day-care centers	China	Established day-care centers and preschool centers at worksites and centers for sibling care at primary schools	Mid-1980s
	Colombia	Supported community-based centers	1987
Provide labor-saving home technologies	Burkina Faso	Distributed labor-saving machines to encourage nonformal education of women	1967
	Nepal	Distributed fuel-efficient stoves	1977
Design flexible school schedules	Bangladesh	Introduced programmed instruction in selected rural schools	1980
	Colombia	Introduced programmed instruction in Escuelas Nuevas	1975
	El Salvador	Introduced programmed instruction	Late 1980s
	Indonesia ⎫	Introduced multigrade teaching using self-taught learning materials	Late 1970s–
	Liberia ⎬		early 1980s
	Philippines ⎭		
Provide alternative schooling	Bangladesh	Built lower primary schools in rural areas, known as BRAC schools	1983
	India	Established nonformal evening schools for out-of-school youths	1979

(Table continues on the following page.)

289

Table 8-1 *(continued)*

Intervention	Country	Description and funding agency (if known)	Year started
Educate community	Mali	Launched media campaigns to advertise value of education for girls	1989[a]
	Morocco	Developed materials and extension service promoting girls' education	1989[a]
Delay childbearing	Guatemala	Used girls' scholarship program to reward avoidance of pregnancy	1987
Improve girls' nutrition	Jamaica	Provided school breakfast program	n.d.
Offer training in nontraditional occupations	Chile	Built vocational centers to train middle-level male and female technicians	1968
	Morocco	Established industrial and commercial training program for men and women	1979
	Tanzania	Established training centers near primary schools for unemployed females	1975
	Yemen, Arab Rep.	Built vocational training centers	1987
Promote gender-neutral instruction	Bangladesh China India Kenya	Revised textbooks to improve perception of women's roles in family and society	1988 1980s
Alleviate poverty	Bangladesh	Established women's income-earning programs	1970s

n.d. No date.

a. Although the project has been launched, the specific intervention pertaining to girls or women is just now starting.

Source: Internal World Bank, USAID, and UNESCO documents; see chapter text.

schools was launched. Overall enrollment is reported to have *declined* by 1.5 percent a year between 1982 and 1986 despite increases of 3 percent in the number of schools, 14 percent in the number of classes, and 21 percent in the number of teachers (Haughton 1986). Female enrollment for the same period fell even faster—by 2.6 percent a year, according to the Ministry of Education. Haughton's report concludes that "there is probably relatively little unsatisfied demand for public schooling, as it currently exists, in this region. In that case an upper limit on net public school enrollments of about a quarter can be expected in rural areas if the only policy pursued is expansion in the number of schools."

The inadequacy of expanding the number of places as a strategy for raising female enrollment is also evident in vocational programs. In the former Arab Republic of Yemen the government committed itself to increasing the role of women in economic development. This commitment, coupled with an anticipated critical shortage of skilled technicians and clerical workers, led to the establishment of a network of fourteen vocational and technical centers to meet the needs of the industrial, agricultural and commercial sectors. The intention was that female students would occupy 15, 20, and 75 percent of the available places in the industrial, agricultural, and commercial programs, respectively. The outcome was disappointing. By 1984 only 7 of the 166 commercial students and none of the industrial and agricultural students were women.

Two project evaluations pointed to the same reason for this outcome: project designers did not take into consideration the preferences of Yemeni girls and their families, cultural norms, or the economy. Women preferred to work in manufacturing and fishing, which provided a reasonable income without requiring a diploma. Those who did attend secondary or postsecondary school did not work in agriculture or industry unless it was in the central government in Aden. Parents outside Aden opposed coeducation, and early marriage prevented many girls from continuing in school (UNESCO 1985a).

These experiences demonstrate that simply expanding education programs may be insufficient to increase female enrollment. For programs to be fully utilized, the demand for education must emanate from families and the community. When parents are concerned about the physical and moral safety of their daughters, when the direct and opportunity costs of attendance are too high, and when the benefits of an education are too few, school expansion policies will be effective only if they are accompanied by policies that lower the cultural, direct, or opportunity costs of education or raise the benefits.

Providing Culturally Appropriate Facilities

Schools must conform to communities' cultural standards, especially the standards of propriety to which females are held. In parts of the Middle East, North Africa, East and South Asia, and Africa's Sahelian region, girls' and young women's activities are governed by social practices that restrict their presence in public places and their interaction with males. Parents may insist that their daughters be separated from males at school, and they may be more concerned with the availability of closed latrines than with the supply of desks and chairs.[2] Pakistan has responded to these concerns by building boundary walls around girls' schools. Bangladesh has responded by providing sanitary facilities in schools; this has had a positive influence on the attitudes of the

---

Box 8-2. *Is "Clean and Safe" Enough? Pakistan's Mosque Schools*

There is no light, no fan. It is very depressing and dreary and suffocating. . . . There is no toilet, no sweeper in any of the schools. When they need a latrine, the girls have to go home during school hours, wasting a considerable amount of time.

Headmistress, Pakistan primary school

In grim terms a Pakistani headmistress describes her school. In Pakistan 29,000 schools lack roofs; 16,000 consist of only one room. Some are so far away that children must walk 4 kilometers to get to them. Worse, 67 percent of the teachers are male. These are serious drawbacks to parents who think it is not "respectable" for their daughters to attend school if there is no female teacher, if they must walk alone, if there are no boundary walls or latrines.

School conditions, coupled with the overall low status accorded women, conspire to limit girls' educational opportunities. In 1985–86 the enrollment rate of girls was only 32 percent, the eighth lowest rate in the world. To encourage female enrollment, the prime minister in 1986 introduced the Five Point Program for Economic and Social Development, which called for the opening of 26,700 mosque schools. This is how the Ministry of Education described the features of the mosque school:

The Mosque will be used as a place of learning for children, for out of school youth and for adults. In addition to Islamiyat, the children will study the modern curricula for primary school. . . . In order to teach modern subjects, a primary school teacher will be appointed . . . who in cooperation with the Pesh Imam will teach children and adults at hours convenient to the community. Free books and teaching aids would be supplied to children

community, teachers, and students toward school and addresses an important parental objection to girls' attendance.

Some countries have also addressed parents' concerns about propriety by supporting the expansion of Koranic schools or by actively recruiting and training female teachers. The evidence suggests that low-quality programs may limit the success of Koranic schools (see box 8-2), whereas increasing the number of female teachers is a promising strategy for raising female enrollment.

Koranic schools are under the control and supervision of an imam, a religious leader revered by the community.[3] Strongly rooted in tradition, these schools provide a proper sheltered environment and a religious education that is acceptable to many parents. Historically, Koranic schools offered instruction only in the Koran and in Islamiyat

---

going to mosque schools. This will ensure rational utilization of the mosque and re-establish its traditional role of spreading the light of knowledge. (quoted in Warwick, Reimers, and McGinn 1989, p. 19)

The government believed parents would enroll daughters in institutions that affirmed cultural traditions and had long provided religious instruction to both boys and girls. The imam, a respected religious figure in the community, would allay parents' fears about sending their daughters to classes taught by men. Sheltered, clean facilities with fresh water and within easy walking distance of home would provide a "respectable" environment for girls still subject to female seclusion.

Since 1985 about 26,700 mosque schools offering education through the third grade have been opened. Opinions regarding their success are mixed. By June 1986 they had succeeded in enrolling 630,000 pupils, but only 30 percent were girls, a slightly smaller percentage than in government schools. A 1989 study of mosque schools in the Sind province revealed that only 26 percent of those enrolled were girls.

Of more concern are questions about the quality of the education provided. A study of mosque schools cites a district official's claim that "imams are poor teachers because they are illiterate" (Warwick, Reimers, and McGinn 1989, p. 26). The report goes on to say that "mosque schools can be rated high on financial efficiency, cultural acceptability, and quantitative success, low on the capability of implementors, and doubtful on the quality of schooling provided."

"Clean and safe" may be necessary to encourage parents to send daughters to school, but is it enough?

(other teachings of the Prophet Muhammad). Bangladesh, Pakistan, Kenya, and Mali have supported the accreditation of Koranic schools by introducing the primary school curriculum and a trained teacher to supplement religious education.[4] Mauritania experimented with a pilot program to teach mathematics and reading in Koranic schools by using radio broadcasts and by providing learning materials and supervisory support from the Ministry of Education. The Gambian government also hopes to improve female school attendance by raising the quality of education in Koranic schools. It is working with Muslim organizations to establish a school calendar, introduce a broader curriculum, and provide better-trained teachers.

The results of these efforts are mixed. In recent years, girls' enrollment in Mali's Koranic schools has grown rapidly, and such schools currently enroll 23 percent of all primary students. Girls account for 47 percent of this enrollment but for only 32 percent of the enrollment in government primary schools. In contrast, Pakistani parents have not responded as enthusiastically as expected to their government's initiative to expand mosque schools. In 1986 girls constituted only 30 percent of the students in these schools, compared with 32 percent in government primary schools. Supporters of the expansion say that mosque schools provide places that could not ordinarily be provided by public schools. Others question the benefits, however, claiming that the quality of education provided in mosque schools is lower than that provided in government primary schools.

Recruiting Female Teachers

Interviews and anecdotal evidence in some countries suggest that increasing the number of female teachers will boost girls' enrollment. Female teachers are in short supply, however, especially in African countries. These shortages arise in part from the requirements for admission into teacher training programs. Although these requirements are minimal—sometimes as little as an eighth-grade diploma—the majority of women still cannot meet them. And the predominantly urban location of teacher training facilities makes it hard to attract young rural women. Those who do become teachers are therefore more likely to be urban residents. They are often unwilling to accept posts in rural areas where living and working conditions are less desirable, where housing and medical facilities are inadequate, where good schools are lacking, where the supply of food and clothing may be limited, where piped water, electricity, and modern household technologies are absent, and where single women may find it difficult to meet desirable mates (Dove 1982; Seetharamu and Ushadevi 1985).

To enlarge the pool of female teachers, some countries have modified their uniform salary schedules to provide extra compensation in the form of housing subsidies and free travel to teachers' hometowns (Dove 1986; Murnane 1987). Other countries have deployed recruiters to rural areas. Neither approach alone, however, substantially increased the number of female teachers in Pakistan or Somalia because other constraints were not addressed.

Pakistan attempted to attract female teachers to rural areas by building residences where several young women could live together. The residences were unpopular except in Baluchistan, where they were occupied by married couples. In the other provinces they remained unoccupied because sociocultural attitudes dictate against single women living alone. Somalia attempted to recruit rural girls to become teachers, hoping that after being trained they would want to serve in rural schools. But the only teacher training institute in the country was located in the capital, Mogadishu, so rural girls had either to travel long distances daily or to move closer to the city. Rural parents, reluctant to release their daughters entirely from domestic responsibilities, refused to send them to the institute. Those who did attend the training program came from areas surrounding Mogadishu, a city that already had a surplus of teachers (USAID 1989).

Both of these strategies implicitly assumed a degree of mobility that girls and women did not have. In another effort, Pakistan addressed this constraint by introducing a teacher training program that combined recruiting girls from rural areas with training them close to home. The program, begun in Punjab province in 1984, introduced primary teacher training in units attached to local secondary schools. Of the ninety Primary Teacher Certificate units started, eighty were exclusively for women. The units were instrumental in raising the proportion of female teachers in the country. In 1985–86, 85 percent of the 5,040 students in these units were female, compared with only 19 percent at the normal school (a teacher training institute) and 38 percent at the government colleges for elementary teachers. In that year alone, the units trained 67 percent of all new female teachers. Locating the training close to home not only weakened parental opposition but, by eliminating the need for boarding facilities, made the program less costly than the conventional one.[5]

Although active local recruitment combined with local training appears to be effective in increasing the supply of female teachers in rural areas, a coherent strategy requires other features as well, including lowering minimum educational qualifications, subsidizing secondary and teacher education, and giving female teachers the option of being posted to a school near home. Nepal successfully implemented such an integrated program (see box 8-3). A similar program has been

Box 8-3. *Learn and Earn: Recruiting Female Teachers in Nepal*

In the 1970s in Nepal posters, booklets, newspapers, and radio programs deluged rural villages with information targeted at socially and economically disadvantaged families in an effort to motivate them to take advantage of a primary teacher training program. The program sought to promote equal educational opportunity for all, and it identified female teachers as key agents in reaching this goal. The main strategy was to train rural girls as primary school teachers. Hostels were constructed so that girls from conservative families in remote areas could participate.

The program functioned on two levels. Girls with secondary school leaving certificates were trained at campuses attached to Tribhuvan University. Hostel accommodations were provided, along with a monthly stipend, travel expenses, medical care, materials, and tutorial assistance. The year-long program offered courses in professional education, general education, and methods. To relate studies to women's roles in community life, supplementary courses in health, nutrition, and gardening were provided at the hostels. Because the teacher training centers were part of Tribhuvan University, the project could be replicated on several campuses. It expanded from its initial site in Polchara in 1971 to Dhankuta in 1973, Nepaljung in 1976, and Jumla in 1978.

Girls who did not have more than a tenth-grade education were lodged in feeder hostels and sent to nearby secondary schools, where they gained the skills to qualify them for the teacher training program. They too were provided with a monthly stipend, travel expenses, medical benefits, and tutorial assistance.

Under a directive from the Ministry of Education, district education officers were instructed to give priority to the women who had graduated from the teacher training program when making assignments to posts in primary schools. Follow-up workshops at campus sites provided monitoring and also refresher courses for former students.

Between 1971 and 1981 the program trained 1,193 girls. The share of female teachers in Nepal increased from 3 percent in 1972 to almost 10 percent in 1980, with 35 percent of the new female teachers coming from the four small campus programs. In the same period primary school enrollment increased from 17 to 28 percent. The combination of active recruitment, dual entry levels, subsidies, and the prospect of a teaching job near home was instrumental in adding females to Nepal's teaching force.

introduced in the former Arab Republic of Yemen in 1987; three centers have been set up as temporary additions to existing postprimary schools to provide teacher training to rural girls with a sixth-grade education. Buses transport participants to and from each center, and each trainee receives a stipend. On completion of the three-year course, the new teachers are placed in local schools, and the program moves to another area. The first course was attended by eighty rural girls, only two of whom had dropped out by the end of the second year.[6]

Reducing Direct Costs

Location and propriety are not the only things parents consider when deciding whether they should educate their daughters. Costs also influence their decisions. Although public schooling often implies free or subsidized tuition, parents still incur the costs of transportation, uniforms, books, and school supplies; in addition, schools may request cash or in-kind donations. These expenses can be prohibitive for poor parents, especially at the secondary level, where tuition is often high. Bangladesh and Pakistan have responded to these constraints by lowering the cost of uniforms, and several countries have introduced scholarship programs for girls.

Lowering the Cost of Uniforms

Providing free uniforms did not substantially raise girls' enrollment in Bangladesh. Beginning in 1981, uniforms were to be distributed to 500,000 girls ages six to ten.[7] The intended recipients were daughters of landless agricultural workers, fishermen, and other low-income parents. As it turned out, only 150,000 to 200,000 girls received free uniforms. Anecdotal evidence suggests that enrollment among girls increased slightly, but the scheme was discontinued after only two years because manufacturers were unable to meet quality standards, because principals distributed uniforms to pupils who were ineligible, and because wealthy parents withdrew their daughters from school, since they had been excluded from the program (UNESCO 1989).

In the Sind region of Pakistan, where school uniforms are compulsory, a different approach to the problem is being tried. Instead of providing free uniforms, the region is experimenting with abolishing the required uniforms in rural areas. This strategy is less costly and more easily administered, but whether the experiment will reduce the direct costs enough to raise girls' enrollment remains to be seen.

Providing Scholarships

Bangladesh has had greater success with its scholarship program for girls in the first three years of secondary school (grades six through eight) than it had with its free uniform program. The scholarship program was established in 1982 by the Bangladesh Association for Community Education, a local nonprofit organization. By the beginning of the 1988 school year 20,085 girls had taken advantage of the program, and the benefits were many (see box 8-4). Encouraged by these results, the government announced in early 1990 that it would

---

Box 8-4. My Daughter Won't Need a Dowry: Bangladesh's Scholarship Program

Anjuman Ara received a scholarship to attend Chitoshi High School. She was thirteen years old, with nine brothers and sisters. Her father finished primary school and is a rice farmer; her mother is illiterate. Her friend, Majeda, was already married and expecting a baby. In the poor Sharasti upazila, a rural region in the Comilla district of Bangladesh, Majeda was the rule rather than the exception. She, unlike her brothers, was an economic burden to her family; at fourteen, she was married and shipped to her in-laws.

Given parental attitudes about daughters, it is not surprising that the 1981 census reported that the average age of marriage was 16.8 years for females but 23.9 years for males and that only 4.7 percent of females but 10.6 percent of males had some secondary schooling. This information is even less surprising in a country where the main reason for not sending children to school is poverty, where fewer than 2 percent of secondary schools are operated by the government, and where parents must bear the cost not only of tuition but also of transportation, books, supplies, uniforms, admission fees, examination fees, the poor fund, and snacks. No wonder Majeda's family was anxious to ship her off to in-laws so she could fulfill her role as obedient wife and fertile mother. Majeda can be expected to bear seven children, contributing to an alarming 3 percent annual rate of population growth in the country.

In an effort to curb that growth, and inspired by population literature documenting that secondary education decreases fertility, the Bangladesh Association for Community Education (BACE) piloted the Female Secondary Education Scholarship Project in January 1982. The project sought to encourage girls to enter and remain in secondary school, thereby delaying marriage and increasing contraceptive use.

Initially all female students in grades six through ten who lived in the Sharasti upazila were eligible for a scholarship, which reduced tuition by half. In January 1985 the project was extended to the Gopalganj upazila and, in the same year scholarships were limited to girls from families earning less than 1,200 taka (about $47) a month. This new approach caused problems. Fieldworkers had difficulty finding enough girls who met the family income test; staff was burdened with reviewing and verifying applications; and influential middle-income members of the community, whose daughters had previously qualified for scholarships, were antagonized. Notwithstanding the negative

waive all fees for girls during the first three years of secondary school and would provide scholarships to girls in the higher grades.

Assessments of Guatemala's scholarship program for primary school girls are equally encouraging. This program, modeled after the one in Bangladesh, was tested in an area, the Indian *altiplano*, where

impact of the selection criterion, the overall success of the program resulted in its expansion to four additional upazilas. By September 1988, 20,085 women had benefited from receiving a scholarship. Anjuman Ara was one of them.

As a result of her experience, Anjuman says she won't get married before she is twenty. She'll have only two children and she'll use birth control pills. Anjuman and other scholarship girls have increased the percentage of female enrollment in secondary schools in the project area from 27.3 percent before the project began—a figure similar to the national average—to 43.5 percent in 1987, more than double the national average. The dropout rate for female secondary school students in the project area declined sharply from 14.7 percent before the project began to 3.5 percent in 1987. Anjuman and her friends encourage their sisters to attend school, so primary school enrollment is up as well. Anjuman went to school regularly; the scholarship program mandates 75 percent attendance. She did well in English, Bengali, religion, social studies, and science. She also learned about banking and savings by managing the scholarship account set up in her name; twice a month, accompanied by a teacher, Anjuman could go to the local bank and withdraw her money. Anjuman, in fact, wants to be a banker.

Timely tuition payments by Anjuman and others like her improved her school too. It now has a toilet and money for equipment and supplies. Knowing they will be paid regularly, more qualified teachers have come to the high school, stabilizing a once-transient staff.

And how does Anjuman's family feel about all this? Her mother responds:

I could not give education to my elder daughter who was married while in class 3. I had to pay dowry. Thanks to the scholarship . . . I received many offers of marriage and could pick and choose. None demanded dowry. Some even wanted to bear my expenses. I could marry my daughter to a household which is socially superior to mine. She visits me more often than my elder daughter and brings me presents. Evidently my younger daughter is happier than my elder daughter to whom I could not give proper education.

At a cost of $44.43 a year, the project transformed Anjuman Ara from family liability to family asset.

only 53 percent of school-age girls attended primary school and only 17 percent completed the cycle. It began in 1987 with one village and fifty scholarship girls, then expanded to twelve villages. By 1988 the families of 600 girls between the ages of seven and fifteen, most of whom were enrolled in grades three, four, and five, had received a payment of 15 quetzales ($4) a month for each daughter who did not become pregnant and who attended classes at least 75 percent of the time.[8] Since parents paid no tuition and schoolbooks were free, the monthly scholarship payment partially compensated parents for other school-related expenses and for the loss of their daughters' time. The project was so successful in retaining girls in school that, according to Guatemala's Ministry of Education, more than 90 percent of the scholarship girls completed the year. At the time this book was written, the government was planning to fund 550 new scholarships for eleven additional communities.

Scholarship programs sponsored by the government were also implemented in India and Nepal, but little is known about their impact (UNESCO 1986). In the early 1980s Nepal tested a scholarship program in two of its poorest rural areas. For three years all girls who attended primary school received a small sum of 5 rupees a month. Although its importance to the cash-poor parents was never evaluated, data on girls' enrollment suggest that the program did not increase the number of girls entering school. Those who entered, however, did stay in school longer. Whether this was the only positive outcome of the program is unknown. Nevertheless, the government was willing to invest additional resources in a program under which 5 percent of the girls in each district would receive a scholarship (Butterworth 1989).

The experiences of Bangladesh and Guatemala with scholarship programs are encouraging, yet the use of such programs to boost girls' enrollment raises several questions that only country-specific research and experience can answer. For example, can a scholarship program be financially sustained for the length of time or extent of coverage necessary to make a difference? Can a country afford to support a growing number of female students even if the cost per student is low? Which girls should receive scholarships? What is the appropriate amount of the award—should it cover tuition only or include other school-related expenses? For how many years should a student receive a scholarship? Should awards be given more selectively as the program continues? What kind of targeting is most cost-effective? The answers to these questions differ from country to country. Effective program design requires an understanding of both the local demand for girls' education and the resources that households and governments are willing to allocate to it.

Reducing Opportunity Costs

The resources that households must allocate for girls' education include not only cash outlays but also the girls' time. Women in developing countries spend many hours each day performing household chores. Girls often share this work with their mothers; they care for siblings, prepare meals, and carry water and firewood. Some earn an income from outside jobs. It may be necessary, therefore, to lower the opportunity cost of girls' schooling to increase their participation.

There are at least four ways to accomplish this. First, as we have already discussed, scholarship programs can ease the barrier that high opportunity costs create by offering monetary compensation to parents for the loss of their daughters' time. Second, allowing girls to bring younger siblings to school, establishing day-care centers nearby, or introducing simple technologies in the home can reduce the amount of time girls must spend working. Third, more flexible schedules for instruction in formal schools can accommodate girls' work schedules. Fourth, alternative schools can provide educational opportunities at times when girls are free to attend. These four approaches have been implemented with varying degrees of success.

Establishing Day-Care Centers

Colombia and China are actively expanding day-care in communities, at schools, and at worksites. In Colombia, where one-fifth of the poorest households are headed by single mothers and where 44 percent of poor children between the ages of seven and eleven do not attend school, the community day-care program—Hogares de Bienestar Infantil—has freed many girls and women to attend school or join the work force. The first centers were established in 1987 in poor neighborhoods. Within a few years they were serving about 400,000 children under the age of seven. The children are provided with 60 percent of their daily nutritional requirements and are supervised by "community mothers" selected by the local women. The community mothers are trained in nutrition, health, hygiene, and recreation, are paid a salary, and receive assistance in obtaining home improvement loans. The program is hoping to reach 1.5 million children by 1992.

China, in its efforts to increase girls' enrollment, has established day-care centers at schools and worksites. In Gansu province, for example, some schools allow girls to bring their younger siblings to class, and worksite day-care centers for the young children of employed mothers have improved girls' enrollment in urban areas (Coletta and Sutton 1989). China has also expanded preschools, which not only relieve girls from childcare duties but also provide an educational advantage for their younger siblings (Lockheed, Verspoor, and associates 1991).

Modifying Home Technologies

Often simple improvements in home production technology can save hours of time—time that can be devoted to school. In the hills of Nepal, for example, where deforestation has made wood scarce, women walk for miles, sometimes for days, into the forest searching for leaves, branches, and twigs for heating and cooking. A hill woman of the Magar ethnic group explains:

> Once it wasn't too difficult to find wood on the ground. But now there is not even enough left over to fill one headload [35 pounds], unless you walk for miles and miles. . . . As it is now, I must bring my daughter with me to help collect fuel and fodder, so she often skips school to help me. . . . If fuel gets even more scarce, I will have to take my daughter out of school completely so she can help me with my other tasks.

> The better woods are getting much scarcer. I must collect other species that burn very poorly. . . . Some woods make my eyes burn and give the rice a bitter taste my husband can hardly stand. (quoted in Molnar 1989, p. 101)

The government of Nepal distributed fuel-efficient, smokeless, wood-burning stoves to 15,000 families as part of the 1977 Forest Act, which was designed to check deforestation, improve the forest cover, and increase the amount of fuel, fodder, and timber available for subsistence. Staff from the Forest Department trained female "stove promoters" who, in turn, taught village women how to use the stoves and how to conserve fuel. Families using the stoves consumed 28 percent less wood on average, thereby reducing the amount each female had to haul by about 2,000 pounds a year (Molnar 1989).

The introduction of labor-saving technologies may be sound policy in some settings but may still not guarantee greater school attendance. Even when the technologies are affordable and appropriate—that is, simple, adaptable to local conditions, and easily maintained—factors other than time may interfere with schooling. In Burkina Faso, for example, a program begun in 1967 was aimed at freeing girls to go to school and promoting nonformal education for women. It introduced mechanical grain mills, accessible water wells, and carts for hauling wood in villages located in three geographic zones (McSweeney and Freedman 1980). The labor-saving technologies did not boost girls' enrollment in the project areas, probably because the formal schools were still too far away. They did reduce the amount of time women needed for certain chores, but instead of using the time saved to attend literacy classes, the women did other work—such as preparing better meals or weaving.

Adopting Flexible School Schedules

Programmed instruction is often advocated as a way of making formal education more responsive to children's work schedules, ensuring that all children get the same quality of instruction, and reducing the penalty for absenteeism. It is also a low-cost way of expanding school places because it facilitates multigrade teaching. Programmed instruction allows the curriculum to be organized in sequential units so that students can learn at their own pace.

Bangladesh, Colombia, El Salvador, Indonesia, Liberia, and the Philippines have experimented with programmed instruction. Despite the rational underpinnings of these efforts, the results suggest that this approach may be disadvantageous for girls if the use of self-learning materials turns out to require more individual attention from teachers, rather than less, and if additional time must be spent on homework.

Bangladesh and Liberia illustrate the problem. In 1980 under Project Impact Bangladesh introduced programmed instruction in eighteen rural schools.[9] Liberia introduced multigrade teaching and programmed instruction under the Improved Efficiency of Learning (IEL) project in five schools in 1979 and expanded it to fifteen schools in 1984. Both programs used self-learning materials organized into modules. In addition, Project Impact relied on teachers and students in grades three, four, and five to guide younger students through their lessons.[10]

Both projects were generally unsuccessful. In Bangladesh the program neither increased enrollment rates nor reduced dropout rates. Despite government efforts to elicit support for the program through home visits by district education officers, parents were not convinced that older students could properly direct the learning of their children. The project did not make learning less dependent on the teacher as planned because the instructional modules, although intended to be self-learning, were not. They required the supervision of a teacher or literate parent; both were in short supply.

The results in Liberia were equally discouraging. An evaluation of the project compared gender differences in mathematics and English test results among third, fourth, and fifth grade students in the IEL schools with test results by students in conventional schools and in schools that participated in a textbook distribution project. The study found that although IEL students scored higher than either of the comparison groups—13.5 percent higher in mathematics and 5.5 percent higher in English—gender differences were greatest in the IEL schools and least in the schools that received textbooks. A possible explanation is that "the improved opportunity to learn is paralleled by increased demands on students, especially in terms of study time to complete assignments. In Liberia, as in many developing countries, numerous demands are placed on daughters. These expectations may have limited their ability to take full advantage of the enriched learning environment" (Boothroyd and Chapman 1987).

Colombia's Escuela Nueva program seems to have been more successful, perhaps because it is better at accommodating children's work schedules or because it is less dependent on the teacher's input and allows more self-learning, thereby penalizing students less for absenteeism. It may also be that programmed instruction is more effective when parents themselves are literate; adult literacy in Colombia is six times higher than in Bangladesh and two and a half times higher than in Liberia. Given the reported success of Colombia's approach, the conditions under which programmed instruction benefits girls merit further research (see box 8-5).

Offering Alternatives to Formal Schooling

Nonformal programs offered before or after the working day provide an alternative for children unable to attend regular school. Although early morning or evening school may not be an ideal way to improve girls' education, it is a strategy that has worked well in parts of India and Bangladesh.

India's nonformal evening education program was designed to bring school dropouts back into the primary education mainstream and to give those who had never attended school another chance. Evening classes for youths ages nine to fourteen were staffed by teachers drawn from and trained in the local community. Two years into the program 1,431 students were enrolled, 1,040 of them girls. The convenient time schedule, community contributions to the school centers, and recruitment and training of local teachers were key ingredients in the success of this program (see box 8-6).

A similar program was launched in Bangladesh in 1983. There the Rural Advancement Committee established twenty-three pilot schools in selected rural areas to offer the first three years of primary education. School sessions ran two and a half hours a day, 271 days a year. Parents decided on the basis of their work schedules whether the school in their community would be open in the early morning or late

Box 8-5. *Work Today, Study Tomorrow: Colombia's Escuela Nueva*

In a remote village a young girl wets down the mud floors of her hut. Her parents are in the fields harvesting grain. A baby cries. The girl drops her pail and lifts the infant from his mat. This young girl, like so many others in developing countries, will not make it to school today. The school schedule interferes with her chores—chores that are critical to her family's welfare. When she does get to school, she may be far behind her classmates. Faced with repeating a grade, she may well drop out.

For girls who do not have the leisure to spend six hours in school every day, Colombia's Escuela Nueva program offers hope. Conceived as a way to provide a full five-year primary education in rural areas where small enrollments and limited resources make conventional classrooms with one teacher for each grade impractical, the program was officially launched in 1976. By July 1989 it was operating in 15,000 rural schools. Not only has the Escuela Nueva increased the relevance of primary education in poor rural communities; it has improved student achievement, enhanced girls' self-esteem, and reduced dropout and repeater rates.

Based on the principles of multigrade teaching and flexible promotion, the Escuela Nueva presupposes student absences when agricultural work is pressing. It allows students to resume their studies after such absences through the use of semiprogrammed materials arranged in sequential learning units. To make learning relevant, the curriculum is oriented to rural life and is readily adapted to the circumstances of a particular community. It promotes problem-solving rather than rote learning, encouraging students to apply what they study at home and in the community. "Resource corners" allow students to work alone or in small groups on assignments appropriate to their grade and progress. A small library of 100 books provides resource material to encourage a project approach to learning. With the assistance of popularly elected student "leaders," the teacher is able to handle up to five grades simultaneously. And the student is able to care for her brothers and sisters one day and learn better ways of doing it the next.

---

afternoon. Of the teachers, 67 percent were female. So strong was the demand for this program that parents tried to enroll "tiny tots who could barely hop on one foot" (Mallon 1989). So great was the enthusiasm that by 1988, 731 centers were operating and 21,903 children were enrolled. And so successful was the program in attracting girls that they made up 63 percent of the enrollment, fewer than 1 percent dropped out, and 83 percent continued their education at government primary schools (Begum, Akhter, and Rahman 1988).

Box 8-6. *Night School for Nine-Year-Olds: India's Nonformal Alternative*

In 1978 only 63.5 percent of girls in India between the ages of six and eleven were in school, compared with 97.3 percent of the boys. In the upper primary grades the enrollment rate of girls was less than half that of boys (24.5 and 48.7 percent, respectively). Most of the children not in school either had never entered or had dropped out soon after entering. They came from poor families, and they shouldered burdensome household chores or worked outside the home to add to the family income. They did not have time for a six-hour school day. Another problem was India's single-point entry system, under which a child could enter school only in the first grade, even if she or he was eight or nine years old. Compelled to mingle with younger children, older boys and girls felt uncomfortable and quit. The insistence on single-point entry and full-time attendance has been a big hurdle in universalizing primary education for children from poor rural families, especially girls.

A nonformal education project, designed by the Indian Institute of Education, discovered that if classes were scheduled at night, after chores were completed, preadolescent girls would attend, even if it meant challenging ghosts and man-eating tigers. This project, supported by central and state governments and the local authority of the Pune district, began in November 1979. Eighty-six classrooms, provided by the communities, were established in seventeen villages. Enrollment was restricted to illiterate children from nine to fourteen years of age. Classes, limited to twenty students, were ungraded and were based on the principle of mastery learning. They were scheduled 300 evenings a year, from 7 p.m. to 9 p.m. To build links with the community,

---

Increasing the Benefits

Important as the costs of schooling are when parents weigh educational decisions, the potential benefits are also crucial. Most past efforts to raise female enrollment have focused on lowering the costs. But if parents do not believe that education will benefit their daughters as much as it will their sons, they may not be inclined to send them to school no matter how much the costs are reduced. Girls may seem to gain less from being educated than boys, in the eyes of many parents, because it is not readily apparent that schooling enhances women's productivity in nonmarket work. But girls may actually gain less from being educated than boys—if they learn less in school or if they study subjects that do not enable them to find jobs or earn a reasonable income. Both the perception and the reality need to be addressed if the gender gap in education is to shrink. Strategies that have been tried include launching information campaigns to advertise the bene-

teachers were recruited from the villages or hamlets where the classes were located. They were paid a small stipend of 2,000 rupees ($250) a year. Sixty-four men and twenty-four women, most from the farming caste, with some secondary education, were trained by members of the project team. The men teachers were called "Bhau" (elder brother) and the women "Tai" (elder sister). Teachers, community leaders, and project officers chose these names because they underscored the responsibility of educated rural youths to pass down learning to the next generation. During the week-long training sessions, the emphasis was on preparing and using educational materials that were relevant to rural life and would encourage peer-group teaching. Annual exams were replaced by an evaluation "fair" called Bal Jatra. Teachers and children from all the project classes met in a central village where, for half the day, they played games, sang, danced, and listened to stories. For the rest of the day they read, calculated numbers, told stories, and answered a quiz.

In January 1981, among the 1,431 enrolled students, 1,040 were girls. A year later 196 girls and 86 boys had quit, a dropout rate far lower than the usual 50–70 percent dropout rate in the first grade. Girls' attendance was much higher than expected. To understand why, project staff interviewed the girls and their parents. Both said that attending school would help the girls learn to keep accounts, to write and read letters, and to manage daily transactions; learning would make them "wise." Parents added that the girls could marry educated young men. Parents and daughters agreed that the most convenient time for class was in the evening after the girls had finished their day's work.

fits of education, providing meals to girls in school, training girls and women for occupations that will lead to jobs and reasonable incomes, and supplying textbooks that are free of gender bias. These strategies can be used as alternatives or as complements to the cost reduction measures we have been discussing.

Informing the Community

From the parents' perspective, girls may benefit less than boys from education. When girls are expected to become mothers and wives and work on the family farm, time spent in school is time taken away from working and from learning the skills needed for these roles. In Somalia, for example, mothers are committed to training their daughters to perform household and domestic activities at an early age (USAID 1989). Schools will not teach them how to dry dung sticks for fuel or grind spices for cooking. Similarly, parents in villages in Mali are not convinced that schooling will help girls become better farmers. Indeed, the few parents who send their daughters to school do so because schooling is obligatory, not because they perceive any long-term advantages for their daughters (Ainsworth 1983).

Education and information campaigns have been successful in raising the demand for health and family planning services in developing countries,[11] but they have rarely been used to promote girls' education. Mali and Morocco are exceptions. In Mali media campaigns advertise the value of education as an investment. In Morocco materials are being developed to promote girls' education; they are to be distributed by extension workers who visit rural communities to encourage local participation in the construction and maintenance of primary schools.

Providing School Feeding Programs

Another reason that girls may gain less from education than boys in some countries is that they are more likely to be undernourished or malnourished. In Matlab thana, a rural district in Bangladesh, malnutrition is substantially higher among girls than among boys, and the mortality rate for girls exceeds the rate for boys by an appalling 50 percent (D'Souza and Chen 1980).[12] Girls are more likely to be malnourished than boys in Guatemala, India, and Pakistan. A study of ninety-four Latin American countries found that girls up to the age of four attained a significantly lower percentage of the ideal weight for their age than boys did (Schofield 1979; Safilios-Rothschild 1979).[13]

Iodine and iron deficiencies are also more prevalent among women. A review of gender differences in iodine deficiency showed that in seventeen countries the incidence of goiter was greater among females than among males (Simon, Jamison, and Manning 1990). At least one study has detected a stronger association between goiter and IQ scores in girls than in boys (Levin and others, forthcoming). Data on hemoglobin concentration also indicate that at least half of all women, and sometimes the entire female population, is anemic (Levin 1986).

Such nutritional deficiencies place children at risk. Malnourished children are less active, less attentive, less motivated, and less responsive than their better-nourished peers. They perform significantly lower on assessments of achievement, IQ, psychomotor skills, and social behavior. They are absent from school and repeat grades more often. Hungry and iron-deficient children have shorter attention spans; iodine-deficient children are slower at processing information and suffer from impaired visual-perceptual and motor coordination (Pollitt 1990).[14] Given this evidence, school feeding programs (SFPS) are often advocated as a means of reducing absenteeism and improving children's ability to benefit from instruction by relieving hunger or nutritional deficiencies. They are also often suggested as an incentive to raise girls' enrollment and attendance by offsetting some of the costs of attending school.

Despite the sound reasoning behind SFPs, most evaluations in both industrial and developing countries have failed to establish a strong link between school meals, on the one hand, and enrollment, attendance, retention, or achievement, on the other hand.[15] Reviews by Halpern and Meyers (1985), Levinger (1984), and Pollitt (1990) point to two main reasons for the inability of past research to reach firm conclusions about the effectiveness of SFPs. First, most evaluations of SFPS are methodologically flawed because they are based on preexisting and nonexperimental programs, which precludes adequate control of confounding factors. Second, the students' health and nutritional status, the program's design, and the social, economic, and school environments interact to produce the observed outcomes. A stimulating school environment can compensate for the effects of hunger and malnutrition, and greater intellectual development can be achieved when diets as well as the psychological and social environments are enriched. Conversely, an unstimulating school environment can negate the educational benefits of SFPs (Levinger 1984). School meals will accomplish little, therefore, unless accompanied by improvements in the quality of education (Halpern and Meyers 1985). An inappropriately designed program may also lessen the benefit of school meals and weaken their influence on parents' decisions about schooling for their children. Levinger notes, for example, that in poor communities where the opportunity costs of schooling are high and the benefits unclear, SFPs may be more effective in raising enrollment when food rations are large enough to be viewed by parents as a significant income transfer. But in communities where the opportunity costs are not high and the economic benefits are clear, SFPs are likely to have little impact on enrollment or attendance.

Although research has not succeeded in establishing a link between SFPS and schooling, enough is known about the relation between a child's health and nutritional status, on the one hand, and that child's school attendance and ability to learn, on the other hand, to warrant launching experimental feeding programs in an effort to boost girls' attendance. To be effective, SFPs should be designed as part of a broader intervention that also addresses other school and environmental factors contributing to learning deficiencies. Moreover, evidence suggests that nutritional intervention may be more effective in promoting mental development when directed to preschool children. A two-year supplementation program in Kingston, Jamaica, for 129 children from nine months to two years old resulted in significantly improved locomotor skills among stunted children (Grantham-McGregor and others 1991).

Training Women for Nontraditional Occupations

Even if the health and nutritional needs of all children were met, girls would still be likely to gain less from their education than boys. Women face wage and employment discrimination in the labor market that limits the economic benefit they can expect to get from their education. Girls' career choices also lead them into education programs that are unlikely to gain them access to well-paid jobs. Earmarking secondary and postsecondary scholarships to train girls in areas that prepare them for occupations in growth sectors of the economy is a strategy that has been successful in many industrial countries. A second option is to provide occupational or vocational training directly linked to employment, with a strong recruitment and guidance component. Past experience suggests that vocational training programs without these characteristics are unlikely to attract females.

The Post-Primary Technical Schools Programme established in 1975 in Dar es Salaam typifies an unsuccessful occupational training program. Spurred by concern over the increasing number of girls with a primary education unable to find employment, the government of Tanzania established twelve training centers on the premises of existing primary schools. The centers offered home economics subjects such as cooking, housecraft, needlework, childcare, and laundry. The program did not guarantee employment, and as a result the centers were greatly underutilized, enrolling only 37 girls although they were designed to accommodate 240 (UNECA 1984).

In Chile the absence of recruitment and guidance components undermined an otherwise sound six-year pilot program to train midlevel technicians. The program, begun in 1968, was introduced into two schools in Santiago—La Cisterna, a technical school for girls, and La Renca, a mechanics school for boys. Both schools were made coeducational and their course offerings were broadened. At La Cisterna chemistry, computer programming and data processing, textiles, and bilingual secretarial training were added to the curriculum; at La Renca chemistry and electronics were added. Close cooperation between pilot schools and industry was also established for curriculum development, practical training, and job placement.

The results of this pilot program were decidedly mediocre. Although it did expand girls' access to training, boys' enrollment in all programs increased faster than girls' enrollment. By 1973 the chemistry program at La Renca enrolled 88 girls and 214 boys, compared

with 47 girls and 37 boys in 1969. During the same period boys' enrollment in electronics grew from 87 to 499, whereas girls' enrollment
increased from 9 to only 42. Similar patterns were observed at La
Cisterna, where the majority of girls continued to enroll in secretarial
courses. Project evaluators attributed the low female enrollment to the
lack of guidance counseling in primary schools and the absence of
recruitment efforts (Ferreri 1974; Pilain 1975).

In contrast to this program, recruitment and counseling strategies
were central to the success of an industrial and commercial job training program in Morocco. Women were actively encouraged to compete with men for admission into training programs that they had
been reluctant to attend previously (see box 8-7).

Ensuring Gender-Neutral Instruction

It is often argued that girls' decisions to enter low-paid, traditionally
female occupations are reinforced by teachers who maintain stereotypical notions of girls' inabilities in science, math, and other traditionally male fields and by textbooks that depict women in occupations with little job mobility and low pay (Finn, Dulberg, and Reis
1979; Whyte 1984). These stereotypes, the argument goes, dampen
girls' aspirations and so discourage their attendance and achievement.
Such observations have led to the conclusion that education programs
would yield larger benefits for girls if teachers were made aware of the
stereotypes they hold, if they modified their interactions accordingly,
and if gender-neutral textbooks were made available.

Empirical evidence is lacking from developing countries to support
or refute the hypothesis that teachers' interactions with female students discourage girls' attendance or achievement, and we are unaware of efforts to sensitize teachers to long-held stereotypes or to
modify their behavior in the classroom. Evidence of the effect of gender bias in textbooks is also lacking. Nevertheless, several countries
have initiated large-scale projects to broaden the ways in which
women and girls are depicted in textbooks. Bangladesh, for example,
is revamping textbooks to show women in roles other than the traditional ones of mother and housewife. Kenya (Herz 1989), China, and
India have implemented similar programs, but no information on
their impact is available (UNESCO 1985c).

If the assumption about the effect of gender-biased textbooks is
correct, such changes should make a difference. But in relation to
other investment options, the cost-effectiveness of revamping textbooks to raise female educational attainment and achievement is
questionable, especially in countries where the status of women is low
and where textbooks of any kind are in short supply. As countries

Box 8-7. *No Diploma Needed: Morocco's Job Training Program*

The composition of the labor force in Morocco is changing as many women, driven by economic necessity, search for paid work. In response to a large increase in the number of women looking for work, an unemployment rate for women of 20 percent, and severe shortages of trained technicians and skilled industrial workers, Morocco's Office of Technical Training and Job Development (OFPPT) initiated the Industrial and Commercial Job Training Program for Women.

This five-year program began in 1979 in Casablanca and Fez, following a review of nonformal education programs for women and a study of women's training needs and resources. Young women with at least twelve years of schooling were recruited to the commercial centers for training in accounting and secretarial skills; those with nine years of schooling were recruited to the industrial centers for training in drafting, electricity, and electronics, fields which women had been reluctant to enter.

To gain admission into these programs, women had to compete with men on the national entrance examination, but they were sometimes given priority in certain fields. OFPPT made special efforts to inform women about the examination and to encourage them to take it. State-owned radio and television stations, which advertised the programs and announced the examination schedule, informed the public that women were eligible and should be encouraged to apply. Notifications were also published in newspapers and distributed to all secondary schools.

OFPPT provided counseling to guide women into areas that best suited their aptitudes and preferences. To facilitate employment after graduation, OFPPT was to establish a formal job placement service. Although the formal service never made it off the drawing board, an informal mechanism was introduced and worked well. OFPPT persuaded employers to accept women for their mandatory two-month apprenticeship. Typically, employers were pleased with the apprentices, offered them permanent jobs, and requested more female apprentices the following year.

A 1983 evaluation showed that female enrollment in the project centers had reached their targets, increasing from 0 to 99 in the industrial centers, from 30 to 144 in the commercial centers, and from 20 to 51 in a construction program. Dropout rates were about the same for men and women. Employment rates were high: 70 percent of women graduates got jobs, a rate much higher than that for women with the same amount of formal education but no vocational training. But best of all, graduates were earning as much as, if not more than, they could have earned in the public sector, where salaries are based on years of formal education and attainment of the baccalaureate diploma—which none of these women had.

continue to develop curricula and instructional materials more sensitive to the circumstances of female students, it is reasonable to expect that they will simultaneously revise how girls and women are portrayed. But in the short run, improving the quality of education for everyone by putting books into the hands of children and instructional materials into the hands of teachers may accomplish much more. Abundant research shows that children with textbooks learn more than those without them (Fuller 1985; Heyneman and Loxley 1983) and that children who learn more stay in school longer. Moreover, having any kind of textbooks may matter more to girls than to boys if girls receive less attention from teachers and less instructional support at home and if their outside work necessitates more frequent absences. Whether girls do in fact benefit more than boys from having textbooks available has not been adequately researched. One study on Peru did find that the availability of textbooks had a larger positive impact on the educational attainment of girls than on that of boys,[16] suggesting that parents' decisions to educate their daughters may be more sensitive to the quality of instruction provided than are their decisions to educate their sons.

Improving the overall quality of education may be the most productive investment for attracting girls to school and keeping them there. Subsidizing girls to attend low-quality schools or establishing alternative low-quality educational institutions, such as Pakistan's mosque schools, are measures unlikely to close the gender gap. Moreover, since girls are likely to spend fewer years in school than boys, they should benefit disproportionately from improvements in the quality of schooling offered.

Alleviating Poverty

No discussion of female education in developing countries is complete if it does not address the role poverty plays in undermining efforts at improvement. Absolute poverty is a condition of many children in Bangladesh, India, and Pakistan. These three countries alone account for 40 percent of the world's child deaths, 45 percent of malnourished children, 35 percent of children out of school, and more than 50 percent of children living in absolute poverty (UNICEF 1990). Simply lowering the costs of education or raising its benefits will probably do little to rescue poor children. Their survival depends on the education of their parents and on their parents' ability to support them. But often the immediate need for income prevents women from participating in literacy, family planning, health and nutrition, and training programs that could eventually raise their families' living standards.[17] Attracting women to these programs demands efforts even greater than those needed to attract their daughters to school. It requires offering them an immediate opportunity to increase their income, as experience in Bangladesh illustrates.[18]

In the aftermath of the 1971 war and the famine of 1974, Bangladesh faced problems of crisis proportions. Families were destitute, literacy was low, and the population was growing at an alarming 3 percent a year. In response, an integrated and multifaceted women's program was launched in 1975 to raise the incomes of rural mothers and thereby motivate them to accept family planning voluntarily, acquire reading and writing skills, and learn more about health, nutrition, maternal care, and childcare.[19] The program had three main components. The first—vocational training centers—targeted mothers and children affected by the war. The centers taught women weaving, tailoring, embroidery, knitting, working with jute, and food preparation. They provided free day-care, education, food, and medical attention for the women's children, and a "scholarship" of 2 to 2.5 takas a day for attending. When the women completed the program, they were invited to work in affiliated production centers. The second component—women's cooperatives—increased the earning capacity of agricultural laborers by exploiting skills that women presumably already had. The cooperatives offered loans, training, and nutrition and literacy classes. The third component—mothers' centers—targeted wives of landless laborers. The centers offered programs in health, literacy, home economics, family planning, and recreation. Classes were held four or five afternoons a week, and programs lasted from six months to a year. To attract women, some mothers' centers also offered training in various skills.

The results of the three programs have been positive.[20] Several evaluations have reported that a majority of participants raised their incomes and that the rate at which participants accepted family planning was almost double the national average.[21] As a result of their success, the programs continue to expand: 100 production units in 20 upazilas employ 11,000 women; 1,500 women's cooperatives in 100 upazilas have 60,000 members; and 1,600 mothers' centers in 40 upazilas have 40,000 members. Cumulatively, the programs have recruited an estimated 230,000 family planning acceptors.[22]

Bangladesh's programs demonstrate that poor women will participate in education programs if they can increase their income. The money earned also boosts their self-confidence and gives them greater decisionmaking authority at home and more control over reproductive choices. One Indian woman, asked whether her participation in an association of vendors had any effect on her husband's attitude toward her, responded, "Yes, my husband doesn't beat me any more and he can't leave me, because I'm the one who brings the loan from the bank" (UNESCO 1976, p. 5).

Making Interventions More Successful

We set out to identify and assess the approaches that have been used to reduce, circumvent, or eliminate the barriers to girls' and women's education in developing countries. Our investigation has been limited and shaped by the information available to us in documents on education projects and in the literature on educating women. Other possible strategies for expanding access to education for girls and women, or for increasing demand, have been omitted because of lack of information. Such strategies include eliminating school policies that bar the enrollment of pregnant or married girls, encouraging girls to delay pregnancy and marriage, and instituting hiring quotas to counteract wage and employment discrimination in the labor market.

The approaches we were able to assess have two striking and perhaps related characteristics. First, most efforts began and ended as pilot projects, with short-term funding and help in implementing them provided by donors and NGOs. These efforts have rarely resulted from a country's policymaking and planning processes and have rarely become an integral part of its national education plan. Second, although we located abundant materials related to this review of education projects, the dearth of systematic evaluations was striking, and the absence of any cost information was even more discouraging. For this reason, few strong conclusions can be drawn about the relative effectiveness, especially the cost-effectiveness, of various measures designed to raise girls' and women's participation in education programs. It is tempting to propose adoption of a package of interventions as the ideal approach, given the lack of conclusive evidence about many programs, but this could simply mask the need to collect more information.

Notwithstanding the absence of sound evaluations, our review does show that some strategies have been effective, some have failed, and some have yielded mixed results. For others, no evidence exists to confirm or dispute their effectiveness (see table 8-2). Parents have responded positively to monetary incentives in the form of scholarships. They have also been influenced by the availability of culturally appropriate facilities and of female teachers where cultural norms make this important. Alternative schools have proved attractive to girls who missed the chance to attend regular primary school or whose work schedules conflict with the regular school day. Improving the quality of schools and training women for occupations in growth sectors of the economy—when combined with strong recruitment and

Table 8-2. *Summary of the Effectiveness of Strategies to Improve Girls'
and Women's Education, Based on Country Experiences*

Objective	Effective strategies	Ineffective strategies	Insufficient evidence to draw a conclusion
Lower the cost of education	Scholarship Culturally appropriate facilities Female teachers Alternative schools; flexible schedules	Free uniforms	Programmed instruction Home production technologies Day-care
Raise the benefits of education	Vocational training for growth sectors of the economy when directly linked to employment and strong recruitment	Vocational training for nongrowth sectors of the economy not directly linked to employment and no recruitment effort	Gender-neutral curricula and books School feeding programs Information campaigns

placement efforts—also appear to be promising strategies. But distributing free uniforms and providing vocational training not directly linked to employment and with little if any effort at recruitment have not yielded the expected results.

Little information is available by which to judge the effectiveness of programmed learning, revamped curricula and textbooks that introduce broader roles for females, home technologies, day-care, school feeding programs, and information campaigns. More experiments are necessary before it will be possible to identify the circumstances under which these initiatives can benefit girls and women. Expanding school places is an inadequate strategy when the cultural and monetary costs are too high or the benefits too few.

Three broad guidelines need to be imparted to policymakers and practitioners who want to address the problem of improving women's education in developing countries. (a) To be sustainable, programs must be administratively feasible and cost-effective, and they must be consistent with other objectives in the education sector. (b) Sound research and information to underpin policy prescriptions are sorely needed in this area. (c) Raising women's education should be the concern of national education policy, not just of special projects, and it is influenced by other policies—for example, on population and the labor market.

Approaches Should Be Appropriate and Affordable

Programs should be appropriate. Interventions should not be so complex to implement that they unduly tax the administrative capacity of education ministries and of local education officials responsible for monitoring them. For example, although scholarship programs have occasionally succeeded, they tend to place a heavy burden on administrative resources. Determining who qualifies, how much money to grant, and how to monitor the recipients can be complex. Moreover, successful programs may require combining several interventions at once or in sequence to address different barriers. For example, establishing schools closer to home in rural communities may not be sufficient to raise girls' enrollment if parents see no benefit from formal education; an information campaign (perhaps through extension services) may have to be launched at the same time. As argued earlier, however, the package approach should not be used simply to avoid hard-headed diagnosis of the problem.

Programs should also be affordable. Some programs are too expensive to be sustained for long. In the poorest countries, where national budgets are often severely constrained by competing demands, meeting this criterion is essential. For example, building primary and secondary boarding schools for rural girls entails large construction and maintenance costs and thus cannot serve as the cornerstone of government efforts to increase enrollments in rural areas. Cheaper alternatives should be explored. Sharpening programs to target those with a real need also increases cost-effectiveness by reducing total program costs and ensuring that those who would benefit the most are reached. Even targeted subsidy programs should have a well-defined lifetime, at the end of which they are evaluated.

How funds are spent can be critical. Budgeting too little for recurrent expenditures results in badly maintained buildings, crowded classrooms, and a shortage of textbooks and qualified teachers. These conditions, as we have seen, erect specific barriers to female education. Limited government funds, cuts in the social sectors, and rapidly growing populations exacerbate the problem. But using funds freed up by reducing spending on other social programs that benefit girls and women may run counter to the policy objectives of the intervention. Another spending issue is which programs should receive support from the central government and which should be financed, as well as administered, locally.

The success of interventions depends on clear policy goals and strong central leadership. But experience shows that vital, effective programs have also relied heavily on local support. Policy and program choices are not always rational or based on cost-benefit calculations by the government. Choices are often made on the grounds of social or community pressure. In both urban and rural areas, community organizations exist that can be mobilized to support local efforts. Resources for female education can be expanded by cultivating the participation of such groups. Support does not have to mean financing capital investments or major recurrent budget items; it can mean assisting in administering and monitoring programs. It can also mean arguing energetically for improving women's education so that the issue receives attention at all levels of government. Furthermore, local organizations concerned with women and the poor can provide guidance in formulating policy and in planning programs by drawing on their insights about the communities in which they live and work.

Knowledge Matters: Monitor, Evaluate, and Inform

For governments, education policymakers, and development specialists faced with the challenge of closing the gender gap in education, understanding the nature and causes of the problem is essential. Information is needed to diagnose the barriers confronting girls and women and to identify which strategies work and which do not. Ministries of education do not often gather, tabulate, or report data on enrollment, dropout, and repetition by gender. Yet gender-specific data collected over many years are essential for monitoring change and evaluating progress. Moreover, a comparison of school data across geographic regions and demographic groups within a country is often required to analyze the problem and isolate those areas where the need for policy and program interventions is most acute. Research is needed on the conditions under which expanding opportunities for girls and women to attend school increases levels of attainment, on the design of strategies to accompany a supply-side approach, and on the importance that parents and girls place on the quality of education when making schooling decisions. Programs of low quality can undermine otherwise sound strategies, as illustrated by Pakistan's mosque school effort. If the quality of programs already in existence is raised, fewer special efforts may be required, and scarce resources can be more effectively targeted toward groups that require special attention.

As the preceding chapters have shown, the answer to why the gender gap in education persists lies in a complex mix of economic and cultural factors that derive from homes, schools, communities, and nations at large. From anecdotes, research, and practical experience one can easily assemble a long list of these factors. Such lists already exist. The challenge is to identify which barriers are the prime ones in specific settings or subpopulations and which policy measures are appropriate and affordable. It is not enough to know that parents care about whether a school has female teachers. How many of the teachers in a primary school must be women to increase the enrollment and achievement of girls? Half? Or is the presence of at least one female teacher in a primary school in problem areas adequate?

Deciding which strategies to pursue requires that the cost-effectiveness of competing measures be compared, which implies knowledge of the benefits as well as the costs associated with each. This necessitates significant efforts in research and experimentation. A variety of data collection methods, including household, community, and school surveys, can provide this information. But designing and implementing surveys can use up considerable time and funds, and analyzing and interpreting the data can require a cadre of skilled scholars. Since developing countries often lack the equipment, personnel, and money to collect extensive data or even to maintain reliable basic data, it is unrealistic to expect the systematic gathering and analysis of information to be a government priority. This is an area in which outside assistance from NGOs, donor agencies, and communities can be useful. International NGOs and donor agencies can sponsor both the transfer of knowledge about how to design and implement surveys and the sharing of software, thereby reducing the cost to a country of data collection. Involving communities and local organizations can help ensure that the data collected is reliable and complete, and it can exert sufficient political pressure on the government to guarantee the timely analysis and reporting of such data.

Ongoing projects on girls' and women's education and local organizations can be a valuable source of information on the determinants of enrollment, attendance, and completion. A thoughtful and systematic evaluation of performance can provide important insights into these determinants. Local organizations can help identify target groups, assess a community's needs and resources, and determine its willingness to undertake specific action.

Broad Policies Make a Difference

Intervention through programs targeted specifically to girls and women is neither the only nor necessarily the most cost-effective way by which a government can influence female education. Broad education policies matter. Even policies that seem entirely neutral with respect to gender can affect girls and boys differently. For example, the more the government supports primary education, the greater the relative benefit to girls because girls are more likely than boys to quit school after the primary level. Also, improvements in the quality of rural primary schools can have a greater marginal impact on girls' learning because girls are less likely than boys to attend better schools farther from home. The goal of extending basic education to all cannot be achieved without focusing on girls, especially those in rural areas.

Policies outside the education sector also affect women's schooling. The delivery of family planning programs and childcare services can alter the lives of young women profoundly. In many Sub-Saharan countries with high fertility rates among fifteen-to-nineteen-year-old girls, family planning programs can make it possible for girls to postpone childbearing and continue their secondary education. As discussed in earlier chapters, teen-age pregnancy is a common reason why girls drop out of high school. Because the responsibility for children still falls primarily to women, childcare services make employment outside the home feasible, indirectly increasing the appeal of higher education. Labor market trends can also be decisive. Wide disparities in the work opportunities and wage rates of men and women with comparable schooling are likely to dampen girls' educational aspirations. A study in several Latin American countries found that, on average, only 20 percent of the wage differential associated with gender is attributable to differences in education or training; another 20 percent may be due to the pull of the home and how this affects women's willingness to work, given the available wage offers, and the rest is due to unexplained factors including sex discrimination (Psacharopoulos and Tzannatos 1992). Employment policies designed to overcome the social barriers to women's working in better-paying jobs will induce not only larger school enrollments among girls but also better performance.

Notes

We are grateful to Maureen Petronio, who wrote most of the boxes in this chapter. Material for the boxes was drawn from the following sources: box 8-1, World Bank (1988b, 1989b); box 8-2, Teachers' Resource Center (1989), Warwick, Reimers, and McGinn (1989), and internal World Bank reports; box 8-3, UNDP (1982); box 8-4, Ather (1984), Martin, Flanagan, and Kleinicki (1985), and Thein, Kabir, and Islam (1988); box 8-5, internal World Bank reports; box 8-6, Naik (1982); and box 8-7, Lycette (1985, 1986), and USAID (1978, 1983).

1. In Jamaica, for example, 36 percent of households are headed by women and in El Salvador, 40 percent. In Ghana, according to 1987–88 data, 44 percent of households with children are headed by women.

2. A survey of 2,000 Pakistani parents reported that they did not mind the absence of desks and chairs in girls' schools, but two-thirds criticized the absence of latrines (Culbertson and others 1986).

3. "Koranic schools" refers to schools run by Islamic institutions. Different names are used for such schools in different countries, including mosque schools, *madersas*, and *madrassas*.

4. See Eisemon and Wasi (1987); Harley (1979); Haughton (1986); Warwick, Reimers, and McGinn (1989); UNESCO (1985b).

5. According to Pakistan's Ministry of Education, the cost per trainee in the home-based program amounted to about Rs. 14,000 (or Rs. 19,000 with central office costs) in 1988, compared with Rs. 23,000 in the conventional program.

6. The final year is spent in supervised teaching.

7. This represents 10 percent of all girls in this age group. Only 54 percent of school-age girls were enrolled at the time. The project was funded by the World Bank, UNICEF, and bilateral donor agencies.

8. The project is administered by a local NGO, Guatemalteca de Educación Sexual (AGES). A village woman "promoter" verifies attendance prior to paying parents each month.

9. Under the World Bank's Second Primary Education Project, Project Impact in Bangladesh was extended to 300 schools.

10. In the IEL project, teachers in grades one to three instruct students in groups of fifteen. The children then break into groups of five for peer practice sessions to ensure content mastery. In grades four to six, learning takes place primarily in peer groups of five to eight children, with some opportunities for independent self-learning.

11. In Egypt, for example, through a campaign launched by the Ministry of Health in 1984, television, radio and newspapers have played a decisive role in boosting public understanding of and demand for oral rehydration salts and vaccinations. Today knowledge of oral rehydration therapy is almost universal among mothers, and more than 80 percent of Egypt's young children are immunized against the six main childhood diseases (UNICEF 1990).

12. Mortality rates are for children ages one to four. In-depth dietary surveys also show that males consume more calories and protein than females of all ages even when nutrient requirements that vary by body weight, pregnancy, lactation, and physical activity are considered (Chen, Haq, and D'Souza 1980).

13. In Sub-Saharan Africa, in contrast, girls do not appear to be at a disadvantage compared with males in anthropometric status (Svedberg 1990).

14. Severe iodine deficiency is often accompanied by cretinism and deaf-mutism. Chronic vitamin A deficiency impairs vision, often causing blindness and preventing afflicted children from attending formal schools.

15. See Halpern (1986); Halpern and Meyers (1985); Levinger (1983, 1984); Pollitt (1990); Powell, Grantham-McGregor, and Elston (1983). One exception is a school breakfast program in Jamaica where 115 undernourished school children with a mean age of 12.5 years were given a government school meal at the beginning of the day. Breakfast had no effect on the children's weight, height, or reading and spelling scores, but it improved arithmetic scores and attendance.

16. The availability of reading or mathematics books was associated with 0.5 years of additional education for males and 0.7 years for females (King and Bellew 1989).

17. A discussion of programs to alleviate poverty is outside the scope of this chapter. Readers are directed to World Bank (1990) for a review of these programs.

18. Descriptions of these programs were drawn from Alauddin and Faruqee (1983); CIDA (1985); Gerard, Islam, and Jahan (1977); Huq and Mahtab (1978); Rahim and Mannan (1982); Rahman (1977); UNICEF (1977).

19. At the same time, there were numerous other women's projects such as cooperatives, cottage industries, Food for Work, and income-generating training projects run by governments and NGOs and supported by many international organizations, including the Canadian International Development Agency (CIDA), the Norwegian Agency for International Development (NORAD), OXFAM, UNICEF, the U.S. Agency for International Development, and the World Bank, to name just a few.

20. Unsuccessful centers were those where women could not substantially increase their earnings. This occurred when the demand for the products was slack, when quality control was weak, when no marketing mechanisms were available to sell the products, and when no income-earning skills were taught. In some of the mothers' centers, for example, training was limited to producing jute crafts which the slack internal and external markets could not absorb. These centers attracted middle-class women with leisure time to spare for educational and recreational activities.

21. A United Nations study also showed a 48 percent reduction in fertility among members of the mothers' centers.

22. The estimates by program are: vocational training centers, 112,000; women's cooperatives, 20,000; and mothers' centers, 98,000.

References

Ainsworth, Martha. 1983. "The Demand for Health and Schooling in Mali: Results of the Community and Service Provider Survey." Discussion Paper 1983-7. World Bank, Country Policy Department, Washington, D.C.

Alauddin, Mohammad, and Rashid Faruqee. 1983. *Population and Family Planning in Bangladesh: A Study of the Research.* World Bank Staff Working Paper 557. Washington, D.C.

Ather, S. A. 1984. "US-AID Scholarship Programme for Female Students in Sharasti Upazila, Comilla," Evaluation Report PD-AAY-603, Dhaka.

Begum, K., S. Akhter, and S. Rahman. 1988. "An Evaluation of BRAC's Primary Education Programme." Report submitted to the World Bank. Dhaka: Institute of Education and Research.

Boothroyd, R. A., and D. W. Chapman. 1987. "Gender Differences and Achievement in Liberian Primary School Children." *International Journal of Educational Development* 7(2):99–105.

Butterworth, Barbara (Ministry of Education, Nepal). 1989. Telephone conversation, November 10.

Chen, Lincoln C., E. Haq, and S. D'Souza. 1980. "Sex Bias in the Family Allocation of Food and Health Care in Rural Bangladesh." *Population and Development Review* 7(1):55–70.

CIDA (Canadian International Development Agency). 1985. *Report on the Women's Programs Population III Bangladesh (Phase 1).* Ottawa.

Coletta, Nat J., and Margaret Sutton. 1989. "Achieving and Sustaining Universal Primary Education: International Experience Relevant to India." Policy,

Research, and External Affairs Working Paper 166. World Bank, Population and Human Resources Department, Washington, D.C.

Culbertson, R., and others. 1986. "Primary Education in Pakistan." Development Associates, Washington, D.C.

Dove, Linda A. 1982. "The Deployment and Training of Teachers for Remote Rural Areas in Less-Developed Countries." *International Review of Education* 28(1):3–27.

————. 1986. *Teachers and Teacher Education in Developing Countries.* London: Croon Helm.

D'Souza, S., and L. C. Chen. 1980. "Sex Differentials in Mortality in Rural Bangladesh." *Population and Development Review* 6(2):257–70.

Eisemon, Thomas, and A. Wasi. 1987. "Koranic Schooling and Its Transformation in Coastal Kenya." *International Journal of Educational Development* 7(2):89–98.

Ferreri, R. 1974. "Acceso de las Mujeres a las Carreras Técnicas." UNESCO, Paris.

Finn, Jeremy D., Loretta Dulberg, and Janet Reis. 1979. "Sex Differences in Educational Attainment: A Cross-National Perspective." *Harvard Education Review* 49(4):477–503.

Fuller, Bruce. 1986. *Raising School Quality in Developing Countries: What Investments Boost Learning?* World Bank Discussion Paper 2. Washington, D.C.

Gerard, R., M. Islam, and H. Jahan. 1977. *Training for Women in Bangladesh.* Dhaka: UNICEF, Women's Development Program.

Grantham-McGregor, S. M., C. A. Powell, S. P. Walker, and J. H. Himes. 1991. "Nutritional Supplementation, Psychosocial Stimulation, and Mental Development of Stunted Children: The Jamaican Study." *Lancet* 338(8758):1–5, July.

Halpern, Robert. 1986. "Effects of Early Childhood Intervention on Primary School Progress in Latin America." *Comparative Education Review* 30(2):193–215.

Halpern, Robert, and Robert Myers. 1985. *Effects of Early Childhood Intervention on Primary School Progress and Performance in the Developing Countries.* Washington, D.C.: U.S. Agency for International Development.

Harley, Barry. 1979. "Mohalla Schools." UNICEF Education Briefing Paper 2. New York.

Haughton, Jonathan. 1986. "Educational Finance and Reform in Mali." World Bank, Africa Office, Washington, D.C.

Herz, Barbara. 1989. "Women in Development: Kenya's Experience." *Finance and Development*, June:43–45.

Heyneman, Stephen P., and William A. Loxley. 1983. "The Effect of Primary-School Quality on Academic Achievement Across Twenty-nine High- and Low-Income Countries." *American Journal of Sociology* 88(6):1162–94.

Huq, J., and M. N. Mahtab. 1978. *Report on Income-Generating Skills for Women.* Dhaka: International Labour Office, Asian Regional Skills Development Program.

King, Elizabeth M., and Rosemary Bellew. 1989. "The Effects of Peru's Push to Improve Education." Policy, Planning, and Research Working Paper 172.

World Bank, Population and Human Resources Department, Education and Employment Division, Washington, D.C.

Levin, Henry M. 1986. "Economic Dimensions of Iodine Deficiency Disorders." In B. S. Hetzel, J. T. Dunn, and J. B. Stanbury, eds., *The Prevention and Control of Iodine Deficiency Disorders.* New York: Elsevier.

Levin, Henry M., Ernesto Pollitt, Rae Galloway, and Judith McGuire. Forthcoming. "Micronutrient Deficiency Disorders." In Dean T. Jamison and W. Henry Mosley, eds., *Disease Control Priorities in Developing Countries.* New York: Oxford University Press.

Levinger, Beryl. 1983. "School Feeding Programs in Less Developed Countries: An Analysis of Actual and Potential Impact." U.S. Agency for International Development, Office of Evaluation, Bureau for Food and Voluntary Aid, Washington, D.C.

————. 1984. "School Feeding Programs: Myth and Potential." *Prospects: Quarterly Review of Education.*

Lockheed, Marlaine, Adriaan Verspoor, and associates. 1991. *Improving Primary Education in Developing Countries.* New York: Oxford University Press.

Lycette, Margaret. 1985. "An Evaluation of Industrial and Commercial Job Training for Women in Morocco." Project 608-0147. International Center for Research on Women, Washington, D.C.

————. 1986. "The Industrial and Commercial Job Training for Women Project in Morocco." U.S. Agency for International Development, Washington, D.C.

Mallon, Nacha. 1989. "The Community Classroom." *World Education Reports* 28 (Spring):15–18.

Martin, Linda G., Donna R. Flanagan, and Ana R. Klenicki. 1985. "Evaluation of the Bangladesh Female Secondary Education Scholarship Program and Related Female Education and Employment Initiatives to Reduce Fertility." International Science and Technology Institute, Inc., Washington, D.C.

McSweeney, Brenda G., and Marion Friedman. 1980. "Lack of Time as an Obstacle to Women's Education: The Case of Upper Volta." *Comparative Education Review* 24(2):S124–S139.

Molnar, Augusta. 1989. "Forest Conservation in Nepal: Encouraging Women's Participation." In Ann Leonard, ed., *Seeds.* New York: Feminist Press, City University of New York.

Moock, Peter, and Joanne Leslie. 1985. "Childhood Malnutrition and Schooling in the Terai Region of Nepal." EDT Discussion Paper 17. World Bank, Education and Training Department, Washington, D.C.

Murnane, Richard J. 1987. "Education Policy and Economic Incentives: Tailoring Incentives to Desired Responses." Paper presented for the World Bank Seminar on Teacher Costs and Effectiveness, April.

Naik, Chitra. 1982. "An Action-Research Project on Universal Primary Education—The Plan and the Process." In Gail P. Kelly and Carolyn M. Elliott, eds., *Women's Education in the Third World: Comparative Perspectives.* Albany: State University of New York.

Pilain, A. C. 1975. *Women, Education, Equality: a Decade of Experiment.* Paris: UNESCO.

Pollitt, Ernesto. 1990. *Malnutrition and Infection in the Classroom.* Paris: UNESCO.

Powell, Christine, Sally Grantham-McGregor, and M. Elston. 1983. "An Evaluation of Giving the Jamaican Government School Mean to a Class of Children." *Human Nutrition* 37:381–88.

Psacharopoulos, George, and Zafiris Tzannatos, eds. 1992. *Women's Employment and Pay in Latin America: Overview and Methodology.* Washington, D.C.: World Bank.

Rahim, M. A., and M. Mannan. 1982. *An Evaluation of the Women's Vocational Training Programme for Population Education and Control.* Dhaka: Planning Commission, External Evaluation Unit.

Rahman, J. 1977. "Social Welfare Mothers Club." Bangladesh, Social Welfare Department, Dhaka.

Robinson, Wade, N. Makary, and Andrea Rugh. 1987. "Fourth Annual Report of the Study of USAID Contributions to the Egyptian Basic Education Program." Creative Associates, Washington, D.C.

Safilios-Rothschild, Constantina. 1979. "Access of Rural Girls to Primary Education in the Third World: State of the Art, Obstacles, and Recommendations." U.S. Agency for International Development, Office of Women in Development, Washington, D.C.

Schofield, Sue. 1979. *Development and the Problems of Village Nutrition.* London: Croon Helm.

Schultz, T. Paul. 1989. "Benefits of Educating Women." World Bank, Background Papers Series, Education and Employment Division, Population and Human Resources Department, Washington, D.C.

Seetharamu, A. S., and M. D. Ushadevi. 1985. *Education in Rural Areas: Constraints and Prospects.* New Delhi: Ashish Publishing House.

Simon, Paul A., Dean T. Jamison, and M. A. Manning. 1990. "Gender Differences in Goiter Prevalence: A Review." University of California at Los Angeles.

Svedberg, P. 1990. "Undernutrition in Sub-Saharan Africa: Is There a Gender Bias?" *Journal of Development Studies* 26(3):469–86.

Teachers' Resource Center. 1989. "A Study of Mosque Schools in Sind with Special Reference to Girls Education." Paper prepared for the World Bank. Karachi.

Thein, Tin-Myaing, M. Kabir, and Mahmuda Islam 1988. "Evaluation of the Female Education Scholarship Program Supported by the Asia Foundation." U.S. Agency for International Development, Dhaka.

UNDP (United Nations Development Programme). 1982. "Nepal: Teacher Training (Equal Access of Women to Education). Project Findings and Recommendations." Paris.

UNECA (United Nations Economic Commission for Africa). 1984. "Training and Employment Opportunities for Out-of-School Girls in Dar Es Salaam." Addis Ababa.

UNESCO (United Nations Educational, Scientific, and Cultural Organization). 1976. "The Continuing Effort for Women's Rights." UNESCO Features 697. Paris.

————. 1985a. "People's Democratic Republic of Yemen. Completion Report of the Second Education Project Credit 865-YDR." Educational Financing Division, Paris.

————. 1985b. "Training of Educational Personnel Focused on Girls and Women." Report of a Subregional Workshop for the Training of Educational Personnel Focused on Girls and Women. Katmandu, Nepal, September 19–27, 1984. Regional Office for Education in Asia and the Pacific, Bangkok.

————. 1985c. "Towards Equality of Educational Opportunity." Report of the Visits of the Regional Panel on the Education of Girls, 27 May–10 June. Regional Office for Education in Asia and the Pacific, Bangkok.

————. 1986. "Education of Girls in Asia and the Pacific: Report of the Regional Review Meeting on the Situation of Education of Girls for Universalization of Primary Education." Regional Office for Education in Asia and the Pacific, Bangkok.

————. 1988. *Statistical Yearbook*. Paris.

————. 1989. "Bangladesh Completion Report First Primary Education Project Credit 1054-BD." Paris.

UNICEF (United Nations Children's Fund). 1977. *Report of a Feasibility Survey of Productive/Income Generating Activities for Women in Bangladesh*. Dhaka.

————. 1990. *The State of the World's Children*. New York.

United Nations Statistical Office. 1988. *Women's Indicators and Statistics (WISTAT)—User's Guide*. New York.

USAID (U.S. Agency for International Development). 1978. "Project Grant Agreement between the Kingdom of Morocco and the United States of America for Industrial and Commercial Job Training for Women." Washington, D.C.

————. 1983. "Industrial and Commercial Job Training for Women in Morocco, Final Report." Washington, D.C.

————. 1989. *Policy Research Initiative, Somalia Teacher Incentive Systems: Final Report*. Improving the Efficiency of Educational Systems Project. Washington, D.C.

Warwick, Donald, Fernando Reimers, and Noel McGinn. 1989. "The Implementation of Reforms in the Primary Schools of Pakistan." Harvard Graduate School of Education, Cambridge, Mass.

Whyte, J. 1984. "Encouraging Girls into Science and Technology: Some European Initiatives." Paris: UNESCO.

World Bank. 1989. *Bhutan: Development Planning in a Unique Environment.* Washington, D.C.

————. 1989. *Women in Pakistan: An Economic and Social Strategy*. Washington, D.C.

————. 1990. *World Development Report 1990*. New York: Oxford University Press.

Subject Index

Absenteeism: of pupils, 114, 164, 232; of teachers, 165, 231

Access to education, 1, 286–87, 291; in Middle East and North Africa, 150; in South Asia, 229–30, 231; in Sub-Saharan Africa, 127–29

Afghanistan, 2

Africa. *See* Middle East and North Africa; Sub-Saharan Africa; *names of individual countries*

Age, self-employment and, 90

Agriculture: influence of, on dropout rate, 119; school calendar and, 200–01

Alternative schooling, 128, 287, 304–05, 306–07

Arab states. *See* Middle East and North Africa

Argentina: literacy in, 178–79; preschool education in, 200; women in higher education in, 186

Bangladesh: alternative schooling in, 304–05; educational expenditures in, 218; gender differences in nutrition and mortality in, 308; gender gap in education in, 218; literacy of rural women in, 220–21; locally recruited female teachers in, 231–32; programmed instruction in, 303; rural-urban disparity

in education in, 220; scholarships for girls in, 297–300; women's anti-poverty program in, 314

Benefits of education, 1–2; gender and, 26–29. *See also* Returns to education; Market returns to education; Nonmarket returns to women's education

Bhutan, 287

Boarding schools, 154, 160

Bolivia, 179

Botswana: female students in, 104; gender gap in literacy in, 2; school enrollment in, 114

Brazil: educational expansion in, 179; teacher quality in, 194; teacher training and salaries in, 195

Breastfeeding, 72–73

Burkina Faso, 2

Chad, 13

Childcare, 200, 301–02, 320

Child labor: in Latin America and the Caribbean, 198–99; in Sub-Saharan Africa, 114–15, 119

Children: investment in, 78–79; mothers' education and well-being of, 12–13, 68–73

Chile: gender differences in university admission tests in, 202–03; lit-

Author Index